BLACK, WHITE, AND CHROME:

The United States and Zimbabwe

1953-1998

Andrew DeRoche

Africa World Press, Inc.

P.O. Box 1892   P.O. Box 48
Trenton, NJ 08607   Asmara, ERITREA

Africa World Press, Inc.

P.O Box 1892
Trenton, NJ 08607

P O Box 48
Asmara, ERITREA

Book Design: Wanjiku Ngugi
Cover Design: Ashraful Haque

Library of Congress Cataloging-in-Publication data

DeRoche, Andrew
    Black, White, and Chrome : The United States and Zimbabwe, 1953 to
1998 / Andrew DeRoche
    p. cm.
    Includes bibliographical references and index.
    ISBN: 0-86543-791-2 -- ISBN: 0-86543-792-0 (pbk.)
    1. United States - -Foreign relations - -Zimbabwe. 2. Zimbabwe-
-Foreign relations- -United States. 3. Afro-Americans - - Politics and
government. 4. United States - -Race relations - - Political aspects-
-History - - 20th century. 5. Chromuium industry - -Political aspects -
-Zimbabwe - -History - -20th century 6. Copper industry and trade-
-Political aspects - - Zimbabwe - -History - - 20th century. 7. Chromium
industry - -Political aspects - -United States - - History - - 20th century.
8. Copper industry and trade - - Political aspects - - United States-
-History - - 20th century. I. Title.
E183. 3. 8. Z55D47 1999
327. 7306891 - -dc21   99-31452
                                                                    CIP

CONTENTS

1

WHY STUDY U.S. RELATIONS WITH ZIMBABWE?

Zimbabwe, a small country in southern Africa, was known as Southern Rhodesia until 1980. Why study the history of United States relations with Zimbabwe? The first reason is that doing so reveals much about the influence of race on U.S. foreign relations. American policy towards Southern Rhodesia evolved from an extremely low priority in the early 1950s to a very high priority in the late 1970s. This change reflected the fact that the fight by African Americans for civil rights increasingly extended onto the stage of international affairs. In the early 1950s, black leaders in the United States strongly criticized the institutionalized racism in Southern Rhodesia, and by the 1970s African Americans constituted a powerful constituency that helped drive U.S. opposition to Ian Smith's white government of Southern Rhodesia. Simultaneously, white southern senators who had resisted domestic desegregation staunchly supported Smith's regime.

Senators such as Harry F. Byrd, Jr. (I-Va.) and Strom Thurmond (R-S.C.) skillfully assisted Smith during the early 1970s; however, the Jimmy Carter Administration enacted a policy towards Southern Rhodesia that sought majority rule. Carter himself greatly contributed to building black African faith in the U.S. commitment to justice in Southern Rhodesia. Carter's actions reflected both the debt he owed the African-American community for supporting his election and his personal convictions that the United States should pursue a moral foreign policy. Carter's efforts were supported by several of his top advisers.

The 1977 appointment of Andrew Young, a southern black, as United Nations Ambassador symbolized Carter's desire for human rights and his relationship to the African-American community. Trained as a minister, Young had served as an assistant to Martin Luther King during the 1960s. His 1972 election to Congress personified the rising influence of the civil rights movement within the American government. As UN ambassador, Young established a close relationship with the leaders of the liberation forces in Southern Rhodesia, Robert Mugabe and Joshua Nkomo. Ultimately, the positive atmosphere Carter and Young fostered helped to end the fighting and bring about the formation of an independent Zimbabwe in 1980. This represented a triumph for Carter's human rights initiatives in foreign policy and a victory for the civil rights constituency; moreover, Carter's policy towards Zimbabwe helped initiate the downfall of apartheid in South Africa.

Indeed, there were many links from the U.S. efforts in support of Zimbabwe in the 1970s to the anti-apartheid struggle of the 1980s. The most important of these was TransAfrica, the African-American lobby group founded by Young and other leading blacks in 1976. In 1984, TransAfrica sparked the grassroots activism that eventually resulted in the 1986 passage of strong sanctions against South Africa. These sanctions added to the pressure on the South African government that ultimately led to multiracial democracy. In many respects, U.S. relations with Zimbabwe had set the stage for the successes of the anti-apartheid movement. In briefly examining U.S. relations with southern Africa in the 1980s, my study details this connection.

In addition to discovering how race increasingly influenced U.S. foreign policy, examining relations with Zimbabwe provides insight into a number of other issues. Ranking second only to racial issues in importance was U.S. interest in Southern Rhodesia's and neighboring Zambia's strategic minerals, mainly chrome and copper. This study analyzes the intense debates waged between 1953 and 1980 over these strategic minerals. Another key topic is U.S. interaction with Great Britain, since Southern Rhodesia was officially a British colony until 1980. My work, therefore, provides another perspective on Anglo-American relations during the Cold War. Finally, my study gives new insight into the side-effects of

Cold War ideologies such as anti-communism and Cold War events such as the Vietnam War.

HISTORIOGRAPHY

First and foremost this study documents the gradual rise of black influence on foreign policy from the 1950s to the 1980s. In doing so it adds to the work assembled by scholars such as Brenda Plummer, whose *Rising Wind* broke much new ground. Initially confronted by skeptics who believed that blacks and diplomacy had no more in common than "chalk and cheese," Plummer demonstrated that the topic offers rich perspectives on both the history of blacks and of foreign relations. Plummer showed that many black leaders provided insightful critiques of U.S. foreign policy. As early as 1900, for example, W.E.B. DuBois had opposed U.S. expansionism and pointed out the link between colonialism and racism.[1]

Plummer was correct in her assertion that the primary role of blacks before 1960 was oppositional, and that key black leaders criticized the direction of U.S. policy. She also argued that electoral politics had little to do with the black influence on foreign policy.[2] That may well have been true before 1960, but it was definitely not the case in later years. As my study demonstrates, the rising black vote became a factor in U.S. foreign policy in the mid-1960s, when the Lyndon Johnson Administration considered black opinion while formulating policy towards Southern Rhodesia. In the 1970s and 1980s black influence in electoral politics contributed to the formation of Zimbabwe and the demise of apartheid, respectively. My study does not dispute Plummer's conclusions about the relative unimportance of black votes in the 1950s; however, it demonstrates how much things changed by the 1980s.

Penny Von Eschen has also examined the role of blacks in U.S. foreign policy. Like Plummer, Von Eschen's major research covers the period before 1960.[3] Michael Krenn analyzed the relationship between African Americans and the State Department, from 1945 to the end of the 1960s.[4] All three scholars contributed to a 1996 issue of *Diplomatic History*, which focused on race and foreign relations. In her essay, Plummer identified a need for more studies that examine both race and diplomacy.[5] My work attempts to answer her call.

At the same time, my work disputes the findings of other scholars such as Gerald Horne. He has argued that African Americans' support for liberation movements in places like southern Africa engendered suspicion among officials in Washington. Leading blacks were silenced because of their support for southern African nationalists, which were perceived to be in league with the Soviet Union. Horne implied that because the liberation forces in Southern Rhodesia were considered communist, they were not supported by African Americans or the U.S. government.[6]

Horne's general point that the American government had silenced blacks such as W.E.B. DuBois and Paul Robeson partly because of their communist views was true. However, on the specific case of Zimbabwe he missed the mark. Beginning in the late 1950s, State Department diplomats realized that men like Joshua Nkomo and Robert Mugabe were primarily nationalists, not communists influenced by Moscow. They also understood that racism in the United States was a liability in foreign relations. In the early 1960s, President John Kennedy established good relations with southern African nationalists like Kenneth Kaunda (Zambia) and Hastings Banda (Malawi), and this continued under Lyndon Johnson. Carter, of course, took this to another level in the late 1970s, consulting with Julius Nyerere (Tanzania) and even visiting Nigeria.

As U.S. presidents recognized more clearly that southern African liberation movements had merit, black leaders' views on the subject received more attention. A. Philip Randolph's statement in support of Southern Rhodesian blacks in the early 1950s was ignored. Martin Luther King's criticism of southern African regimes in the early and mid-1960s, however, was acknowledged by Kennedy and Johnson. Black leaders such as Jesse Jackson, Coretta Scott King, and especially Young achieved an unprecedented level of influence during the Carter Administration. Conservatives such as Jesse Helms (R-N.C.) did accuse Young and others of supporting communists. Carter, though, agreed with the black leadership that Southern Rhodesia should attain majority rule, and he worked closely with them to help achieve it. Fine articles by Ronald Walters and Herschelle Challenor clearly identify this increasing black influence.[7]

Surprisingly, some otherwise sound works such as Michael Hunt's influential *Ideology and U.S. Foreign Policy* entirely missed the significance of Carter's relations with Zimbabwe. Hunt briefly discussed the "Tar Baby" policy of the Nixon Administration, but made no mention of Kissinger's 1976 diplomacy in southern Africa, Andrew Young, or Carter's dedication to sanctions.[8] Because he ignored this important aspect of Carter's foreign policy, Hunt's conclusions about the Carter years have been viewed as being a little too negative. My work helps to rectify such interpretations.

However, this study is by no means the first to examine the role of the Carter Administration in the transition to majority rule and independence for Zimbabwe. In his important overview of American and European relations with southern Africa, *King Solomon's Mines Revisited*, William Minter credited the Carter Administration with drastically breaking with the policies of its predecessors. He lauded Carter for returning the United States to compliance with sanctions against Southern Rhodesia, also praising Young for helping to keep negotiations alive in 1977 and early 1978.[9]

So far so good; but when describing U.S. relations with Southern Rhodesia from mid-1978 to the end of 1979 Minter was too critical of Carter. He emphasized the support in Washington for Abel Muzorewa, who was elected Southern Rhodesian Prime Minister under a Smith compromise plan.[10] Minter ignored Carter's determination that Muzorewa was not a legitimate ruler, and his successful fight to maintain sanctions until a settlement was reached.

Minter also contended that after Young's resignation, no support for southern African nationalists remained in Washington. By December 1979, "any semblance of sympathy to Third World interests had virtually disappeared."[11] Carter's actions, as well as those of Secretary of State Cyrus Vance and Representative Stephen Solarz (D-N.Y.) in the fall of 1979 clearly proved otherwise. They maintained U.S. support for a settlement in Southern Rhodesia that was acceptable to the liberation forces, thereby contributing to the final deal at Lancaster House and the election of Robert Mugabe in 1980. Minter, then, accurately depicted the initial thrust of Carter's policy, but misjudged its ultimate effectiveness.

Other scholars have disagreed with Minter regarding the strength of Carter's support for liberation in southern Africa. In his study of the importance of race in international affairs, *Power and Prejudice*, Paul Lauren praises Carter and Young for both their general pronouncements against racism and their accomplishments regarding Zimbabwe.[12] In *Morality, Reason & Power*, a study of foreign relations during the Carter Administration, Gaddis Smith singles out policy towards Southern Rhodesia as the best result of Carter's intention to treat Africa on its own merits rather than as a Cold War battlefield. Smith cites Mugabe's 1980 visit to the White House as "a rare occasion for optimism."[13] In his study of Young's UN career, *Flawed Triumphs*, Bartlett Jones judges Carter's policy towards Zimbabwe to be successful, reflecting a consensus among Carter, Young, and Vance.[14]

Both Lauren and Smith summarize Carter's relations with Zimbabwe accurately, in general, but neither investigate the events or the background in any detail. Jones discusses Young's actions at some length; however, he pays much less attention to the roles of others and provides little background. This study does not challenge their basic interpretations regarding Carter's policy, but it does provide a much more nuanced account than those mentioned above. Furthermore, this study traces U.S. policy towards Zimbabwe back to the 1950s, thereby providing insight into a number of other issues besides race.

The first chapter of this text examines relations with the Rhodesian Federation during the Eisenhower Administration. It demonstrates that while Eisenhower himself paid no attention to southern Africa, the State Department and some members of Congress were very interested in the strategic minerals from the area. As the United States imported great quantities of copper and chrome, its relations with Northern and Southern Rhodesia revolved around securing access to these materials. This section of the text builds on Daniel Volman's dissertation, which documents the concern over copper and chrome very well.[15] Furthermore, my findings reinforce the conclusions of Thomas Borstelmann, whose *Apartheid's Reluctant Uncle* emphasizes the centrality of minerals in U.S. relations with southern Africa during the Truman Administration.[16]

Borstelmann also underlines the similarities between segregation in the American south and the apartheid system in South Africa. He argues that U.S. policymakers opted to support the white regimes of southern Africa, mainly because strategic minerals for the fight against the Soviet Union were more important than racial justice.[17] While that may have been true of the Truman Administration and South Africa, it would be an exaggeration to accuse the Eisenhower Administration of actively supporting the white minority in the Rhodesian Federation in order to get strategic minerals.

By the late 1950s, the civil rights movement had reached a level of influence where the U.S. government could not pursue a blatantly racist policy. American officials instead determined that they must balance Cold War concerns such as minerals with moderate support for racial justice in Africa. In his *Cold War and Black Liberation*, Thomas Noer convincingly describes U.S. relations with southern Africa in the 1950s as a struggle to balance anticommunism with support for majority rule. Furthermore, it became increasingly clear in the 1960s that standing on the side of racial justice actually benefitted the United States in its competition with the Soviets. So, the Kennedy and Johnson Administrations followed a middle course in southern Africa.

This middle course guaranteed that the United States would not become bogged down in a military struggle in Africa, but at the same time would reap some gains. In the short run, moderate opposition to southern African racism helped maintain support from black leaders such as King. In the long run, it kept alive the possibility that when the black Africans eventually triumphed, they would look favorably on the United States. Thus, access to strategic minerals for the future was guaranteed by the middle course, risking little. That was the heart of Noer's argument, and it correctly explained U.S. relations with Southern Rhodesia during the 1960s. The United States applied moderate economic pressure against the white regimes, but would not commit its "power and prestige to black liberation."[18] Only in the 1970s would U.S. power and prestige be brought to bare in southern Africa.

My chapters on the Kennedy and Johnson Administrations do not challenge Noer's basic thesis. However, by utilizing documents that were not available to him, I am able to demonstrate in much greater detail the lengths to which U.S. officials would go in support of racial justice. Midlevel officials such as G. Mennen Williams and George Ball took more aggressive stands against the white regimes than Noer describes. My research shows that even Kennedy and Johnson displayed a personal interest in the Southern Rhodesian conflict, but not to an extent that overturns Noer's middle-course thesis.

Noer's work concentrated on the 1950s and 1960s, only offering a brief commentary on the period after 1968. In *The "Tar Baby" Option*, Anthony Lake adds a piece to the puzzle by examining U.S. relations with Southern Rhodesia from 1965 to 1974. Lake concurrs with Noer that American policy towards Southern Rhodesia under Johnson was "cautious but generally correct." However, Lake stresses the major change in U.S. policy initiated by the Richard Nixon Administration. American policy in the early 1970s, particularly the Byrd Amendment, pleased southern African whites. Lake's lengthy explanation of that legislation was his most important contribution to the literature on U.S. relations with Africa.[19]

My treatment of the period from 1965 to 1974 does not dispute the substance of Lake's argument, but it does challenge certain points of emphasis. He insinuated that some Johnson Administration officials may have resisted a stronger policy because of their racism. My research in the George Ball Papers reveals a much more complex picture in which circumstances constricted policy options. I also identify a few examples of U.S. officials actually being more aggressive than the British in opposing Smith in 1965, whereas Lake contends that they strictly followed the British lead. Regarding the enactment of the Byrd Amendment in 1971, I agree with Lake's version. He rightly underlines Senator Harry Byrd's skill and attributes Nixon's inertia on Southern Rhodesia more to disinterest than racism. If anything, I further highlight the point that Nixon was obsessed with Vietnam and re-election and was not a racist. Ultimately, the only substantive weakness of Lake's book is that he wrote it in 1975, before the United States really became involved in the Southern Rhodesian conflict.

In 1976, Secretary of State Henry Kissinger intervened in the Southern Rhodesian conflict. He delivered a remarkable speech in Zambia in April, then practiced his "shuttle diplomacy" across southern Africa in September. Scholars from all sides have agreed that Kissinger succeeded in forcing Ian Smith to accept the principle of majority rule.[20]   Furthermore, everyone agrees that Kissinger's initiative broke down at the Geneva Conference without a final resolution.

Thus, the debate centers on how Kissinger achieved his limited success, and why he failed to obtain a final deal. In *Kissinger*, Walter Isaacson praises the former Secretary of State for securing an initial agreement through "ambiguity." He goes so far as to credit Kissinger with building "trust" among black Africans.[21] As my research demonstrates, Kissinger clearly crossed the line from ambiguity to dishonesty. Furthermore, by doing so he alienated key black Africans like Joshua Nkomo and Julius Nyerere. Kissinger had also angered General Olusegun Obasanjo of Nigeria to the point where Obasanjo would not allow him to visit his country.

I agree with the scholarly consensus; that Kissinger's getting Smith to accept majority rule was significant. However, I strongly disagree with Isaacson's point that Kissinger also succeeded in building trust with black African leaders. If anything, he raised the barrier between the U.S. government and African blacks. Breaking this barrier down was one of the most significant accomplishments of the Carter Administration, due primarily to the efforts of Young and Carter himself. Making this point clear, in fact, is the focal point of my work. My research and writing show the crucial difference between Kissinger's approach and that of Carter and Young.

My penultimate chapter thoroughly investigates U.S. relations with Southern Rhodesia between 1977 and 1979. Cyrus Vance, Stephen Low, and Stephen Stedman detail the diplomacy of those years in depth, highlighting particularly the work of individuals in the State Department and the White House.[22] Bartlett Jones covers the actions of Andrew Young quite well.[23] I incorporate their work into my discussion of those aspects of the topic. However, I add a detailed treatment of the role of Congress. Utilizing materials from the Carter Library and the Harry F. Byrd, Jr. Papers allows me to document the fierce opposition to Carter's policy from Byrd, Jesse Helms, and Bob Dole (R-Ka). I also describe the crucial support that Carter received from Representative Stephen Solarz.

In addition to analyzing Carter's battle with Congress over sanctions, I provide considerable context regarding the domestic circumstances in the United States, and the military situation in southern Africa. Combining these topics with a discussion of the diplomacy allows me to show the complicated interplay of events that lead to the settlement at Lancaster House in fall 1979. The resulting chapter is the most comprehensive treatment of the U.S. role in the transition from Southern Rhodesia to Zimbabwe.

My final substantive chapter traces U.S. relations with southern Africa through the 1980s. Because most archival materials for this period remain classified, my sources were mostly published primary sources and secondary works. The scholars whose work proved most useful were Peter Schraeder and Robert Massie.[24] I do not attempt to challenge their conclusions in any way. Instead, I use their convincing discussions of the U.S. role in ending apartheid to demonstrate the long-term significance of American relations with Zimbabwe.

NOTES

1. Brenda Gayle Plummer, *Rising Wind: Black Americans and U.S. Foreign Affairs, 1935-1960* (Chapel Hill: University of North Carolina Press, 1996), 2, 4, 10, and 15.

2. Plummer, *Rising Wind*, 24.

3. Penny Von Eschen, *Race Against Empire: Black Americans and Anticolonialism, 1937-1957* (Ithaca: Cornell University Press, 1997).

4. Michael Krenn, *Black Diplomacy: African Americans and the State Department, 1945-1969* (Armonk: M.E. Sharpe, 1999).

5. Brenda Gayle Plummer, "'Below the Level of Men': African Americans, Race, and the History of US Foreign Relations," *Diplomatic History* (Fall 1996), 641. The article by Michael Krenn in that same issue is particularly insightful.

6. Gerald Horne, "Race for the Planet: African-Americans and US Foreign Policy Reconsidered," *Diplomatic History* 19 (Winter 1995), 159-160.

7. Ronald Walters, "African-American Influence on US Foreign Policy Toward South Africa," in Mohammed Ahrari, ed., *Ethnic Groups and U.S. Foreign Policy* (New York: Greenwood Press, 1987), 65-82; Herschelle Challenor, "The Influence of Black Americans on US Foreign Policy Toward Africa," in Abdul Aziz Said, ed., *Ethnicity and U.S. Foreign Policy* (New York: Praeger, 1981), 143-181.

8. Michael Hunt, *Ideology and U.S. Foreign Policy* (New Haven: Yale University Press, 1987), 182-186. While there is no question of the overall merit of Hunt's work, I believe he misses the significance of Zimbabwe.

9. William Minter, *King Solomon's Mines Revisited: Western Interests and the Burdened History of Southern Africa* (New York: Basic Books, 1986), 298-299. See also William Minter and Elizabeth Schmidt, "When Sanctions Worked: The Case of Rhodesia Reexamined," *African Affairs* 87 (April 1988), 207-237.

10. Minter, *King Solomon's Mines*, 300-301.

11. Ibid., 300-304.

12. Paul Gordon Lauren, *Power and Prejudice: The Politics and Diplomacy of Racial Discrimination* 2nd Edition (Boulder: Westview Press, 1996), 266-268.

13. Gaddis Smith, *Morality, Reason & Power: American Diplomacy in the Carter Years* (New York: Hill and Wang, 1986), 133-135, 142. The point that Carter's Zimbabwe policy represented a unique break from the Cold War is also made in Peter Schraeder, "The Faulty Assumptions of U.S. Foreign Policy in the Third World," in Ted Carpenter, ed., *Collective Defense or Strategic Independence: Alternative Strategies for the Future* (Washington: Cato Institute, 1989), 151-174.

14. Bartlett C. Jones, *Flawed Triumphs: Andy Young at the United Nations* (Lanham: University Press of America, 1996), 72-73.

15. Daniel Henry Volman, "United States Foreign Policy and the Decolonization of British Central Africa (Zimbabwe, Zambia, and Malawi), 1945-1965," UCLA, 1991. Volman's study is excellent on the early 1950s, but its treatment of the period after 1956 suffers from a paucity of primary sources. He was unable to utilize the latest two volumes of the *FRUS* for Africa, and also did not use the rich materials at the Eisenhower Library. As a result, his study was too critical of the racial views of State Department diplomats.

16. Thomas Borstelmann, *Apartheid's Reluctant Uncle: The United States and Southern Africa in the Early Cold War* (New York: Oxford University Press, 1993), 198-199.

17. Borstelmann, *Apartheid's Reluctant Uncle*, 200-204.

18. Thomas J. Noer, *Cold War and Black Liberation: The United States and White Rule in Africa, 1948-1968* (Columbia: University of Missouri Press, 1985), 254. For a critique of Noer, see David Gibbs, "Political Parties and International Relations: The United States and the Decolonization of Sub-Saharan Africa," *The International History Review* 17 (May 1995), 306-307, 326-327. Gibbs argues that

there was a substantive difference between the Africa policies of Eisenhower and Kennedy. My research regarding the Rhodesian Federation tends to support Noer and to refute Gibbs, in that neither Eisenhower nor Kennedy took strong action.

19. Anthony Lake, *The "Tar Baby" Option: American Policy Toward Southern Rhodesia* (New York: Columbia University Press, 1976), 5. The chapter on the Byrd Amendment spans 40 pages, from 198 to 238.

20. For examples, see David Martin and Phyllis Johnson, *The Struggle for Zimbabwe: The Chimurenga War* (Boston: Faber and Faber, 1981), 263; Martin Meredith, *The Past Is Another Country: Rhodesia UDI to Zimbabwe* (London: Pan, 1980), 270; Stephen Low, "The Zimbabwe Settlement, 1976-1979," in Saadia Touval and I. William Zartman, eds., *International Mediation in Theory and Practice* (Boulder: Westview, 1985), 92. Martin and Johnson are Zimbabwean scholars, Meredith is a British journalist, and Low is a former State diplomat.

21. Walter Isaacson, *Kissinger: A Biography* (New York: Simon and Schuster, 1992), 691-692.

22. Cyrus Vance, *Hard Choices: Critical Years in America's Foreign Policy* (New York: Simon and Schuster, 1983), especially 256-270, 285-289, 293-297, appendix I and appendix V. Low, "The Zimbabwe Settlement, 1976-1979," 91-109. Stephen Stedman, *Peacemaking in Civil War: International Mediation in Zimbabwe, 1974-1980* (Boulder: Reiner, 1991). Stedman's criticism of Kissinger is insightful, but his criticism of Carter is too harsh.

23. Jones, *Flawed Triumphs: Andy Young at the United Nations*, 59-73.

24. Peter Schraeder, *United States Foreign Policy toward Africa: Incrementalism, Crisis and Change* (Cambridge: Cambridge University Press, 1994), especially pp.189-246; Robert Massie, *Loosing the Bonds: The United States and South Africa in the Apartheid Years* (New York: Doubleday, 1997).

2

COPPER MINES, BLACK NATIONALISTS, AND WHITE SUPREMACISTS: U.S. RELATIONS WITH THE FEDERATION RHODESIA AND NYASALAND, 1953-1961

Dwight Eisenhower's assumption of the presidency in January nearly coincided with the creation of the Federation of Rhodesia and Nyasaland, which the British parliament approved on 27 July 1953. The Federation combined the colony of Southern Rhodesia and the protectorates of Northern Rhodesia and Nyasaland under one government. British support for the decision revolved around potential economic benefit, with greater stability in Southern Rhodesia expected to result in more investment and immigration from Europe and the United States.[1] From 1953 to 1961, the U.S. government avoided any major policy initiatives towards the Rhodesian Federation.[2] President Eisenhower opted to leave such formulations to Great Britain; as the Federation was a British colony, it was a British problem.[3] Rather than grapple with politics, U.S. relations with the Federation focused on economic strategic issues. Motivated by Cold War concerns, America desired access to the Federation's strategic minerals (i.e., copper and chrome), and preferring to stay out of the complex racial disputes that simmered ominously.[4]

To a great extent, American foreign relations in the early 1950s sought to preserve national security.[5] That security was closely connected to developments in the Soviet Union, Europe, and Asia. Africa, posing virtually no potential threat to U.S. security, ranked far behind other areas on the American agenda. What importance Africa did have regarding U.S. security involved strategic minerals such as uranium, found in the Congo and South Africa.[6] American relations with the Federation during the Eisenhower Administration also revolved around strategic minerals. Acquisition of the minerals did not require a military presence or formal colonization by the United States, but could be facilitated by positive interaction. During his second term, Eisenhower recommended cultural relations, as opposed to military operations, as a better way to make friends in Africa.[7] However, events at an American-owned theater in Southern Rhodesia illustrated how race relations complicated American hopes of improving its international reputation by exporting culture.

These events also demonstrated that U.S. investment did not always foster progressive race relations. Because of such incidents and their threat to U.S. aquisition of minerals, American officials paid increasing attention to race relations within the Federation.

Lower- and middle-level U.S. officials recognized the centrality of race relations in the success or failure of the Federation. They also realized that race relations and nationalism were closely intertwined. Indeed, ongoing racial discrimination in all spheres of life—social, economic, and political—motivated the opposition to Federation by black African nationalists. If these nationalists opted for widespread violence, mining operations could be disrupted. Furthermore, if they eventually gained power they could restrict access to the minerals.

While some diplomats and intelligence personnel understood the importance of race relations and rising nationalism in the Federation, President Eisenhower and Secretary of State John Foster Dulles paid virtually no personal attention to such matters.[8] Vice President Richard Nixon, who led the move during Eisenhower's second administration to pay more attention to Africa, remained aloof from the concerns of Federation blacks. State's first Assistant Secretary for African Affairs, Joseph Satterthwaite, demonstrated some knowledge of nationalism in the Federation, but misjudged its urgency and tilted towards Great Britain's preferences.

In general, the Eisenhower Administration gradually focused more on Africa during its second term.[9] Eisenhower began advocating aid for developing nations in 1957 and called for additional funds for Africa in 1960. In February of that year he spoke in favor of greater assistance to southern Africa in particular.[10] It was primarily because of Nixon's efforts that the State Department established a separate bureau for Africa in 1958. The higher priority for Africa took shape very slowly, however, and was never very inspired. Despite its "deathbed conversion" regarding Africa, the Eisenhower Administration's policy remained one of "passivity, caution, and hesitant reaction."[11] Eisenhower's policies never dealt with Africa for its own sake, but always for Africa's role in the U.S. Cold War strategy of containment.[12] Moreover, in the context of U.S. relations with Africa during the 1950s, the Federation ranked far behind nations such as the Congo, Ghana, and South Africa.

EISENHOWER'S FIRST TERM: 1953-56

The Eisenhower Administration defended the British parliament's decision to form the Rhodesian Federation from the start. Margaret Joy Tibbetts, Second Secretary at the U.S. Embassy in London, outlined this position in 1953.[13]

> Admittedly Federation is a gamble and there are many rocks in the road ahead. It is the Embassy's conviction, however, that the responsible leaders and officials of the British Government would not have been convinced of its necessity if they had not seen in the Federation the possibility of creating in Central Africa a stable society which would ultimately strengthen Britains' position throughout East and Central Africa.[14]

The conviction of the American embassy in London to stand behind the "responsible leaders and officials of the British Government" held sway throughout Eisenhower's first term. In fact, it would constitute U.S. policy until after 1961.[15] White Southern Rhodesian politicians Godfrey Huggins and Roy Welensky led the pro-Federation forces and would become, respectively, the Federation's first and last prime ministers. Moreover, some liberal whites in Southern Rhodesia, Great Britain, and the United States professed optimism about the Federation's racial policy of partnership. Partnership was to allow for gradual economic and political advancement of blacks, and its defenders praised it as a progressive alternative to South African apartheid. Indeed, white liberals hoped that the success of the Federation and its policy of partnership would keep Southern Rhodesia from aligning more closely with Pretoria's openly racist regime.

Black leaders in the Federation expressed no such hopes however. From the first discussion of Federation, blacks such as Joshua Nkomo and Harry Nkumbula voiced skepticism about the motives of Southern Rhodesian white politicians. Nkomo, Nkumbula, and their followers in the nascent nationalist movements of Southern and Northern Rhodesia hedged at joining in a partnership involving Southern Rhodesian whites. They viewed federation as a method by which Southern Rhodesia would expand its racial discrimination to Northern Rhodesia, while profiting from closer contact with its booming copper mines.[16]

Black nationalists' pessimism about the Federation and partnership was understandable considering some of the statements made by white Southern Rhodesian politicians. In a speech in 1952 while still Prime Minister of Southern Rhodesia, Roy Welensky had warned: "I say to the Africans... if they do not come with us, they will meet the same fate which came to Red Indians in the U.S.A."[17] During debates in the Federal parliament on 20 July 1954, a proposal that segregation in public facilities be abolished throughout the Federation was described by then-obscure Southern Rhodesian representative Ian Smith as "a most ungracious act."[18] Federal Prime Minister Godfrey Huggins agreed with Smith's position favoring segregation, and on 29 July 1954 Huggins exclaimed:

> You cannot expect the European to form up in a queue with
> dirty people, possibly an old umfazi (African woman) with
> an infant on her back, mewling and puking and making a
> mess of everything.[19]

Clearly, Welensky and Huggins were not likely to lead the Federation down the path to true racial partnership. African nationalists like Nkomo and Nkumbula understood this and thus opposed Federation from the start. Neither side in this debate affected the initial policy of the Eisenhower Administration regarding the Federation. Since Nyasaland and the Rhodesias were British possessions, the U.S. State Department followed Great Britain's lead in those areas. American diplomats were cognizant of racial issues and hoped partnership would be a success; however, much more attention was paid to strategic minerals.

Between 1953 and 1956, the United States' economic interest in the Federation of Rhodesia and Nyasaland increased substantially. This involvement took two basic forms: government loans and private investment. Three major public loans were made during this period. In 1953 the Export-Import Bank of Washington lent Northern Rhodesia $22.4 million for a hydroelectric project, and the World Bank lent $14 million for railroad construction. In 1956 the World Bank lent the Federation $80 million to build the Kariba Dam, which also would be used for hydropower.[20]

Bitterly opposed by blacks and whites in Northern Rhodesia, the Kariba project forced 27,000 Batonga people to abandon their homelands. The Kariba location was chosen by Southern Rhodesian whites who stood to gain from its proximity to Salisbury and the potential tourism generated by the resulting lake.[21] A black Southern Rhodesian later described Kariba as the Federation's greatest achievement, but added that he had "yet to meet one African who regards that (Kariba) with common national pride of achievement."[22] In the decision to build Kariba, however, as in the decision to form the Federation, the views of blacks were not considered. The World Bank followed the lead of the British parliament, which was convinced by the arguments of the white Southern Rhodesians.

The World Bank's loan for Kariba and the two aforementioned loans all financed operations directly linked to Rhodesian copper and chrome mines. Mining concerns partially owned by the American Metal Company and Union Carbide, however, virtually dominated the political-economy of the Federation.[23] In 1955 the American Metal Company held 51 percent interest in the Rhodesian Selection Trust, one of two groups that controlled Rhodesia's copper production. In the chrome industry, Union Carbide played a central role throughout this period.[24]

During Eisenhower's first term, the combination of substantial loans and private investment meant that America's economic stake in the Federation was large. What did the United States receive in return? Not surprisingly, the major returns were tremendous shipments of copper and chrome. For example, in 1954 the Federation exported over 260,000 tons of chrome to America, nearly double the amount that U.S. mines produced. Northern Rhodesia supplied over 60,000 tons of copper to America in 1954, approximately 7 percent of the amount mined in the United States.[25] Both copper and chrome were being stockpiled as a Cold War precaution. Since airplane production required large amounts of copper wire, the United States wanted to stockpile it not only for American use but to keep it from the Soviets. Chromium was a key element in stainless steel, an important component of submarines and automobiles. Thus the central position of the mining industry in relations with the Federation exemplified the effect of more than just economics, as the mining was driven by Cold War concerns. At the same time, mining in the Federation touched on another crucial topic: race relations.

Just over seven million blacks inhabited the Federation states of Southern Rhodesia, Northern Rhodesia, and Nyasaland in the 1950s. A white population of about two hundred thousand, mostly living in Southern Rhodesia, governed all internal affairs. In 1955, Southern Rhodesia included 2.4 million blacks and 165 thousand whites. Northern Rhodesia claimed 2.08 million blacks and 65 thousand whites. Nyasaland featured 2.55 million blacks and 6 thousand whites.[26] With black nationalists striving for independence in Ghana and Kenya, the issue of race relations within the Federation was crucial. How much attention did U.S. officials and private investors pay to this issue? Were they influenced by the civil rights movement emerging in the United States?

In December 1953, the U.S. intelligence agencies predicted problems in the Federation because of racial conflict.[27] The Central Intelligence Agency (CIA) emphasized the value of minerals in the area, however, and advised that the issue of race should not hinder U.S. economic and political support for the Federation. The U.S. Consul General in Southern Rhodesia, John Hoover, rated minerals as America's number one interest in Rhodesia. He listed race relations fourth.[28]

A. Philip Randolph, the African-American head of the Sleep-
ing Car Porters' Union, argued that Washington's priorities should
be different. When the British created the Federation in 1953,
Randolph believed that the United States should oppose the British plan. He wrote to Eisenhower that the Federation scheme should
"be postponed and referred to the Trusteeship Council of the United
Nations for study and appraisal, since it is bitterly and practically
universally opposed by African chiefs of these territories."[29] As a
leader of the civil rights movement in the United States, Randolph
desired that racial justice be the key factor in relations with the
Federation. He advocated heeding the desires of black Africans,
but Eisenhower was relatively unconcerned with the views of blacks
in Africa or America during his first term.[30] The White House
delegated Randolph's letter to a low-level State Department official.[31]

In order to support African independence movements, Randolph
joined the American Committee on Africa (ACOA). This group
had been founded in May 1953 in Manhattan, by a small group
that included George Houser, Norman Thomas, Donald Harrington,
and James Farmer. Harrington, pastor of the Community Church
of New York, became the first chairman of the ACOA, and Houser
became the first secretary. With Houser traveling through Africa
in 1954, the ACOA got off to a slow start. His return to active duty
in March 1955, with one assistant, launched the ACOA's full-time
program. In their first year they succeeded in raising funds to keep
open a South African school that would not be controlled by the
racist government. Houser spent much of his time at the United
Nations lobbying against apartheid and met African nationalist
Julius Nyerere of Tanzania. Houser and the ACOA thus began to
play the important role of friend and supporter for African nationalists visiting the United States.[32] In reality, however, during
Eisenhower's first term the ACOA was a fledgling group with no
influence on U.S. policy.

The one channel through which positive steps regarding race
sometimes occurred was private investment. Throughout 1953 the
Rhodesian Selection Trust, an American-owned copper mining
concern, conducted negotiations with the white miners' union in
order to open up skilled and semi-skilled jobs to black workers.
With encouragement from the owner in New York, the Trust's di-

rector convinced the white union to create twenty four job categories for blacks.[33] Black urban workers in the Federation gained in real income in the 1950s, due in part to the efforts of American investors. This also reflected the lack of an extreme Afrikaner interest group, which was stifling any gains for blacks in South Africa.[34]

Private U.S. investors helped to improve the lives of some blacks in the Federation, and they considered progressive race relations to be crucial to the survival of the Federation. After visiting the copper mines of Northern Rhodesia in 1955, Congresswoman Frances Bolton (R-Ohio) reported: "In fact, in many areas our businessmen abroad can teach our diplomatic representation the true avenues of creating goodwill. Our thanks to our American businessmen who are showing the way so courageously in Africa."[35] Many officials in the Eisenhower Administration, however, did not give race relations as high a priority as Bolton and some American businessmen in the Federation did.

In 1956, despite pessimistic predictions by the CIA and others, American officials continued to hope for the Federation's success. The State Department officer for southern African Economic Affairs, David Longanecker, wrote: "The Federation has a very favorable balance of trade and of payments with the United States and is therefore a large net earner of dollars."[36] Longanecker, like the U.S. government in general during Eisenhower's first term, paid more attention to economics than race when pondering relations with the Federation.

In addition to economics, another major factor that overshadowed race in U.S. relations with the Federation was the Cold War. One scholar of Soviet foreign relations has speculated that the USSR established contacts with Southern Rhodesian nationalists as early as 1958, but supplied no evidence.[37] In any case, the Eisenhower Administration perceived no real threat of Soviet operations in southern Africa. Rather, it desired that strategic minerals from the Federation augment U.S. stockpiles, and that such minerals not reach the Soviets.

The interest in Northern Rhodesian copper among members of the Congress, moreover, emerged clearly in 1956. In February and March the Senate's Subcommittee on Investigations held hearings on East-West trade. The Senators' questions regarding the trade of

Northern Rhodesian copper elucidated the influence of the Cold War on U.S. relations with the Federation. Margaret Tibbetts later recalled that "the worst thing that anybody ever could do anywhere was the way we looked at Africa in terms of the Cold War....we were idiots to think of it in terms of the Cold War, but we were obsessed with the Cold War."[38] Nevertheless, the U.S. government viewed Africa through a Cold War lens throughout the Eisenhower Administration.

The Senate's examination of the trade of Northern Rhodesian copper began on 15 February 1956 with the testimony of the subcommittee's counsel Jerome Adlerman. Adlerman explained that airplane production required large amounts of copper wire. For this reason primarily, the Soviets imported copper wire. According to Adlerman, "They have made very, very strenuous efforts in the past to get copper." The United States mined a lot of copper internally, but Adlerman pointed out that domestic copper production was "insufficient for our demands, and we must get copper from the outside."[39] Thus Washington invested in Federation copper to supplement its internal supply and also sought to prevent the shipment of copper to the Soviets in order to hinder their aircraft production.

Regardless of U.S. efforts to keep copper from getting to the Soviets, large quantities were reaching them in the form of copper wire. Curiously the embargo blocked copper, but not copper wire. The subcommittee hoped to discover what companies were shipping this wire and if possible to stop them. Some members suspected that copper from Northern Rhodesian mines was shipped to England, where it was rolled into wire and then shipped to the USSR. Senator Joseph McCarthy (R-Wisc.) held such a view, as his cross-examination of assistant counsel Adlerman illustrated.

> McCarthy: Is this correct, that we supplied the money to develop the mines from which the copper wire went to the Soviet Union?
> Alderman: Yes, sir. We extended a loan of $22.4 million to the Rhodesian Congo Border Power Company.
> McCarthy: In other words... American money under the foreign aid program was used to finance the shipment of copper wire to the Soviet Union?[40]

The loan under scrutiny was the one made by the Export-Import Bank in January 1953 to Northern Rhodesia. The Federation repaid the loan with copper shipments to the United States. In addition private U.S. investors profited, since the American Metal Company held the majority of shares in one of the two major copper concerns. McCarthy ignored such benefits and focused on the chance that some copper from these mines reached the Soviets. His accusation that American loans financed "the shipment of copper wire to the Soviet Union," exaggerated the case.

In truth, the U.S. financed the construction of hydroelectric plants and railroads, and received copper in return. The defense industry used this copper, and with Eisenhower's blessing they stockpiled it as a Cold War precaution. Relations with the Federation during the Eisenhower Administration reflected the Cold War concern with strategic minerals, as had relations with South Africa during the Truman Administration.[42] As much as anything else, the importance of strategic minerals compelled the United States to loan money to the Rhodesias. The 1953 loan of $22.4 million had not garnered enough copper or chrome to meet the stockpile goals, so Cold War concerns remained influential in 1956.

These hearings demonstrated the impact of the Cold War on U.S. policy towards the Federation. The most important aspect of Washington's policy as of 1956 was to stockpile copper and chrome. To further these ends, the World Bank loaned the Federation $80 million dollars in June 1956 for the Kariba Dam. This loan came near the end of Eisenhower's first term, during which economics and the Cold War outweighed race in relations with the Federation. The civil rights movement in the United States accelerated during Eisenhower's second term, and racial divisions in the Federation widened. The question became: Would these changes substantially alter U.S. policy?

EISENHOWER'S SECOND TERM: 1957-61
The economic component of relations with the Federation remained significant during Eisenhower's second term. The World Bank issued two major loans to the Federation: $19 million for railroad improvements in 1958; $5.6 million for agricultural development in 1960. The importation of large amounts of strategic minerals continued. For example, in 1959 Southern Rhodesia shipped over

450,000 tons of chromite to the United States, where it was mainly used in stainless steel. American industry utilized more Southern Rhodesian chrome than from any other source, and American mines only produced around 100,000 tons. However, annual copper shipments steadily declined as loans were repaid and imports from Chile and Peru increased.[43]

By 1957, economic growth in the Federation, boosted by new dams and improved railroads, impressed important American officials. In August the U.S. Consul General in Southern Rhodesia, Loyd Steere, advised the State Department to open full diplomatic relations with the Federation, thus upgrading the consulate to an embassy. He reasoned that America could thereby influence racial policies more strongly.[44] In October mid-level officials at the State Department replied. State's cable began by praising the Federation's economy: "In recent years its rate of economic development has been unsurpassed by any other country in the world. American private investment has reached a high level and can be expected to grow further."[45] While it is unclear whether the State Department realized it, the Federation's economic growth primarily benefited the white minority. In any case, when weighing economic factors, State favored full diplomatic relations.[46]

On the other side of the coin, State Department officials believed that racial problems discouraged full recognition. In order for the Federation to succeed, the white government had to win the loyalty of the black population. However, American diplomats acknowledged that to the contrary; black resistance and opposition were increasing as time passed. As of 1957, Federation blacks were not allowed in hotels or restaurants and were not trusted to drink European beer. In that year Southern Rhodesian blacks founded their branch of the African National Congress, joining the branches in Northern Rhodesia and Nyasaland in criticizing the Federation.[47] Federation nationalists such as Joshua Nkomo and Harry Nkumbula "all regarded it (Federation) as a failure because, in their opinions, it had increased racial discrimination."[48] State bureaucrats dealing with Africa felt that such nationalist resistance discouraged full recognition of the Federation. Their view of race relations in the Federation, in any case, was clear.

The officially professed policy of the Federation Government is one of 'racial partnership,' but its implementation to date has apparently been inadequate to counter the opposition of the African nationalists. The white minority electorate, which has a virtual monopoly of political power, does not appear to be willing in the near future to endorse any political concessions which would be apt to placate the African inhabitants.[49]

The State Department carefully weighed whether full diplomatic recognition, which would entail establishing an embassy in Salisbury, would help or hinder race relations within the Federation. The Department decided that it would not be appropriate for the United States to be the first country to recognize the Federation. As it turned out, no other Western power would initiate full recognition. In State's opinion, U.S. primacy in recognition "might be construed as a gratuitous endorsement of the racial status quo in the Federation and serve to encourage the latter country's pressures on the United Kingdom to grant full independence before the future political and social position of the Africans is adequately clarified."[50]

The department contended that the Federation was unpopular with African nationalists, and the general struggle of nationalists against colonialism had been important to State officials—including John Foster Dulles—since the Suez Crisis of the previous year. Dulles never demonstrated interest specifically in southern African nationalism, but strongly opposed the colonialism of Great Britain regarding Suez.[51] State officials would not support independence for Southern Rhodesia, Northern Rhodesia, and Nyasaland until the status of blacks was established. The diplomats' position did not spell out exactly what they thought the blacks' status should be, but it illustrated the influences of race relations and nationalism on the decision not to recognize the Federation in 1957.

Simultaneously, domestic civil rights possibly influenced their thinking, as the integration crisis raged in Little Rock, Arkansas. On 4 September 1957, Arkansas Governor Orval Faubus commanded the National Guard to prevent nine blacks from entering previously all-white Central High School. When Faubus withdrew the Arkansas troops, two days of mob violence broke out, injuring two black reporters and effectively keeping Central High segregated. Faubus had finally pushed President Eisenhower too far, and he reluctantly ordered in Federal troops on 24 September. If Eisenhower was going to use troops, no matter how reluctantly, he would do it right. By nightfall a thousand soldiers from the riot-trained 101st Airborne Division arrived in Little Rock to allow the black students to enter school.[52] Reports from Asia and Africa criticizing the resistance to integration in Little Rock reached Eisenhower, making it clear that segregation in the South hurt the foreign reputation of the United States.[53]

Policy towards Africa in general became a higher priority of the Eisenhower Administration in its second term. During March 1957, Vice President Richard Nixon visited several African countries. African-American E. Frederick Morrow, Eisenhower's administrative officer for special projects, accompanied Nixon. The primary occasion for the trip was the Independence Celebration in Ghana, to be held at midnight on March 6. Morrow and Nixon met with Ghana's first prime minister, Kwame Nkrumah, on March 4. Nkrumah welcomed Nixon graciously and was very happy to meet Morrow. He observed that they each were breaking difficult ground in the advancement of blacks.[54]

While Nixon was initially received graciously, he had very little to offer the new nation of Ghana in return; indeed, Eisenhower had authorized him to present Nkrumah only one fellowship for a Ghanian student to study in the United States. Nkrumah responded to this slight by seating Nixon in the back of the hall at the formal Independence dinner. Martin Luther King, Jr., an unofficial American delegate who had been personally invited by Nkrumah, upstaged Nixon at the dinner by challenging him to inspect the poor conditions of southern blacks in the United States and report on the violence to Eisenhower. After King spoke, Nixon invited King to visit the White House, and he did so later in 1957.[55]

Returning to Washington on March 21, the vice president submitted a report stressing the importance of Africa in the struggle against the Soviet Union.[56] His report has been praised as "a milestone in the development of American policy toward Africa...

(which) brought African affairs out of bureaucratic limbo." However, Nixon's report implied that Africa was not important for its own sake, but only as a new arena in which to achieve U.S. anticommunist goals.[57] In August 1958, the government formed a separate Bureau for African Affairs within the State Department: previously Africa had been included in the Bureau for Near Eastern Affairs. Nixon had been instrumental in the formation of the African Bureau, convincing Congress that it was necessary as Africa became more of a Cold War battleground.[58]

Eisenhower appointed Joseph Satterthwaite as the first Assistant Secretary of State for African Affairs. Satterthwaite's 30 years with State made him a safe choice for the new post. He had considerable experience with African issues, most recently as Consul General in Tangiers. A career foreign service officer like Satterthwaite would not be likely to revolutionize U.S. relations with Africa overnight, and his first speech as assistant secretary in September 1958 echoed the cautious approach State had taken towards Africa throughout the 1950s.[59]

In December 1958, Ghana again took center stage in the decolonization of Africa, when Kwame Nkrumah hosted an All African People's Conference (AAPC). Over 300 delegates from 65 parties or groups attended the AACP, to discuss the struggle for independence in Africa. George Houser led a group from the American Committee on Africa (ACOA), and the AFL/CIO and Associated Negro Press also sent representatives. African-American Congressman Charles Diggs (D-Mich.) was present as an observer. Diggs expressed dismay that the Eisenhower Administration had sent no official message of greetings or goodwill for the conference's opening, and succeeded in cajoling a message from Nixon which arrived on the last day.[60]

The conference in Accra fostered developments that would have important ramifications for U.S. relations with Southern Rhodesia. Participants decreed that April 15 would be celebrated as African Freedom Day.[61] Perhaps more importantly, the American Committee on Africa's George Houser met Joshua Nkomo for the first time in Accra. He described Nkomo as follows:

> Nkomo was not easily forgotten partly because of his huge
> size. He was tall and heavy, even at 42, yet he carried his

weight with great ease. He walked with a rythmic sway, almost like a glide. He had a kind of mischievous smile and soft laugh that gave him an appearance of good humor and jollity, although he could be very stern.[62]

Houser and the ACOA provided Nkomo with useful support beginning in 1959, when Nkomo visited the United States, and would remain his ally through the 1960s and 1970s.

Mason Sears, the U.S. representative on the Trusteeship Council at the United Nations, witnessed the Accra Conference. About a month after returning to the United States, Sears submitted a report on African nationalism to Henry Cabot Lodge, the American representative at the United Nations. Sears' report accurately summarized the concerns of nationalists in the Federation. He contended that Prime Minister Roy Welensky would be unable to hold the Federation together. The root of the problem was the racism of the whites in Southern Rhodesia, whom he judged nearly as segregationist as the leaders of South Africa. Indeed, one possibility Sears foresaw was that Southern Rhodesia would try to join the Union of South Africa. However, Sears argued that the future of the Federation states would be determined by black Africans, and he identified Hastings Banda of Nyasaland as the most influential nationalist. Sears rightly predicted that primary among the nationalists' demands would be universal suffrage.[63]

Sears explained why African nationalism was a major concern for the U.S. government. In his view, the Soviets were likely to begin seeking the allegiance of the nationalists. Rather than allowing the Soviets control of Africa's valuable resources, the United States should beat the Soviets to the punch in gaining the nationalists' allegiance. In order to accomplish this, Sears proffered four recommendations. First, State should encourage U.S. embassies and consulates to increase contact with nationalist leaders. Second, State should occasionally send a representative to Africa specifically to meet with nationalist leaders. Third, Congress should fund visits to the United States by African political leaders. Finally, Sears suggested that the United States adopt a more supportive stance towards African nationalism at the United Nations. If it adopted such strategies, Sears concluded, then the United States could "ride along with the Nationalist bandwagon without actually climbing on board, or without taking sides against its European allies."[64]

Sears' conclusion illuminated the crux of the U.S. dilemma regarding nationalism. On the one hand, supporting the "Nationalist bandwagon" was useful and necessary in the propaganda battle with the Soviet Union. Gaining the allegiance of African nationalists accomplished containment in Africa. For Eisenhower, Dulles, and Satterthwaite, however, containment in Europe took precedence over containment in Africa. Therefore, when African nationalists boldly challenged the French in Algeria or the British in the Federation, the Eisenhower Administration stuck by the metropole, thus avoiding "taking sides against... European allies."[65] When an African nationalist went so far as to seek Soviet support, as in the case of Patrice Lumumba in the Congo, Eisenhower ordered his removal from power.

Not surprisingly, Sears' report had little impact. Henry Cabot Lodge, U.S. ambassador to the UN, forwarded the report with great praise to Dulles.[66] Dulles did not get to read the report before leaving on a trip to Europe, and passed it on to the African Bureau.[67] In fact, Dulles probably never read it, as he died from stomach cancer in April. Whether or not the Assistant Secretary for Africa, Joseph Satterthwaite, read it is less clear; however, if he did read it he did not take it to heart.

When it came to the question of decolonization and independence for African nations, Satterthwaite believed that the process should be very gradual. Whenever there was a choice between siding with the nationalists or the metropole, he opted for the latter. At the only meeting of the Senate's Subcommittee on Africa in 1959, Satterthwaite and Senator John Kennedy discussed Africa. Kennedy had made a controversial speech supporting independence for Algeria in 1957, advocating U.S. support for nationalism around the world.[68]

In their off-the-record discussion at the 1959 subcommittee meeting, Kennedy asked why the State Department did not put more pressure on the French to grant independence to Algeria. Satterthwaite replied that because the defense of Europe against the Soviets was so important, the amount of pressure that State could put on France was limited. The European Bureau and Secretary Dulles, he added, hesitated to pressure France about Algeria.[69]

Indeed, though Kennedy championed anticolonialism as a senator, as president he would at times support the metropoles over the African nationalists.[70]

The fact that Kennedy, one of the few members of Congress to have spoken out on Africa, called only one meeting of the subcommittee in 1959 illustrated how Africa still trailed far behind Europe, Asia, and South America in the minds of U.S. senators. Similarly, the House of Representatives showed little enthusiasm. Congressman Charles Diggs urged his fellow African Americans to take an interest in the struggles of African nationalists, and decried U.S. policymakers for only viewing Africa in terms of the Cold War.[71] Congresswoman Frances Bolton was one of very few other interested members of the House. She met informally with Satterthwaite on 28 February 1959, explaining to him that the House Subcommittee on Africa had not met at all in 1958. However, she had succeeded in getting a meeting scheduled for March 5.[72]

At the meeting on 5 March 1959, Satterthwaite demonstrated his less-than-stellar grasp for the realities of the situation in the Federation. In discussing its racial policy of partnership, Satterthwaite remarked that "quite a bit of progress had been made along these lines." Nationalists in the Federation clearly disagreed. Indeed, during February, protests in Nyasaland against the Federation had resulted in a state of emergency being declared. On 25 February the African National Congress was banned throughout the Federation. Nationalist leaders Hastings Banda and Kenneth Kaunda had been imprisoned in Southern Rhodesia. Satterthwaite mentioned these events briefly, but did not emphasize their seriousness.[73]

The State Department refrained from criticizing the Federation's use of excessive force to quell the disturbances in Nyasaland. George Houser and the American Committee on Africa, to the contrary, denounced the racial discrimination in the Federation and called for its dissolution.[74] In a letter to Federation Prime Minister Roy Welensky, Houser protested the state of emergency and banning of the ANC. In reply, Welensky argued that any progress in the Federation was because of European efforts, and that all the nationalists were thugs.[75]

A few months later, during a dinner speech, Welensky manifested his view that the nationalists did not have any worthy grievances. Instead of considering some type of reform as a response to the riots, he pondered forming a riot squad. "Perhaps the most cogent lesson we learned from the disturbances in Nyasaland is the need for adequate policing of the right sort, properly trained, with its concomitant of an effective intelligence service operating all the time."[76] Welensky's reactions to the blacks' struggle for social and political equality closely resembled those by southern U.S. governors Orval Faubus in 1957 and George Wallace in the 1960s.

The strategies of segregationists in southern Africa in 1959 certainly resembled those of segregationists in the southern United States. Martin Luther King, Jr., commented on this resemblance more than once during that summer. In June he wrote to the editors of *Dissent* magazine in Southern Rhodesia: "Although we are separated by many miles we are closer together in a mutual struggle for freedom and human brotherhood."[77] During a July dinner for Kenyan Tom Mboya in Atlanta, King explained to Mboya that "there is no basic difference between colonialism and segregation... our struggles are not only similar; they are in a real sense one."[78]

Such similarities between race relations in the Federation and the United States became clear to Joshua Nkomo in 1959. Nkomo, leader of the Southern Rhodesian ANC, fortunately was outside of the country during the February crackdown. Rather than return to be jailed, he decided to visit the United States in hopes of rallying some support for the ANC cause. About this time he first caught the eye of the State Department in Washington, and as a result State officials requested the U.S. consul general in Salisbury to cable Nkomo's biographical information. Consul general Joseph Palmer responded with a brief memo detailing Nkomo's life, which reached Foggy Bottom on May 9.[79]

Nkomo traveled across the United States in 1959, speaking about the struggle for independence in Africa. During a fall stop at the State University of New York in New Paltz, he mentioned casually that he enjoyed apples and rock music. A group of students who overheard him rushed out and bought him a bag of apples and a record album. Such kindness greatly pleased Nkomo, and the support of such individuals and the ACOA demonstrated that African nationalism had friends in the United States. On the other hand, Nkomo also experienced what he referred to as one of the "pinpricks" of U.S. racism when a barbershop in Manhattan denied him service because of his color.[80]

Abel Muzorewa was learning the same lessons in 1959. While studying religion in Missouri, a restaurant in St. Louis refused to serve him. Nevertheless, Martin Luther King's battle against segregation inspired Muzorewa.[81] Also in 1959, Ndabaningi Sithole published his book *African Nationalism*. While studying in the United States the American civil rights movement impressed Sithole, and he cited King's view on nonviolence in *African Nationalism*.[82] Nkomo, Muzorewa, and Sithole understood that while some U.S. citizens held racist views similar to the leaders of the Federation, many others such as King would be helpful. The role that the U.S. government would play in the struggle for independence and freedom in southern Africa, however, was not clear.[83]

In Africa as a general rule in the late 1950s, Cold War concerns encouraged the U.S. to support the desires of blacks. As countries like Ghana and Nigeria gained independence and blacks took power, the possibility of them aligning with the Soviets emerged. The case of the Federation, however, differed from the general rule in one fundamental way: Great Britain retained control of the Federation throughout the 1950s. As a result, Washington did not want to initiate significant policy changes on its own, and instead supported Great Britain's policy.

While U.S. officials walked softly in the Federation so as not to step on Britain's toes, their policy did not differ greatly from their general strategy for gaining influence throughout Africa. The developmental loans and technical cooperation grants supplied to the Federation typified U.S. policy during the 1950s, which avoided military involvement in Africa. President Eisenhower had explained this reasoning at a 1958 meeting of the National Security Council: "Military activity is usually ineffective as the first step in establishing close relations with a country.... We should first work through education and cultural relations... We must win Africa, but we can't win it by military activity."[84]

In order to establish close relations with African countries, therefore, Eisenhower advocated improving cultural relations. His special President's Fund Program sent outstanding American athletes and artists to Africa and the Middle East. Mal Whitfield, an African-American sprinter who had won three gold medals, visited

Northern Rhodesia in 1955. He instructed some young African runners and demonstrated his blazing speed before an enthusiastic audience, and the trip was quite successful.[85]

In addition to athletes, the U.S. government paid for tours by outstanding black musicians, known as "jambassadors." Dizzy Gillespie played in Iran, Pakistan, and Turkey, and the State Department planned to send Louis Armstrong on such a tour. After the crisis at Little Rock, however, Armstrong refused to represent the United States. He exclaimed: "The way they are treating my people in the South, the government can go to hell."[86] Armstrong did not tour, and the State Department also stopped sponsoring such trips for athletes.[87]

Furthermore, events in the Federation revealed the potential negative impact of cultural relations that were privately funded. On 7 September 1959, the American-owned Royal Cinema in Salisbury, Southern Rhodesia, staged a grand opening and benefit for the Red Cross. The extravaganza excluded all black Africans. The fact that a "whites only" event occurred at an American movie theater infuriated Clarence Randall, the chairman of Eisenhower's Council on Foreign Economic Policy.[88] Randall remarked that the incident "greatly damaged the image which Africans have of our country."[89]

According to Joseph Palmer, the American Consul General in Salisbury, the really important point was not the isolated event of the Red Cross benefit at the Royal Cinema. Rather, the more serious problem existed in the ongoing exclusion of nonwhites from several American-owned theaters in Salisbury. In December of 1959, Palmer pointed the finger of blame at American movie mogul Spyros Skouras, the president of 20th Century Fox.[90] Skouras controlled the Royal Cinema and other theaters in Salisbury. The theaters were operated by the African Consolidated Theaters group, but widely recognized as American-owned. Skouras claimed that local government policy in Salisbury necessitated the exclusion of nonwhites. In fact, if the theaters simply provided separate restrooms for nonwhites, then the laws of Salisbury would allow multiracial audiences. Palmer concluded that Skouras himself was responsible for the policy and hoped that the State Department could convince him to correct the situation. Palmer also made the following observation.

> Incidentally, "The Ten Commandments" is to be shown to
> European only audiences at the Royal Cinema beginning
> next week. I think we can be confident that this will give
> rise to some wry comments by African Christians who will
> note a gap between their own understanding of those rules
> of behavior and their interpretation by an American-con-
> trolled company.[91]

Palmer clearly objected to Skouras's ongoing policy of banning blacks from his theaters in Southern Rhodesia. Palmer explained the situation to Joseph Satterthwaite, the Assistant Secretary of State for African Affairs. Satterthwaite replied: "Because of the public identification of African Consolidated as an 'American' firm, I certainly agree that its policy is most unfortunate... However, as the issue has been pointed out to Mr. Skouras... I frankly doubt whether there is much more we can properly do at this juncture." Satterthwaite decided that since Skouras had already been advised of the situation, nothing more could be done. He thought that his hands were tied, and emphasized that "the U.S. Government has no control over the American parent firm."[92]

The parent firm in this case, 20th Century Fox, conducted business in a manner that several American officials considered injurious to the reputation of the United States. The U.S. government lacked the power to control the policies of 20th Century Fox, and this inability exemplified the potential dangers of private investment in foreign countries. Eisenhower had recommended increasing cultural relations in order to establish good will in African countries. However, the American-owned theaters in Southern Rhodesia demonstrated that cultural relations could do more harm than good.

The events surrounding the theaters, moreover, illuminated the increasingly complicated role of race in relations between the United States and the Federation in 1959 and 1960. An American-owned company excluded blacks in Rhodesia, harming America's reputation, but the U.S. government refrained from any action stronger than a verbal warning. Similar racial discrimination existed in the southern United States, and the Eisenhower Administration also refrained from any extended or massive intervention in those events.

While the State Department discussed the proper course of action regarding the Rhodesian theaters, students initiated a grass roots sit-in movement against segregation in the South. Young Americans such as John Lewis and James Bevel formed the Student Nonviolent Coordinating Committee (SNCC), and 1960 ushered in a new era of direct confrontation.[93] On 1 February 1960 Joseph McNeill, a college freshman, initiated a sit-in at a Woolworth's cafeteria in Greensboro, North Carolina. This sparked active involvement by SNCC in a sit-in campaign that quickly spread to Richmond, Nashville, Chattanooga, and other cities. By year's end some 50,000 blacks participated in the effort, forcing the integration of 126 southern cities.

While the Justice Department provided some helpful mediation on behalf of the movement, President Eisenhower never strongly endorsed the direct action strategy. When violence flared up in Jacksonville, pleas for Federal help went unheeded. Such lukewarm enthusiasm typified the civil rights policies of the Eisenhower Administration from 1953 to 1961. While some progress had been made, Eisenhower generally refused to actively confront southern white resistance to racial equality. Eisenhower supported the removal of laws requiring segregation, but opted to leave anything more progressive to the private sector.[94]

Leaving the onus with the private sector meant the job would not get done, whether in the United States or in the Federation. Martin Luther King, Jr., and A. Philip Randolph urged Eisenhower to provide Federal protection against brutal police repression of the direct action campaigns in 1960 and also joined in calling for a stronger stand against racial injustice in southern Africa. They co-chaired the American Committee on Africa's Freedom Day, which featured speeches by Federation nationalists Hastings Banda and Kenneth Kaunda.[95]

Meanwhile, a March massacre of 69 blacks who had been nonviolently protesting pass laws in Sharpeville, near Johannesburg, provided a horrible example of what could occur in the Federation.[96] A group of outraged State Department officials issued a statement strongly condemning the Sharpeville tragedy and apartheid. The State employees had not cleared their statement with the Eisenhower Administration, or even with Secretary of State Christian Herter. Herter explained to the White House that he disagreed with the statement. Eisenhower and high officials at State and Defense similarly refused to defend the statement.[97] As with the crackdown in Nyasaland in 1959, the leaders of the Eisenhower Administration refrained from censuring southern African whites after Sharpeville.

In July 1960, the Federation nationalists launched their own direct confrontation against white resistance. The National Democratic Party (NDP), which replaced the banned African National Congress on 1 January 1960, had organized numerous large and spirited demonstrations against the Federation throughout the spring. On 19 July, Southern Rhodesian Prime Minister Edgar Whitehead ordered the arrest of three NDP leaders. This was the first of many blunders by Whitehead, about whom the U.S. Consul General Joseph Palmer opined: "Edgar is almost blind and deaf and... unmarried, all of which remove him from a lot of reality.... He has practically no contact with Africans."[98] Whitehead's repressive tactics mirrored those of southern U.S. governors Orval Faubus and George Wallace, and similarly caused far more problems than they solved.[99] Whitehead overestimated the security threat posed by the NDP, and by arresting three leaders triggered widespread violence in Southern Rhodesia.[100]

After the arrests on 19 July, seven thousand Africans gathered in the township of Highfield and marched eight miles into Salisbury to confront Whitehead the next day. Whitehead refused to talk to the demonstrators and called in a battalion of troops to control the crowd that had swollen to 40,000. Police waded into the crowd to break up the assembly, with jeeps speeding among the pedestrians and planes buzzing overhead. A riot erupted, and three Africans suffered gunshot wounds. A similar scenario unfolded the following weekend in Bulawayo, Southern Rhodesia's second-largest city, leaving eleven Africans dead. Whitehead's tactics of arresting NDP leaders and sending in troops against unarmed civilians reaped a tragic harvest - the first Africans killed by government forces in Southern Rhodesia since 1896.[101]

The July riots added to the conviction of African nationalists that the Federation must go. Joshua Nkomo explained that the NDP did not recognize Whitehead's government and advocated immediate independence for the three states of Nyasaland, Northern

Rhodesia, and Southern Rhodesia.[102] In the United States, Assistant Secretary for Africa Joseph Satterthwaite discussed the riots with British officials. While Satterthwaite may have attributed more seriousness to these events than he had the earlier Nyasaland riots, he still hoped that reform could hold the Federation together.[103] Similarly, the manager of Eastman Kodak's operations in Salisbury expressed optimism for the future of the Federation. He complained that pessimism and negative press about violence in Southern Rhodesia would discourage American investment. He contended that industrial expansion, such as that proposed by Kodak, was the key to the success of the Federation.[104]

A leading Southern Rhodesian nationalist explained to a State official, however, that reform and industrial expansion would not be enough. Federation blacks would not be satisfied until they had political equality and independence.[105] The bureau of intelligence at the State Department concluded in October 1960 that the Federation would inevitably dissolve. Northern Rhodesia and Nyasaland were well on their way to majority rule, and Southern Rhodesia would eventually follow. However, unless the British moved the transition along more rapidly, additional violence would break out. If brutalities similar to the South African tragedy at Sharpeville resulted, then the Federation would take on the status of a true international crisis.[106]

At the time of the July riots Joseph Palmer, the U.S. Consul General in Salisbury, provided a chilling picture of one potential outcome from replications of Sharpeville. If the Federation disintegrated too quickly, bedlam would result. Palmer believed that only fundamental political reform instigated by Great Britain combined with significant financial aid from the United States could guarantee stability in the region. Otherwise, the Federation could conceivably descend into chaos resembling that in the Congo.[107] Such a development would preclude foreign investment, endanger U.S. access to the copper and chrome mines of Northern and Southern Rhodesia, and possibly result in Soviet intervention.

Palmer's allusion to the Congo was a powerful one in the summer of 1960, and the Congo was the one part of Africa to which Eisenhower paid personal attention.[108] The influx of Soviet supplies and possibility of Soviet military intervention in the Congo evidently infuriated Eisenhower to the point where he may have ordered the CIA to assassinate Premeir Patrice Lumumba.[109] While the CIA did not actually kill Lumumba, the United States had rebuffed his call for help and driven him to the dire straits that led to his demise; moreover, Eisenhower foiled Lumumba's nation-building efforts and effectively sided with the Belgian metropole's move to regain the riches of Katanga.[110]

THE ELECTION OF 1960 AND SOME APPRAISALS

Aside from worrying about Soviet influence in the Congo, Eisenhower paid virtually no attention to Africa in the late summer and fall of 1960. The summer violence subsided, and the Federation suffered no Sharpeville; therefore, it remained out of the international spotlight and off Eisenhower's agenda. As his second term wound down, he focused his energies on getting Nixon elected. Eisenhower's neglect of Africa proved a campaign liability that Kennedy exploited skillfully, referring to Africa over 500 times in his speeches. He accurately criticized the Eisenhower Administration for failing to accept African nationalism.[111]

As a senator, John F. Kennedy had spoken out against colonization and for independence in Algeria. So, there was some belief that if he became president, his policies towards Africa would be not only higher priority but also more progressive. In other words, many voters hoped Kennedy would deal with Africa for the sake of the Africans fighting for independence rather than as a Cold War arena. Martin Luther King, Jr., believed that in contrast to Eisenhower, Kennedy understood the moral aspect of racial issues in the U.S. and Africa. King also respected Kennedy's advisers regarding Africa such as G. Mennen Williams and Chester Bowles.[112]

When the State Department rejected Kenyan nationalist Tom Mboya's request for $100,000 to fly 222 African students to the United States, Kennedy supplied the funds from the Kennedy Foundation. Nixon, hearing of the Kennedy offer and not wanting to concede the points Kennedy would gain among black voters, convinced State to offer the funds. However, Mboya had already agreed to Kennedy's grant, so Nixon lost out.[113] As the election loomed, Nixon's advisers sensed that Kennedy had scored highly with the electorate regarding Africa and asked Eisenhower to meet publicly with African diplomats. Eisenhower responded with an unenthusiastic reception at the White House the night before the election.[114]

Kennedy's outflanking Nixon regarding Africa was ironic considering Nixon's 1957 visit to Ghana and role in the formation of the African bureau. Similarly, Kennedy gained crucial black support with an eleventh-hour maneuver within the civil rights arena— another area where Nixon had been a leader in the Eisenhower Administration. The October 1960 incarceration of King in Georgia (for violating terms of a suspended sentence for a traffic offense) garnered no sympathy from the Eisenhower Administration, as a draft message of condolence never was sent. Nixon would only respond to questions about King with "no comment." Kennedy on the other hand, at the suggestion of one of his advisers, phoned Coretta Scott King and expressed his sympathy. His brother Robert called the sentencing judge and stated his opinion that King should be released on bail. King was free the next day, and the resulting publicity spurred by King's father influenced blacks across the country to support Kennedy.[115]

Partly because of issues of race and relations with Africa, then, the first new president in the 1960s to tackle those challenges would be John Kennedy. The legacy of relations with the Federation that he inherited was not a progressive or dynamic one. American relations with the Federation during the 1950s emphasized the importance of strategic minerals for U.S. national security, and American policy generally seconded British policy. Although racial issues and African nationalism took on increasing importance during Eisenhower's second term, these issues did not become primary factors in U.S. relations with the Federation. Nonetheless, the Eisenhower Administration's relations with the Federation distilled the elements that would remain central into the 1970s, balancing concerns for strategic metals against race relations and nationalism, while following Great Britain's policy.

NOTES

1. Prosser Gifford, "Misconceived Dominion: The Creation and Disintegration of Federation in British Central Africa," 399-401, in Prosser Gifford and Wm. Roger Louis, eds., *The Transfer of Power*

in Africa: Decolonization, 1940-1960 (New Haven: Yale University Press, 1982), 387-416.

2. The limited attention paid to Africa in the major works on the Eisenhower Administration reflects the low priority that Eisenhower and his advisers gave African issues. Stephen Ambrose, *Eisenhower: The President* (New York: Simon and Schuster, 1984) details the 1960 Congo crisis, 586-89. Wm. Roger Louis, "Dulles, Suez, and the British," in Richard Immerman, ed., *John Foster Dulles and the Diplomacy of the Cold War* (Princeton: Princeton University Press, 1990) touches on Dulles' views on African nationalism in relation to the Suez crisis. Stephen Ambrose, *Nixon: The Education of a Politician, 1913-62* (New York: Simon & Schuster, 1987) examines Nixon's 1957 trip to Africa, 431-433.

3. For an overview of U.S. policy towards British colonialism in Africa, see James Mayall, "Africa in Anglo-American Relations," in Wm. Roger Louis and Hedley Bull, eds., *The 'Special Relationship': Anglo-American Relations Since 1945* (Oxford: Clarendon Press, 1986), 321-340.

4. The Eisenhower Administration's desire for Federation minerals fits into the World Systems notion of how the U.S. sought to integrate the periphery into the core for raw materials. For an analysis of U.S. foreign relations during the Cold War from this perspective see Thomas J. McCormick, *America's Half-Century: United States Foreign Policy in the Cold War* (Baltimore: Johns Hopkins University Press, 1989).

5. See Melvyn P. Leffler, *A Preponderance of Power: National Security, the Truman Administration and the Cold War* (Stanford: Stanford University Press, 1992).

6. William Minter, *King Solomon's Mines Revisited: Western Interests and the Burdened History of Southern Africa* (New York: Basic Books, 1986). Thomas Borstelmann, *Apartheid's Reluctant Uncle: The United States and Southern Africa in the Early Cold War* (New York: Oxford University Press, 1993).

7. For a discussion of how to study the effects of culture in U.S. foreign relations, see Akira Iriye, "Culture and International History," in Michael Hogan and Thomas Paterson, eds., *Explaining the History of American Foreign Relations* (Cambridge: Cambridge University Press, 1991), 214-225.

8. Many scholars contend that Eisenhower and Dulles generally ignored nationalism in Africa. For example, see Robert D. Schulzinger, *American Diplomacy in the Twentieth Century*, 2nd ed. (New York: Oxford University Press, 1990), 232, 258.

9. Thomas J. Noer, *Cold War and Black Liberation: The United States and White Rule in Africa, 1948-1968* (Columbia: University of Missouri Press, 1985), 48-60.

10. Burton Kaufman, *Trade and Aid: Eisenhower's Foreign Economic Policy, 1953-1961* (Baltimore: Johns Hopkins University Press, 1982), 108, 197, 250.

11. Waldemar Neilsen, *The Great Powers and Africa* (New York: Praeger, 1969), 271-272, 279.

12. The classic analysis of the containment strategies of Eisenhower and other U.S. presidents is John Lewis Gaddis, *Strategies of Containment* (New York: Oxford University Press, 1982).

13. Margaret Joy Tibbetts served as U.S. ambassador to Norway from 1964 to 1969, and then as Deputy Assistant Secretary for European Affairs until 1971. For information and photographs of Tibbetts, see Homer L. Calkin, *Women in the Department of State: Their Role in American Foreign Affairs* (Washington: State Department, 1978), 109-111, 172, and 215.

14. Despatch from Margaret Joy Tibbetts to the State Department, July 30, 1953, State Department Decimal File, 745.00/7-3053, NA2.National Archives II, College Park. During her stint in London, Tibbetts sent eight despatches to Washington regarding Rhodesia, beginning on 1 May 1952. They were very detailed, running to as many as seven pages in length.

15. See Mayall, "Africa in Anglo-American Relations."

16. The actions of supporters and opponents of the Federation, particularly Welensky, Huggins, and Nkomo are documented in great detail in J.R.T. Wood, *The Welensky Papers: A History of the Federation of Rhodesia and Nyasaland* (Durban: Graham, 1983). Nkomo's views on the Federation and experiences at a 1952 London Conference are described in Joshua Nkomo, *Nkomo: The Story of My Life* (London: Methuen, 1984), 46-60.

17. Quoted in George Houser, *No One Can Stop the Rain: Glimpses of Africa's Liberation Struggle* (New York: Pilgrim, 1989), 101.

18. Quoted in Colin Leys, *European Politics in Southern Rhodesia* (Oxford: Clarendon, 1959), 267-268.

19. Quoted in Wood, *The Welensky Papers*, 419.

20. Loans discussed in Daniel Volman's 1991 UCLA dissertation, "United States Foreign Policy and the Decolonization of British Central Africa (Zimbabwe, Zambia, and Malawi), 1945-1965," 90-91.

21. See Harry Franklin, *Unholy Wedlock: The Failure of the Central African Federation* (London: George Allen, 1963), 105-119, and

Robert Rotberg, *The Rise of Nationalism in Central Africa: The Making of Malawi and Zambia, 1873-1964* (Cambridge: Harvard University Press, 1965), 274.

22. Herbert Chitepo, "Developments in Central Africa," in David P. Currie, *Federalism and the New Nations of Africa* (Chicago: Chicago University Press, 1964), 9.

23. For a detailed study of the centrality of mining in the political economy of all southern Africa, beginning with gold mines in 19th century South Africa, see Minter, *King Solomon's Mines Revisited.*

24. For discussion of initial U.S. investment in Rhodesian copper and chrome during the 1920s, see Mira Wilkin, *The Maturing of Multinational Enterprise: American Business Abroad from 1914 to 1970* (Cambridge: Harvard University Press, 1974), 110-113 and 167-173.

25. Bureau of Mines, *Minerals Yearbook 1954*, Volume 1 (Washington: U.S. Government Printing Office, 1958), 304, 313, 381, 399.

26. Figures from A.J. Wills, *An Introduction to the History of Central Africa: Zambia, Malawi, and Zimbabwe*, 4th edition (New York: Oxford University Press, 1985), Appendix vii.

27. National Intelligence Estimate on "Conditions and Trends in Tropical Africa," December 22, 1953, in *FRUS, 1952-4* Volume XI, 82-83.

28. Despatch from John Hoover in Salisbury to the State Department, May 8, 1953; in *Foreign Relations of the United States 1952-1954* [hereafter *FRUS*] Volume XI, 318-323. Hoover ranked the Federation's potential as a safety valve for Europe's surplus population second, and the potential contribution of the Federation's military forces in defending the free world third.

29. Letter from A. Philip Randolph to Eisenhower, June 17, 1953, State Department Decimal File, 770.00/6-1753, NA2]. For evidence of African blacks' opposition to the Federation, see T. David Williams, *Malawi: The Politics of Despair* (Ithaca: Cornell University Press, 1978), 141-146; Wood, *Welensky Papers.*

30. African American Congressman Adam Clayton Powell, during a 1955 meeting with Eisenhower, argued for a U.S. stand against colonialism at the UN - to no avail. See Adam Clayton Powell, Jr., *Adam by Adam: The Autobiography of Adam Clayton Powell Jr.* (New York: Dial Press, 1971), 116.

31. See John Jernegan, Deputy Assistant Secretary for Near Eastern, South Asian, and African Affairs, letter to Randolph, State Department Decimal File, 770.00/6-1753, NA2. For analysis of the treatment of Randolph by the Eisenhower Administration see Volman,

"United States Foreign Policy and the Decolonization of British Central Africa," 147-150.

32. George Houser, *No One Can Stop The Rain: Glimpses of Africa's Liberation Struggle* (New York: Pilgrim Press, 1989), xi, 63-68.

33. The negotiations over black advancement, and role of the American Metal Company in them, are discussed in Jane L. Parpart's *Labor and Capital on the African Copperbelt* (Philadelphia: Temple University Press, 1983), 20, 137-8, 176n, and 205n.

34. Minter, *King Solomon's Mines*, 100-101. For an excellent discussion of the rise of apartheid in the 1950s, see Robert Massie, *Loosing the Bonds: The United States and South Africa in the Apartheid Years* (New York: Doubleday, 1997), 45-54.

35. *U.S. Congress. House. Committee on Foreign Affairs. Report of the Special Study Mission to Africa, South and East of the Sahara; by Honorable Frances P. Bolton* (Washington: U.S. Gov. Printing Office, 1956), 132. Bolton visited 24 African countries between September and December 1955, covering about 20,000 miles in 99 days. Her lengthy report contains fascinating descriptions of many aspects of southern Africa. For a summary of the trip, see David Loth, *A Long Way Forward: The Biography of Congresswoman Frances P. Bolton* (New York: Longmans & Green, 1957), 286-292.

36. Memo from David Longanecker to the Director of Southern African Affairs, October 31, 1956; in *FRUS, 1955-7*, XVIII, 51-52.

37. Keith Somerville, "The Soviet Union and Zimbabwe: The Liberation Struggle and After," in R. Craig Nation and Mark Kauppi, eds., *The Soviet Impact in Africa* (Lexington: Heath, 1984), 196.

38. Margaret Joy Tibbetts, interview with the author, Bethel, Maine, 22 December 1993.

39. February 15, 1956, testimony of Jerome Adlerman at the hearing on East-West trade, *Hearings Before the Permanent Subcommittee On Investigations of the Committee On Government Operations United States Senate* Part 1: February 15,16,17,20 and March 6, 1956 (Washington: U.S. Government Printing Office, 1956), 16-18.

40. February 15, 1956, testimony of Jerome Adlerman, *Hearings Before the Permanent Subcommittee*, 17.

41. Throughout his presidency, Eisenhower advocated the stockpiling of essential materials for national security. See the Cabinet Debriefing, "Stockpiling of Copper," 4/24/1959, Box 7, Christian Herter Papers, Dwight Eisenhower Library.

42. For the Truman Administration, see Borstelmann, *Apartheid's Reluctant Uncle.*

43. Bureau of Mines, *Minerals Yearbook 1960*, Volume 1 (Washington: Government Printing Office, 1961), 341 and 348.

44. Loyd Steere despatch to Washington, August 1, 1957, State Department Decimal File, 601.0045c/8-157, NA2.

45. Instruction from State to Salisbury, Bonn, Paris, Lisbon, London, 15 October 1957, State Department Decimal File, 601.0045c/10-1557, NA2. The cable was drafted by J.P. Nagoski of African Affairs and approved by C. Vaughan Ferguson. It went out over John Foster Dulles' name.

46. See Rotberg, *The Rise of Nationalism in Central Africa*, 257.

47. For a description of the formation and spread of the Southern Rhodesian ANC by a founding member, see Nathan M. Shamuyarira, *Crisis in Rhodesia* (New York: Transatlantic, 1966), 45-56. Shamuyarira also discusses the precursors to the ANC, the City Youth Leagues, 26-44.

48. Eshmael Mlambo, *Rhodesia: The Struggle for a Birthright* (London: Hurst, 1972), 116-7, 119; for a similar conclusion see Rotberg, *The Rise of Nationalism*, 255.

49. State to Salisbury, et.al., 15 October 1957, State Department Decimal File, 601.0045c/10-1557, NA2.

50. *Ibid.*

51. For discussion of Dulles' support of nationalism and opposition to colonialism, see Wm. Roger Louis, "Dulles, Suez, and the British," 153-154.

52. Taylor Branch, *Parting the Waters: America in the King Years, 1945-63* (New York: Simon and Schuster, 1988), 222-224.

53. Noer, *Cold War and Black Liberation*, 50-52.

54. For Morrow's view of the Africa trip, see E. Frederick Morrow, *Black Man in the White House: A Diary of the Eisenhower Years By the Administrative Officer for Special Projects, The White House, 1955-1961* (New York: Coward-McCann, 1963), 125-154.

55. The banquet described in Ambrose, *Nixon: The Education of a Politician 1913-1962*, 431-433. For a thorough treatment of the Eisenhower Administration's dealings with King in 1957, the Civil Rights Act of 1957, and Eisenhower's general handling of civil rights, see Robert F. Burk, *The Eisenhower Administration and Black Civil Rights* (Knoxville: University of Tennessee Press, 1984).

56. See Nixon's 69 page "Report to the President on the Vice President's Visit to Africa," WHCF, Confidential Files, Box 100, "VP's Africa Trip," DDE.

57. Neilsen, *The Great Powers in Africa*, 267.

58. *FRUS, 1958-1960, XIV, Africa*, 23; Noer, *Cold War and Black Liberation*, 49.

59. Neilsen, *The Great Powers and Africa*, 271.

60. The AAPC and Diggs' efforts described in George Houser, *No One Can Stop the Rain*, 69-72. Charles Diggs would remain one of the few members of Congress actively involved in relations with Africa until the Carter Administration. His papers in the Moorland-Spingarn Library at Howard University, though unprocessed, are filled with useful materials on U.S. relations with Africa in the 1960s and 1970s.

61. Events at the conference and resulting Africa Freedom Day in the U.S. described in Brenda Plummer, *Rising Wind: Black Americans and U.S. Foreign Affairs, 1935-1960* (Chapel Hill: University of North Carolina Press, 1996), 278-280.

62. George Houser, *No One Can Stop the Rain*, 103. In an interview with the author in Denver on 11/13/95, former U.S. ambassador to Zambia Stephen Low expressed similar opinions of Nkomo. Low described Nkomo as much friendlier than Mugabe, and so big that he took up a whole couch.

63. Mason Sears, "U.S. Relationship With African Nationalism," 29 January 1959, pp 1-5, 770.00/1-3059, State Department Decimal File, NA2.

64. *Ibid.*, 6-8.

65. For an excellent discussion of how the U.S. position on nationalism and colonialism in the 1950s related to containment and varied depending on the circumstances, see Cary Fraser, *Ambivalent Anti-Colonialism: The United States and the Genesis of West Indian Independence, 1940-1964* (Westport: Greenwood, 1994), 9-30.

66. Lodge sent the report to Dulles under a cover letter instructing that Sears' views be carefully considered to "Dear Foster," 30 January 1959, 770.00/1-3059, State Department Decimal File, NA2..

67. John Foster Dulles to Henry Cabot Lodge, 3 February 1959, 770.00/1-3059, State Department Decimal File, NA2. Dulles informed Lodge in this letter that "I have not yet had a chance to read the report. In the meantime, I am passing it along to Joe Satterthwaite."

68. Kennedy speech of 2 July 1957 described in Noer, *Cold War and Black Liberation*, 50-51.

69. Joseph Satterthwaite, oral history interview with William Moss, 2 March 1971, John F. Kennedy Library, Boston, MA.

70. Thomas J. Noer, "New Frontiers and Old Priorities in Africa," in Thomas G. Paterson, ed., *Kennedy's Quest for Victory: American*

Foreign Policy, 1961-63 (New York: Oxford University Press, 1989), 253-283.

71.   Charles C. Diggs, Jr., "The Role of the American Negro in American-African Relations." Address before the American Society of African Culture, 26 June 1959, reprinted in Adelaide Hill and Martin Kilson, eds., *Apropos of Africa: Sentiments of Negro American Leaders on Africa from the 1800s to the 1950s* (London: Frank Cass, 1969), 382-385.

72.   J.C. Satterthwaite, memorandum of conversation with Frances Bolton, 28 February 1959, 770.00/2-2859, State Department Decimal File, NA2.

73.   Statement of Joseph Satterthwaite, 5 March 1959, *Hearings Before the Subcommittee on Africa of the Committee on Foreign Affairs House of Representatives* (Washington: U.S. Government Printing Office, 1959). The Nyasaland disturbances and resulting state of emergency described in Colin Baker, *State of Emergency: Crisis in Central Africa, Nyasaland 1959-1960* (London: Tauris, 1997).

74.   American Committee on Africa, "Statement on Crisis in Central African Federation," 9 March 1959, Folder 10, Box 124, Martin Luther King, Jr. Papers, Martin Luther King, Jr. Library, Atlanta, GA.

75.   Houser, *No One Can Stop the Rain*, 102.

76.   Roy Welensky speech at Ndola dinner, 20 June 1959, enclosed in Joseph Palmer airpouch to State, 24 August 1959, 745c.5/8-2459, State Department Decimal File, NA2.

77.   Stephen B. Oates, *Let the Trumpet Sound: The Life of Martin Luther King, Jr.* (New York: Harper and Row, 1982), 114.

78.   David J. Garrow, *Bearing the Cross: Martin Luther King, Jr., and the Southern Christian Leadership Conference* (New York: Vintage, 1986), 118.

79.   Airgram, Salisbury to State, 20 March 1959, 745c.521/3-2059, State Decimal File, NA2.

80.   Houser, *No One Can Stop the Rain*, 104-5.

81.   Abel Muzorewa, *Rise Up and Walk: An Autobiography* (London: Evans Brothers, 1978), 48-49.

82.   Ndabaningi Sithole, *African Nationalism* (London: Oxford University Press, 1959). For the King quotation, see page 54.

83.   See Mayall, "Africa in Anglo-American Relations."

84.   Memorandum, discussion at the 375th meeting of the National Security Council, August 7, 1958, pp.12-13, Ann Whitman file, DDE.

85.   President's Fund Program and Whitfield's visit to Northern Rhodesia described in Vernon McKay, *Africa in World Politics* (New York:

Harper & Row, 1963), 384; Whitfield's career detailed in James A. Page, *Black Olympian Medalists* (Englewood: Libraries Unlimited, 1991), 122-3.

86. Penny Von Eschen, *Race Against Empire: Black Americans and Anticolonialism, 1937-1957* (Ithaca: Cornell University Press, 1997), 177-180.

87. Secretary of State Christian Herter explained his reasoning in a 1960 response to a suggestion that African-American athletes make extended visits to Africa as unofficial cultural ambassadors. "Prominent Negro athletes, of whom there are many in this country, will, I think, find it difficult to make visits of the length that you indicate and still remain effective." Instead, Herter advocated utilizing literature and films documenting the successes of black American athletes. Christian A. Herter to Martin Sommers, 20 October 1960, Christian Herter Papers, Chronological File, Box 9, Folder "10/60," DDE.

88. The Council on Foreign Economic Policy had been created in December 1954. Clarence Randall, president of Chicago's Inland Steel Company, became chair of the CFEP in 1956. For a brief history of the CFEP, see the finding aid to the papers of the CFEP, DDE. Abilene, KS (hereafter DDE).

89. Clarence B. Randall to Eric Johnston, 19 October 1959, Box 1, 10/59, Chronological File, The Council on Foreign Economic Policy, Records, DDE. Johnston was president of the Motion Picture Association of America. The opening is detailed in *The New York Times*, 9/23/1959, 5.

90. Evidently, Skouras' was as disrespectful of women as he was of blacks. According to Joan Collins, Skouras had aggressively attempted to blackmail sexual intercourse from her in exchange for a part in *Cleopatra* in 1958; see Joan Collins, *Past Imperfect: An Autobiography* (New York: Simon and Schuster, 1978), 143.

91. Joseph Palmer to Joseph Satterthwaite, 8 December 1959, Box 1, Africa #2, Randall Series, Subject Subseries, the Council on Foreign Economic Policy, Chairman, DDE.

92. Joseph Satterthwaite to Joseph Palmer, 20 January 1960, Box 1, Africa #2, Randall Series, Subject Subseries, the Council on Foreign Economic Policy, Chairman, DDE.

93. The sit-ins are described in Taylor Branch, *Parting the Waters: America in the King Years 1954-63*, 272-311.

94. Robert Burk, *The Eisenhower Administration and Black Civil Rights*, 253-255, 262-263.

95. Houser, *No One Can Stop the Rain*, 108.

96. For a discussion of the events at Sharpeville, see Jackie Grobler, *A Decisive Clash: A Short History of Black Protest Politics in South Africa, 1875-1976* (Pretoria: Acacia Books, 1988), 122-126.

97. Noer, *Cold War and Black Liberation*, 54-55.

98. Joseph Palmer to State, 27 July 1960, 745c.00/7-2760, State Decimal File, NA2.

99. Ultimately, however, the tactics of Wallace and Faubus may well have enabled the civil rights movement to be successful. It can be argued, along these lines, that the tactics of Whitehead and his successor Ian Smith ultimately sparked enough resistance to result in an independent black-ruled Zimbabwe. For a discussion of the role of Wallace and Faubus, see Michael J. Klarman, "How *Brown* Changed Race Relations: The Backlash Thesis," *The Journal of American History* (June 1994), 81-118.

100. Joseph Palmer, U.S. Consul General, downplayed the threat posed by the NDP. He correctly identified Joshua Nkomo as the leader in exile in London, thus concluding that the NDP carried on the goals and methods of Nkomo's previous group, the ANC. Actually, it seems that Palmer considered beer halls to be a greater threat to the security of the Federation than the NDP. See Palmer to State, 23 July 1960, 745c.00/7-2360; Palmer to State, 1 July 1960, 745c.00/7-160, State Decimal File, NA2.

101. Shamuyarira, *Crisis in Rhodesia*, 63-64.

102. Stephen Gebelt, Second Secretary U.S. Embassy in Accra to State, 19 August 1960, 745c.00/8-1960, State Decimal File, NA2.

103. Memorandum of conversation between Joseph Satterthwaite and Harry Jeffreys, British Minister for Federation Affairs, 19 August 1960, 745c.00/8-1960, State Decimal File, NA2.

104. The views of S.D. Gent, manager of Kodak's Salisbury operations, described in Edward Mulcahy to State, 27 October 1960, 845c.05111/10-2760, State Decimal File, NA2.

105. Memorandum of September conversations between F.T. McNamara of the State African bureau and Nathan Shamayurira, Southern Rhodesian editor, 19 October 1960, 745c.00/10-1960, State Decimal Files, NA2.

106. Hugh Cumming, director of State Department Intelligence to the Secretary of State, 19 and 26 October 1960, 745c.00/10-1960 and 745c.00/10-2660, State Decimal File, NA2.

107. Joseph Palmer to State, 26 July 1960, 745c.00/7-2660, State Decimal File, NA2.

108. Ambrose, *Eisenhower: Volume Two*, 586-589.

109. Peter Grose, *Gentleman Spy: The Life of Allen Dulles* (Boston:

Houghton Mifflin, 1994), 500-506. Ambrose found no evidence that Eisenhower ordered the assassination. Grose, however, concluded that Eisenhower knew it was being considered and never stopped the CIA. For the view that the CIA was somehow involved in the assassination, see Richard D. Mahoney, *JFK: Ordeal in Africa* (New York: Oxford University Press, 1983), 71.

110. For a detailed examination of the CIA's efforts against Lumumba, see U.S. Congress, Senate, Select Committee to Study Governmental Operations with Respect to Intelligence Activities, *Alleged Assassination Plots Involving Foreign Leaders*, 94th Cong., 1st Sess., 1975, S.Rpt. 465, pp 13-70.

111. Noer, *Cold War and Black Liberation*, 58.

112. Oral history interview with Martin Luther King, Jr., 9 March 1964, Atlanta, GA, Oral History Project, John F. Kennedy Library, Boston, MA., 6, 21.

113. Gordon Hagberg interview with Thomas Mboya, 10 March 1965, Oral History Project, John F. Kennedy Library.

114. Noer, *Cold War and Black Liberation*, 59.

115. Branch, *Parting the Waters*, 362-370; Burk, *The Eisenhower Administration and Black Civil*

3

INTERNATIONAL RACE RELATIONS:
JOHN F. KENNEDY AND THE CAUTIOUS DECOLONIZATION OF THE RHODESIAN FEDERATION

From its inception, the John F. Kennedy Administration assigned Africa a higher priority than had the Eisenhower Administration. After his victory in November, Kennedy appointed G. Mennen Williams as Assistant Secretary of State for African Affairs. It was surprising that his first appointment would be the head of the African bureau, rather than Secretary of State or some other position. Williams had doubts about the position, but Kennedy mollified him somewhat by emphasizing the importance that would be placed on Africa. As governor of Michigan, Williams had been a key Kennedy supporter and was associated with liberal Democrats such as Chester Bowles and Adlai Stevenson, whom Kennedy named Undersecretary of State and ambassador to the UN, respectively.[1]

Joseph Satterthwaite, whom Williams replaced, did not embrace the progressive views that Williams brought to the African bureau. Satterthwaite became the U.S. ambassador to South Africa and would be one of many within the State Department who would differ with Williams regarding Africa policies.[2] Chief among these "Europeanists" at State during the Kennedy years was George Ball, who was initially Undersecretary for Economic Affairs and then replaced Bowles as Undersecretary of State in December of 1961. Dean Acheson, leader of the unofficial foreign policy establishment, also criticized Williams and the "Africanists," and supported Ball's rise.[3]

Ball, Acheson, Satterthwaite, and others questioned the wisdom of backing black rule in Africa. Instead, they favored maintaining close ties with the white minority regimes of southern Africa and good relations with the metropoles.[4] While Williams recommended direct U.S. action to prevent a crisis in the Federation of Rhodesia and Nyasaland, other senior policy makers downplayed the importance of decolonization. Secretary of State Dean Rusk, Secretary of Defense Robert McNamara, and National Security Adviser McGeorge Bundy argued that defusing nationalist movements like the National Liberation Front in Vietnam was more important than supporting decolonization, because such nationalists were supported by the Soviet Union.

The looming breakup of the Federation necessitated choosing between aspirations of the Southern Rhodesian whites led by Roy Welensky, and those of the black nationalists including Hastings Banda, Kenneth Kaunda, and Joshua Nkomo. This "contentious issue... divided the foreign policy apparatus of the Kennedy Administration" roughly along the Africanist/Europeanist fault line.[5]

During the transition period after Kennedy's 1960 election, however, it was not clear that there would be such a strong resistance to the progressive Africanist agenda regarding the Federation. In order to overhaul relations with Africa, Kennedy turned to a panel of experts for advice. They formed a "Task Force on Africa," led by Robert Good and Vernon McKay, both associated at the time with Johns Hopkins University.[6] On 31 December 1960 the Task Force submitted a report to Kennedy. The task force concluded that the United States should only continue to support the Federation if it was "reconstituted along lines clearly acceptable to the principal African leaders."[7] The task force, moreover, stipulated a very complex approach to the Federation that included qualified support for British policy, and a pledge of U.S. economic assistance to the Federation if the wishes of leading African nationalists were being met.[8]

Thus the panel of experts provided a plan for a nuanced long-term policy towards the Federation that would foster independence and racial equality. Williams appreciated the high quality of the experts' advice and had matters been left to him much of the Task

Force's report may have been implemented.[9] Foreign relations during the Kennedy years did not emphasize long-term nuanced plans, focusing instead on a series of crises that were handled ad hoc by the president and his advisers.

In a sharp departure from Eisenhower's policy, the Kennedy Administration made decisions regarding Africa at the highest levels. The content of the policies aside, personal involvement may have been the single most important difference between the Eisenhower and Kennedy approaches to Africa. The President met with numerous African leaders one-on-one, and greatly impressed them with his interest in their countries' problems. As Williams later recalled: "The president was really excellent with these Africans. They were able to get together on a very informal basis and talk."[10] This human touch that Kennedy brought to the Oval Office did not necessarily translate into more enlightened policies though. He met not only with black nationalists like Dr. Hastings Banda, the leading African in Nyasaland who became the first president of Malawi, but also with white supremacists like Roy Welensky, the last prime minister of the Federation.

In general, U.S. relations with the Rhodesian Federation during the Kennedy Administration were moderate and cautious. The U.S. followed the British lead and refrained from any major initiatives. The United States stayed on the sideline as the Federation disbanded in 1963, and Nyasaland and Northern Rhodesia gained independence relatively smoothly. Southern Rhodesia, however, loomed as a potential crisis. Because of the efforts of Williams and American blacks, Kennedy was aware of the difficult situation in Southern Rhodesia. He displayed potential to serve as a mediator in the escalating Southern Rhodesian conflict, but he was assassinated before the crisis actually erupted.

ECONOMICS

The economic component of relations between the United States and the Federation reflected the caution of the Kennedy Administration. Since the Federation was expected to disintegrate, with possible widespread violence, the U.S. government refrained from any large loans or grants. The Eisenhower Administration had made several substantial loans to the Federation, most notably $80 million for the Kariba Dam. Between 1961 and 1963, however, Washington made no major loans to the Federation, or to the individual states after dissolution. Therefore, in the early 1960s the U.S. government did not have a lot of money at stake in the Federation.

The two most important strategic minerals acquired from the Federation during the 1950s were copper and chrome. Imports of Rhodesian copper dwindled rapidly, beginning in the late 1950s, and in 1961 the United States imported no Rhodesian copper. Rising domestic production and shipments from Chile, Peru, and Canada replaced Rhodesia's contribution.[11] Nonetheless, overall private U.S. investment in the Federation in 1961 totalled $72 million, and most of this involved the copper mines in Northern Rhodesia. Private American investment overseen by the American Metal Climax corporation held the biggest shares of the Rhodesian Selection Trust and Roan Antelope, the two leading copper concerns in the Federation.[12] Although private American investors retained a large stake in the copper industry, this investment did not directly influence U.S. policy, which mainly attempted to come to grips with the break-up of the Federation and the threat of a Southern Rhodesian unilateral independence.[13]

Chrome persisted as an important element of relations, however, for both sides. The United States utilized chrome primarily in the production of stainless steel, an important component in the production of automobiles and various turbines, including those in submarines. Southern Rhodesian mines yielded the highest quality chrome in the world. Therefore, between 1961 and 1963, the United States imported chrome from Southern Rhodesia in large quantities and ceased domestic production. In 1962 the Federation shipped over 300,000 tons of chrome to the United States, which represented about 75 percent of Southern Rhodesia's chrome exports.[14] Chrome exemplified the type of concrete return that justified aid and was a fundamental part of relations with the Federation through 1963.

The Kennedy Administration overhauled the system of foreign aid, replacing the International Cooperation Administration with the Agency for International Development (AID). Congress enabled this with the Foreign Assistance Act of November 1961. Under AID, the emphasis in assistance to Africa switched to long-term loans repayable in U.S. currency, a change from the previous emphasis on grants and loans repayable in local currency. In 1962, the inaugural year of AID, American assistance programs in Africa cost $312 million. This money funded programs in thirty African countries, but the Congo and Ghana each accounted for over $60 million of the total. The United States alloted the Federation $2.8 million in development grants, a relatively meager sum.[15] In 1963 succor to Africa through AID dropped to $261 million, and the Federation's share fell to $1.8 million—again in development grants.[16] During the Kennedy years Americans put less money into the Federation, either in the form of grants or loans. While the valuable minerals, cheap labor, and impressive new power source at Kariba meant that the Federation was still very attractive from a purely economic standpoint, political realities dissuaded foreign investment.

POLITICAL REALITIES: 1961

Events in 1961 illuminated the fact that the Federation would not long survive. How the dissolution would play out in the three territories of Nyasaland, Northern Rhodesia, and Southern Rhodesia remained to be seen. Many middle- and lower-level bureaucrats in the Eisenhower Administration had perceived events in the Federation relatively accurately. Intelligence reports, for example, correctly had predicted that failure to improve race relations within the Federation and provide blacks with significant political gains would lead to the Federation's downfall. Bureaucrats in the Kennedy Administration continued to describe the Federation's future presciently. On 11 April 1961 the CIA and the government's other intelligence agencies issued a joint national intelligence estimate on "Probable Developments in Colonial Africa." Regarding the Federation, the analysts concluded:

> We expect that within two years the Federation of Rhodesia and Nyasaland will break up into its constituent parts....
> In Southern Rhodesia the white population will probably be able to maintain its supremacy for several years and will probably move towards close association with South Africa.[17]

Analysts argued that the United States should by no means be expected to initiate any substantive actions regarding the Federation, which was primarily Great Britain's responsibility. Probably no high-level policy makers in the Kennedy Administration read the above estimate. In any case, the President and his close advisers Robert Kennedy, Robert McNamara, and McGeorge Bundy had other things on their mind. Events in the Federation dodged the spotlight that illuminated high profile international crises like Cuba and Germany in the spring of 1961.[18]

Of course, for the participants on the ground in the Federation, events rushed ahead and attitudes remained tense. While the Federation ranked very low on President Kennedy's foreign policy agenda, any little signal he sent indicating a U.S. position on the Federation had serious impact on the attitudes of the people there. On May 2, he met at the White House with Dr. Hastings Banda of Nyasaland, one of the eleven African leaders Kennedy hosted in 1961.

Kennedy welcomed Banda, who opened the conversation by briefly outlining the progress towards independence being made in Nyasaland. The President shifted the conversation to the Congo, and he and Banda agreed that the UN forces were performing a positive service. In reference to remaining neutral in the Cold War, Kennedy offered his view that "none of the new African states wanted to be in anyone's pocket." The president introduced Banda to the members of the cabinet and concluded the meeting by promising his continued personal interest in the developments in Nyasaland and his understanding of Nyasaland's "needs for assistance in education and other fields."[19]

Banda returned to Nyasaland glowing from his encounter with the President and expecting succor from the United States after independence. His interview with Kennedy infuriated white Southern Rhodesians, however, including Federation Prime Minister Roy Welensky, who complained that U.S. interest in black Africans would contribute to the undermining of the position of white Africans like himself. Tellingly, Welensky had never met with Banda or the other black nationalist leaders in the Federation.[20] The subject of Banda's White House sojourn reduced Welensky to "emotion, bitterness, and anger." Banda's trip fueled discontent among Southern Rhodesian whites in general, who complained in their newspapers and conversations about U.S. support for revolution and self-determination.[21]

John Emmerson, U.S. consul general in Salisbury, summarized the political situation in the Federation at the end of May. He praised Kenneth Kaunda of Northern Rhodesia as a moderate who would probably maintain control of the nationalist party after the July party congress. While he expected Banda to win the August elections in Nyasaland, he criticized him as overconfident and unrealistic, both about the future of his country and the amount of help the United States would provide. He saved his most severe criticism, however, for Joshua Nkomo, the leading nationalist of Southern Rhodesia. Emmerson disparaged him for spending too much time out of Africa, contending that "Nkomo and his cohorts are totally incompetent to assume positions of responsibility."[22]

Nkomo, in fact, had made less progress towards independence for Southern Rhodesia than nationalist leaders had made in Northern Rhodesia and Nyasaland. Of course, that was probably more a reflection of the intransigence of the Southern Rhodesian whites than of Nkomo's "incompetence." As for Nkomo spending too much time abroad, that was an often difficult reality he faced in order to raise foreign support for the liberation of Southern Rhodesia.[22] Furthermore, all of the Federation's nationalist leaders including Banda and Kaunda had spent considerable amounts of time in London.

If any government could coerce the white leaders of the Federation to grant political equality to blacks, it was Great Britain. Southern Rhodesian nationalist Nathan Shimayurira explained this view in *Foreign Affairs*. Only Great Britain could force enough reform in the Federation to prevent a violent showdown. Shimayurira expressed a slender hope that if the British impelled Welensky and his followers to legislate significant political advances for blacks, the Federation could even stay together and prosper.[24]

Shimayurira's colleague Nkomo, who had just attended a December 1960 London conference on the Federation, held no such hopes. Nkomo later recalled: "The British had no intention of doing anything other than hand back power to the settler electorate that had been allowed to run Southern Rhodesia since the 1920s." Indeed, when the British sent a representative to Southern Rhodesia in February 1961 for a constitutional conference, he advocated a small increase in black representation that would not have challenged the domination of the whites. Nkomo and his National

Democratic Party (NDP) refused to accept the document. In July, the NDP urged the few elegible black voters to boycott the referendum on the new constitution. The whites approved it by a nearly two-to-one margin. In a separate unofficial poll organized by the NDP, blacks rejected the constitution by a remarkable count of 467,189 to 584.[25] The constitution went into effect, and the Southern Rhodesian nationalists' struggle for freedom and independence went on.

Welensky also maneuvered the British into accepting a constitution for Northern Rhodesia that would make little difference in the status quo. In early August, riots erupted. Crowds of angry blacks blew up bridges and burned public buildings, first in the Northern Province. On 18 August similar outbursts began in the Luapula Province, prompting the dispatch of a Federal army battalion and two platoons of the Police Mobile Unit. During 12 separate incidents in August the security forces fired on the crowds, killing 20 blacks. One other rioter and eight police officers were drowned when a police boat capsized on the Zambesi, and two other protestors died by "misadventure."[26] Kenneth Kaunda blamed the violence on the Federation security forces, arguing that the ongoing repression had finally driven the people of Northern Rhodesia beyond the breaking point.[27] Africans could not be blamed for rioting, he explained, because talking even to the British was almost pointless.[28]

In hopes of getting Kennedy to lean on the British, Kaunda cabled the White House on 22 August as follows:

> Killing of Africans and total uprooting of villages in Northern and Luapala provinces by so-called security forces of Northern Rhodesia continues. Implore you in the name of God and humanity intervene by raising this matter at UN emergency session and also directly with Macmillan.[29]

Before receiving any reply from Washington, Kaunda flew to London for more talks with the British. While he considered such talks unlikely to do any good, he had nowhere else to turn. Meanwhile, Williams arrived in Northern Rhodesia for a visit. He had achieved notoriety during a February address in Kenya by declaring that "Africa is for the Africans." The statement, which he felt had been taken out of context by the media, raised quite a rumpus in Europe. Kennedy privately expressed concern that it could upset European allies.[30]

There was no doubt, however, that William's remark upset Federation whites. At the Lusaka airport just before his departure on 28 August, Stuart "Zambesi Jim" Finlay-Bissett strode up to the Assistant Secretary and punched him in the nose. Finlay-Bissett, a 58-year-old business man, openly espoused white supremacy and had recruited mercenaries from the Federation to support the secession of the Katanga province in the Congo civil war.[31] He quite obviously did not think Africa was for black Africans. The State Department opted not to press any formal charges in hopes of avoiding a publicity fiasco, and left Finlay-Bissett's case to the Northern Rhodesian judicial system.[32]

The local authorities prosecuted him on an assault charge and fined him 50 pounds, which was approximately $140. One of Finlay-Bisset's white supremacist cohorts contributed $5,600 for his defense and exclaimed that it would have been "cheap at twice the price." Finlay-Bissett claimed to have gotten congratulatory mail from many places, particularly Michigan (where Williams had been governor).[33] Sir Evelyn Hone, the governor of Northern Rhodesia, wrote Williams a personal letter of apology. Williams responded that the incident was forgotten, and that he preferred "to remember only the many kindnesses shown to me in Northern Rhodesia."[34]

Kenneth Kaunda had still not been sent any reply to his 22 August message to the White House regarding the aforementioned crackdown by Federation security forces in Northern Rhodesia. While in the Federation, Williams pondered how best to react to Kaunda's message. At first he had suggested no personal reply from Kennedy. After being attacked by Finlay-Bissett, however, he changed his mind and recommended a short reply. In hopes of not exacerbating tension in the Federation and thus making Great Britain's efforts more difficult, the State Department drafted a vague and noncommital reply, which the White House approved.[35]

In Dar Es Salaam, Tanzania, on 15 September American diplomats handed Kaunda the offical reply from the State Department, signed by Dean Rusk.

> President Kennedy has asked me to let you know that he
> has received your message and regrets to hear of the loss of
> life resulting from the recent violence in Northern Rhode-
> sia. It is his hope that law and order can be restored in such
> a way as to be mutually advantageous to all concerned.[36]

While such a moderate and neutral message could hardly have been
very encouraging to Kaunda, it was another sign of the higher priority that the Kennedy Administration gave to African nationalism. It is difficult to imagine the Eisenhower Administration sending such a message.

Kennedy also differed from Eisenhower in his policy towards
the former Belgian Congo. In the fall of 1961, George Ball emerged
as the high-level official most interested in the Congo crisis. Ball
pointed out to Kennedy how the Federation and the Congo were
connected. The Katanga secession movement was receiving significant assistance "from Rhodesian interests, and particularly from
Sir Roy Welensky, the white supremacy Prime Minister of the
Rhodesian Federation."[37]

Ball explained how the United States could lean on Welensky
to stop aiding the Katanga secession by offering to withhold judgement regarding the Federation's own problems. "Sir Roy Welensky
has his own difficulties in the Rhodesian Federation and there is
recent evidence that he is worried about our reaction to his activities there. We may therefore be able to deflect his interest from
Katanga or at least moderate his support for Katanga separatism."[38]
Evidently, Welensky wanted to visit the United States, and Ball
felt that gave the Kennedy Administration some leverage on him.[39]

Nonetheless, Welensky continued to support the Katanga secession through the end of 1961. The situation in the Congo in
November and December heated up dramatically. With Ball, Williams, and Stevenson all espousing U.S. backing for a major UN
onslaught against Katanga, Kennedy complied. American transport aircraft moved supplies, and American dollars paid the largest
share of the expenses. Heavily armed UN troops, with the support
of UN fighter-bombers, launched an offensive in mid-December.
The UN forces wrought havoc on the Katanga forces and mercenaries (many from the Federation), but various factors induced
Kennedy to halt the operation before it entirely stifled the seces-

sion. The UN force declared a cease-fire on 19 December, and Katanga remained a rebel province as 1961 drew to a close.[40]

In the Federation itself during the fall of 1961, events transpired that were much less dramatic, yet illustrative of the link between race relations in the United States and Southern Rhodesia. In a 13 October ruling the Supreme Court of Southern Rhodesia opened all public swimming pools to members of any race. The court based its decision partly on the 1954 U.S. Supreme Court case, *Brown v. Board of Education of Topeka*, which had prohibited segregation in U.S. schools. Integrated pools represented a very sensitive area among Federation whites, and thus it seemed remarkable to the U.S. Consul General that on this issue Southern Rhodesia progressed "faster and with less difficulty than some sections of the United States."[41]

People of different races swimming together in Southern Rhodesia surely surprised and pleased many people in 1961. However, as the U.S. Consul General realized, alleviation of social discrimination in public places did not satisfy Southern Rhodesian nationalists. They wanted political equality. As the Consul General explained: "Their demands can now be assuaged only by lowering the franchise qualifications sufficiently to give them, as the representatives of the majority of the Africans of Southern Rhodesia, control of the Colony's parliament."[42] In response to the opening of the pools, Joshua Nkomo explained: "We don't want to swim in your swimming pools. We want to swim with you in parliament."[43]

Nkomo's desire for blacks to "swim" with whites in parliament underlined parallels between Southern Rhodesia and the southern United States. Civil rights workers opened a voter registration school in Mississippi in August 1961 to begin addressing the very severe lack of black voting. In much of Mississippi, and in parts of other deep south states, virtually no blacks voted. This denial of democracy had reigned since approximately 1900, and whites enforced it by intimidation, literacy tests, and poll taxes. As the American Consul General had suggested when discussing swimming pools, parts of the United States still featured extensive segregation of public facilities. Freedom Riders bravely fought for integration of interstate transportation during the summer, and Student Nonviolent Coordinating Committee (SNCC) members sat-in to desegregate theatres in Nashville.[44] In South Carolina, Alabama, and Mississippi, not a single black child attended an integrated public school.[45]

The widespread segregation and racial discrimination in the United States not only paralleled the situation in the Federation, it directly hindered relations between the two. According to the American Consul General in Salisbury, John Emmerson, blacks generally respected the United States, but, he added, "Alabama does not help."[46] Assistant Secretary Williams believed that blacks' struggles in Alabama and elsewhere profoundly affected the opinions that Africans had of the United States. He thought that "you could make a barometric chart of how civil rights were going through the relationships you had with many Africans."[47] A Ghanian diplomat summed up the impact of racial discrimination in the United States during a October 25 speech:

> Africans feel that despite the nice words which come from America... the American on the whole is not prepared to accept the African as an equal.[48]

A high percentage of white Americans in 1961 may have not respected black Africans as equals. However, U.S. diplomats in the Federation labored to earn the respect of the black nationalists. In September John Emmerson conversed with several leaders of Nkomo's National Democratic Party (NDP), including Ndabaningi Sithole and Robert Mugabe. Emmerson believed such meetings were crucial since one of his key duties was "providing the necessary dialogue between the two races which is essential to a peaceful solution" of the Federation's problems.[49]

Emmerson thought highly of Mugabe, the NDP's Publicity Secretary. Mugabe had studied in South Africa and just returned from a few years of teaching in Ghana. Emmerson characterized him as "one of the best educated members of the National Council." After a nebulous Nkomo speech in October Emmerson consulted Mugabe for clarification.[50] In a December conversation with a black Southern Rhodesian businessman, moreover, Emmerson gained insight into the potential split within the nationalist movement pitting Nkomo's group against a group led by Mugabe, Sithole, and others. So, while many Americans may have held prejudicial or ignorant views of Federation blacks, U.S. diplomats in Salisbury offered significant insight into the nationalist movement. Emmerson's 1961 faith in Mugabe would prove providential in 1980.

While there is no extant record of what Mugabe thought about Americans in 1961, Joshua Nkomo undoubtedly believed that some were on his side. In November, he detailed recent events to his friend George Houser, head of the American Committee on Africa (ACOA). Nkomo requested legal defense funds for over 500 people whom the Federation's government had imprisoned.[51] Houser and the ACOA had assisted Nkomo during his profitable speaking tour of the United States in 1959 and 1960. Before Houser could respond to Nkomo's plea in 1961, however, Federal Prime Minister Roy Welensky banned Nkomo's National Democratic Party (NDP).

Nkomo traveled to Tanzania for the 9 December independence ceremony as a representative of the NDP. During a lull in the festivities Julius Nyerere, the first president of independent Tanzania, approached Nkomo with a smile and said that he should not be there, since he no longer represented anyone. Nyerere's joke did not really amuse Nkomo, who returned to Southern Rhodesia to find that in fact the NDP had been banned.[52] Roy Welensky announced that he had "permanently abolished the NDP for the sins it committed," banning it under the 1959 unlawful organizations act because of its steady drift towards violence.[53]

Welensky outlawed the NDP, but did not prohibit the formation of other nationalist parties. About a week later, therefore, Nkomo announced the formation of the Zimbabwe African People's Party (ZAPU). ZAPU, led by the same people and consisting of the same membership as the banned NDP, sought the same goals. The U.S. Consul General in Salisbury observed that ZAPU carried on the "NDP attitude of cautious friendship with U.S., of frustrated disappointment with UK, of uncompromising opposition to a constitution which gives Africans only 15 of 65 assembly seats."[54]

RISING NATIONALISM: 1962

Throughout 1962 the general situation in the Federation remained the same. Nyasaland neared independence under black majority rule, with Northern Rhodesia not too far behind. Southern Rhodesia toiled on through the quagmire that pitted ZAPU against the whites. By the end of the year, the opposing positions further polarized and all hopes of compromise evaporated. As the struggle turned violent in Southern Rhodesia, the United States stayed in the background and followed the British lead. Questions of the status of Southern Rhodesia and the role of the British received considerable attention at the UN, where the United States supported British refusal to take any forceful initiatives towards resolving the Southern Rhodesian dispute.

Problems in Africa stayed at the bottom of the Kennedy foreign relations agenda throughout 1962, with much higher priority going to Laos, Vietnam, and especially Cuba. On the domestic front, Kennedy faced daunting challenges in 1962 over the black Americans' fight for civil rights. During the summer the efforts of Martin Luther King and his followers in Georgia climaxed, and Kennedy refrained from intervening.[55] When James Meredith, an African-American student, entered the University of Mississippi in September, however, the ensuing violence prompted Kennedy to send in troops.[56] Kennedy disliked the negative impact racial discrimination in the United States had on his relations with black Africans. His actions on behalf of Meredith garnered their respect, demonstrating the link between race relations in the United States and relations with Africa. The relationship between the U.S. civil rights movement and the struggle for equality in Africa was a complex one, though, and it played out in many different ways during the last two years John Kennedy sat in the Oval Office.

As for relations with the Federation of Rhodesia and Nyasaland in 1962, the focus remained on how best to deal with the expected dissolution. In January, State bureaucrats requested information about the status of the Federation. They wanted news regarding any alterations in Great Britain's policy, changes in the relations between the three territories, and updates on the nationalist leaders, particularly Banda and Kaunda. They emphasized that:

> The future of the Federation experiment appears to depend to a great extent on a rapid racial accomodation in Southern Rhodesia.... they must either grant Africans a full voice in government, with early prospects of African control, or face the break up of the Federation.[57]

The State Department realized that Southern Rhodesia presented the most serious situation in the Federation. Indeed, as it became more and more clear in 1962 that the Federation would dissolve, the concern zeroed in on the future of Southern Rhodesia. Northern Rhodesia and Nyasaland attracted less attention, as they progressed steadily toward black rule.[58] In mid-May, Banda convinced British representatives that independence for Nyasaland could not be denied. At year's end, the British Government proclaimed to the House of Commons that it would "accept in principle that Nyasaland shall be allowed to withdraw from the Federation."[59]

Northern Rhodesia did not escape the control of the Federation government as quickly as Nyasaland, but blacks would control a majority of the cabinet posts in Northern Rhodesia by the end of 1962. On 28 February the British revealed the new constitution, which called for elections in the fall. Kaunda criticized the constitution; nonetheless, he decided to participate in the elections, and instead of protesting the Federation he turned his energies to registering voters.[60]

In April, Kaunda flew to Washington, where he met with President Kennedy's special assistant Ralph Dungan. Kaunda explained that the United States could be most helpful by pressuring the British to guarantee that the elections take place. In the long run, Kaunda desired increased U.S. support for education in Northern Rhodesia.[61] The general elections took place as scheduled on 30 October with nearly 90 percent participation, "in an orderly atmosphere and no major breaches of the peace were reported." Kaunda's party won 14 seats on the Legislative Council, giving blacks the majority. In the new government, Kaunda's party headed three departments including the key Labour and Mines Bureau.[62]

Events during 1962, then, demonstrated pretty clearly that Nyasaland and Northern Rhodesia would be independent and majority-ruled in the near future. These two territorries provided little anxiety for U.S. policymakers. In Southern Rhodesia, though, black nationalists and the white government remained divided, and the situation sparked concern and debate among officials in the U.S. government. Two questions dominated the discussion: (1) Should the new Southern Rhodesian constitution proposed by the British in 1961 be implemented? (2) Should the UN investigate Southern

Rhodesian domestic policies and rule on whether it deserved "self-governing" status?

In February 1962, Joshua Nkomo came to New York as a representative of the new Zimbabwe African People's Union (ZAPU), and made his feelings on these questions absolutely clear. Before doing so, however, he submitted a memo emphasizing ZAPU's general goal of "one man, one vote."[63] As for the proposed new constitution, Nkomo adamantly opposed it. Indeed, he had instigated the informal referendum among blacks the previous summer that had overwhelmingly rejected it. He explained to the U.S. ambassador to the UN, Adlai Stevenson, that the new constitution would result in an "early outbreak of trouble." He urged Stevenson to convince the U.S. government to pressure the British into suspending the constitution, and to replace it with one that would guarantee a black majority.[64]

Regarding the possible UN investigation of Southern Rhodesia's status, Nkomo believed it imperative. The British admitted Southern Rhodesia was not independent but contended that it was "self-governing," an argument Nkomo found absurd. Britain was responsible for Southern Rhodesia's foreign relations, and for implementing the new constitution. Furthermore, if a territory's government was not representative of its population, then under UN rules it was not eligible for self-government. So, Nkomo wanted the UN to investigate and fully expected a ruling against Southern Rhodesian self-government.[65]

American officials expressed their concern that the investigation would be seen as "UN meddling" by Welensky and the Southern Rhodesian white leaders and would actually lead to a unilateral declaration of independence. Nkomo discounted this argument and reiterated that the British had a responsibility to bring about majority rule.[66] Nevertheless, the State Department had reached a decision about the UN investigation. Basically, State opposed UN investigations into circumstances where the colonial power was making progress (which was how they saw Southern Rhodesia), as this could foil all hopes of a moderate solution. They also believed it would set a bad precedent, resulting in the tying up of the UN with investigations of all similar territories.[67]

While in New York, Nkomo dined at the home of Jonathan Bingham, the American overseer of colonial questions at the UN.[68]

He and Bingham's family conversed about the scenario in Southern Rhodesia. Bingham's daughter queried: "Surely you are going to vote for Mr. Nkomo, aren't you, Daddy?" Bingham responded: "I'd vote for him if the vote were mine, but unfortunately my vote belongs to the United States."[69] In fact, the United States did vote against Resolution 1745, the "United Nations Investigation of the Measure of Self-Government Attained by the Territory of Southern Rhodesia." Despite U.S. opposition, on 23 February the Resolution passed the UN General Assembly vote by a count of 57 to 21.[70]

Back in Southern Rhodesia, the ZAPU leadership rejoiced at the vote, but criticized the United States for opposing it. A ZAPU press release complained that the United States had "made a positive stand against us by the manner in which it voted."[71] Shortly thereafter, American diplomats in Salisbury met with ZAPU officials and argued that the UN vote was really just procedural, and that the United States still very much supported majority rule in Southern Rhodesia. Some ZAPU members seemed to believe this and agreed that U.S. actions in the next few months would be much more indicative of its true position.[72]

Other ZAPU leaders, however, continued to find fault with the U.S. vote. Robert Mugabe, ZAPU's Publicity Secretary, advocated a ZAPU boycott of a delegation visiting Salisbury from the U.S. Naval War College.[73] Mugabe contended that the vote demonstrated how various countries felt about ZAPU's struggle, pointiing out that the Soviet Union had voted in ZAPU's favor. However, he added that ZAPU was a nonaligned neutral group with no allegiance to the Soviets. They appreciated the Soviet vote, and they would accept Soviet aid but not Soviet domination.[74] Average blacks in Salisbury were aware of the UN vote, and thus grateful to the Soviets. They were disappointed with the United States, but at the same time knew how Americans had assisted Nkomo during his trips. The typical perception of the United States among Southern Rhodesian blacks in the spring of 1962, then, was mixed, ranging from disappointment to guarded optimism.[75]

Williams and like-minded Africanists hoped to rectify the sometimes negative image of the United States held by nationalists like Mugabe. As Williams prepared for another African trip, President Kennedy asked him for a brief summary of events in the Rhodesias.

Williams asked his assistant, Wayne Fredericks, to get such a memo to Kennedy promptly. Williams instructed Fredericks: "I have in mind that we should encourage the British to retain some strategy so as to give the Southern Rhodesian Nationalists hope for a better constitution some day than the one now under consideration."[76]

In this secret correspondence with Fredericks, Williams advocated the eventual replacement of the proposed constitution with one more favorable to ZAPU. Bingham publicly attempted to regain the faith of the black nationalists. He pronounced that the United States still favored greater black participation in Southern Rhodesian politics and did not consider Southern Rhodesia to be self-governing. The United States had voted against a UN investigation along procedural lines, because they thought it might do more harm than good for the cause of majority rule in Southern Rhodesia.[77] State diplomats in Salisbury distributed copies of Bingham's speech among the members of ZAPU, and it did impress them favorably.[78]

Stevenson also sought to reassure ZAPU; he placed the burden of blame for Southern Rhodesia's problems on the shoulders of the whites. Like Bingham, Stevenson ameliorated somewhat the views towards the United States of the nationalists. Roy Welensky, the leader of the Federation, reacted very differently. He responded to Stevenson a few days later at a Northern Rhodesian political gathering. He contended that whites had in fact brought civilization to Southern Rhodesia. He reminded Stevenson that blacks in the United States were discriminated against in all aspects of life and argued that race relations in the Federation had progressed faster than they had in the United States.[79]

Welensky and other white politicians in Southern Rhodesia were very upset with Stevenson and Bingham, and they also criticized the activities of American diplomats in the Federation. By June the U.S. Consul General in Salisbury, John Emmerson, had been recalled to Washington and replaced. *The London Daily Telegraph* attributed Emmerson's early recall to Welensky's displeasure with Americans' support for black nationalists. The *Telegraph* displayed British support for Welensky's position against U.S. meddling in the Federation.[80]

The British government placed its hopes for Southern Rhodesia in successful implementation of the new constitution. They did not believe that outside influence, whether by themselves, the United States, or the UN, could do any good in Southern Rhodesia. The British Ambassador to the United States, David Ormsby-Gore, explained that the British had never exercised their powers over affairs inside Southern Rhodesia, and that they had only very tenuous rights to intervene. All things considered, the best that blacks could reasonably expect was a gradual improvement of their situation under the new constitution. Ormsby-Gore discounted the possibility that Nkomo and his followers would resort to widespread violence.[81]

In June the UN committee investigating Southern Rhodesia submitted its report. The committee thoroughly undermined the British position that Southern Rhodesia was self-governing, and it recommended replacing the proposed constitution with one much more favorable to the black majority.[82] The report precipitated increasingly complicated verbal gymnastics by the British delegation to the UN in the summer and fall of 1962. One British representative, Hugh Foot, eventually resigned out of frustration with the unrealistic position he was expected to defend. The U.S. delegates were also embarrassed by the British position, which the Soviets found quite amusing.[83]

The investigatory committee intended for the General Assembly to vote on a resolution calling for a new Southern Rhodesian constitution. Stevenson notified Secretary Rusk that he favored U.S. abstention on such a resolution. He added that the United States should suggest to the British that they sidetrack the proposed constitution.[84] The British insisted on implementing the constitution as it was, which brought a lop-sided rebuke at the UN. The General Assembly adopted Resolution 1747, "United Nations Request for the Drafting of a New Constitution for Southern Rhodesia," by a vote of 73 to 1. The United States and 26 other countries abstained.[85]

Despite the vote, however, the British went forward with their plans for implementing the constitution. The U.S. delegation to the UN worried that the British policy might result in a unilateral declaration. They felt it was time for "high level approach to UK on SR." Before resigning, Hugh Foot told Jonathan Bingham that he hoped the U.S. government would intervene to convince the British to drastically alter their blueprint for Southern Rhodesia.

He convinced the U.S. delegation that the present course of action might result in a rebel white regime in closer alliance with South Africa.[86]

State Department analysts agreed with the views of U.S. officials in New York. The Policy Planning Staff observed that the British were: "trapped in a morass of maneuver and counter-maneuver in the Federation." They felt that when the impending fragmentation of the Federation occurred: "The worst eventuality would be a union of sorts between Southern Rhodesia and South Africa."[87] The Policy Planning Staff explained that the Federation's future hinged on race relations:

> As in South Africa, the political and social status of the Black as contrasted with the White is the key issue in the Federation and nowhere is the cleavage between the two races more sharply drawn than in Southern Rhodesia. In the Federation, as in South Africa, the problem is complicated by U.S. investment (about $200,000,000 in Northern Rhodesia alone) and the presence of U.S. nationals in considerable numbers.[88]

Most private investment was in Northern Rhodesia's copper mines, but it still behooved the United States to prevent Southern Rhodesia from joining forces with South Africa. An alliance of white regimes - the "White Redoubt" - had been made more likely by the recent UN investigation and vote against the proposed constitution. To prevent it the State Department suggested several means: (1) Pressure Great Britain to deal with the threat of a Southern Rhodesia-South Africa alliance; (2) Develop goodwill among Federation leaders through AID programs; (3) Continue to encourage American companies to practice racial justice in hiring and advancement; (4) Mediation by State Department officials of negotiations between black leaders and the British.[89]

There is no question that an acceptable settlement of the dispute over the Southern Rhodesian constitution, especially regarding the political role of blacks, was very high on the African bureau agenda in the summer of 1962. Its priority list of the top 20 African issues placed Southern Rhodesia third, that is, after the Congo and Algeria.[90] The Policy Planning Staff and Assistant Secretary Williams believed that it was necessary for the U.S. government to pressure the British into replacing the proposed constitution with a more progressive one. Supporters of this position included Stevenson and Bingham at the UN, the Consul General in Salisbury, and nationalist leader Robert Mugabe.[91] Policy Planning also suggested U.S. mediation as a potential facilitating role.

From the options proposed by Policy Planning, the Kennedy Administration chose only to provide AID funds to the Federation and encourage American companies to continue their practices of black advancement. High-level U.S. officials opted against pressuring the British. Undersecretary of State George Ball instructed President Kennedy along these lines before a lunch meeting with Foreign Secretary Home. Ball advised Kennedy to relate to Home that "we recognize this is a thorny problem for the United Kingdom and that we do not propose to tell them what to do about it."[92]

During the meeting, Home informed Kennedy that the British could not do anything until after the next elections in Southern Rhodesia. They hoped that Edgar Whitehead would be re-elected and would then pursue reform. They refrained from intervening with another new constitution, or from criticizing Whitehead, because that might contribute to the election triumph of the extreme right wing. Home concluded: "Nothing should be done to make Whitehead's task more difficult, particularly at this time, since the only alternative to Whitehead was apartheid."[93]

For the most part, the U.S. government accepted the British assessment that the best course on Southern Rhodesia was to hope for Whitehead's re-election and then go from there. In a follow-up message to Lord Home after the White House meeting, Ball explained: "We fully appreciate the prime importance of Sir Edgar Whitehead's election, and we do not wish to compound your difficulties by offering advice from the sidelines." He elaborated on U.S. wishes, however, by crediting Stevenson for identifying the potential problems for the British at the UN. Ball requested that Home consider Stevenson's idea that the British make a public statement pledging to retain sovereignty in Southern Rhodesia until the majority was satisfied with the government. Doing so would make it easier for the United States to support the British in New York.[94]

The British rejected Ball's suggestion that they listen to Stevenson and attempt to mollify their critics at the UN. Home explained that doing so would fan the fires of reactionary criticism in Southern Rhodesia, precluding a Whitehead victory.[95] In October the UN General Assembly approved Resolution 1760, "United Nations Request for Suspension of the 1961 Constitution for Southern Rhodesia and the Convening of a Constititional Conference to Formulate a New Constitution," 81 to 2. Unwilling to support the British in their losing cause, the United States abstained.[96] American policy in the fall of 1962, then, was mildly critical of the British but basically supportive of their decision to wait for elections.

High level U.S. officials, in fact, would not initiate measures on Southern Rhodesia independent of the British until Henry Kissinger's brief foray into Southern African diplomacy in 1976. The Kennedy Administration also decided not to mediate between the Southern Rhodesian nationalists and whites.[97] High-level mediation by the United States between blacks and whites in Southern Rhodesia would not occur until Andrew Young led such efforts during the Jimmy Carter Administration.

In late 1962 leading American blacks, however, hoped Kennedy would act forcefully for justice in Southern Rhodesia. He had recently deployed Federal troops to the University of Mississippi to quell the rioting against the admission of Ole Miss's first black student, James Meredith.[98] Kennedy's armed intervention in Mississippi on behalf of racial justice encouraged black Americans that he might take strong action towards southern Africa. In November, the American Negro Leadership Conference on Africa (ANLCA) convened for three days at Columbia University. The group, founded a few months before, was led by a committee that included Whitney Young of the Urban League, Roy Wilkins of the NAACP, A. Philip Randolph, and Martin Luther King, Jr. Among the approximately 60 participants were many other influential blacks such as E. Frederic Morrow, a former Eisenhower adviser, and Louis Martin, a high-ranking member of the Democratic Committee and later an adviser to Jimmy Carter. SNCC Representative John Lewis, later a U.S. congressman, was one of the observers. Background paper contributors included George Houser and Eduardo Mondlane, a leader of the liberation movement in Mozambique.[99]

The ANLCA espoused a U.S. policy towards the Federation of Rhodesia and Nyasaland that would contribute to: (1) dismantling of the Federation; (2) universal suffrage in the three territories; (3) removal of the present government of Southern Rhodesia; (4) a new constitution for Southern Rhodesia. At conference end, the leadership was urged to meet with Kennedy in December and present its policy suggestions to him.[100] King and several others did indeed meet with the President on 17 December 1962. They requested that he increase diplomatic pressure in order to end colonial rule throughout Africa. The meeting lasted three hours and encouraged King, but it did not transform policy towards the Federation.[101]

By the time King and Kennedy spoke, events in Southern Rhodesia had rendered talk of constitutional reform obsolete. Between August and December 1962, the narrow peninsula of common ground joining the positions of Nkomo and Whitehead vanished into a sea of violent resistance and reactionary racism. During August and September, it became evident that ZAPU's leadership had reached two key decisions: (1) They would wage an armed struggle; (2) They would send cadres abroad for revolutionary training. Their turn to violence resulted in the banning of ZAPU in September, and contributed to the political victory in December of the white supremacist Rhodesian Front.

During June and July, ZAPU leaders had debated whether or not to resort to armed revolt. Robert Mugabe strongly supported a strategy of violence, and Joshua Nkomo was leaning in that direction. Ndabaningi Sithole and Dr. Samuel Parirenyatwa cautioned against it, wanting to give British constitutional reforms a chance.[102] In August Dr. Parirenyatwa died under mysterious circumstances, quite possibly at the hands of whites.[103] Parirenyatwa's death silenced one of the strongest voices for moderation within the Southern Rhodesian nationalist movement. Because the death seemed to have been perpetrated by whites, it convinced Nkomo that ZAPU must take up arms.[104]

Black African leadership including Ghana and Mali had agreed to set up a military command for African liberation in Egypt. So, in September Nkomo went to Cairo to pick up ZAPU's first shipment of guns. He returned via Air France, stowing rifles in the cargo hold and carrying ammo and grenades as carry-on baggage.[105]

September featured a series of violent strikes across Southern Rhodesia against government buildings such as schools and beerhalls, mostly with petrol bombs. The violence generally seemed to be of a grass-roots nature, but a few high-profile strikes against power lines and bridges were masterminded by ZAPU leaders. Paul Geren, the U.S. Consul General, suspected Mugabe of being the chief architect.[106]

Geren also reported residual anti-American sentiment among middle-level members of ZAPU. Top leaders like Nkomo understood that the United States was at minimum a lukewarm supporter of their cause, but some of his followers were not convinced and dealt rudely with American visitors to their headquarters.[107] At the same time, the first ZAPU cadres trained in the Soviet Union rejoined the liberation force.[108] Events in Southern Rhodesia during the fall of 1962 could concievably have been interpreted by U.S. officials as a Soviet-inspired communist revolt, hostile to the West. Such an interpretation would have fit nicely with the U.S. view of events in the Congo, Vietnam, Cuba, and elsewhere. British diplomats in Washington, moreover, espoused this view to Assistant Secretary Williams. He disagreed and explained that the U.S. government considered the drive for self-determination in Southern Rhodesia "an indigenous movement." The Soviets would try to capitalize on any such movement, but they had not instigated it.[109]

This was a critical distinction. Because the African Bureau did not blame the revolt in Southern Rhodesia on the Soviet Union, they saw no reason to intervene on the side of the white regime. The black versus white nature of the struggle further discouraged aligning against the revolt, and the perception that it was a British problem tended to dissuade significant action anyway. Had Southern Rhodesia been high on Kennedy's agenda, however, the U.S. may well have decided to oppose ZAPU extremists like Mugabe.

The extremists' anti-American views and tenuous links to the Soviets would have made a U.S./ZAPU alliance problematic at best in the Cold War context of 1962. While Williams and other Africanists understood the indigenous nature of the nationalist movement, it is not clear how Robert McNamara, McGeorge Bundy, and other high-level officials would have proceeded had it gotten to that level. It is not difficult to imagine the United States choosing a moderate leader, perhaps Sithole or Nkomo, and arming him to the teeth against Mugabe and the more extreme elements. One need only remember what happened in Vietnam to believe that such events could have happened in Southern Rhodesia.

Considering such alternatives, then, it was probably fortunate that Southern Rhodesia remained a low priority for the Kennedy Administration late in 1962. Even after the banning of ZAPU and restriction of its leaders, the African Bureau continued to support Southern Rhodesia's Prime Minister Edgar Whitehead and his program of constitutional reform.[110] They urged Whitehead to accelerate political gains for Africans but were not particularly demanding. They wished him luck in the upcoming elections and recognized the validity of Whitehead's desire to progress slowly in order to maintain a majority in the legislature.[111]

American diplomats' best wishes did not help Whitehead in the December 1962 elections, and right-wing candidate Winston Field replaced him as Southern Rhodesia's prime minister. Field belonged to the extremist Rhodesian Front that would rule Southern Rhodesia until 1979. Poor white farmers had more influence in the Rhodesian Front than they previously had.[112] With their support, Field intended to make Southern Rhodesia more like South Africa and to build an alliance with Pretoria and the Portuguese colonial governments in Mozambique and Angola. There were indirect benefits to the nationalist movement, though, as Nkomo later recalled.

> In some ways Field's election made our task easier. We no longer had to struggle to make clear to outsiders that the regime in our country really was different from those in the other colonies that the British were abandoning.... The fight was on.[113]

Whitehead himself, of course, was disappointed with the result. Yet, he was grateful that he would not have to preside over the fast approaching break up of the Federation, with its negative effect on the white elites in Salisbury.[114] He foresaw that the Southern Rhodesian economy would suffer significantly from the loss of direct ties to the Northern Rhodesian copper mines, since the offices of the mining companies were planning to vacate Salisbury. The author of Southern Rhodesia's development plan, Professor John

Phillips, had expressed optimism about receiving money from the World Bank and the Agency for International Development if Whitehead won. Field's victory meant that he would not bother to seek international funding since there was "little hope of success."[115]

Robert Mugabe was also gloomy. He stressed to Consul General Geren that the ideology of the Rhodesian Front was "thinly veiled apartheid." He informed Geren of his fear that Field would gain total independence from Great Britain for Southern Rhodesia and asked what Geren thought the United States might do to help the nationalists.[116] Field's victory dismayed the African Bureau. In a position paper they prepared for the President, they characterized Southern Rhodesia as a "drastically changed situation."[117] With the rise of the Rhodesian front and the beginning of armed revolt late in 1962, the situation in Southern Rhodesia was "drastically changed." Would the Kennedy Administration respond with any "drastic changes" in their policy towards Southern Rhodesia, and the other Federation states, in 1963?

THE END OF FEDERATION: 1963

Of course, 1963 is best remembered for the assassination of John Kennedy in November. The tragedy was magnified by the fact that during Kennedy's last year he began to demonstrate real potential as a progressive president. Responding to events in Birmingham, he delivered a forceful address in June advocating equal rights for all Americans, calling civil rights a moral issue rooted in the Bible and the Constitution. He then requested that Congress pass measures that would give the executive branch sufficient power to protect individuals' civil rights. A small part of his motivation was a hope to diminish the damage to the U.S. image in Africa caused by news coverage of violence in the South. More importantly, though, he finally had realized that the civil rights activists were deserving of support, and that the Federal Government was unable to provide it.[118]

Arguably the most important African issue during the Kennedy Administration was the civil war in the former Belgian Congo. Led by Moise Tshombe, the mineral-rich Katanga province there had seceded from the rest of the new republic. Buoyed by U.S. funds and utilizing U.S. planes, the UN force successfully quelled the Katanga secession for good on 17 January 1963. In some ways this followed Cold War patterns, because American officials hoped that ending the secession would bring stability and preclude a Soviet or Chinese intervention.[119]

At the same time, though, the policy contradicted the wishes of the former colonial power, Belgium, and its allies in support of the secession. Roy Welensky had been their chief supporter.[120] Indeed, the U.S. assistance facilitated the plans of the Afro-Asian block at the UN and earned praise from black African leaders. Kenneth Kaunda, the leading nationalist in Northern Rhodesia, explained his view to Adlai Stevenson during a visit to the UN in May. According to Kaunda, ending the secession had been a "master stroke which changed the course of history." He believed it was the first step to ending white domination of southern Africa, because the secession had been an important component of the white redoubt desired by Welensky, Salazar, and Verwoerd of South Africa.[121] By opposing the goals of Cold War allies in Salisbury, Lisbon, and Pretoria, therefore, U.S. policy towards the Congo represented an exception to the Cold War pattern.

In February 1963, Assistant Secretary Williams once again travelled across Africa, stopping in the Congo and the Federation. Upon returning to Foggy Bottom he delineated his view of Africa to Secretary Rusk. His number one conclusion was that U.S. policy towards the Congo was popular with all of Africa except the white regimes. His second point was:

> Southern Rhodesia is (the) new African time bomb. If Nationalist aspirations do not get some hope and if Nationalists are not brought into constitutional dialogue instead of belligerent hostility, there will be major flare-up.

Williams added that Southern Rhodesia "may wreck Britain's decolonization record and produce white-black showdown."[122]

Among the states that had made up the Federation, then, only Southern Rhodesia appeared to have a potentially disastrous future. While in Salisbury, Williams had discussed Northern Rhodesia with a wide range of British and African officials. They all agreed that the prospects for Northern Rhodesia were bright, and that Kenneth Kaunda possessed "excellent character and intelligence."[123] These officials, and Williams, all expected Kaunda to become the leader of an independent Northern Rhodesia shortly. The first step was to achieve separation from the Federation, and thereby get out from the control of the white elites in Southern Rhodesia.

In his summary of the trip, Williams predicted a Northern Rhodesian break from the Federation before long. Indeed, the British Minister for Central African Affairs, R.A. Butler, informed Welensky on 29 March of the British decision that Northern Rhodesia had the right to secede.[124] Thus Butler sounded the "actual death knell of the Federation," as a State bureaucrat later described this decision.[125] With Nyasaland already gone and Northern Rhodesia free to follow suit, the Federation's end was nigh. British officials publicly announced the final decision to end the Federation after a conference at Victoria Falls in July, and it would cease to exist on 1 January 1964.[126]

During his May trip to the United States, Kaunda explained to Stevenson that he hoped for U.S. assistance in establishing an independent Northern Rhodesia.[127] He sent an autographed copy of his book *Zambia Shall Be Free* to President Kennedy. Kennedy wrote Kaunda: "Wish you and all people of Northern Rhodesia peace, happiness and success in your efforts [to] build [a] new nation."[128] While a letter signed by Kennedy no doubt gratified Kaunda—as personal attention from Kennedy had gratified other African leaders—Kaunda hoped for much more from the United States than best wishes. While U.S. officials discussed various potential aid programs for Northern Rhodesia in 1963, mostly related to education, they would not be implemented until after Northern Rhodesia became Zambia in 1964.[129]

In Nyasaland, however, the Kennedy Administration could implement educational aid programs, since that territory attained independence in 1963. On 1 February, Banda was sworn in as the first prime minister of independent Nyasaland.[130] Williams opined a few weeks later that "Dr. Banda still seems to have things pretty well under control in Nyasaland." Banda's challenge would be tackling a deficit of about $17 million. Evidently, Banda expected Great Britain and the United States to succor him substantially in this regard, and Williams tried to clarify that U.S. aid would strictly be earmarked for projects, not his national budget.[131]

In fact, the Agency for International Development intended to provide about $2 million for Nyasaland in 1963, for agricultural and educational projects. The primary AID project would be construction of the Blantyre Polytechnic School. Help also took a human form, and on 15 January a group of Peace Corps volunteers arrived in Nyasaland. The 42 volunteers would serve as teachers, doubling the number of secondary school teachers in Nyasaland.[132]

Banda himself had initiated the project in June 1962. State officials informed Banda that the project had been approved and would be handled by the Peace Corps director Sargent Shriver.[133] The volunteers' arrival in January 1963 represented the culmination of several months of diplomatic wrangling by U.S. officials, who had to secure the necessary immigration documents from the Federation government in Salisbury. Leaders of the Federation disliked the idea of Americans helping Banda. They argued that Banda would brainwash the volunteers against the Federation. Geren managed to secure the required documents in spite of their concerns. By the time the volunteers arrived, moreover, Nyasaland had seceded and the objections of Federation officials were moot.[134]

The Peace Corps volunteers not only provided much-needed classroom instruction, they worked in hospitals and on community building projects in their spare time. Banda informed Kennedy of their achievements in a May letter in which he also requested additional volunteers in the future. Kennedy responded:

> I entirely share your enthusiasm for the work the Peace Corps Volunteers are doing, but it was particularly gratifying to learn that the volunteer teachers in Nyasaland have not only made a contribution to secondary education, but have also gone beyond their classrooms to work in hospitals and community projects.... It is this kind of mutually rewarding experience that I hope will always characterize the relations of our two governments and our two peoples.[135]

Kennedy praised the Peace Corps' effort in Nyasaland as a "mutually rewarding experience." The U.S. Consul General similarly described it as a "visible sign of the American desire to help."[136] While the Peace Corps in general did represent these things to some extent, it also served as another avenue for the United States to promote democracy and compete with the Soviet Union. While that was not a serious concern regarding Nyasaland, with a leader as pro-American as Banda, it was a major part of the equation in other nations.[137] In Nyasaland the Peace Corps' role was pretty straightforward, and for the most part was a "mutually rewarding experience" for the teachers and the students.[138]

With Nyasaland's assumption of internal self-rule in 1963, and total independence as Malawi in 1964, the United States was able to play a small but constructive role in helping to build a new nation. Personified by the Peace Corps volunteers and solidified by the personal relationship of mutual respect between Banda and Kennedy, U.S. relations with Nyasaland were the simplest and most positive of those with any of the three Federation territories in 1963. On the other hand, U.S. relations with Southern Rhodesia were much more complicated.

The Federation's demise begged questions of the status of Southern Rhodesia. Would it be allowed independence in the near future, as was the case for both Nyasaland and Northern Rhodesia? Independence under the new constitution and the leadership of the Rhodesian Front would mean that 250,000 whites exercised virtual political and economic domination over about 4 million blacks. White and black leadership increasingly polarized their followers, with the whites defending their priviledges and the blacks espousing violent revolt.

In February, Williams had conversed with white leaders in Salisbury.[139] He concluded that if greater political power were not granted to the blacks quickly, major violence would ensue. Newly elected Prime Minister Winston Field and his Rhodesian Front cronies doubted the ability of the blacks to mount a serious revolt. Williams accepted Field's prognosis that Joshua Nkomo was a weak leader of the nationalist movement, and that ZAPU would not be very effective until he was replaced.[140] White leaders seemed more concerned with economic troubles and requested that Williams work to curb U.S. imports of Soviet chrome. Of Southern Rhodesian chrome exports in 1962, 75 percent had gone to the United States. The Soviets were threatening this key outlet, however, by undercutting their prices.[141] Williams forwarded their concerns, but he himself clearly believed the critical issue was political rights for blacks.

Back in Washington in March, Williams prepared for discussions with the British regarding Southern Rhodesia. He strongly manifested his alarm to his subordinates at the African Bureau about the situation in Southern Rhodesia and called for increased efforts to devise better methods for the United States to push Great Britain into "executing a more forthcoming Southern Rhodesia program." He reiterated that blacks and whites were diverging dangerously, and that if the British did not take some action immediately, "the apparent collision course will result in an explosion." Such a chain of events would tarnish the British record on decolonization in Africa as well as their reputation around the world. Williams did not desire this and wanted the United States to do its best to help prevent it.[142]

President Kennedy certainly did not consider Southern Rhodesia to be the high priority that Williams did; however, he was interested in developments there. He requested updates on two areas of concern in Africa; the Congo and Southern Rhodesia. His Deputy Special Assistant for National Security Affairs Carl Kaysen forwarded Kennedy a situation report on Southern Rhodesia for his weekend reading. Kaysen emphasized: "We are going to hear more of this, and more noisily, in the future."[143]

The main argument of the report was that Southern Rhodesian whites insisted on independence from the British no later than it was granted to Nyasaland and Northern Rhodesia. If the British denied them independence, they might very well declare it unilaterally. Southern Rhodesia would simmer ominously no matter what, but a unilateral declaration of independence (UDI) would exacerbate the situation. The white regime would move closer to South Africa, and the blacks would fight more fiercely. British officials had already informed U.S. diplomats in London that they would not consider using force to prevent UDI. As a result, it would turn into a very complicated problem at the United Nations for the British and the United States.[144]

Whether or not Kennedy read the situation report is unclear. The fact that it was included in his weekend reading illustrated his desire to stay informed, and even if he did not absorb the information therein, some of his top advisers on the Security Council did. As of mid-April 1963, then, high-level members of the U.S. government were well aware of the approaching crisis in Southern

Rhodesia. Williams wanted them to put greater pressure on the British to achieve a settlement acceptable to blacks, but this option was not chosen. Instead, the U.S. government basically sat back and let the British handle Southern Rhodesia.

Williams continued working to promote a more active role by the United States. He explained his view on Southern Rhodesia to Ndabaningi Sithole, one of the leading nationalists. Sithole wanted the United States to lean on the British. While Williams probably sympathized, he could be no more reassuring than to hope all sides in the dispute would continue a dialogue.[145] Sithole's request that the United States put leverage on the British was echoed by Robert Mugabe. Back in January, Mugabe had explained to Consul General Geren that in order to avert war in Southern Rhodesia, the United States should convince the British to mandate equal political rights for blacks there.[146]

Mugabe and Sithole were not only disappointed with the efforts of the British and the Americans, they were also disgruntled over Nkomo's leadership of ZAPU. At an April meeting between ZAPU leaders and Julius Nyerere in Tanzania, the disagreements surfaced. Sithole and Mugabe criticized the amount of time that Nkomo spent abroad and wanted to focus on raising support for liberation among the people in Southern Rhodesia. A split between Nkomo and the Sithole/Mugabe group was imminent.[147]

Through the summer of 1963, the struggle for control of the nationalist movement became more pronounced. The State Department felt it was important enough to brief McGeorge Bundy on it, suggesting the President might want to be more informed before he talked with Julius Nyerere in July.[148] On August 8, the Sithole/Mugabe group formed the Zimbabwe African National Union (ZANU). Sithole took the reigns as ZANU's first president, and Mugabe was named secretary-general. The official split sparked a horrible spree of black-on-black violence across Southern Rhodesia.[149] Internationally, the split created concern. American supporters of the nationalists decided to maintain contact with both groups, but sadly realized that this development would weaken the movement.[150]

During the final days of the Kennedy Administration, doubt remained at the highest levels as to how the United States was dealing with southern African nationalists. Robert Kennedy spelled this out to McGeorge Bundy just two days before President Kennedy's death. The Attorney General considered southern Africa an area that deserved the close attention of the National Security Council's Standing Group. He wrote:

> About ten days ago we talked about having the Standing Group discuss what should be the attitude and policy of the United States toward the individuals and organizations attempting to gain independence in Mozambique, South Africa, Angola, and Rhodesia.... It seems to me these areas are going to be extremely important in the future and that some serious thought should be given to what we are going to do.[151]

That the President's brother considered the southern African liberation movements to be "extremely important" was not a new phenomenon in 1963. According to historian Arthur Schlesinger, Robert Kennedy "supported independence movements in black Africa."[152] For example, in 1962 he talked with Eduardo Mondlane, a leader of the struggle against the Portuguese in Mozambique. Mondlane made a positive impression on Kennedy, who as a result got the CIA to pay for Mondlane's visit. It appeared that the Attorney General was interested in becoming similarly involved in the struggle in Southern Rhodesia in November 1963, but the tragedy in Dallas intervened. We will never know what might have been if the Kennedy Administration had not been shattered. As things turned out, Robert Kennedy engineered no major alterations in relations with Southern Rhodesia.

Instead, the groundwork for the protracted struggle in Southern Rhodesia was laid during the last few months of the Kennedy Administration. ZANU initiated its contacts with the Chinese, which would produce training and weapons for the long fight against the Salisbury regime. What remained of Nkomo's ZAPU established ties with the Soviets and set up headquarters in Northern Rhodesia. The Southern Rhodesian government established its own intelligence agency, the Central Intelligence Organization (CIO), separate from the Federation's security apparatus. The Terrorist Desk of the CIO's dreaded Special Branch began its operations against ZANU and ZAPU that continued until the struggle's end in 1980.[154]

Southern Rhodesia had made its way onto President Kennedy's foreign relations docket one last time, on October 8. For about a half-hour that morning at the White House, Kennedy discussed the Southern Rhodesian situation with Roy Welensky, the Federation's lame duck prime minister who was visiting the United States on his way to London.[155] Briefing papers given to Kennedy before the meeting provided him with details about Welensky and Southern Rhodesia, encouraging him to express the U.S. government's disapproval of a unilateral declaration of independence (UDI).[156]

During the conversation with Welensky, Kennedy did not directly bring up the subject of a UDI. He did, however, ask Welensky a series of questions about the possible sequence of events in Southern Rhodesia. He wondered if blacks and whites could work together to reach a solution. Welensky responded that such a solution was unlikely considering the distance separating the two sides. Kennedy inquired if the whites were aligning more closely with Pretoria, to which Welensky said no. The President asked what specific steps could lead to a settlement, and Welensky explained that only new constitutional proposals by the British could do it. Kennedy wondered what would happen if no such settlement transpired, alluding to a possible UDI. Welensky insisted that the British must bring about a settlement, and that not finding a solution was "unthinkable."[157]

Their conversation turned from Southern Rhodesia to more general issues regarding Africa. Kennedy queried Welensky on the role of communism there, to which Welensky replied he did not think it was particualarly appealing to most Africans. He added, however, that nonalignment was appealing, and that it represented something of a victory for the Eastern Bloc since it prevented total access to Africa by the West. President Kennedy concluded that "the tide of African nationalism is so strong that as a practical matter we can only try to moderate and influence, not stop it."[158]

This meeting with Welensky showed Kennedy at his best. His questions and comments demonstrated an impressive knowledge of events in Southern Rhodesia and Africa in general. After returning to Salisbury, Welensky praised the President as "very friendly and very, very knowledgeable on our affairs." Welensky suggested that the understanding of Kennedy and State officials with whom he had met was just one more reason that a reasonable solution could be worked out in Southern Rhodesia. The inclination of whites there to consider Western critics ignorant of the Southern Rhodesian situation was misguided.[159]

Welensky's attitude indicated that real potential existed for the United States to play a very helpful role in facilitating a British-led negotiated settlement in Southern Rhodesia. Kennedy's ability to deal realistically with white leaders like Welensky, coupled with his excellent relationship with black leaders like Dr. Banda and Kenneth Kaunda, added up to a great prospect for U.S. influence in negotiating a settlement in Southern Rhodesia. Had Kennedy been president until 1969 or even just 1965, with his Administration's relatively high priority on Africa and his contacts with white and black leaders, events in Southern Rhodesia may well have turned out differently. Of course, Lyndon Johnson became president shortly after Kennedy's talk with Welensky, and the United States refrained from influencing a British settlement in Southern Rhodesia. Instead, the Johnson Administration would have to deal with Ian Smith and his 1965 UDI.

NOTES

1. Thomas Noer, *Cold War and Black Liberation: The United States and White Rule in Africa, 1948-1968* (Columbia: University of Missouri Press, 1985), 62-63. Bowles had made a name for himself among Africanists with his *Africa's Challenge to America* (Berkeley: University of California Press, 1956).

2. Interview with Joseph Satterthwaite, Washington, 2 March 1971, Oral History Project, John F. Kennedy Library, Boston, MA (hereafter JFK), 5-6.

3. Douglas Brinkley, *Dean Acheson: The Cold War Years, 1953-1971* (New Haven: Yale University Press, 1992), 306, 309.

4. The Europeanist/Africanist split in the Kennedy Administration is discussed in Noer, *Cold War and Black Liberation*, 62-66.

5. Daniel Henry Volman, "United States Foreign Policy and the Decolonization of British Central Africa (Zimbabwe, Zambia, and Malawi), 1945-1965" (UCLA Dissertation, 1991), 212, 261-264.

6. McKay was one of the leading Africanists in academia, and his

Africa in World Politics (New York: Harper and Row, 1963) is still useful. Good served as U.S. ambassador to Zambia from 1965 to 1968, and his *U.D.I.: The International Politics of the Rhodesian Rebellion* (Princeton: Princeton University Press, 1973) provides an insider's view into the events of the Southern Rhodesian unilateral declaration of independence.

7. "Report to the Honorable John F. Kennedy by the Task Force on Africa," 31 December 1960, "Africa 12/31/60 Parts I & II," Box 1, James C. Thompson Papers, JFK. Quotation from the first page of part one.

8. *Ibid.*, 49-52.

9. G. Mennen Williams interview, Oral History Project, JFK, 37-38. Throughout his tenure at the State Department, Williams maintained contact with Vernon McKay.

10. *Ibid.*, 65.

11. Bureau of Mines, *Minerals Yearbook 1965*, Volume 1 (Washington: U.S. Government Printing Office, 1966), 361, 373-374.

12. John Emmerson, American Consul General in Salisbury, Air Pouch to the State Department, 22 December 1961, 845c.053/12-2261; Emmerson to State, 10 March 1961, 845c.05111/3-1061. One example of U.S. investment unrelated to the mines was a $2.8 million luxury casino and hotel near Victoria Falls in Northern Rhodesia, planned by Rendell Mabey, a former State Legislator from Utah. For discussion, see Frederick Dutton to Senator Carl Yarborough, 12 April 1962, 845c.05111/4-362, State Decimal File, National Archives II, College Park, MD (hereafter NA2).

13. For an analysis of the potential profits to U.S. investors from the expanding African market for consumer goods in the Federation, see air pouch from Edward Mulcahy, American Consulate, Salisbury, to State, 17 November 1961, 845c.055/11-1761, Decimal File, NA2. Mulcahy's report specified tomato sauce as very popular among Africans, a prescient point since Heinz would become the only U.S. company with a plant in Zimbabwe during the 1980s. Mulcahy revealed his dismissive view of Africans by explaining that they need not be featured in advertisements, because they would buy anything Europeans bought.

14. Volman, "United States Foreign Policy and the Decolonization of British Central Africa," 171.

15. *Report to the Congress on the Foreign Assistance Program for Fiscal Year 1962* (Washington: U.S. Government Printing Office [hereafter USGPO], 1963), 1, 31.

16. *The Foreign Assistance Program: Annual Report to the Congress for Fiscal Year 1963* (Washington: USGPO, 1964), 67.

17. National Intelligence Estimate Number 60/70-61, "Probable Developments in Colonial Africa," 11 April 1961, "60/70, Africa," Box 8-9, National Security File, National Intelligence Estimates, Lyndon B. Johnson Library, Austin, TX, 2.

18. Arthur M. Schlesinger, Jr., *A Thousand Days: John F. Kennedy in the White House* (Boston: Houghton Mifflin, 1965), 558-560.

19. Memorandum of conversation between the President and Dr. Hastings K. Banda, 2 May 1961, *Foreign Relations of the United States, 1961-1963*, Volume XXI, Africa (Washington: USGPO, 1995), 508-509.

20. Nathan Shamuyarira, "The Coming Showdown in Central Africa," *Foreign Affairs* 39, #2 (January 1961), 293.

21. John K. Emmerson, American Consul General in Salisbury, air pouch to the State Department, 31 May 1961, 745c.00/5-3161, State Decimal File, NA2, College Park, MD, 3-4.

22. I*bid.*, 1,4. Daniel Volman contends that Emmerson was a racist, and that his racism had a significant impact on U.S. relations with the Federation. See Volman, "United States Foreign Policy and the Decolonization of British Central Africa," 319.

23. For some discussion of the difficulties of his time in exile, see Joshua Nkomo, *Nkomo: The Story of My Life* (London: Methuen, 1984), 73-89.

24. Shamuyarira, "The Coming Showdown," 297.

25. Nkomo, *Nkomo*, 92-96.

26. *Northern Rhodesia 1961: Colonial Office, Report on Northern Rhodesia for the Year 1961* (London: Her Majesty's Stationery Office, 1962), 5.

27. Kenneth D. Kaunda, *Zambia Shall Be Free: An Autobiography* (New York: Frederick A. Praeger, 1963), 155-160.

28. Kenneth Kaunda in London *Tribune*, 24 August 1961, quoted in J.R.T. Wood, *The Welensky Papers: A History of the Federation of Rhodesia and Nyasaland* (Durban: Graham Publishing, 1983), 942.

29. Kuanda to the President, the White House, Washington, 22 August 1961, "CO 250 Rhodesia," Box 68, White House Central File, JFK.

30. Reaction to William's speech described in Noer, *Cold War and Black Liberation*, 69; and Schlesinger, *A Thousand Days*, 555-6.

31. Salisbury to Secretary of State, 29 August 1961, "Rhodesia and Nyasaland," Box 123b, President's Office File, Countries, JFK.

32. C. Vaughan Ferguson, Jr., State Department African Affairs Desk, to Consul General in Salisbury, 29 August 1961, 745c.00/8-2961,

Decimal File, NA2.

33. Quotations from "Sock-On-Jaw Site Visited," *Baltimore Sun*, 18 February 1963, in "Feb. 1963 Trip - G. Mennen Williams," Box 24, Trips File, 1961-66, Records of G. Mennen Williams; Salisbury to Secretary of State, 12 September 1961, 745c.00/9-1261, Decimal File, NA2.

34. Governor Evelyn Hone to Williams, 29 August 1961; Williams to Hone, 16 September 1961, "Administration - Organization File, 1961," Box 2, Records of G. Mennen Williams, NA2.

35. Memorandum from State to McGeorge Bundy, "Proposed Telegram to Kenneth Kaunda," 2 September 1961, 745c.00/9-261, State Decimal File, NA2; note from Bromley Smith to State, saying "White House approved suggested message," 9/4/61, attached to ibid.

36. The message from Kennedy to Kaunda went out over Rusk's name, but was actually signed by William Wight of the African bureau. It was sent in a telegram from State to Dar Es Salaam, 8 September 1961, 745c.00/9-861; the delivery to Kaunda is described in Dar Es Salaam to State, 16 September 1961, 745c.00/9-1661, State Decimal File, NA2.

37. Memorandum From the Under Secretary of State for Economic Affairs (Ball) to President Kennedy, 23 September 1961, *FRUS, 1961-1963*, Volume XX, 236. For a U.S. diplomat's description of Welensky's racism see John Emmerson, U.S. Consul General, Salisbury, to State, 18 July 1961, 745c.oo/7-1861, State Decimal File, NA2.

38. *FRUS, 1961-1963*, Volume XX, 236.

39. See Emmerson to State, 18 July 1961 for Welensky's remarks about a U.S. visit. Wayne Fredericks, Deputy Assistant Secretary for African Affairs, explained that the State Department would keep in mind the "delicate question of a Welensky visit to the United States," in a letter to John Emmerson, U.S. Consul General, Salisbury, 19 July 1961, 745c.00/7-1961, State Decimal File, NA2.

40. For discussion of the events in the Congo in late 1961, see David Gibbs, *The Political Economy of Third World Intervention: Mines, Money, and the U.S. Policy in the Congo Crisis* (Chicago: University of Chicago Press, 1991), 132-133. Gibbs argues that the pro-Katanga lobby in the U.S. and British pressure combined to convince Kennedy to hault the UN operation.

41. Consul General, Salisbury, to State, 7 November 1961, 745c.00/11-761, State Decimal File, NA2.

42. *Ibid.*, 2.

43. Nathan Shamayurira, *Crisis in Rhodesia* (New York: Transatlantic, 1966), 77.

44. For a detailed narrative of U.S. civil rights events during 1961, see Taylor Branch, *Parting the Waters: America in the King Years, 1954-63* (New York: Simon and Schuster, 1988), 379-561.

45. Michael Klarman, "How *Brown* Changed Race Relations: The Backlash Thesis," *Journal of American History* 81 (June 1994), 81-118. In this article Klarman links *Brown* to a white southern backlash which ultimately led to political equality in the mid-1960s.

46. John Emmerson to State, 31 May 1961, 745c.00/5-3161, State Decimal File, NA2.

47. Williams Oral History Interview, JFK, 77.

48. E.M. Debrah, Counselor, Embassy of Ghana, Washington, DC, *The Effect of the Existence of "Segregation" in the US on the American Image in Africa*, 25 October 1961, "Speech, Embassy of Ghana, 10/25/61," Papers of Pedro San Juan (no box number), JFK.

49. John Emmerson to State, 26 September 1961, 745c.00/9-2661, State Decimal File, NA2.

50. John Emmerson to State, 31 October 1961, 745c.00/10-3161, Decimal File, NA2. For details of Mugabe's youth, education, and early activism, see Richard Worth, *Robert Mugabe of Zimbabwe* (New York: Julian Messner, 1990), 19-29.

51. Nkomo's letter to Houser in November 1961, described in George Houser, *No One Can Stop the Rain: Glimpses of Africa's Liberation Struggle* (New York: Pilgrim Press, 1989), 224.

52. Nkomo, *Nkomo*, 97.

53. Salisbury to State, 11 December 1961, 745c.00/12-961, Decimal File, NA2.

54. John Emmerson to State, 18 December 1961, 745c.00/12-1861, Decimal File, NA2.

55. The events in Albany, Georgia, during the summer of 1962 and the reactions of the Kennedy Administration are described in Taylor Branch, *Parting the Waters*, 601-632.

56. *Ibid.*, 647-672.

57. Department of State Instruction, "Reporting Needs - The Federation of Rhodesia and Nyasaland," 25 January 1962, 745c.00/1-2562, Decimal File, NA2.

58. "Federation of Rhodesia and Nyasaland," Memorandum for Mr. McGeorge Bundy, National Security Adviser, from Walter Collopy, State Department, 7 May 1962, "Rhodesia General 2/62-7/62," Box 155a, NSF, JFK. The above memo, with an attachment from Will-

iams, can be found at 745c.00/4-1662, Decimal File, NA2. The memo alone is also in *FRUS 1961-63*, Volume XXI, 516-518.

59. See Philip Short, *Banda* (London: Routledge & Kegan Paul, 1974), 166-7; Great Britain Colonial Office, *Nyasaland: Report for the Year 1962* (London: Her Majesty's Stationery Office, 1964), 1-2.

60. Great Britain Colonial Office, *Report on Northern Rhodesia for the Year 1962* (London: Her Majesty's Stationery Office, 1963), 3.

61. Memorandum of conversation between Kenneth Kaunda and Ralph Dungan, 13 April 1962, "Rhodesia General 2/62-7/62," Box 155a, NSF, JFK. President Kennedy sent Kaunda his regrets that he had not been able to meet with him during his visit in a letter of 30 April 1962.

62. Colonial Office, *Report on Northern Rhodesia, 1962*, 4.

63. Nkomo memo to UN, February 1962, in Christopher Nyangoni and Gideon Nyandoro, eds., *Zimbabwe Independence Movements: Select Documents* (New York: Harper and Row, 1979), 54-55.

64. Adlai Stevenson to the State Department, 23 February 1962, 745c.00/2-2362, Decimal File, NA2.

65. Nkomo, *Nkomo*, 99.

66. Adlai Stevenson to State, 21 February 1962, 745c.00/2-2062, Decimal File, NA2.

67. For a detailed explanation of the State Department's position, see "Southern Rhodesia," Woodruff Wallner, Head of International Affairs, to Undersecretary George Ball, 22 February 1962, 745c.00/2-2262, Decimal File, NA2.

68. Schlesinger, *A Thousand Days*, 563.

69. Nkomo, *Nkomo*, 85.

70. *FRUS 1961-1963*, Volume XXI, 515n.

71. American Consul General, Salisbury, to State, 13 March 1962, 745c.00/3-1362, Decimal File, NA2.

72. American Consul General, Salisbury, to State, 14 March 1962, 745c.00/3-1462, Decimal File, NA2.

73. American Consul General, Salisbury, to State, 23 March 1962, 745c.00/3-2362, Decimal File, NA2.

74. Memo of conversation with Robert Mugabe, American Consul General Salisbury, to State, 18 April 1962, 845c.062/4-1862, Decimal File, NA2.

75. AmConGen, Salisbury, to State, 15 May 1962, 745c.00/5-1562, Decimal File, NA2.

76. Memorandum, "Angola and Rhodesia," Williams to Fredericks, 16 April 1962, 745c.00/4-1662, Decimal File, NA2. The paper on the Rhodesias requested by Williams was sent to McGeorge Bundy by

Walter Collopy on 7 May 1962. It is printed, without the above memo, in *FRUS, 1961-1963*, 516-518; it is also in the Decimal File at NA2 and in the NSF at the JFK Library. The paper contains interesting insights regarding Nyasaland and Northern Rhodesia, discussed earlier in this chapter. It also contains prescient material on Southern Rhodesia being taken over by reactionary right-wing whites, but there is no indication that Kennedy read it or acted upon it.

77. Excerpts of Bingham's speech in State to Salisbury, 19 March 1962, 745c.00/3-662, Decimal File, NA2.

78. AmConGen, Salisbury to State, 4 May 1962, 745c.00/5-462. In September U.S. Consul General in Salisbury, Paul Geren, gave a copy of Bingham's speech to a young ZAPU lawyer who was very critical of the U.S. The lawyer, Enoch Dumbutshena, had not seen it before and "admitted that it helped put things in a different light." AmConGen, Salisbury to State, 18 September 1962, 745c.00/9-1862, Decimal File, NA2.

79. AmConGen, Salisbury to State, 19 April 1962, 745c.00/4-1962, Decimal File, NA2. The dispute between Welensky and Stevenson was discussed in several other cables and is summarized in Wood, *The Welensky Papers*, 1037.

80. *London Daily Telegraph* article summarized in AmEmbassy, London, to State, 5 June 1962, 745c.00/6-562, Decimal File, NA2. Another *Daily Telegraph* article critical of U.S. diplomats in the Federation is detailed in Luanda to State, 27 June 1962, "Rhodesia General 2/62-7/62," Box 155a, NSF, JFK. Welensky told Emmerson's replacement: "I liked Emmerson. I am sorry he left under a cloud." See Paul Geren, AmConGen, to State, 13 July 1962, 611.45c/7-1362, Decimal File, NA2.

81. MemCon, Williams and Ormsby-Gore, 1 March 1962, 745c.00/3-162, Decimal File, NA2.

82. Eshmael Mlambo, *Rhodesia: The Struggle for a Birthright* (London: Hurst, 1972), 175.

83. Nkomo, *Nkomo*, 100. Foot's resignation also discussed in Wood, *The Welensky Papers*, 1088.

84. Stevenson to Rusk, 15 June 1962, 745c.00/6-1562, Decimal File, NA2.

85. *FRUS, 1961-1963*, 518n.

86. Plimton, US Rep to UN, to Rusk, 3 July 1962, 745c.00/7-362, Decimal File, NA2.

87. State Department Planning Group, "The White Redoubt," June 28, 1962, on microfiche in *South Africa: The Making of U.S. Policy,*

1962-1989 (Washington: National Security Archive, 1991), 9, 13.

88. State Department Planning Group, "The White Redoubt," 14.

89. *Ibid.*, 15-16.

90. See the final draft of the "AF Priority List for August-September, 1962," 21 August 1962, and two previous drafts, in "Priority African Issues," Box 29, Miscellanous Files, 1961-66, Records of G. Mennen Williams, NA2.

91. Mugabe's view in AmConGen, Salisbury to State, 31 August 1962, 745c.00/8-3162; Consul General Geren's view in his cable to State, 14 September 1962, 745c.00/9-1462. In a 29 September 1962 note to Foreign Secretary Lord Home, Stevenson requested that the British make a public statement of their intent to keep control of Southern Rhodesia until it has a government acceptable to the majority. See Stevenson to Home, 745c.00/9-2962, Decimal File, NA2.

92. George Ball, Memorandum for the President, "Your September 30 Luncheon with Lord Home: Southern Rhodesia," 29 September 1962, 745c.00/9-2962, Decimal File, NA2.

93. MemCon, 30 September 1962, President Kennedy and Foreign Secretary Home, et.al., 745c.00/9-3062, Decimal File, NA2; reprinted in *FRUS, 1961-1963*, Volume XXI, 520.

94. Dean Rusk to Alec Home, signed by Ball, 5 October 1962, "Rhodesia General, 9/62-11/62," Box 155a, NSF, JFK Library; reprinted in *FRUS, 1961-1963* volume XXI, 521-22.

95. Home to Rusk, 18 October 1962, summarized in *FRUS, 1961-1963*, Volume XXI, 521n.

96. *FRUS, 1961 1963*, Volume XXI, 522.

97. State to AmConGen Salisbury, 19 September 1962, 745c.oo/8-3162, Decimal File, NA2.

98. The showdown at Ole Miss is described in Carl Brauer, *John F. Kennedy and the Second Reconstruction* (New York: Columbia University Press, 1977), 191-197; also see Taylor Branch, *Parting the Waters*, 647-672.

99. For a discussion of the formation and ultimate shortcomings of the ANLCA, see George Houser, *No One Can Stop the Rain*, 266; for the list of participants at this conference, see ANCLA, "Resolutions," Arden House, Campus of Columbia University, Harriman, New York, November 23, 24, 25, 1962, Folder 9, Box 125, Martin Luther King Papers, MLK Library, Atlanta, GA.

100. ANCLA, "Resolutions," Folder 9, Box 125, MLK Papers, MLK Library. One of the ANCLA conference's background papers was submitted by Dr. John Davis of the American Society of African Culture. Davis and the State Department exchanged interesting let-

ters that fall. Davis wrote Rusk on 25 October 1962, criticizing the Southern Rhodesian constitution. A note dated 31 October, attached to State's reply, identified Davis as an influential negro leader. The note added that Davis deserved a thoughtful response, because it would probably be used at the ANCLA conference. State's response was thoughtful, but not sent until 4 December, after the conference. The two letters and attached note are numbered 745c.00/10-2562, Decimal File, NA2.

101. Branch, *Parting the Waters*, 684.

102. AmConsul, Salisbury to State, 21 June 1962, 745c.00/6-2162; AmConsul, Salisbury to State, 30 July 1962, 745c.00/7-3062, Decimal File, NA2.

103. Parirenyatwa's death detailed in Shamuyarira, *Crisis in Rhodesia*, 75-76. The only witness was Edward "Danger" Sibanda, who was driving Dr. P to meet with Nkomo on the day Dr. P died.

104. Nkomo, *Nkomo*, 101.

105. *Ibid.*, 101-102.

106. AmConsul, Salisbury to State, 14 September 1962, 745c.00/9-1462, Decimal File, NA2.

107. One of the visitors, Chester Bowles' son Sam, was told by a ZAPU member that he was "not wanted in ZAPU headquarters." See AmConsul, Salisbury to State, 7 August 1962, 745c.00/8-762, Decimal File, NA2.

108. Daniel Kempton, *Soviet Strategy Toward Southern Africa: The National Liberation Movement Connection* (New York: Praeger, 1989), 100. The first ZAPU member trained in the USSR, Bobylock Manyonga, was arrested in the fall of 1962 transporting weapons. He resisted interrogation, protecting his fellow revolutionaries, and remained imprisoned for 14 years. See Joshua Nkomo, *Nkomo*, 104-105.

109. MemCon, G. Mennen Williams and O.B. Bennet of the British Embassy, 12 September 1962, 745c.00/9-1262, Decimal File, NA2.

110. Whitehead announced the banning of ZAPU on 20 September 1962. Mugabe was restricted immediately, and the police found large quantities of explosives in his house. Nkomo was restricted as soon as he returned from Tanzania. Geren concluded that the banning and restrictions would only enhance their prestige among the nationalists in Southern Rhodesia. See AmConGen, Salisbury to State, 21 September 1962, 745c.00/9-2162; and AmConGen, Salisbury to State, 10 November 1962, 745c.00/11-1062, Decimal File, NA2.

111. State telegram to the U.S. Consulate in Salisbury, 30 November 1962, 745c.00/11-1062, Decimal File, NA2. Drafted by Dunham

and approved by Williams, the message was sent over Rusk's name, with instructions to pass it on to Whitehead. Geren gave Whitehead the message on December 7 when he returned from campaigning.

112. For discussion of the differences between the United Party and the Rhodesian Front, see James Scarritt, "Zimbabwe: Revolutionary Violence Resulting in Reform," in Jack Goldstone, ed., *Revolutions of the Late Twentieth Century* (Boulder: Westview, 1991), 238-239.

113. Nkomo, *Nkomo*, 106.

114. Geren discussion with Whitehead in Salisbury to State, 20 December 1962, "Rhodesia, General 12/62," Box 155a, NSF, JFK Library.

115. AmConGen, Salisbury to State, 7 December 1962, 845c.10/12-762, Decimal File, NA2.

116. Salisbury to State, 19 December 1962, 745c.00/12-1962, Decimal File, NA2.

117. State to Salisbury, 18 December 1962, "Rhodesia, General 12/62," Box 155a, NSF, JFK.

118. Carl Brauer, *John F. Kennedy and the Second Reconstruction*, 230-264. Kennedy's concern for the U.S. image abroad is discussed on 240-241, and his 11 June speech is analysed on 259-263. The role of televised violence in bringing about Kennedy's new position on civil rights is analysed in Michael Klarman, "How *Brown* Changed Race Relations," 110-114.

119. Gibbs, *The Political Economy of Third World Intervention*, 140-144.

120. Welensky's support for the Katanga secession did waver somewhat by the end. According to Paul Geren, U.S. Consul General in Salisbury who perhaps should have been a sportswriter, Welensky was not "the Beelzebub who has (supposedly)... turned over all the Federation's anti-aircraft guns to Katanga." Instead he was "a paunched and aging boxer who was once the great white hope, and who recently considered whether he might seek to be the manager of a rebellious Negro boxer but gave up the effort." Geren to State, 3 January 1963, 745c.00/1-363, Decimal File, NA2.

121. Stevenson to State, 24 May 1963, "Rhodesia General 1/63-9/63," Box 155a, NSF Countries, JFK.

122. Memorandum, Williams to Rusk, "Major Conclusions of Williams Africa Trip," 25 February 1963, "Feb. 1963 Trip," Box 24, Trips File, 1961 - 1966, Records of G. Mennen Williams, NA2.

123. Williams to Rusk, from Salisbury, 20 February 1963, "Trip Feb. 1963," Box 24, Trips File 1961-66, Records of GMW, NA2.

124. This meeting, which infuriated Welensky, is described in Wood, *The Welensky Papers*, 1175-1176.

125. Paper prepared by State, "Situation Report on Southern Rhodesia," 6 April 1963, forwarded to McGeorge Bundy by Brubeck, *FRUS, 1961-1963*, Volume XXI, 527.

126. Colin Legum, ed., *Zambia: Independence and Beyond, The Speeches of Kenneth Kaunda* (London: Thomas Nelson, 1966), 49.

127. Stevenson to Rusk, 24 May 1963, "Rhodesia General 1/63-9/63," Box 155a, NSF Countries, JFK.

128. John F. Kennedy to the Honorable Kenneth D. Kaunda, 20 May 1963, "CO 250 Rhodesia," Box 68, White House Central File, JFK. Kennedy's personal secretary later sent Kaunda a letter thanking him for the book. The University of Denver has a copy of this book signed by Kaunda for the publisher, discovered in the stacks by the author and now in Special Collections.

129. As plans to send Peace Corps volunteers to Nyasaland progressed late in 1962, the subject of sending PCVs to Northern Rhodesia came up. See AmConGen, Salisbury to State, "Peace Corps Possibilities in Northern Rhodesia," 7 August 1962, 845c.00PC/8-762, Decimal File, NA2.

130. Short, *Banda*, 167.

131. Williams to State from Salisbury, 20 February 1963, "Rhodesia General 1/63-9/63," Box 155a, NSF Countries, JFK. In a memo to Wayne Fredericks, Williams reiterated: "Nyasaland seems overly optimistic on US aid." Memo, Williams to Wayne Fredericks, "First Draft of a Position Paper..." 5 March 1963, "US-UK Talks," Box 29, Miscellanous Files, Records of GMW, NA2.

132. Memo from Howard Furnas, State, to McGeorge Bundy, 28 January 1963, *FRUS, 1961-1963*, Volume XXI, 525-26. Blantyre School mentioned in Geren to State, 28 January 1963, 845c.00PC/1-2863; Arrival of volunteers noted in Geren to State, 15 January 1963, 845c.00PC/1-1563; their specific school assignments detailed in Geren to State, 23 January 1963, 845c.00PC/1-2363, Decimal File, NA2.

133. Banda to Kennedy, 5 June 1962, attached to a memo from Brubeck to Bundy, 26 June 1962; State's reply over Kennedy's name, 29 June 1962, "Rhodesia and Nyasaland," Box 123b, President's Office File, JFK.

134. See especially Geren to State, 21 September 1962, "Interview with Acting Federal Prime Minister and Deputy Prime Minister on the Peace Corps," 845c.00PC/9-2162; also 845c.00PC/9-1462, 845c.00PC/7-2062, and 845c.00PC/6-2862, Decimal File, NA2. Basically, arranging for the volunteers to work in Nyasaland in 1963

required dealing with Banda as ruler of an independent state in 1962, before Nyasaland was independent.

135. Banda to Kennedy, 3 May 1963; Kennedy to Banda, 4 June 1963, "Rhodesia and Nyasaland," Box 123b, President's Office Files, JFK.

136. Geren to State, 28 January 1963, 845c.00PC/1-2863, Decimal File, NA2.

137. The role of the Peace Corps in Kennedy's foreign policy has received much recent attention. For evidence that truly good intentions, outside of Cold War competition, underlay the program see Elizabeth Cobbs, "Decolonization, the Cold War, and the Foreign Policy of the Peace Corps," *Diplomatic History* (Winter 1996), 79-105. For a view with more emphasis on the Cold War impetus behind the PC see Gary May, "Passing the Torch and Lighting the Fires: The Peace Corps," in Thomas Paterson, ed., *Kennedy's Quest for Victory: American Foreign Policy, 1961-63* (New York: Oxford University Press, 1989), 284-316.

138. At least one of the relatively few black PCVs, Esther White, worked in Nyasaland. She was dismayed that her Afro hairstyle was criticized by one of her students. See Jonathan Zimmermann, "Beyond Double Consciousness: Black Peace Corps Volunteers in Africa, 1961-1971," *Journal of American History* (December 1995), 999-1028; White's story on 1018.

139. The trip to Africa was the fifth in two years for Williams and his wife Nancy. His visit and his overall work regarding Africa received laudatory coverage in the 18 February 1963 *Salisbury Daily News*. Clipping enclosed in "From Salisbury Feb. Trip `63," Box 24, Trips File 1961-66, Records of GMW, NA2.

140. Williams to State, 20 February 1963, ibid. Portions of this message are reprinted in *FRUS 1961-1963*, Volume XXI, 526-27.

141. MemCon of Williams and Federation Economic ministers, ibid.; *The Rhodesia Herald*, 19 February 1963, ibid.

142. Memo, Williams to Fredericks, 5 March 1963, ibid.

143. Memo, Carl Kaysen to Kennedy, 11 April 1963, "Rhodesia General 1/63-9/63," Box 155a, NSF Countries, JFK. This interesting memo, which proves that the situation report did get as far as the President, was not mentioned in *FRUS, 1961-1963*.

144. "Situation Report on Southern Rhodesia," attached to a memo from State for McGeorge Bundy, 6 April 1963, "Rhodesia General 1/63-9/63," Box 155a, NSF Countries, JFK. Handwritten on the memo to Bundy is the note: "(Taken from Pres. weekend reading dtd 4/11/63 - *Tab 3*)."

145. Williams to Sithole, 16 April 1963, *FRUS, 1961-1963*, Volume XXI, 530-32. The letter was in reponse to a letter from Sithole to Kennedy left at the U.S. embassy in London on April 8, summarized on 530n.

146. Geren to State, 11 January 1963, 745c.00/1-1163, Decimal File, NA2. The airgram was entitled "Mugabe Sees Violence Ahead in SR." Ironically, Mugabe explained to Geren that he believed a one party socialist system with a single powerful leader would be best for Southern Rhodesia when it became Zimbabwe. He became precisely that in 1980, and remained so in 2000.

147. Shamuyarira, *Crisis in Rhodesia*, 176-177. Nkomo places the first signs of the split in May, and blames Leopold Takawira for turning Mugabe against him. See Nkomo, *Nkomo*, 112-114.

148. Brief, "Struggle for Leadership in the Zimbabwe African People's Union (ZAPU) of Southern Rhodesia," attached to a memo from William Brubeck to McGeorge Bundy, 15 July 1963, "Rhodesia General, 1/63-9/63," Box 155a, NSF Countries, JFK. For a brief description of Nyerere's meeting with Kennedy in 1963 see, Julius Nyerere, *Crusade for Liberty* (Dar Es Salaam: Oxford University Press, 1978), 47-48.

149. Nkomo, *Nkomo*, 117; David Martin and Phyllis Johnson, *The Struggle for Zimbabwe: The Chimurenga War* (London: Faber and Faber, 1981), 70-71; Nyangoni and Nyandoro, eds., *Zimbabwe Independence Movements*, 57-64.

150. Houser, *No One Can Stop the Rain*, 225-227.

151. Memo from Robert Kennedy to McGeorge Bundy, November 20, 1963, on microfiche in *South Africa: The Making of US policy*. The original is in the Robert Kennedy Papers and is cited in Arthur Schlesinger, *Robert Kennedy and His Times* (New York: Ballantine, 1978), 606.

152. Schlesinger, *Robert Kennedy and His Times*, 801.

153. Noer, *Cold War and Black Liberation*, 85. G. Mennen Williams described RFK as very important in developing U.S. relations with African liberation movements. See Williams Oral History, 63-65, JFK.

154. First contacts between ZANU and China discussed in Martin and Johnson, *The Struggle for Zimbabwe*, 11; ZAPU's Soviet connection in Kempton, *Soviet Strategy*, 100; CIO formation in Henrick Ellert, "The Rhodesian Security and Intelligence Community 1960-1980," in Ngwabi Bhebe and Terrence Ranger, eds., *Soldiers in Zimbabwe's Liberation War* (London: James Currey, 1995), 87-103.

155. The decision to receive Welensky at the White House had been a difficult one. It was agreed that Kennedy would see him, but it would

be made clear that Kennedy had not invited Welensky to the U.S. Furthermore, it would be balanced by visits from black African leaders, and the meeting would receive "the minimum possible publicity." See memo from Carl Kaysen to William Brubeck, 27 March 1963, "Rhodesia General, 1/63-9/63," Box 155a, NSF Countries, JFK.

156. Memo from State to McGeorge Bundy, 4 October 1963; memo from William Brubeck for President Kennedy, "Meeting with Sir Roy Welensky," 7 October 1963, "Rhodesia General 10/63," Box 155a, NSF Countries, JFK.

157. MemCon, President Kennedy and Roy Welensky, 8 October 1963, *FRUS, 1961-1963*, Volume XXI, 536-538.

158. *Ibid.*, 537.

159. Welensky's 24 October speech to the Salisbury Rotary Club described in Geren to State, 25 October 1963, "Rhodesia General, 10/63," Box 155a, NSF Countries, JFK. Welensky also spoke highly of Senator Barry Goldwater, who had indicated to him that he might have relatives in Southern Rhodesia. Welensky's positive appraisal of his visit to the U.S. is briefly described in Wood, *The Welensky Papers*, 1221.

4

THE JOHNSON ADMINISTRATION
AND SOUTHERN RHODESIA'S
DECLARATION OF INDEPENDENCE

With the assassination of John Kennedy, Lyndon Johnson became president on November 22, 1963. G. Mennen Williams, Assistant Secretary of State for Africa from 1961 to 1966, believed that Johnson intended "to try and do the same things" as Kennedy had done regarding Africa.[1]

Through speeches and votes at the United Nations, the Johnson Administration mirrored the Kennedy policy of moderate symbolic support for the aspirations of nationalist movements in southern Africa.[2] Agency for International Development funds for Africa dwindled to $202 million in 1964, down from $261 million the previous year and $312 million in 1962.[3] Focusing on a domestic agenda featuring a "war on poverty" and civil rights legislation, while simultaneously becoming bogged down in Vietnam, top officials in the Johnson Administration paid scarcely any attention to Africa.

With a few brief exceptions, Africa remained at the bottom of Johnson's foreign policy agenda.[4] The anomalous Congo attracted some high-level attention, and the United States employed mercenaries to defeat yet another rebellion there in 1964-65.[5] Southern Rhodesia joined the Congo in the spotlight on 11 November 1965, when Prime Minister Ian Smith announced Southern Rhodesia's unilateral declaration of independence (UDI) from Great Britain.

Smith's critics believed that he sought to preserve white control of the predominantly black nation forever, and his illegal action earned worldwide condemnation. The British denounced UDI and applied sanctions to Southern Rhodesia, and the United States staunchly supported the British position.

For about a month following UDI, high-level officials in the Johnson Administration paid considerable attention to Southern Rhodesia. George Ball, the Undersecretary of State, organized a crack team of experts headed by William Rogers, to coordinate U.S. reaction to UDI with British policy. The resulting U.S. policy towards Southern Rhodesia reflected a variety of influences: economic concerns, strategic issues, and race relations both in the United States and in Africa. Because Southern Rhodesia was perceived primarily as a British responsibility, the most drastic course of action - U.S. military intervention to oust Smith - was never considered an option. Nevertheless, by participating in an airlift of oil to Zambia and prohibiting imports of Southern Rhodesia's products, the Johnson Administration demonstrated its commitment to racial justice in Africa, its responsiveness to African-American constituents, and its support for Cold War ally Great Britain.

UDI BACKGROUND: 1963-64

The Kennedy Administration supported the British policy of gently urging the white regime of Southern Rhodesia to grant political rights to its black population. In the last days of Kennedy's presidency, the fate of Southern Rhodesia was unclear. The Rhodesian Federation, which had linked Southern with Northern Rhodesia, was being disbanded. Northern Rhodesia was slated to become the independent nation of Zambia. The Southern Rhodesian government hoped for similar independence from Great Britain, but faced resistance because of its institutionalized racism. The Kennedy Administration seconded the British policy of insisting on advancement for blacks in Southern Rhodesia before independence.

As Washington adjusted to its new president in December 1963, a major transition was also occurring in Salisbury. After ten rocky years, the Federation of Rhodesia and Nyasaland had entered its final month.

The British had hoped their three territories in central Africa, Southern Rhodesia, Northern Rhodesia, and Nyasaland, could join together in a prosperous, multiracial state. The U.S. government had supported the British decision to form the Federation from the start and invested more than $200 million in the ten-year experiment.[6] The white ruling elite, headquartered in Salisbury, benefitted from access to the immense wealth of the Northern Rhodesian copper mines.[7] Blacks in Northern Rhodesia and Nyasaland opposed the arrangement from the first, however, and their opposition finally convinced the British to disband the Federation.

The Federation officially dissolved at midnight on 31 December 1963.[8] The results of ten years of Federation were in many ways contary to London's aspirations. Nyasaland and Northern Rhodesia gained independence as Malawi and Zambia, respectively, but were both economically weaker than before. Southern Rhodesia, on the other hand, featured a stronger economy and an entrenched minority regime.[9] Winston Field and the white supremacist Rhodesian Front party presided in Salisbury, while Southern Rhodesian black nationalists posed relatively little threat in the short run.

Seeing the developments in the other two territories, moreover, the Southern Rhodesian government demanded independence from Britain. British Prime Minister Alec Douglas-Home countered with a suggestion that independence might not be granted until Southern Rhodesia implemented majority rule. Duncan Sandys, the British Colonial Secretary, reiterated this position before parliament and during a meeting with U.S. Secretary of State Dean Rusk in December. Rusk inquired about the odds of UDI, and Sandys replied that it was unlikely.[10] At the end of 1963 the situation was at an impasse and CIA analysts viewed Southern Rhodesia as Britain's "thorniest decolonization problem to date."[11]

During the first few months of 1964, no major changes occurred in the Southern Rhodesian scenario. In April 1964, however, Britain's "thorniest decolonization problem" got significantly thornier. The Rhodesian Front, exasperated by the inertia of their Prime Minister Winston Field, replaced him with Ian Smith. Stubborn, combatative, and politically cunning, Smith was the first Rhodesian-born prime minister of the country.[12] He flew a fighter jet during World War II, and when shot down over Italy, he joined the guerrillas in their struggle against the Germans. Most importantly for his fellow "cowboys" in the Rhodesian Front, he firmly advocated white rule in Southern Rhodesia and seemed unafraid of a unilateral declaration of independence.[13]

Ian Smith's ascension caused a stir in the U.S. State Department and even caught the attention of Undersecretary George Ball, who usually focused on Europe or Vietnam. Ball warned U.S. ambassadors throughout Africa that Smith's victory practically erased any chances for a negotiated settlement and greatly increased the likelihood of UDI. Ball added that there was nothing substantive that the United States could do to influence events in Southern Rhodesia, and that the onus was on the British. The British government offered no concrete plan, however, and again explained to Rusk that it doubted Smith would actually declare independence.[14]

It appeared that the British would not do anything to hinder Smith, who in turn proceeded to guarantee that black nationalists could not do anything. Using the Law and Order Act for justification, the Smith government restricted without trial approximately 400 blacks in Gonakudzingwa. Jane Ngwenya of the Zimbabwe African People's Union (ZAPU), who served six years there, described Gonakudzingwa as a flat, semidesert area that became extremely hot during the days. It was a game park populated by wild animals, located in the wilds about 400 miles southeast of Salisbury, so no prisoners seriously considered escaping.

Among those detained was Joshua Nkomo, ZAPU's leader. Nkomo entered prison on 16 April 1964, and at first kept his spirits high. He wrote in May to his friend and supporter in the United States, George Houser: "We are adjusting ourselves well and becoming friendly to lions and elephants." His spirits slowly sank, though, and he would not exit prison until 3 December 1974, over ten years later.[15] Nkomo's incarceration, soon followed by the incarceration of other chief activists including Ndabaningi Sithole and Robert Mugabe, effectively crippled the liberation struggle until the early 1970s.[16]

A few days after Nkomo's arrest the U.S. Consul General in Salisbury summarized the situation for the State Department. He emphasized that Southern Rhodesia was rapidly deteriorating towards a violent upheaval and that recent events—the rise of Smith and the restriction of Nkomo—did not change the circumstances there but made them more urgent. So far the British had done little to bring the whites and blacks to the negotiating table, and time was running out before Smith would declare independence. He suggested that U.S. negotiators join with the British, along with other key outside parties like Zambian leader Kenneth Kaunda, in a "well-planned concerted diplomatic effort" to achieve majority rule in Southern Rhodesia peacefully.[17]

The Johnson Administration did no such thing, and few people in the United States cared. In general, Southern Rhodesia did not capture the attention of the American public before UDI. There were a few nongovernmental organizations, however, that kept a close eye on Africa and pressured the Johnson Administration to take action. The American Committee on Africa (ACOA) consistently urged the U.S. government to support African nationalism. Headed by George Houser, the ACOA frequently sent position papers to members of Congress and occasionally organized rallies espousing racial justice in Africa. While Houser himself was a classic white liberal, many key members of the ACOA were black, including A. Philip Randolph and Martin Luther King.

Black Americans, led by Randolph and King, helped form a separate organization called the American Negro Leadership Conference on Africa (ANCLA) to provide a forum for influential blacks to discuss Africa. They first met in 1962 in New York, and their second gathering took place in Washington from 24 September to 27 September, 1964. The ANLCA participants expressed pride in the recent achievements of black Americans in securing their civil rights in the United States, and in the fact that King would be receiving the Nobel Peace Prize in December. These successes, moreover, underscored the potential of African Americans to influence events in southern Africa.

African Americans had a "special responsibility to urge a dynamic African policy" from the U.S. government. Ongoing injustice in southern Africa required more forceful efforts by the United States, and the ANCLA suggested several. They advocated sanctions against South Africa in order to end apartheid. To prevent the catastrophe of a UDI by Ian Smith, they prompted the U.S. government to oppose Southern Rhodesia's independence without majority rule in the United Nations. They also requested the Johnson Administration to work for the release of the political prisoners such as Nkomo.[18] While the ANCLA's resolutions manifested the desire of African-American leaders that racial justice be extended to southern Africa, they basically failed to influence U.S. policy towards Southern Rhodesia in the fall of 1964.

Indeed, the Johnson Administration continued to support the British do-nothing policy. Some observers hoped all that would change after the British elections in October. Labor party victory made Harold Wilson the new British prime minister, and he quickly warned Ian Smith that UDI without majority rule would be viewed as a rebellion against Great Britain. He added that UDI would result in isolation and economic disaster for Southern Rhodesia. Dean Rusk applauded Wilson's stance and reiterated that the United States would not recognize a Southern Rhodesian government before majority rule.[19]

These statements from Wilson and Rusk, while forceful, deterred Ian Smith not at all. He reassured his constituents that while some sacrifice would be necessary, an independent Southern Rhodesia could survive. They would find non-British outlets for the tobacco crop, their main agricultural product. They could utilize the leverage of their stranglehold on Zambia's copper industry to dissuade international measures against them. Even if the British or the United Nations imposed sanctions on them, neighboring South Africa surely would help them over any rough spots in the road ahead. Smith's message placated the fears of white Southern Rhodesians, and they headed into 1965 determined to gain independence.[20]

Smith roused support because his message was what white Southern Rhodesians wanted to hear. Many of his points, moreover, sounded unpleasantly realistic to analysts in other concerned nations. For example, top U.S. government personnel worried about the fate of Zambia in case of a UDI. Zambia formally attained independence on 24 October 1964, and a wide spectrum of Americans attended. A controversial member of the official U.S. delegation was Charles Engelhard, a millionaire with massive investments in South Africa, who supposedly inspired novelist Ian Flemming's villain Goldfinger.[21] Young SNCC leader John Lewis witnessed the event, a highlight of his African tour that had begun in Guinea with Harry Belafonte and Fannie Lou Hamer.[22]

Zambian President Kenneth Kaunda visited Washington at the end of November and met with Johnson. Before the meeting, Rusk briefed Johnson on the U.S. relationship with Kaunda and the importance of Zambian copper.

> While publicly espousing a neutralist line, Kaunda is decidedly pro-West. He is a devout Christian, a sincere advocate of multiracialism, a man of democratic instincts and one who generally prefers compromise to conflict. Kaunda should be treated as a good friend of the U.S. whose attitudes on the whole parallel our own. Zambia's outstanding feature is its huge copper resources. American investment in the industry runs to about $100 million.[23]

When Zambia had been known as Northern Rhodesia and was part of the Rhodesian Federation, the copper deposits there had been the primary impetus for U.S. investment in the Federation. With Zambian independence, copper continued to be a central factor in U.S. interest in the entire region—not just in Zambia. While dissolution of the Federation saw the heads of the copper industry move from Salisbury to Zambia's capital of Lusaka, the industry remained linked to Southern Rhodesia for power and transportation.[24]

Kaunda feared that after a UDI, Smith would cut off Zambia's coal, electricity, and port access, thus halting copper production. World prices would in turn skyrocket, possibly prompting consumers to switch to aluminum, thus devastating Zambia's economy permanently. The U.S. government, sharing Kaunda's fears, contemplated measures to keep world copper prices down and also sought alternative sources of coal for Zambia. Kaunda proposed a rail link to Tanzania, which would sever his ties to Southern Rhodesia. Rusk summarized the U.S. position towards such a railroad at the time of Kaunda's 1964 visit as "open-minded," but a final decision hinged on feasibility studies.[25] Indeed, the U.S. would not make a decision whether or not to back the project until the following summer. The intertwined fates of Zambia and Southern Rhodesia remained up in the air as 1964 drew to a close.

UDI DRAWS NIGH: JANUARY TO OCTOBER 1965

Johnson's first full year as elected president, 1965, contained many watershed events for U.S. history—some triumphant, some tragic. Reacting to brutal attacks on civil rights activists in Selma, Alabama, in March, Johnson submitted a tough bill to Congress that would result in the Voting Rights Act.[26] This law forbade literacy tests and empowered the federal government to register voters in districts where discrimination persisted, thus constituting the crowning achievement of the Second Reconstruction. Also in March, two battalions of U.S. Marines landed at Danang, and the escalation of direct U.S. intervention in Vietnam began.[27] At the end of April 33,000 U.S. troops invaded the Dominican Republic to crush a rebellion.[28]

These events influenced U.S. relations with Africa in a variety of ways. Black African leaders noted the Johnson Administration's championing of civil rights. The president of Kenya, Jomo Kenyatta, wrote Johnson: "... in view of the wide interest and sympathy roused by incidents in the southern part of your country and the close connections between the Negro people and the people of Africa, I am writing to offer you my support in your government's efforts to remove all forms of discriminatory practices."[29] Clearly, Johnson's civil rights record scored points with President Kenyatta.

American diplomats also recognized the ongoing possibility that U.S. race relations could negatively affect African opinion. Despite the progress, some black leaders continued to criticize American society. Malcolm X, the outspoken Muslim minister, explicity linked American racism to U.S. policies in southern Africa that supported white supremacy. In a fierce speech in London, he advocated the overthrow of Ian Smith and his regime. Within two weeks Malcolm was dead. After the assassination, Ball worried that the incident would be used as anti-American propaganda by radicals in Africa. He wanted Carl Rowan, the respected black director of the U.S. Information Agency, to inform U.S. embassies in Africa that other blacks had killed Malcolm X, not whites.[30]

The major U.S. foreign policy operations of 1965, Vietnam and the Dominican Republic, also held a variety of ramifications for U.S. relations with Africa. Robert Komer, a National Security Council staffer, identified some potential connections between Africa policy and the U.S. stance towards other areas. In midyear he described American foreign relations as a "catalogue of horrors." He suggested the Johnson Administration:

offset the impact of Vietnam and Santo Domingo by a series of measures deliberately calculated to show that we're
still for peace and progress. A new gambit to rescue the
UN, new disarmament initiatives, a stronger line on racism
in Africa are possibilities.[31]

Komer suggested that America's rapidly declining reputation
around the world could be partially resuscitated if Johnson took a
stronger stand against racism in Africa. Southern Rhodesia, in many
respects, offered the best situation for such a U.S. stance. South
Africa's apartheid was the most obvious target, but its tremendous
economic and strategic importance mitigated any steps to undo it.
Indeed, Ian Smith's slightly less draconian system of institutionalized racism would become the recipient of U.S. criticism and economic punishment, but not until it illegally declared independence
in November.

Although the U.S. government would not make a preemptive
strike against Smith, the decision came early in 1965 that Southern
Rhodesia qualified as an attractive candidate for a U.S. diplomatic
stand against racism. With Smith and the Rhodesian Front party in
office, the 219,000 whites in Southern Rhodesia would maintain
virtual political and economic control of the approximately four
million blacks for the foreseeable future. Despite comprising less
than five percent of the population, in the mid-1960s, whites were
guarantors of fifty of the sixty-five seats in the Southern Rhodesian parliament. Moreover, the average income of whites was ten
times that of blacks.[32]

With its leaders in prison, the nationalist movement posed little
immediate threat to Smith. However, cadres of Joshua Nkomo's
Zimbabwe African People's Union were undergoing training in
the Soviet Union, China, and North Korea in 1965.[33] If Smith did
not negotiate a new constitution favorable to the nationalists, they
would launch a protracted armed struggle.

While the Johnson Administration never intended to intervene
directly in a military struggle in Southern Rhodesia, it determined
by mid-1965 that the United States could benefit politically by
firmly opposing Smith economically. American intelligence op-
eratives made it clear that in taking a hardline against Smith, the
United States risked nothing that was "essential to U.S. security."[34]

If the United States imposed total sanctions on Southern Rhodesia, the only significant loss to the U.S. economy would be chromite. The United States imported over 300,000 tons of Southern Rhodesian chromite in 1965, which represented more than 20 percent of the chromite shipped into the United States.[35] Cutting off this source would necessitate a heavy reliance on Soviet chromite, which was the only other source for high-grade ore. Yet, the existence of stockpiles of chromite guaranteed that relying on the Soviets for it would not endanger U.S. security.

The United States stood to lose very little by joining an international effort to oust Smith. On the other side of the ledger, much could be gained. Siding with the black majority in Southern Rhodesia would align the United States on the side most of the world viewed as morally and ethically correct. That made it just the type of position that NSC-staffer Komer was advocating. The effort against Smith after UDI would be led by the British and would certainly involve the United Nations, so the Johnson Administration could be seen as supportive of a key ally and of the UN. As Johnson drew increasing criticism over the Vietnam intervention, particularly from the less-developed nations who dominated the UN General Assembly, anything that could be done to counter it was useful.

Black Americans, destined to become more influential after the Voting Rights Act, would also applaud an anti-Smith policy. While Southern Rhodesia policy would not be a crucial issue for domestic American politics, black support would probably outweigh any opposition. Finally, the black majority in Southern Rhodesia clearly had the odds on its side. According to the CIA, the white minority "will find it difficult to cope with an increasingly restive black population which outnumbers it 20-1."[36] Majority rule would probably win out in the long run. With no such odds in Vietnam, the Johnson Administration was undoubtedly glad to put its money - albeit not much money—on the favorite horse for a change.

The United States stood to lose nothing crucial by slapping an embargo on Smith, but American officials did worry about the potential damage to the world copper market if Southern Rhodesia retaliated by cutting off Zambia. The Zambian copper belt's annual exports of 700,000 tons amounted to over 20 percent of free world copper production. From March to May 1965, British and

U.S. planning teams met in Washington and considered all manners of schemes to keep the copper belt running. The planners agreed that Zambia could survive UDI, but suggested surveying the infrastructure linking Zambia to Tanzania to determine how best to help get the copper out.[37]

As he had made clear during his visit the previous fall, Zambian President Kenneth Kaunda wanted the United States to fund a thousand-mile railroad to Tanzania. Williams and the African Bureau strongly advocated U.S. funding for the project.[38] The estimated costs totaled about four hundred million dollars, however, and therefore met firm opposition from the economically minded Ball.[39] Johnson concluded that with the mounting costs of intervention in Vietnam, Congress would never acquiesce in such an expensive project in Africa. In a May meeting with Rusk, Johnson shot down the proposal. The railroad received financing from communist China instead, taking nearly eight years to complete.[40]

Southern Rhodesia inched closer to declaring independence throughout 1965. Campaigning for re-election, Smith stressed independence—including a possible unilateral declaration. The British warned that they would respond to UDI by cutting Southern Rhodesia off from the Commonwealth, which meant closing the main markets for Southern Rhodesian tobacco. Johnson's ambassador to the United Nations, Adlai Stevenson, elucidated the administration's intention to join efforts against Smith after UDI. British and American warnings dissuaded few white voters, however. In the May 7 general elections, more than two-thirds of the electorate backed Ian Smith, and his Rhodesian Front party captured all fifty seats on the exclusively white "A" roll.[41] Whatever U.S. diplomats proposed doing about Southern Rhodesia, clearly they would be dealing with a confident Smith.

Stevenson's pledge in May that the United States would oppose UDI had not undermined Smith's support among his white constituency, nor had it satisfied black Africans. Nigerian foreign minister Nuhu Bamali, meeting with Rusk in September, accused the United States of sitting on the fence regarding Southern Rhodesia. He argued that Americans could do far more to influence Smith than the British, and that sanctions alone would not be enough. Rusk responded that the United States "has not straddled the fence on this issue, but has publicly stated its opposition to

UDI."[42] He added that people tended to over-estimate American influence, and that the best policy would be for the Johnson Administration to reiterate its support for the British efforts against UDI. About a week later Ball did just that:

> It would be a grievous error to assume that the United States could in any way condone an attempt of the Government of S. Rhodesia by unilateral action to deal with such important issues as are involved in the discussions which concern the future of your country.... The United States Government does not intend to deviate from its course of strong support for Her Majesty's Government now and—if it occurs—after a unilateral declaration of independence.[43]

Ball manifested to Smith that the United States would not condone UDI, and would continue to support the British position. Simultaneously, Ball instructed American diplomats in London to explain to the British that U.S. support was not infinite. He was disappointed with British vacillation in their negotiations with Smith. The British wanted the United States to guarantee them shipments of tobacco and pledge to cease importing Southern Rhodesian sugar in the case of UDI. According to Ball, the United States could give the British no such guarantees until they spelled out their planned reaction to UDI more clearly. He approved of them using the promise of U.S. support as leverage against Southern Rhodesia, but did not want them to see it as a "blank check."[44] The official position of the State Department, as put forth by Ball, was that any program for Southern Rhodesia would have to be primarily financed by the British.

The British would have to carry the ball, and their quarterback was Prime Minister Harold Wilson. Wilson had first met Smith at Winston Churchill's funeral in January, and had found him "extremely difficult and sour."[45] In early October, Wilson hosted Smith in London in hopes of negotiating a settlement. According to McGeorge Bundy, Johnson's National Security Adviser: "For Smith to go to London with the idea the Americans don't give a damn about UDI is a mistake.... We have not stated it as strongly as we may want to."[46]

To Bundy's satisfaction, on October 5, Johnson informed Smith of America's firm opposition to UDI. On October 8, the U.S. ambassador in London personally warned Smith that the United States would not recognize any government in Southern Rhodesia that was not representative of the majority.[47] These high-level U.S. diplomatic efforts fell in line with ideas that black African leaders projected, and received praise from Kaunda.[48] Despite praiseworthy American diplomacy, the talks between Smith and Wilson broke down. Ball explained to Vice President Hubert Humphrey that the London negotiations "didn't get anywhere and we may have the UDI thing on our hands."[49]

At this juncture, Ball contended that the United States had done enough and should perhaps wash its hands of the Southern Rhodesian question. What did concern him about UDI, however, were its potential ramifications for the North Atlantic Treaty Organization (NATO). If Portugal recognized Smith's regime after UDI, the British might break relations with Portugal. Ball was apprehensive about the how these developments could affect the NATO operations.[50] He requested that Secretary of State Dean Rusk discuss Southern Rhodesia with Portugal's Foreign Minister Franco Nogueira in their October 9 meeting.

Rusk devoted very little time to the Southern Rhodesia situation, because he had his hands full with the war in Vietnam. Following Ball's suggestion, though, he broached the subject while talking with the Portuguese Foreign Minister in New York on 9 October. He asked Nogueira a series of questions about Southern Rhodesia, and Nogueira explained that the bottom line for Portugal was its desire to stay out of the dispute. Rusk agreed that such a course would be best. He concluded that "it would be very unfortunate if Smith moved to UDI as this would create disturbances and turmoil in Africa at a time when we can well do without them."[51]

Both Rusk and Ball opposed expending more U.S. resources on Southern Rhodesia. Where Rusk simply did not see room for significant action or expenditure while so much was being spent in Vietnam, Ball doubted the efficacy of further inroads when the British where leading so ineffectively. One of the NSC staffers who worked on African issues, Ulrich Haynes, shared Ball's disappointment with the British. Haynes suggested that instead of washing its hands of the situation, however, the United States should take the lead and propose initiatives of its own.[52]

Haynes' espousal of a more aggressive U.S. policy probably reflected, to some extent, his close relationship with Williams—who continued to press Ball to be more forthcoming on the issue.[53] The connection between Haynes and Williams went back to the early days of the Kennedy Administration. Following instructions from Rusk, Williams had recruited qualified blacks to work in the State Department. He considered Haynes among the most talented blacks he hired and regreted that the National Security Council was able to "steal" him.[54]

Haynes enjoyed a moment in the spotlight while still at State, when late in 1963 South Africa denied him a visa to pass through on his way to Swaziland. Upon learning of the slight, Rusk summoned the South African ambassador into his office. He asked if Haynes was being discriminated against because he was black, then demanded that he be issued a visa. The South Africans complied, and Haynes completed an enjoyable and successful journey.[55] The episode demonstrated Rusk's interest in racial justice and his willingness to confront the white regimes of southern Africa.[56] By late 1965, however, the Vietnam war dominated his time to the point that he could do very little else.[57] African issues were left primarily to his subordinates at State and to Haynes on the NSC.

As a high noon showdown between Smith and Wilson approached, U.S. policy towards Southern Rhodesia took on a somewhat higher priority. The bulk of the work was still being done by Undersecretary Ball. While Ball personally wanted to let the issue rest, McGeorge Bundy had pushed him to once again assert the Johnson Administration's opposition to UDI. Ball prepared a telegram that was sent to Wilson a few days before he headed down to Salisbury for more talks with Smith. Ball emphasized that U.S. officials wanted Smith to grasp their condemnation of UDI.

Ball also included a supportive but vague message from Johnson, requesting that Wilson pass it on to Smith, in which he reiterated Johnson's disapproval of UDI and support for the British efforts. Ball further stated: "A unilateral declaration of independence unresponsive to the rights and interests of the majority of the population and in violation of the existing constitution would be a tragic mistake. If such a step should be taken, the United States would feel compelled to sever the traditional close ties that have character-ized its relations with Southern Rhodesia through war and peace."[58]

With this general encouragement from the Johnson Adminis-tration, Wilson flew to Salisbury on 25 October for five days of discussions. He met with ZAPU leader Nkomo and his rival Ndabaningi Sithole, leader of the Zimbabwe African National Union (ZANU). Talking with Nkomo and Sithole did nothing to derail the oncoming train of UDI, however, since Smith and his white constituency considered the nationalist movement a nonen-tity at that point. During Wilson's session with Nkomo, Smith's police dogs mauled nationalist demonstrators. In response to the Archbishop of Canterbury's proclamation in support of Southern Rhodesia's black majority, Southern Rhodesia's white minority burned bibles.[59] The atmosphere was by no means conducive to a negotiated settlement.

On October 29, the final full day of Wilson's futile bargaining, the U.S. government weighed in one last time. The Johnson Ad-ministration notified Smith that:

> we are convinced that a unilateral declaration of indepen-dence would be a tragic mistake which would serve the true interests of no one. The United States would have to make known its strong opposition to any such decision, and we do not intend to change our course of firm support for the position of the British government after any such uni-lateral declaration.[60]

Thus the United States practiced some high-level diplomacy in support of British policy towards Southern Rhodesia. In fact, Bundy telephoned Ball just prior to its transmission to clarify the word-ing.[61] Bundy's interest signified neither a higher priority for, nor an increase in resources allotted to, Southern Rhodesia. More likely, Bundy viewed support for the British on this issue as a cheap bar-gaining chip for British support on the U.S. intervention in Viet-nam. For a variety of reasons, then, as the Southern Rhodesia sce-nario came down to the wire, top American officials labored to ensure that U.S. backing for Wilson was crystal clear to Smith. However, it remained nebulous precisely what concrete maneuvers Wilson and his American backers would carry out if Smith perpetrated UDI.

British diplomats terminated talks with Smith on 5 November, and he imposed a state of emergency. Later that day in a press conference Rusk admonished Smith not to declare independence, still stopping short of spelling out the consequences. On 9 November State officials began preparing a statement for Johnson to deliver should Smith announce UDI, its content little more than the vague pledge of nonrecognition.[62] After nearly two years of debating how best to deal with a UDI, the Johnson Administration still had no concrete plan except to continue diplomatic support for the British policy.

THE JOHNSON ADMINISTRATION AND UDI

On the Armistice Day morning of 11 November 1965, Wilson spoke with Smith on the telephone, but Smith had made up his mind. A few hours later he announced that Southern Rhodesia was thenceforth an independent nation, no longer subject to control by Britain.[63] Whites in Salisbury evidently breathed a sigh of relief that a clear decision - even if it was a risky one - had finally been made. Blacks, whatever they were feeling, refrained from public demonstrations.[64] The eyes of the world turned to London, anxious to see Wilson's response. He deliberated over his options.

Obviously the most aggressive manner to oppose Smith would be a military operation. However, such a step would be very costly for an already weak British economy and would require logistical support from the United States that the British could not count on. Most importantly, public opinion opposed the use of force, and Wilson's Labor party held only a three-vote advantage in Parliament. Economic and political realities, therefore, precluded the use of force.[65]

The next strongest response would be sanctions, aptly defined by British diplomat Robin Renwick as "the imposition of economic penalties to bring about a change in the political behavior of the country against which they are directed."[66] Wilson recognized Southern Rhodesia's high degree of vulnerability to such measures: Southern Rhodesia earned 38 percent of its income from exports, and tobacco constituted 33 percent of its exports. Half of that tobacco went to Great Britain.[67] Furthermore, many of Smith's friends and staunchest supporters grew tobacco. So, directing sanctions against tobacco would inflict serious economic hardship, and in turn could lead to political change. If nothing else, it was hoped that sanctions would give Smith a powerful incentive to negotiate.

With such results in mind, Wilson opted to ban imports of Southern Rhodesian tobacco. Other initial actions included prohibition of British arms shipments and capital transfers to Southern Rhodesia, cessation of British aid to Southern Rhodesia; and passage of the Southern Rhodesia Act, a law that gave Wilson the power to impose more sanctions.[68] Eventually, Wilson would prohibit the purchase of sugar and minerals from Southern Rhodesia and the sale of petroleum to Southern Rhodesia. The success of such extensive measures would depend on the policy of South Africa, as the vast majority of material destined for Southern Rhodesia passed through its powerful neighbor's ports. The evening of UDI, Prime Minister Hendrik Verwoerd unequivocally revealed South Africa's refusal to participate in "any form of boycott" against Southern Rhodesia.[69] Nonetheless, the British pursued their policy of sanctions and sought cooperation from the Johnson Administration.

On November 11, President Johnson hosted his foreign policy advisers at his ranch near Austin, Texas. For six hours, he discussed the international scene with Rusk, Ball, Bundy, Defense Secretary Robert McNamara, and chief Policy Planner Walt Rostow. At some point during the meeting, the African Bureau called and informed Rusk of UDI. Rusk requested that the Bureau's contingency plans be sent to Austin. After Rusk returned to the meeting with the news, the group decided only to recall the U.S. consul general from Salisbury. In a post-meeting press conference, Rusk announced that the U.S. government deplored Smith's action. He explained that the consul general was being recalled, and that further measures would be spelled out the following day by Arthur Goldberg, the U.S. representative at the United Nations.[70]

Part of the reason for delaying more substantive action was that the contingency plans prepared by the African Bureau had not received high-level attention, and they were in transit to Austin on 11 November. During the summer and fall of 1965, Johnson and his advisers committed virtually no time to any foreign policy issue other than Vietnam.[71] Johnson, Bundy, and McNamara simply were not certain of the preferred options in the case of UDI. Moreover, the thrust of U.S. policy towards Southern Rhodesia through-out the Johnson, Kennedy, and Eisenhower Administrations had been to second the British. Therefore, the Johnson Administration needed to find out the British response to UDI before they could proceed with their policy of supporting it.

By the morning of 12 November, Rusk had ascertained Wilson's initial reaction to UDI—which amounted to economic measures and an arms embargo. In a telephone conversation that morning, Rusk and Johnson agreed that the U.S. response should mainly consist of suspending the 1966 import quota for Southern Rhode-sian sugar and an arms embargo.[72] Later that day at the UN Secu-rity Council, Ambassador Goldberg delineated the Johnson Administration's policy. In addition to suspending future sugar imports and ceasing weapons exports, the United States would dis-courage American citizens from traveling to Southern Rhodesia or investing there. These measures joined the steps taken the previ-ous day to recall the consul general from Salisbury and retract dip-lomatic status from representatives of Southern Rhodesia in Wash-ington.[73]

Washington's initial response to UDI, then, amounted to sym-bolic diplomatic changes and support for the British sanctions. This served the wishes of White House aides like Bundy and Komer, who viewed all issues in the context of how they would influence the war in Vietnam. The policy might gain reciprocal British sup-port for the war, and at least might counter some of the criticism at the United Nations. Furthermore, the moderate response meshed with the desires of Undersecretary Ball, who did not want to get ahead of the British policy.

Ball agreed that a forthcoming U.S. response was necessary to ingratiate the United States with black African leaders who were being offered support by communist China. On the other hand, he discouraged too strong a policy until all of the economic ramifica-tions could be studied. Shortly after UDI he expressed his concern that stopping exports to Southern Rhodesia would negatively af-fect the balance of payments.[74] He also proposed that the African bureau convene a meeting with heads of American companies who possessed significant holdings in Southern Rhodesia. Indeed, Ball's pertinent views and actions in the months following UDI consis-tently revolved around the economic aspects of the situation.[75]

Meanwhile, Ball certainly understood who would advocate a more forceful policy against Ian Smith. He explained to Treasury Department official Henry Fowler that: "The American Negro community regards this as a test case of the bona fides of the Administration."[76] In fact, leaders of the African-American community quickly registered their support for strong measures against Smith. National Association for the Advancement of Colored People (NAACP) executive director Roy Wilkins requested that Johnson support the British actions to remove Smith. He concluded: "Negro Americans... fully support whatever measures may be necessary to suppress this racist revolt."[77] Martin Luther King similarly asked that Johnson refuse to recognize the Smith regime and that Johnson impose economic sanctions.[78]

The director of the Congress on Racial Equality, James Farmer, specified serious steps including U.S. leadership at the United Nations in imposing full sanctions against Southern Rhodesia.[79] Representative Adam Clayton Powell suggested that Johnson lead the effort to adopt a world economic boycott of Southern Rhodesia.[80] Powell and Farmer wanted far more than Johnson was inclined to deliver on Southern Rhodesia in November 1965. Moreover, Farmer and Powell were not particularly influential with Johnson. Roy Wilkins, on the other hand, was Johnson's closest contact among the civil rights leaders.[81] While African-American voters never mounted a massive movement to lobby against Smith's rebel regime, the pleas of Wilkins and King for a strong policy against it undoubtedly carried some weight at the White House.[82]

In order to take a firmer line against Smith in the short run, the Johnson Administration opted to focus on Southern Rhodesian sugar. On 12 November, Ambassador Goldberg had announced that the United States would not import any Southern Rhodesian sugar in 1966.[83] A week after UDI, on 18 November, Goldberg spearheaded a movement to prevent the import of the 1965 quota of Southern Rhodesian sugar. While suspending the sugar quota for 1966 was simply replicating the action taken by the British, stopping 1965 imports was actually more than the British were doing. A ship carrying 9,500 tons, the entire quota of sugar for 1965, was en route to Yonkers and scheduled to dock on 10 December. Blocking that shipment would mean the United States was slightly ahead of the British in its opposition to Smith, at least regarding sugar imports.

Ball disagreed with being more agressive than the British, and also disliked the idea of revoking existing contracts for sugar imports.[84] Goldberg explained to Ball, however, that the Afro-Asian representatives at the UN might stage a demonstration against the 1965 shipment and would possibly get the longshoremen to refuse to unload it. Goldberg added that leaders of the labor movement had indicated to him that they wanted a stronger stand against Smith, which suggested that they might well refuse to unload the sugar.[85] Pressure from the labor movement, then, helped convince Goldberg to seek suspension of the 1965 shipment.

State's Executive Secretary, Benjamin Read, summarized the situation regarding the 1965 sugar imports for McGeorge Bundy. Read emphasized Goldberg's opinion, and added that the African Bureau concurred with Goldberg. He estimated that any resulting legal actions against the government for breach of contract would probably not succeed. He suggested expediency, since the ship was due within a few weeks.[86] Robert Komer, an NSC staffer who considered the Southern Rhodesia situation a fine opportunity to alleviate the criticism of Johnson's Vietnam policy, echoed State's recommendation that the president suspend the sugar quotas for 1966 and 1965.[87] Johnson nodded his approval, and on 20 November Goldberg announced at the UN that the 1965 quota of sugar would not be unloaded.[88] While the shipment was only worth about $1 million, the action publicly demonstrated the Johnson Administration's desire to take an aggressive stand against UDI.

While Johnson's decision for the sugar embargo risked very little, it gained some approval from labor and African Americans.[89] Much more was at stake, however, regarding copper. In the days following UDI, Johnson and his advisers gave more attention to the impact of Smith's decision on the copper market than to any other aspect of the crisis. As Ball explained to Bundy, the Southern Rhodesian situation "was getting confused with the copper situation because of the Zambians."[90] If Zambia joined economic sanctions against SR, Smith would respond by closing the railroads that carried Zambian copper to the sea ports. He would also block shipment of coal and oil to Zambia. So, if Zambia joined a strong sanctions effort against Southern Rhodesia, then about 20 percent of the world's copper supply would be in limbo. Cessation of Zambian copper exports would result in a world shortage and drastic price increase.[91]

Such a prospect sounded alarms at the highest levels of power in Washington, including the Oval Office. While discussing the possible ramifications of UDI, President Johnson made it perfectly clear to Bundy that "anything that busts the copper market open is of no use to him."[92] Johnson had already explored the implications of UDI for the copper market with Thomas Mann, the Undersecretary of State for Economic Affairs.[93] Clearly, the President did not like the potential impact on supply and prices. Defense Secretary Robert McNamara concurred, telling Ball that "the last thing we can stand is stoppage of copper from Zambia."[94]

Why did Robert McNamara and Lyndon Johnson care so much about the supply and price of copper? As for the supply, while the United States ranked first in copper production, it imported roughly one-third of the copper it used annually. Any threat to copper supplies could harm a number of key U.S. industries, particularly the electronics industry. In Chicago alone, that industry employed almost 200,000 workers. Those people produced electronic components and finished goods such as color televisions, which required large quantities of copper wire. Cuts in copper supplies could curtail production of high demand items like color television sets, causing massive lay-offs in Chicago. The need for copper did not stop at these shores, however, as American soldiers in Vietnam utilized ammunition strips made from copper.[95] Escalation of the war required more copper, and obviously Johnson did not want to necessitate the firing of thousands of well-paid workers in Chicago because of the war. Therefore, he needed to maintain adequate supplies of copper.

The supply of copper was a very high priority, but the price was also important. By the time of UDI, the copper price had already risen two cents, bringing it up to 38 cents per pound. At that price, some industries would substitute aluminum for copper. Even higher prices would bring more substitution, thereby cutting the profits of copper producers.[96] So, copper producers actually opposed an increase in copper prices after a point. For example, the Anaconda Corporation told the Defense Department that they spoke for the entire U.S. copper industry, and "the last thing they wanted to see was prices going up."[97] One of Johnson's top economic counselors, Gardner Ackley, advised that the President help Anaconda and the other producers by stemming the price increase, thereby preventing large scale substitution with aluminum. It was in the interests of the American economy as a whole, since the profits of the big copper companies outstripped those of the aluminum companies, and the rate of return for copper stockholders was much higher.[98]

In early November, Johnson faced a mounting problem regarding the supply and price of copper. By illegally declaring independence from Great Britain, Smith exacerbated Johnson's concerns over the copper industry. The international community demanded a stern reaction to UDI, and Zambian President Kenneth Kaunda intended to participate fully. Such participation would halt the flow of Zambian copper, possibly hindering production of ammunition belts for U.S. soldiers or laying off American workers who built televisions. Resulting price increases would harm U.S. copper producers by causing shifts to aluminum, thus damaging one of the stronger components of the American economy.

What options did the Johnson Administration have to deal with the copper problem? Ball and Deputy Defense Secretary Cyrus Vance discussed mandating a rollback of copper prices. After Vance pledged to work on getting a rollback in domestic copper prices, Ball commented that "the Zambia thing is really moving."[99] A rollback would be futile, surely, if Zambia's 20 percent were cut off from the world market. In contemplating the copper situation, there was no avoiding the potential of Zambia's being isolated by Smith. Ball hoped that Kaunda would keep Zambia from participating in sanctions against Smith, but Kaunda rejected that notion.

Kaunda informed British and American officials that he believed Zambian participation to be critical to the success of any sanctions against Smith. He would not allow Zambia to be the outlet that allowed Smith to stave off the sanctions. In order to stop its trade with Southern Rhodesia, Zambia would need significant economic and logistical support from Great Britain and the United States. He hoped for Anglo-American assistance in getting fuel into Zambia, and shipping copper out.[100] With Kaunda's plans and the copper problem in mind, Komer and McNamara weighed the Johnson Administration's options on Saturday evening, November 13. They concluded that it would be possible to airlift fuel in and copper out of Zambia.

When informed of their view, Ball doubted the effectiveness of such an airlift. He focused, as usual, on the economic impact of the plan. He explained to Bundy: "We will have a time getting copper out of Zambia on a basis that won't hike world prices."[101] An airlift would be so expensive that it could, in fact, undermine the copper industry and the economy of Zambia by leading to a price hike. Such a price increase could trigger widespread substitution of aluminum for copper, which would deal a devastating long-term blow to the copper industry everywhere, including Zambia. Ball's opposition to Zambian participation in the sanctions did not necessarily constitute sympathy for Ian Smith and UDI, but definitely did reveal his view that Zambia's interests fundamentally rested on the health of the copper market.

The fate of the Zambian copper industry was tangled in the complex web of global politics and economics. The United States had agressively taken the lead in stopping imports of Southern Rhodesian sugar, but with copper far too much would be at stake for hasty action. Johnson's top advisers paid close attention to Zambian copper in the weeks following UDI, but decided that any concrete pledge to help Zambia would have to wait until the British plotted their course. In the meantime, Johnson could not allow the American copper industry to twist in the wind. On 18 November, McNamara announced that because mounting Vietnam war demands and a world shortage were driving up copper prices, the President had released 200,000 tons of copper from the national stockpile.[102]

The British government had inquired about the possibility of such a move while discussing ways of dealing with UDI and had been told that it was not legal. They expressed some displeasure at not being consulted before the sudden shift, and Assistant Secretary Williams suggested that State think about ways to smooth the ruffled feathers in London.[103] Indeed, Johnson's decision to release stockpiled copper demonstrated how a problem threatening both the U.S. economy and war effort took precedence over maintaining a "special relationship" with England. Moreover, the Administration would go to extremes when inflation threatened the national economy, but would not take the same steps simply to facilitate a British policy towards Southern Rhodesia.[104] That is not to say that U.S. officials washed their hands of Southern Rhodesia after the initial decisions to close the embassy, stop arms shipments, and cancel the sugar quotas. Any further decisions, however, required more thought and coordination with London.

THE ROLE OF GEORGE BALL

On 18 November, the same day President Johnson released the stockpiled copper, Ball initiated his search for someone to oversee the details of U.S. policy towards Southern Rhodesia. The first person he asked to take the post was Undersecretary for Political Affairs U. Alexis Johnson. Revealing his doubts about the African bureau, Ball told Johnson that "he was concerned about the Rhodesian matter as nobody in whom he has confidence is on top of it."[105] Johnson declined, as he had previous commitments including an upcoming appearance on *Face the Nation*.

The following day Ball informed McNamara that he wanted to bring in Roswell Gilpatric to work on the problems affecting Southern Rhodesia and Zambia. Gilpatric had served as deputy at the Pentagon from 1961 to 1964, and McNamara welcomed Gilpatric as a "marvelous" choice.[106] Ball explained to McGeorge Bundy that he believed Gilpatric was "sufficiently organized" to coordinate an effective policy on UDI. Bundy felt Gilpatric could "do a good job," but registered concern about his temperamental personality.[107] Ball opted to pursue Gilpatric despite Bundy's reservations.

The next afternoon, Ball asked Gilpatric if he could work for a week or two for State on something "pretty interesting but reasonably complicated." He summarized the basic situation—that if Zambia joined an economic strike against Southern Rhodesia, Smith would isolate the copper belt. He added: "If copper should dry up it would cost the British 2 million pounds a year in foreign exchange and what it would do to world copper market and general world economic situation would be catastrophic." Gilpatric was associated with Corning Industries, and Ball asked if that would create any conflict of interests. Gilpatric replied that it would not, and agreed to decide about the job within two days.[108]

While in London discussing military matters, Ball informed Wilson that Gilpatric had been hired to coordinate U.S. policy, and a delighted Wilson asked to meet with Gilpatric as soon as possible.[109] Wilson summarized his meeting with Ball in a cable to the President, including his enthusiasm for the appointment of Gilpatric. When Johnson read of Gilpatric's hiring, he asked Bill Moyers to check it with Ball. Ball explained that Gilpatric was being contracted by State to coordinate Southern Rhodesian policy. He wasn't really a presidential appointment, and so Bundy, Rusk, and McNamara had agreed that Johnson did not need to be informed. Ball emphasized that Gilpatric was particularly qualified because he had experience in business and at the Pentagon, and also that he knew the State Department well. He could still disengage Gilpatric, but would have trouble finding someone to do the job.[110]

President Johnson evidently feared that Congress would oppose the hiring of Gilpatric, and there may have been a personality conflict as well. Prime Minister Wilson approved wholeheartedly of the choice of Gilpatric as the American pointman, and Ball felt it would be difficult to find someone as capable for the job. Nevertheless, during the afternoon of 29 November, Johnson phoned Rusk from Texas and told him that he did not want Gilpatric on the job. It is not exactly clear how much of the decision was personal, or how much political. Nonetheless, after Johnson called Rusk, Ball complied with the President's wishes and disengaged Gilpatric.[111] Bundy later told Ball that it was the right move, but that he wished they "had known more of the history of the feeling" about Gilpatric.

Bundy and Ball then discussed who should replace Gilpatric. They agreed the best person would be former Attorney General William Rogers, whom they both knew, and who Bundy felt had "great ability." They considered him part of the foreign policy "team" already, and Ball had been holding him in reserve for assignment in the Dominican Republic. They decided they would instead hire him to work on Southern Rhodesia for a few weeks. Not wanting to repeat the fiasco involving Gilpatric, Ball wisely pledged to delay contracting Rogers until Johnson approved the decision.[112]

The following day, while waiting for the go-ahead on Rogers, Ball checked on the progress of the working group that was drawing up the contingency plans for Southern Rhodesia and Zambia. Ball concluded that they had not outlined all the options clearly enough, and that they were being unrealistic about the extent to which the United States could direct the British. Their report needed better organization and more practicality, because "we could not second guess the British on this."[113] Ball wanted a "comprehensive outline of this whole Rhodesian problem with as much hard stuff in it as possible," so that Rusk could go over it with the President, who would be meeting with Wilson soon. Ball felt that Wilson understood the complexities of the situation pretty well, but that President Johnson "really has to begin to understand what is involved more than he does."[114]

In Ball's mind the main questions involved how best to deal with an economic war between Southern Rhodesia and Zambia, with the primary concern being how to keep the copper belt running. He thought the United States should assist the British in this, but not play too large a role and thus risk being blamed for any failure. He explained the circumstances to Rogers on 1 December, underlining the economic aspect of the problem. A lot of work had already been done at the working level by both British and American bureaucrats to outline a plan, and "what is needed is a top man to tie it together." He asked if Rogers could spare a week or two to be that "top man," assuming the White House approved him. Rogers accepted the assignment, and in turn received the President's blessings.[115]

Scholar and sometime government official Anthony Lake has condemned Ball for bringing in Rogers, arguing that he was an old friend whom Ball felt he could control.[116] Lake argued that Ball expected Rogers to moderate plans formulated by the African Bureau regarding Southern Rhodesia, so that his own plans would win out. While Ball undoubtedly favored a less agressive policy than some personnel in the African Bureau, Lake exaggerated the conspiratorial nature of the hiring of Rogers. His portayal of Ball as the ultimate "Europeanist" who opposed the progressive ideas of the "Africanists" is somewhat simplistic and not substantiated by the documentary evidence.

Sloppiness on details by Lake diminishes the credibility of his criticism of Ball, who actually was not plotting to advance his "Europeanist" agenda. Basically, Ball wanted someone who could prepare a useful report to show the President before he met with Wilson. Ball's first choice, U. Alexis Johnson, was not available.

The President rejected Gilpatric, Ball's second choice, unexpectedly. With those circumstances in mind, the choice of Rogers can hardly be seen as part of a scheme by Ball to hamstring the "Africanists." Lake would have us believe that allowing Ball to control the policymaking on Southern Rhodesia was akin to letting the fox guard the henhouse.

The implication of Lake's account is that Ball was a racist who did not care about the plight of blacks in Southern Rhodesia. The reality, however, was that Ball focused almost exclusively on the economic ramifications of UDI, particularly regarding Zambian copper. He advocated a U.S. policy that would keep the copper smelters firing, at a relatively low risk to the credibility of the United States. He believed such a policy was in the best interests of not only the United States, but also the black majorities in Zambia and across southern Africa. He paid attention to the views of African Americans, especially those of Whitney Young and Roy Wilkins.

Pigeonholing Ball as a "Europeanist" ignores his complex understanding of African problems. Indeed, the prototypical "Africanist," G. Mennen Williams, downplayed the efficacy of categorizing Ball as a "Europeanist." He lauded Ball as an outstanding advocate, who dealt with issues on an ad hoc basis in hopes of reaching the most realistic solutions.[117] Williams' description of Ball—as a practical advocate who could see both sides - hits the nail on the head, at least in the case of Ball's role in the American reaction to UDI. He championed a policy that would second the British fight against Ian Smith, while taking low-cost steps to ensure the production of copper.

OIL EMBARGO AND AIRLIFT

Shortly after accepting the assignment as overseer of U.S. policy towards Southern Rhodesia, William Rogers concluded that the circumstances were complex and grave. The British plan would not end Smith's rebellion in the near future. So, taking measures against Smith that would cause him to punish Zambia and cut off its copper would do longlasting damage to the copper industry. Mainly because of the Vietnam War, the United States would be in no position to share its copper. So, the British should think long and hard before taking steps against Smith that would drive him to a retaliatory strike against Zambia. Nonetheless, Rogers asserted that the United States was prepared to join with the British in just the type of measure that would bring such results—an oil embargo.[118]

Support for an oil embargo came from many quarters, including African leaders, civil rights activists, and the UN Security Council. On 20 November, the Security Council called on the British to cut off the flow of petroleum products to the Smith regime. Heads of State from Ghana and Tanzania, among others, demanded ever more loudly that the British take this step in the last weeks of November. A working-group of American and British bureacrats analysed the potential for an oil embargo that would actually cripple the Smith regime and presciently concluded that it would not succeed because "South Africa could pick up the slack."[119]

They did see virtue in slapping an oil embargo on Southern Rhodesia anyway, however, as a diplomatic ploy to please black African leaders. Led by Tanzania's Julius Nyerere, African nations had threatened to sever relations with Britain by mid-December if stronger measures were not taken against Smith.[120] Ball talked with British officials in early December, hoping to formulate the best way of dealing with the African leaders' threat.[121] To head off an African "stampede that would be hard to reverse," Ball favored a British-mandated oil embargo. Bundy advised Ball to inform President Johnson that the United States was considering following the British lead on an oil embargo, primarily intended to "tamp down African reaction."[122]

Bundy evidently felt that Johnson would not want to be perceived as twisting British arms to enact such an embargo. In reality, Ball had urged his British colleagues to do it, in order to forestall the African "stampede" on 15 December. Ball had decided, furthermore, to request U.S. oil companies to comply with the embargo and also to seek compliance from the other major importers to Southern Rhodesia—the Netherlands, France, and Kuwait.[123] The understanding of the President and the public would be that the United States was following the British lead, but in reality the oil embargo had been instigated by Ball. His subordinates at State then embarked on some detailed legwork to see that the sanctions would be as successful as possible.

On 13 December, Economic Undersecretary Thomas Mann informed American partners in the primary oil refinery supplying

Southern Rhodesia of the plans for an oil embargo. He added that he expected the British government to issue a formal order ceasing oil imports into Southern Rhodesia. The oil executives emphasized the tremendous importance of getting the British to issue such an order, since it would greatly facilitate the process of nullifying their contracts. Mann later notified British officials that American companies' compliance in the oil embargo depended on the issuance of a prohibitory order by Her Majesty's Government. The British diplomats replied that before their government would announce such an order, they wanted a firm U.S. pledge to participate in an airlift of petroleum to Zambia.[124]

Ball had grasped early on that an airlift into Zambia would be necessitated by an oil embargo against Southern Rhodesia. As the oil embargo became increasingly likely, he began investigating the logistics. He talked with Cyrus Vance on 11 December about utilizing military planes. Ball suggested possibly using three U.S. planes in an ancillary role in the British airlift of petroleum into Zambia. Vance suspected that a few planes might be available, but that he must explore the situation further before confirming. Vance and Ball agreed to meet the following day.[125]

As it turned out, the Defense Department could not spare any planes, so Ball decided instead to charter some civilian aircraft. Wherever the planes eventually came from, Ball wanted to give the British an affirmative answer on 13 December. He phoned Bundy, reminding the Security Adviser of the stakes. American diplomats had agreed to join the British in an oil embargo against Smith, expecting him to respond by shutting off the pipelines into Zambia. Zambia had meager oil reserves, so the "mines would have to stop pumping and we would be in trouble with copper." Ball's preferred action was to contribute a few U.S. planes and crews to an oil airlift into Zambia for a few months, after which trucks and trains could take over.

Ball estimated the cost to be about half a million dollars, and added that it would not exacerbate the balance of trade problem since the money would go to American airlines and pilots. Furthermore, he intended for U.S. participation in the operation to be public knowledge, so the Johnson Administration could "got some kudos out of the Africans." Since it would be announced publicly, Ball hoped Bundy could get the President's personal approval. This should be done as soon as possible, because the British wanted an answer that night. After posing a few questions about the details of the airlift, Bundy sought the President's approval. About five minutes later he returned to the phone and informed Ball that Johnson "said o.k., go ahead."[126]

Obviously, Ball believed Johnson's decision would be popular among black African leaders. Participation in the oil embargo and airlift would also engender support from African-American spokesmen. Martin Luther King had recently advocated a full international boycott of Southern Rhodesia.[127] On 13 December, Roy Wilkins and the executive committee of the NAACP urged members of Congress to enact an oil embargo against Southern Rhodesia.[128]

Whitney Young, head of the Urban League, discussed the domestic implications of Johnson's Southern Rhodesia policy at great length with Ball. Young differentiated between Southern Rhodesia and Vietnam, emphasizing that the former was "purely a racial matter." In order to earn support from black Americans, Johnson should support the British efforts in full and expand the embargo to include oil. Ball stressed his recent efforts to implement an oil embargo, then outlined the very convoluted nature of the circumstances and importance of access to Zambian copper. Young recognized the complexity of the problem, but maintained that it would be more difficult to keep his fellow African-American leaders in line on Southern Rhodesia than it had been regarding Vietnam.[129]

On 16 December Martin Luther King again spoke out on Southern Rhodesia. He advocated "the strengthening of economic sanctions especially an embargo on oil shipments to Rhodesia." King hoped that stronger nonviolent means would bring about a negotiated settlement and thus avoid the outbreak of violence.[130] That same day Congressman Benjamin Rosenthal (D-N.Y.), a member of the Foreign Affairs Committee who had recently visited Africa, also requested that Johnson impose an oil embargo.[131] The demands for a stronger policy influenced Lyndon Johnson, particularly those voiced by African Americans such as Wilkins, Young, and King. According to scholar Anthony Lake, Johnson was "very concerned with his standing with black leaders."[132]

Wilson had arrived in New York on 15 December. He addressed the United Nations general assembly on the morning of 16 December, but before he began his speech nearly all the African delegations walked out in protest of his Southern Rhodesia policy.[133] Maintaining his composure, Wilson delivered a powerful speech reasserting that Southern Rhodesia was a British problem and that they would continue to focus on economic measures to bring about majority rule. He did not mention an oil embargo during the speech, but in a private discussion with Ambassador Goldberg afterwards he manifested his view that oil was the key for placating the Africans. Goldberg felt U.S. companies would comply if Wilson issued an official ban. Wilson hoped the United States would contribute more to an airlift into Zambia than a few Constellation planes, but Goldberg reminded him that Southern Rhodesia was his responsibility and the United States could only play a supporting role.[134]

After his talk with Goldberg, Wilson flew to Andrews Air Force Base. A limo whisked him to the White House, where Johnson greeted him outside with a handshake. Wilson asked about Johnson's health, then told him he looked fine.[135] Strolling inside, the two proceeded to discuss their chief international concerns, particularly Vietnam. Ball joined them for a long treatment of the problems in southern Africa. Wilson's optimistic presentation and vigorous approach to the challenging Southern Rhodesian situation evidently impressed Johnson, who had not previously thought highly of the prime minister.[136] Johnson pledged U.S. participation in an oil embargo and airlift, if Wilson got an order in counsel forbidding oil shipments. Ball concluded that evening that "the ball is in Wilson's court."[137]

The next day Wilson issued an order banning oil deliveries to Southern Rhodesia.[138] On 18 December Ian Smith terminated the flow of oil into Zambia, and on 19 December the first Royal Air Force planes carrying petroleum landed in Lusaka.[139] Day-to-day management of the U.S. part in the drama passed from Ball to Economic Undersecretary Thomas Mann. Mann doubted that the sanctions would drive Smith out, but realized that political factors had necessitated U.S. participation.[140] Mann layed out his doubts about the effectiveness of the oil embargo to the President, who responded by requesting an analysis of alternative courses of action. Meanwhile, the Agency for International Development attained the necessary authorization to finance the U.S. role in the airlift.[141] On 27 December, the State Department announced that the United States would provide planes and pilots for the airlift into Zambia, officially notifying Kaunda the next day.[142]

It would be necessary for the U.S. planes to land in Katanga, since Zambia could not handle such a big plane, and then the oil would be carried into Zambia by railroad. On 4 January 1966 a Pan-American Airlines 707 touched down in Elizabethville, Katanga Province, and unloaded 120 barrels holding 55 gallons of oil. Ten days later a TransWorld Airlines 707 joined the exercise.[143] Each plane completed two runs per day for the duration of the airlift, and together they dropped off about 3,000 tons of petroleum per month for Zambia.[144]

In late January, Kaunda thanked Johnson for "this great contribution to the maintenance of the Zambian economy." He requested that the airlift continue until after the rainy season ended in mid-April, and the Johnson Administration complied.[145] The two Boeing 707s flew fuel into Katanga until 30 April 1966, hauling a total of 68,921 barrels containing 3.6 million U.S. gallons of oil. The transport costs alone for the oil topped $1 per gallon, and the planes used more fuel than they delivered. Since they refueled on the coast, however, their consumption did not take away from their contribution to the Zambian shortage. The British and American airlift, coupled with the heroic efforts of oil-truck drivers negotiating the treacherous road from Tanzania into Zambia, provided enough fuel for Zambia to ride out the storm and to continue producing copper. Completion of a pipeline in 1968 between Dar Es Salaam and the copperbelt ended Zambia's dependence on Southern Rhodesia forever.[146]

CONCLUSIONS

When Smith declared independence on 11 November 1965, the U.S. government reacted first with only symbolic diplomatic measures—denying recognition and recalling the consul general. After hesitating for a day, the Johnson Administration announced limited sanctions against Southern Rhodesia. These measures included prohibition of weapons sales to Southern Rhodesia and suspension of the sugar quota for 1966, and simply mirrored the British policy. Such inititial responses demonstrated that, at the highest level, the Johnson Administration had not been prepared to react immediately to UDI because Johnson, Rusk, Bundy, and McNamara were preoccupied with the war in Vietnam. It also reflected the tendency, carried on from the Eisenhower and Kennedy Administrations, to follow the British lead regarding Southern Rhodesia.

About a week after UDI, however, Johnson approved the rejection of a shipment of Southern Rhodesian sugar due to land in New York in December. This move actually put the United States slightly ahead of the British as far as their policy on Southern Rhodesian sugar. Cancelling the sugar importation illustrated the sensitivity of U.S. officials to criticism from Africans and Asians at the UN, African-American leaders, and the labor movement. At a time when Johnson was beginning to be beseiged by criticism over the Vietnam intervention, his advisers sought to avoid other problems when feasible. If domestic criticism grew loud enough, the Johnson Administration would preempt the British, even on a traditionally British issue like Southern Rhodesia.

With Rusk involved so extensively with Vietnam policy, oversight of Southern Rhodesia policy fell to George Ball. In the days following UDI, it was clear from Ball's conversations that the most critical issue in his mind was the tremendous copper mines of Zambia. Any strong measures against Smith would result in retaliatory measures against neighboring Zambia, which depended on Southern Rhodesia for fuel and transportation. Ball, formerly the Undersecretary for Economic Affairs, generally viewed events through an "economic lens." Had policy been entirely up to him, harsh sanctions against Smith would probably have been avoided. He felt that in the long run the health of the copper industry was in the best interests of all residents of southern Africa. Closing Zambia's copper mines, in addition, could limit supply and raise prices to the point where American jobs could be threatened as well.

Yet, Ball was a brilliant advocate who could see both sides of any issue. As the weeks passed after UDI, it became clear to Ball that the gravest immediate threat was a "stampede" against the British by black African nations. Furthermore, he sensed the growing dissatisfaction with U.S. policy towards Southern Rhodesia among the civil rights leaders—particularly Whitney Young. For these reasons, then, Ball championed U.S. participation in an oil embargo against the Smith regime. American officials, Ball included, were responsive to the attitudes of black leaders in Africa and the United States.

Moreover, once the decision to embargo oil was reached, Ball did his best to see that the embargo succeeded. Most importantly, he attained Johnson's personal approval for U.S. participation in an airlift for Zambia. This was the bargaining chip he needed to get the British to issue an official ban on oil imports, which in turn allowed American companies to void their contracts and participate. Ultimately, South Africa foiled the effectiveness of the oil embargo, but it was not from a lack of effort by George Ball and other U.S. diplomats.

Finally, the Johnson Administration's policy reflected the desires of black African leaders like Kenneth Kaunda and Julius Nyerere. Their threat to "stampede" at the UN, more than anything else, convinced Ball to support the oil embargo and airlift. Furthermore, Kaunda persuaded the Johnson Administration to keep flying through April. In the overall scope of U.S. foreign relations, this was a relatively small operation; yet, it was one of the first times that the U.S. government responded to black Africans with concrete steps against white Africans.[147] In this sense, the American reaction to UDI set the stage for future policies that helped bring majority rule to Zimbabwe in 1980 and to South Africa in 1994.

NOTES

1. G. Mennen Williams Oral History Interview, Lyndon Johnson Library, Austin, TX (hereafter LBJ), 20.

2. William's replacement as chief of the African Bureau, Joseph Palmer, described both the Johnson and the Kennedy Administrations as "very sympathetic and sensitive to African aspirations," which was certainly an exaggeration but was accurate in so far as it paints the Administrations' Africa policies as similar. See Joseph Palmer Oral History Interview, LBJ, 6.

3. Department of State, *The Foreign Assistance Program: Annual Report To The Congress For the Fiscal Year 1964* (Washington: U.S. Government Printing Office, 1965), 104.

4.   Terrence Lyons, "Keeping Africa off the Agenda," in Warren Cohen and Nancy Tucker, eds., *Lyndon Johnson Confronts the World: American Foreign Policy, 1963-1968* (Cambridge: Cambridge University Press, 1994), 245-278.

5.   Piero Gleijeses, "'Flee! The White Giants Are Coming!': The United States, the Mercenaries, and the Congo, 1964-65," *Diplomatic History* 18, #2 (Spring 1994), 207-237.

6.   This investment, mainly loans by the World Bank, represented the second largest U.S. investment in Sub-Saharan Africa during this period, trailing only the U.S. investment in South Africa. Daniel Henry Volman, "United States Foreign Policy and the Decolonization of British Central Africa (Zimbabwe, Zambia, and Malawi), 1945-1965" (UCLA Dissertation, 1991), 102. For discussion of the reasons behind US loans to southern Africa during the 1950s, see William Minter, *King Solomon's Mines Revisited: Western Interests and the Burdened History of Southern Africa* (New York: Basic Books, 1986), 117.

7.   Many scholars contend that access to Northern Rhodesian copper was by far the most important reason that Southern Rhodesian whites wanted the Federation. See Elaine Windrich, *Britain and the Politics of Rhodesian Independence* (New York: Africana Press, 1978), 12.

8.   The last months of the Federation are described in J.R.T. Wood, *The Welensky Papers: A History of the Federation of Rhodesia and Nyasaland* (Durban: Graham Publishing, 1983), 1201-1231.

9.   Prosser Gifford, "Misconceived Dominion: The Creation and Disintegration of Federation in British Central Africa," in Prosser Gifford and Wm. Roger Louis, eds., *The Transfer of Power in Africa: Decolonization 1940-1960* (New Haven: Yale University Press, 1982), 415.

10. Memorandum of Conversation Between Dean Rusk, Duncan Sandys, et.al., 19 December 1963, London, *Foreign Relations of the United States, 1961-1963, XXI Africa* (Washington: U.S. Government Printing Office, 1995), 539-540.

11. Central Intelligence Agency, "Special Report: Breakup of the Federation of Rhodesia and Nyasaland," 27 December 1963, "Rhodesia Memos, 12/63-1/66," Box 97, National Security File (hereafter NSF), Country File (hereafter CO), LBJ.

12. Robert C. Good, *U.D.I.: The International Politics of the Rhodesian Rebellion* (Princeton: Princeton University Press, 1973), 41.

13. The British press coined the term "Cowboy Cabinet" for the first Rhodesian Front ministry because of the large number of farmers

among them, as well as for their agressive approach to independence. Nathan M. Shamuyarira, *Crisis in Rhodesia* (New York:
Transatlantic, 1966), 211-216.

14. Ball to all U.S. embassies in Africa, 15 April 1964, cited in Thomas
J. Noer, *Cold War and Black Liberation: The United States and
White Rule in Africa, 1948-1968* (Columbia: University of Mis-
souri Press, 1985), 190.

15. Joshua Nkomo, *Nkomo: The Story of My Life* (London: Methuen
Press, 1984), 119; Shamuyarira, *Crisis in Rhodesia*, 219-220; for
Ngwenya's description and Nkomo's message, see George Houser,
No One Can Stop the Rain: Glimpses of Africa's Liberation Struggle
(New York: The Pilgrim Press, 1989), 230.

16. For discussion of Mugabe's prison experiences see Richard Worth,
Robert Mugabe of Zimbabwe (New York: Julian Messner, 1990),
28-38.

17. Pearson to State, 20 April 1964, "Rhodesia Cables, 12/63-1/66,"
Box 97, NSF-CO, LBJ.

18. American Negro Leadership Conference on Africa, "Resolutions,"
24-27 September 1964, Folder 9, Box 125, Martin Luther King
Papers, Martin Luther King Library, Atlanta, GA (hereafter MLK),
1, 5.

19. Wilson's 27 October 1964 statement and Rusk's of the following
day quoted in G. Mennen Williams, *Africa for the Africans* (Grand
Rapids: William Eerdmans Publishing Co., 1969), 111-112.

20. Shamuyarira, *Crisis in Rhodesia*, 222.

21. Robert Massie, *Loosing the Bonds: The United States and South
Africa in the Apartheid Years* (New York: Doubleday, 1997), 214-
215. For the debate over whether or not Engelhard should attend,
see several conversations between 26 September and 1 October,
1964, in "Zambia," Box 6, George Ball Papers (hereafter GB), LBJ.

22. Taylor Branch, *Pillar of Fire: America in the King Years, 1963-65*
(New York: Simon and Schuster, 1998), 480-482.

23. Dean Rusk, Memorandum for the President, "Your Meeting with
President Kaunda of Zambia," 28 November 1964, "Zambia Kaunda
Visit," Box 102, NSF-CO, LBJ.

24. Private American investors controlled the Rhodesian Selection Trust,
one of the two principal copper concerns in the Federation. The
Trust moved its headquarters to Lusaka in 1964. See Mira Wilkins,
*The Maturing of Multinational Enterprise: American Business
Abroad from 1914 to 1970* (Cambridge: Harvard University Press,
1974), 370.

25. Rusk, Memo to the President, 28 November 1964.

26. See David J. Garrow, *Bearing the Cross: Martin Luther King, Jr., and the Southern Christian Leadership Conference* (New York: Vintage Books, 1988), 380-381, 405-407, 438.

27. Marilyn Young, *The Vietnam Wars 1945-1990* (New York: HarperCollins, 1991), 139.

28. Robert D. Schulzinger, *American Diplomacy in the Twentieth Century* (New York: Oxford University Press, 1994), 278-79.

29. Jomo Kenyatta to His Excellency Mr. L.B. Johnson, 8 April 1965, "Kenya-Presidential," Box 30, NSF-Special Head of State Correspondence, LBJ.

30. Malcolm's London speech described in Branch, *Pillar of Fire*, 585. Ball's reaction in memo of telephone conversation (hereafter Telcon), George Ball and Henry Tasca, 22 February 1965, "Africa: General 6/17/64-8/9/66," Box 1, GB, LBJ.

31. Memo, "A Rounded Foreign Policy Stance," R.W. Komer to McGeorge Bundy, 7 July 1965, "Komer Memos, Vol. I," Box 6, NSF-Name, LBJ.

32. Population figures in A.J. Wills, *An Introduction to the History of Central Africa: Zambia, Malawi, and Zimbabwe* (New York: Oxford University Press, 1985), Appendix viii. Parliament and income statistics from James Scarritt, "Zimbabwe: Revolutionary Violence Resulting in Reform," in Jack Goldstone, ed., *Revolutions of the Twentieth Century* (Boulder: Westview, 1991), 239.

33. Daniel Kempton, *Soviet Strategy Toward Southern Africa: The National Liberation Movement Connection* (New York: Praeger, 1989), 100.

34. Director of Central Intelligence, "Problems and Prospects in Sub-Saharan Africa," 22 April 1965, "60-70, Africa," Box 8-9, NSF-National Intelligence Estimates, LBJ, 2.

35. Of 1,518,338 tons of chromite imported by the U.S. in 1965, 328,796 tons came from Southern Rhodesia. This was the second leading source after South Africa, followed by the Philippines and the USSR. See Bureau of Mines, *Minerals Yearbook 1965, vol.1* (Washington: U.S. Government Printing Office, 1966), 303.

36. Director of Central Intelligence, "Problems and Prospects in Sub-Saharan Africa," 15.

37. Good, *U.D.I.*, 88-92.

38. Williams Oral History, LBJ, 16.

39. Ball's view that the railroad was "uneconomic" mentioned in G. Mennen Williams, "Memorandum for the Files," 29 June 1965, "Zambia," Box 28, Records of G. Mennen Williams, Country Files, 1961-66, National Archives II, College Park, MD (hereafter NA2).

40. See Williams, "Memorandum for the Files," 29 June 1965; Good, *U.D.I.*, 93-94; Noer, *Cold War and Black Liberation*, 193.
41. Williams, *Africa for the Africans*, 112-113.
42. Memorandum of Conversation between Dean Rusk, Nuhu Bamali, etal., 22 September 1965, "Rhodesia Memos, 12/63-1/66," Box 97, NSF-CO, LBJ.
43. Oral message for Ian Smith, sent by George Ball to the American Consul General in Salisbury, 29 September 1965, "Rhodesia Cables, 12/63-1/66," Box 97, NSF-CO, LBJ.
44. Ball quoted in Noer, *Cold War and Black Liberation*, 194.
45. Austen Morgan, *Harold Wilson* (London: Pluto, 1992), 274.
46. Telcon, Ball and McGeorge Bundy, 5 October 1965, "Britain III 11/24/64-12/31/65," Box 1, GB, LBJ.
47. Noer, *Cold War and Black Liberation*, 194; Anthony Lake, *The "Tar Baby" Option: American Policy Toward Southern Rhodesia* (New York: Columbia University Press, 1976), 79.
48. Kaunda's message to Lyndon Johnson, included in cable from Robert Good, US Ambassador to Zambia, to Rusk, 9 October 1965, "Haynes Memos," Box 3, NSF-Name, LBJ.
49. Telcon, Ball and Hubert Humphrey, 8 October 1965, "Britain III 11/24/64-12/31/65," Box 1, GB, LBJ.
50. Telcon, Ball and Leddy, 9 October 1965; Telcon, Ball and Rusk, 9 October 1965, "Brit III 11/24/64-12/31/65," Box 1, GB, LBJ.
51. Memorandum of Conversation, Rusk and Nogueira, 9 October 1965, "Portugal, Vol.2," Box 203, NSF-CO, LBJ.
52. Noer, *Cold War and Black Liberation*, 194.
53. Telcon, Williams and Ball, 13 October 1965, "Brit III 11/24/64-12/31/65," Box 1, GB, LBJ.
54. G. Mennen Williams Oral History, John F.Kennedy Library, Boston, MA (hereafter JFK), 50, 74. For a thorough discussion of efforts in the 1960s to increase the number of blacks in the Foreign Service, see Michael Krenn, *Black Diplomacy: African Americans and the State Department, 1945-1969* (Armonk: M.E. Sharpe, 1999), 144-151.
55. Williams Oral History, JFK, 80-81. The incident is also discussed in *FRUS, 1961-63*, Volume XXI, Africa, 660-661; Noer, *Cold War and Black Liberation*, 153.
56. Rusk also acted on behalf blacks in the U.S. He delivered a very powerful testimony before the Senate Commerce Committee advocating Kennedy's civil rights bill in 1963. Racial issues touched him personally in 1967 when his daughter married a black man, and he stood by her. See Thomas J. Schoenbaum, *Waging Peace*

and War: Dean Rusk in the Truman, Kennedy, and Johnson Years (New York: Simon and Schuster, 1988), 382-383 and 460-461.

57. On Rusk and Vietnam, see Thomas W. Zeiler, *Dean Rusk: Defending the American Mission Abroad* (Wilmington: Scholarly Resources, 2000), 107-205.

58. Telegram drafted by Ball and approved by Bundy, from Rusk to the U.S. ambassador in London, 22 October 1965, "U.K. Cables, 10/65-1/66," Box 209, NSF-CO, LBJ. Also see "Draft White House Statement on Southern Rhodesia," 21 October 1965, "CO 250 Rhodesia," Box 65, White House Central File - Countries, LBJ.

59. Rick Haynes to McGeorge Bundy, "Situation Report: Rhodesian UDI," 27 October 1965; ibid., 28 October 1965, "Rhodesia-Memos, 12/63-1/66," Box 97, NSF-CO, LBJ.

60. Johnson's message for Smith, in Rusk to Ross McClellan, U.S. Consul General in Salisbury, 29 October 1965, "Rhodesia Cables, 12/63-1/66," Box 97, NSF-CO, LBJ. In his reply Smith thanked Johnson for his concern but said nothing substantive. See Smith to Johnson, 30 October 1965, "Rhodesia - Ian Smith," Box 47, NSF - Special Head of State Correspondence, LBJ.

61. Telcon, Bundy and Ball, 29 October 1965, "Brit III 11/24/64-12/31/65," Box 1, GB, LBJ.

62. Noer, *Cold War and Black Liberation*, 196.

63. Morgan, *Harold Wilson*, 275.

64. Ross McClelland, U.S. Consul General in Salisbury, to State, 11 November 1965, "Rhodesia Cables, 12/63-1/66," Box 97, NSF-CO, LBJ.

65. Good, *U.D.I.*, 59-65.

66. Robin Renwick, *Economic Sanctions* (Cambridge: Harvard University Press, 1981), 2. Renwick headed the Rhodesia Department of the British Foreign Office during the 1979 Lancaster House negotiations.

67. Harry R. Strack, *Sanctions: the Case of Rhodesia* (Syracuse: Syracuse University Press, 1978), 15-16.

68. Renwick, *Economic Sanctions*, 26-27.

69. Verwoerd's 11 November 1965 speech contained in Joseph Satterthwaite, US Ambassador in South Africa, to State, 12 November 1965, "South Africa - Cables, 11/64-9/66," Box 78, NSF-CO, LBJ.

70. Lake, *The "Tar Baby" Option*, 80-81. Williams sent the recall telegram to Consul General McClelland on 11 November, as well as instructions for consulate officials to warn any U.S. nationals in Southern Rhodesia about the increased likelihood of violence. See

Williams memo, 11 November 1965, "Correspondence with Secretary," Box 29, Miscellanous Files, 1961-66, Records of G. Mennen Williams, NA2.

71. On the same day as the six-hour meeting and UDI, 11 November 1965, U.S. combat casualties in Vietnam passed the one thousand mark as the battle of the Ia Drang valley raged. For mention of the thousandth casualty on the same press release as Johnson's initial condemnatioin of UDI, see untitled UPI announcement, 12 November 1965, "CO 250 Rhodesia, Box 65, WHCF-CO, LBJ. For discussion of Ia Drang, see Young, *The Vietnam Wars, 1945-1990*, 161-162.

72. Conversation between Rusk and Johnson summarized in memorandum, Gordon Chase to McGeorge Bundy, 12 November 1965, "Rhodesia - Memos, 12/63-1/66," Box 97, NSF-CO, LBJ.

73. Williams, *Africa for the Africans*, 114-115.

74. Telcon, Ball and Bundy, 12 November 1965, "S. Rhodesia 10/2/65-5/10/66," Box 6, GB, LBJ.

75. Telcon, Ball and Wayne Fredericks, 12 November 1965, "Zambia," Box 6, GB, LBJ.

76. Telcon, Ball and Fowler, 13 November 1965, "Brit III 11/24/64-12/31/65," Box 1, GB, LBJ.

77. Wilkins to Johnson, 12 November 1965, "CO 250 Rhodesia 11/22/63-1/5/66," Box 65, WHCF-CO, LBJ.

78. Telegram, Martin Luther King to the President, 11 November 1965, "CO 250 Rhodesia 11/22/63-1/5/66," Box 65, WHCF-CO, LBJ.

79. Farmer to Johnson, 12 November 1965, ibid.

80. Powell to Johnson, 15 November 1965, ibid.

81. Nancy J. Weiss, *Whitney M. Young, Jr. and the Struggle for Civil Rights* (Princeton: Princeton University Press, 1989), 148.

82. Some State Department officials predicted that America's "increasingly politically-conscious Negro minority" could develop into a vocal pressure group for stronger policies against Smith. See "Note on the Rhodesian Crisis," enclosed with memo to McGeorge Bundy from Jack Valenti, 19 November 1965, "Rhodesia - Memos, 12/63-1/66," Box 97, NSF-CO, LBJ.

83. For administration justifications for this action, see memo from Ball to Johnson and enclosed directive for the Agriculture Department, 18 November 1965, "Rhodesia - Memos, 12/63-1/66," Box 97, NSF-CO, LBJ.

84. Telcon, Ball and Undersecretary of Agriculture Schnittker, 18 November 1965, "Southern Rhodesia 10/2/65-5/10/66," Box 6, GB, LBJ.

85. Telcon, Goldberg and Ball, 18 November 1965, ibid.
86. Memo, Read to Bundy, 18 November 1965, "Rhodesia - Memos, 12/63-1/66," Box 97, NSF-CO, LBJ.
87. Memo, Komer to the President, 19 November 1965, ibid.
88. Williams, *Africa for the Africans*, 115.
89. There was some criticism of the decision. For example, see Bertrand DeBlanc, District Attorney for Lafayette, LA., to Senator Allen Ellender, 24 November 1965, "CO 250 Rhodesia, 11/22/63-1/5/66," Box 65, WHCF-CO, LBJ. DeBlanc did not think the Johnson Administration had any right to reject the 9,500 tons of sugar for 1965, which was the quota authorized by Congress.
90. Telcon, Bundy and Ball, 13 November 1965, "Brit III 11/24/64-12/31/65," Box 1, GB, LBJ.
91. Memo dictated by Mr. Johnston, assistant to Undersecretary of State for Economic Affairs Thomas Mann, 13 November 1965, "BE4/Copper," Box 10, WHCF-Ex BE4, LBJ.
92. Telcon, Bundy and Ball, 13 November 1965, "Brit III 11/24/64-12/31/65," Box 1, GB, LBJ.
93. Telcon, Ball and Assistant Secretary of Defense Cyrus Vance, 13 November 1965, "Zambia," Box 6, GB, LBJ.
94. Telcon, Ball and McNamara, 13 November 1965, ibid.
95. "The Copper Price Increase," Memo for the President from Gardner Ackley, Chairman of the Council of Economic Advisers, 8 November 1965, "BE4/Copper," Box 10, WHCF-EX BE4, LBJ; Roman Pucinski, Congressman (IL), to the President, 18 November 1965, "BE4/Copper," Box 16, WHCF-Gen BE4, LBJ.
96. Memo dictated by Johnston, assistant to Mann, 13 November 1965.
97. Telcon, Ball and Vance, 13 November 1965.
98. "The Copper Price Incease," Memo for the President from Ackley, 8 November 1965.
99. Telcon, Ball and Vance, 13 November 1965.
100. Memo dictated by Johnston, assistant to Mann, 13 November 1965.
101. Telcon, Ball and Assistant to the President Joseph Califano, 15 November 1965; Telcon, Ball and Bundy, 15 November 1965, "Zambia," Box 6, GB, LBJ.
102. Memo, to Jack Valenti from his office, 20 November 1965, "BE4/Copper," Box 10, WHCF-EX BE4, LBJ; President's Administrative Assistant Henry Wilson to Congressman Roman Pucinski, 19 November 1965, "BE4/Copper," Box 16, WHCF-Gen BE4, LBJ.
103. Williams to Ball, 18 November 1965, "Rhodesia," Box 28, Records of GMW, Country Files 1961-66, NA2.

104. Ball's decision to bring in an outsider to concentrate on Southern Rhodesia and Zambia is discussed in Lake, *"Tar Baby" Option*, 82. Lake mistakenly named Thomas Finletter as Ball's choice, and went on to explain that after Ball told Wilson about Finletter, President Johnson shot down the choice. In fact, Ball's choice whom Johnson rejected was Roswell Gilpatric. Lake's error probably reflected a simple lapse of memory on the part of one of his interviewees, as he cites no documentary evidence.

105. Telcon, Ball and U. Alexis Johnson, 18 November 1965, "Southern Rhodesia 10/2/65-5/10/66," Box 6, GB, LBJ.

106. For a brief description of Gilpatric's technocratic approach and his participation in July 1965 discussions with President Johnson about Vietnam, see Brian Van DeMark, *Into the Quagmire: Lyndon Johnson and the Escalation of the Vietnam War* (New York: Oxford University Press, 1991), 174-5; Johnson's asking Gilpatric for advice on Vietnam in July 1965 is also detailed in George Mct. Kahin, *Intervention: How America Became Involved in Vietnam* (New York: Doubleday, 1986), 360.

107. Telcon, Ball and McNamara, 19 November 1965; Telcon, Ball and Bundy, 19 November 1965, "Southern Rhodesia 10/2/65-5/10/66," Box 6, GB, LBJ.

108. Telcon, Ball and Gilpatric, 20 November 1965, ibid.

109. Telcon, Ball and Bundy, 29 November 1965, "Southern Rhodesia 10/2/65-5/10/66," Box 6, GB, LBJ.

110. Telcon, Moyers and Ball, 29 November 1965, "Southern Rhodesia 10/2/65-5/10/66," Box 6, GB, LBJ.

111. Telcon, Bundy and Ball, 29 November 1965, ibid. Gilpatric claims he had an affair with Jackie Kennedy while she was first lady, but there is no evidence that Johnson knew or cared. See Christopher Andersen, *Jack and Jackie: Portrait of an American Marriage* (New York: William Morrow, 1996), 339-350.

112. Telcon, Bundy and Ball, 29 November 1965, "Southern Rhodesia 10/2/65-5/10/66," Box 6, GB, LBJ.

113. Telcon, Ball and U. ALexis Johnson, 30 November 1965, ibid. Johnson and Ball felt maybe Dan Mayers could help tighten up the report, and that he should talk with Steve Low, who had attended all of the meetings of the working group.

114. Telcon, Ball and U. Alexis Johnson, 30 November 1965, ibid. Dan Mayers was working on the outline that Ball wanted and would be meeting with Steve Low to go over the details.

115. Telcon, Ball and William Rogers, 1 December 1965, "Southern Rhodesia 10/2/65-5/10/66," Box 6, GB, LBJ; Telcon, Ball and Bundy,

1 December 1965, ibid.

116. Lake, *"Tar Baby" Option*, 82.

117. G. Mennen Williams, Oral History, JFK, 56-57.

118. Telegram, Rusk to U.S. embassy in London, drafted by Rogers and others, 4 December 1965, "United Kingdom Cables, 10/65-1/66," Box 209, NSF-CO, LBJ.

119. State Department report, "Outline of Rhodesian Porblem," 1 December 1965, "Rhodesia Memos, 12/63-1/66," Box 97, NSF-CO, LBJ.

120. For a discussion of Nyerere's leadership of the Organization of African Unity's efforts to get Great Britain to act more forcefully against Smith see Directorate of Intelligence, "African Response to the Rhodesian Rebellion," 3 January 1966, "Rhodesia (Codeword)," Box 97, NSF-CO, LBJ.

121. White House aid Ric Haynes saw things more optimistically and argued that many African leaders sought a "face-saving" escape from such a drastic move, however. Haynes to Bundy, "Situation Report: Rhodesian Crisis," 8 December 1965, "Rhodesia Memos, 12/63-1/66," Box 97, NSF-CO, LBJ.

122. Telcon, Ball and Bundy, 9 December 1965, "Southern Rhodesia, 10/2/65-5/10/66," Box 6, GB, LBJ.

123. Rusk to U.S. embassy in London, drafted by Rogers and Mayers, 9 December 1965, "United Kingdom Cables 10/65-1/66," Box 209, NSF-CO, LBJ.

124. Ball to U.S. Embassy London, drafted by Rogers and others, 13 December 1965, "United Kingdom Cables 10/65-1/66," Box 209, NSF-CO, LBJ.

125. Telcon, Vance and Ball, 11 December 1965, "Southern Rhodesia 10/2/65-5/10/66," Box 6, GB, LBJ.

126. Telcon, Ball and Bundy, 13 November 1965, ibid. Ball and Bundy began talking at 7 P.M., and Bundy informed Ball of the President's approval for the airlift at 7:10 P.M.

127. Martin Luther King, speech at the South African benefit of the American Committee on Africa, Hunter College, New York City, 10 December 1965, speech copied and sent to the author by the Martin Luther King Library, Atlanta, GA.

128. "Resolution Urging Embargo On Rhodesia," adopted by NAACP Executive Committee, 13 December 1965, "Rhodesia," Box 194, Charles Diggs Papers, Howard University, Washington, DC.

129. Telcon, Ball and Whitney Young, 15 December 1965, "Southern Rhodesia 10/2/65-5/10/66," Box 6, GB, LBJ. Young also called Arthur Goldberg, who informed Ball that "good people like Young

and Roy Wilkins were feeling the heat." See Telcon, Ball and Goldberg, 16 December 1965, ibid.

130. Martin Luther King to the President, 16 December 1965, "CO250 Rhodesia 11/22/63-1/5/66," Box 65, WHCF-CO, LBJ.

131. Benjamin Rosenthal to Johnson, 16 December 1965, ibid.

132. Lake, *"Tar Baby" Option*, 89. Lake cited "a number" of unnamed individuals who "knew Johnson well."

133. Evidently some of the French African representatives remained. See Ric Haynes to Bundy, "Situation Report: Rhodesian Crisis," 16 December 1965, "Rhodesia - Memos, 12/63-1/66," Box 97, NSF-CO, LBJ; Morgan, *Harold Wilson*, 276.

134. Telcon, Goldberg and Ball, 16 December 1965, "Southern Rhodesia 10/2/65-5/10/66," Box 6, GB, LBJ; Wilson's speech is also summarized in memo, "Visit of Prime Minister Wilson: Southern Rhodesia," 16 December 1965, "United Kingdom Memos, 10/65-1/66," Box 209, NSF-CO, LBJ.

135. Lake, *"Tar Baby" Option*, 89-90.

136. Good, *U.D.I.*, 106, 115. Wilson's optimism that sanctions would work did not convince many U.S. diplomats, who doubted that South Africa would respect them. While he names no one specifically, Good mentions that several high U.S. officials scoffed at Wilson's high hopes for sanctions.

137. Telcon, Ball and Joseph Sisco, Assistant Secretary for International Organization Affairs, 16 December 1965, "Britain III 11/24/64-12/31/65," Box 1, GB, LBJ.

138. Renwick, *Economic Sanctions*, 27.

139. Good, *U.D.I.*, 108. On 2 January 1966, Smith offered to reopen the flow of oil into Zambia, but Kaunda rejected the ploy as an attempt to divert world attention from the central issue - racial justice. See U.S. Consulate Salisbury to State, 2 January 1966, "Rhodesian Cables, 12/63-1/66," Box 97, NSF-CO, LBJ; Haynes to Bundy, "Situation Report: The Rhodesian Crisis," 6 January 1966, "Rhodesia - Memos, 12/63-1/66," ibid.

140. Telcon, Ball and Mann, 20 December 1965, "Southern Rhodesia 10/2/65-5/10/66," Box 6, GB, LBJ. Ball was going to Florida on vacation. He informed Mann that Rogers had returned to his law firm, but that Dan Mayers had worked closely with Rogers and that he could probably answer any questions that Mann might have.

141. Thomas Mann, "Memorandum for the President on the Rhodesian Crisis," 22 December 1965, "CO 250 Rhodesia-Nyasaland," Box 11, WHCF-Confidential, LBJ; McGeorge Bundy, "Memorandum for the Secretary of State, Subject: The Rhodesia Crisis," no date

but apparently around 23 December 1965, "Rhodesia - Memos, 12/ 63-1/66," Box 97, NSF-CO, LBJ; Memorandum for McGeorge Bundy from David Bell, AID Administrator, 23 December 1965, ibid.

142. Noer, *Cold War and Black Liberation*, 205. Kaunda wrote letters to Johnson on 15 and 18 December requesting U.S. participation in an airlift. On 28 December Johnson approved a reply to Kaunda that explained U.S. policy. See the letters and a memo from Ulric Haynes to Johnson in "Zambia - Kaunda Correspondence," Box 61, NSF - Special Head of State Correspondence, LBJ.

143. Thomas McElhiney to Mann, "Rhodesia/Zambia Situation Reports," 4, 5 and 13 January 1966, "Rhodesia - Memos, 12/63-1/66," Box 97, NSF-CO, LBJ.

144. President Johnson to Julius Nyerere, letter sent by cable from State to U.S. Embassy in Dar Es Salaam, 28 January 1966, "Tanzania - Nyerere Correspondence," Box 45, NSF - Special Head of State Correspondence, LBJ.

145. Kaunda to Johnson, 26 January 1966, and Johnson to Kaunda, 10 February 1966, "Zambia - Kaunda Correspondence," Box 61, NSF - Special Head of State Correspondence, LBJ.

146. Good, *U.D.I.*, 110. During the operation, over 100 truckdrivers died on the Great North Road from Tanzania to Zambia, and they referred to the route as the "Hell Run."

147. Major studies regarding race and U.S. foreign policy have missed the significance of the airlift. For example, see Michael Hunt, *Ideology and U.S. Foreign Policy* (New Haven: Yale University Press, 1987), or Paul Gordon Lauren, *Power and Prejudice: The Politics and Diplomacy of Racial Discrimination*, 2nd Ed. (Boulder: Westview Press, 1996).

5

NIXON'S INDIFFERENCE
AND BYRD'S SKILL:
RUSTING THE STAINLESS U.S. POLICY
TOWARDS SOUTHERN RHODESIA,
1966-1972

From 1965 to 1968, the Lyndon B. Johnson Administration carried out an active policy towards Southern Rhodesia, hoping to encourage a nonviolent settlement and transition to majority rule. The U.S. government participated in the sanctions against Southern Rhodesia, staying supportive as sanctions gradually got tougher. Administration officials battled with critics of the sanctions, and Johnson sent his Vice President Hubert Humphrey to Africa to emphasize American support for a just solution in Southern Rhodesia. Johnson's policy did not succeed in ousting Ian Smith or bringing majority rule, but it gained respect from blacks in Africa and the United States and certainly did nothing to harm the chances for a negotiated settlement.

The Richard M. Nixon Administration's policy towards Southern Rhodesia, however, would be a different story. Whereas Johnson and other high officials in his administration had displayed some dynamism on Southern Rhodesia, Nixon and his top aides manifested nothing but inertia and apathy. The incredible ignorance regarding Southern Rhodesia demonstrated by Vice President Spiro Agnew contrasted sharply with his predecessor's African diplomacy. Nixon and National Security Adviser Henry Kissinger never pressed for concrete action on the key issues such as chrome imports or the U.S. consulate's closing, content instead to postpone decisions. While the Nixon Administration's failure to act cannot be attributed to racism or corporate influence, their indifference opened the door for Congress to overturn the Johnson Administration's sanctions. An amendment to the 1971 Military Procurement Act, crafted by Virginia Senator Harry F. Byrd, Jr., eradicated the ban on chrome imports. The Byrd Amendment thoroughly undermined U.S. support for a nonviolent solution and exemplified the impact of Nixon's apathy on Africa and obsession with Vietnam.

VOLUNTARY CHROME SANCTIONS

The Johnson Administration initially reacted to Ian Smith's unilateral declaration of independence (UDI) in November 1965 by banning imports of sugar from Southern Rhodesia. The ban symbolized U.S. intentions to oppose Smith's action, but involved very small economic stakes. A truly substantive sanctions program had to include the most valuable export from Southern Rhodesia to the United States, i.e., chrome ore. Of the approximately $10.4 million worth of American imports from Southern Rhodesia in 1964, chrome ore represented $4.6 million.[1] Southern Rhodesian mines supplied the world's best metallurgical grade chrome ore, a crucial element in the production of stainless steel.[2] American industries used it to make steam turbine blades, nuclear reactors, rockets, nuclear submarines, and mufflers and trim on automobiles, among other things.[3]

In mid-December, State Department officials talked with the major U.S. importers of chrome ore about their willingness to comply with a voluntary embargo.[4] On 20 January 1966 the British government forbade anyone from importing chrome ore from Southern Rhodesia. This order most seriously affected U.S. corporations like Union Carbide, which purchased about half of the chrome ore produced in Southern Rhodesia annually. In the following weeks, several large shipments of Southern Rhodesian chrome ore arrived in the United States. These were allowed to be delivered, since they had been contracted before the order.[5] After these shipments had been unloaded U.S. companies respected the British order, and "at a considerable cost to themselves" ceased importing chrome ore from Southern Rhodesia.[6] Anthony Solomon, Assistant Secretary for Economic Affairs in 1966, later judged that U.S. corporations "all cooperated" with this first wave of voluntary sanctions.[7] Undoubtedly this was because these firms were told that the sanctions would not last very long.

The first three months after UDI offered very little public criticism of the Johnson Administration's policy, while liberals and African Americans expressed general satisfaction with the oil embargo and boycotts of sugar and chrome ore. Government officials perceived the potential for criticism from the start, however, particularly in relation to Vietnam. Thomas Mann, Undersecretary for Economic Affairs, explained to British diplomats in December 1965 that: "as we become more involved in the Rhodesian crisis and as casualties mount in Vietnam, we can only expect increased pressure from the American public and from Congress regarding British commercial assistance to... North Vietnam."[8]

Sanctions against Southern Rhodesia were prime targets for public criticism for a number of reasons. As Mann pointed out, British merchant vessels traded with Hanoi, and as of 1966 the U.S. public generally supported the war effort in Vietnam. So, people wondered why the United States should support British efforts against Southern Rhodesia, when the British traded with the country's enemy. Furthermore, sanctions on Southern Rhodesian chrome ore necessitated purchase of expensive chrome ore from the USSR, our Cold War adversary. With detente still several years away, the U.S. public understandably opposed anything that succored the Soviets. Ian Smith, furthermore, represented a constituency with many attractive characteristics for the majority of the American public. He and his followers were Christian, anti-communist, white, and in rebellion against Great Britian (like Americans in 1776).[9]

PUBLIC CRITICISM
The establishment in Washington of the Rhodesian Information Office (RIO) in February of 1966 sparked a gradual increase in American public criticism of the sanctions. Smith's representatives at the RIO printed a propaganda newsletter, "Rhodesian Commentary," for members of Congress and potential supporters around the United States.[10] The RIO's efforts angered liberals such as

African-American newspaper editor Carl Rowan, but it had secured permission to operate in the United States via regular legal channels. The U.S. government could not peremptorily close it down.

The National Security Council staffer in charge of African matters, Ulrich Haynes, explained to Rowan that the RIO's operations did not signify U.S. recognition of Smith's regime in any way, and that China and Cuba ran similar offices in the United States. Haynes concluded that the most salient fact about the RIO was that it had already begun to rally right-wing American support for Smith.[11] Haynes and his NSC colleague Robert Komer agreed that President Johnson would "be reading a lot more on Rhodesia shortly," and advised their boss on the NSC, McGeorge Bundy, to give Johnson some warning.[12] Komer specified that RIO propaganda would fuel right-wing criticism of Johnson's anti-Smith policy.[13]

In fact, criticism of U.S. participation in sanctions against Southern Rhodesia had already started. As Undersecretary Thomas Mann had predicted in December, it revolved around British merchants' trade with communist states. A group of students at the University of New Hampshire wondered why the Johnson Administration joined sanctions against Southern Rhodesia while the British continued trading with Cuba. The State Department responded that the British Government did not permit the trade of any strategic materials with either North Vietnam or Cuba, and that the United States was trying to get them to stop all trade with those nations.[14]

In the months following the opening of Smith's RIO propaganda press, similar criticism of the sanctions came into Washington from all corners of the United States. Letters from constituents to members of Congress demanded that the United States withdraw from the sanctions against Smith until the British stopped trading with Ho Chi Minh.[15] Senator Edmund S. Muskie (D-Me.) responded to one such constituent that he had some reservations about ongoing British commerce with North Vietnam, but felt that the British were restricting such trade, and therefore he supported the sanctions program.[16] On the other hand, Senator James Eastland (D-Miss.) concurred with the public criticism. On 22 March, he chastised Johnson for imposing sanctions without congressional approval.[17]

Some critics of the sanctions believed that Southern Rhodesia was a de facto nation that deserved independence, and therefore the British, Americans, and United Nations should stay out of Southern Rhodesia's internal affairs. For example, the Mississippi Division of the Sons of Confederate Veterans requested that Johnson recognize Southern Rhodesian independence. The Sons could see that Smith espoused similar principles to those for which many Confederate soldiers had fought, i.e., the right to secede and white supremacy.[18] By far the most outspoken opponent of the Johnson Administration's policy, beginning in May 1966, was former Secretary of State Dean Acheson. He launched his campaign against sanctions in a speech at the University of Virginia, and would wage a campaign advocating independence for Southern Rhodesia until his death in 1971.[19]

JOHNSON'S ACTIVE POLICY

Johnson's representative at the UN, Arthur Goldberg, quickly rebutted Acheson's arguments, and the two jousted for the next year.[20] Goldberg's allies in support of the sanctions in the spring of 1966 included a few interested members of Congress led by Donald Fraser (D-Minn.) and Charles Diggs (D-Mich.), and African leaders such as Jomo Kenyatta of Kenya.[21] The new chief of the African Bureau in the State Department, Joseph Palmer, basically followed the precedent set by Williams. Undersecretary George Ball continued to oversee the U.S. policy towards Southern Rhodesia, a policy that stood firmly behind the British efforts.[22]

The British and the Americans tightened the screws on Smith during the first half of 1966, adding chrome to the list of boycotted items and striving to embargo oil. Their success, however, was limited. The most debilitating failure involved South Africa and the oil sanctions. The South African government refused to prevent resale of oil from their country to Southern Rhodesia. In February, 14 trucks full of fuel from South Africa reached Salisbury, and officials at State and in the White House realized that incoming oil would allow Smith to defy the sanctions indefinitely. Furthermore, the longer Smith's rebellion lasted, the louder the black African leaders would shout for armed UN or British intervention.[23]

While South African actions significantly undermined the success of the oil embargo, the advocates of sanctions did enjoy one major success in the spring of 1966. In March two Greek oil tankers sailed towards Beira, Mozambique, with petroleum for the pipeline that stretched from Beira to Southern Rhodesia. British representatives at the UN proposed a resolution that would allow the British navy to use force to prevent the tankers from unloading. With Goldberg's active participation, the UN Security Council passed Resolution 221 (1966), which determined that the situation in SR was a "threat to international peace." Due to Resolution 221, the pipeline from Beira to Southern Rhodesia remained closed until 1979, representing the single greatest success of the sanctions policy. Moreover, the Security Council's ruling that the situation threatened international peace opened the door for future rulings in favor of more severe measures against Smith.[24]

Smith surely could grasp the ramifications of the resolution, and in a television and radio address on 15 April, he decried the successful British maneuver to close the Beira pipleline.[25] Roy Wilkins, executive director of the NAACP, praised the Johnson Administration for bolstering the British effort at Beira. He expressed concern, however, that the British would negotiate an unacceptable compromise with Smith and requested that Johnson implement a tougher policy against Southern Rhodesia. Assistant Secretary Palmer replied that the U.S. government felt the current sanctions program was the best possible option. Palmer added that Smith's decision to send representatives to London illustrated the success of the sanctions, and that the United States would have to trust the British to reach an acceptable solution to what was primarily their concern.[26]

By mid-1966, it was clear that the U.S. government would stick to its policy of supporting British sanctions and negotiations, but would not endorse a military intervention. The British held firm in their negotiations with Smith's representatives, avoiding concessions over political equality for blacks but having no intention of using force anyway. If the situation was to become an armed struggle, the impetus would have to come from within. However, liberation fighters in the Zimbabwe African People's Union (ZAPU) and the Zimababwe African National Union (ZANU) faced innumerable obstacles.

Many ZAPU and ZANU leaders (including Joshua Nkomo, Ndabaningi Sithole, and Robert Mugabe) were in prison. Smith's security forces utilized a fearsome array of modern weapons and equipment, including helicopters; but, despite the grim prospects, a ZANU guerrilla force penetrated deep into Southern Rhodesia in Spring 1966. On 28 April, they battled the Security Forces at Sinoia, and 7 of 21 guerrillas died in the encounter. This battle marked the beginning of the liberation war (Chimurenga).[27] With defeat in a small battle being the highlight, the liberation struggle obviously posed little threat to Smith in 1966.

The Johnson Administration refrained from any contact with the fledgling liberation movement, and the chief U.S. contribution continued to be supporting the British policy of sanctions and negotiations. On 26 May 1966, Johnson provided a big dose of rhetorical support for Smith's opponents by delivering the first presidential address devoted entirely to Africa. Johnson said:

> We are giving every encouragement and support to the efforts of the United Kingdom and the United Nations to restore legitimate government in Rhodesia. Only when this is accomplished can steps be taken to open the full power and responsibility of nationhood to all the people of Rhodesia—not just 6 percent of them.[28]

The goal, according to Johnson, was a "legitimate government" in Southern Rhodesia that would represent the black majority as well as the white minority. Secretary of State Dean Rusk feared, however, that the British were in fact prepared to define that "legitimate government" as one with Smith still in control and without any guarantees regarding a transition to majority rule. Being associated with such a settlement would seriously damage the reputation of the United States among black Africans. Furthermore, leaving Smith and minority rule intact would probably spark a widespread violent struggle by the blacks in Southern Rhodesia, leading to a "breakdown of law and order." If Wilson asked Johnson to support a settlement with Smith, Johnson should "avoid a commitment pending study of the terms of the agreement."[29]

Rusk believed that Johnson should beware of any British settlement that would amount to selling out to Smith. A group of representatives and senators studying African issues during the summer of 1966 concurred. The group, which included Charles Diggs, Donald Fraser, and Edward Kennedy (D-Mass.), met with Johnson in July. They focused primarily on the situation in Southwest Africa (now Namibia) but also felt strongly about Southern Rhodesia. They opined that "a private American overture to the British government should be made to emphasize that it is now all the more important for it to hold firm on Rhodesia."[30]

Concern about the British selling out to Smith, expressed by Rusk and the Congressional group, proved groundless. In late August, Wilson's representatives terminated talks with Smith when he sought emergency police powers from the Southern Rhodesian parliament. The talks did not prove fruitful in any case. The new NSC staffer in charge of Africa, Edward Hamilton, observed that "the British seem to be sticking to their guns rather more resolutely than might have been expected." The next showdown would be at a Commonwealth Conference the following week, which Hamilton predicted would be "stormy."[31]

MORE ACTION: MANDATORY SANCTIONS

Emotions ran high at the conference. Delegates demanded that the British pledge "No Independence Before Majority Rule," which would become commonly known as the NIBMAR requirement. They wanted direct British rule of Southern Rhodesia in order to bring about majority rule. Wilson did not offer to set up a government in Salisbury, but he did announce a serious ultimatum for Smith. If he refused to end his rebellion before the end of the year, Wilson would request the UN to impose mandatory sanctions.[32]

After the conference Kenneth Kaunda, President of Zambia, asked Johnson to "keep the British honest" and prevent "excessive footdragging" by Wilson. Jomo Kenyatta made a similar request, adding that Johnson should be sure that mandatory sanctions included oil. Johnson replied that the United States was definitely prepared to support a UN resolution for mandatory sanctions, but believed that the decision to include oil should be further studied. He reiterated his rhetorical support for an acceptable settlement of the Southern Rhodesian problem, portraying it as "a matter of basic human rights."[33]

Shortly thereafter, Wilson took action worthy of Johnson's lofty rhetoric. He dispelled Kaunda's fears of "footdragging," meeting for one-on-one discussions with Smith on board the HMS Tiger from 2 to 4 December. Evidently the sanctions had taken enough of a toll to force Smith back to the table, but he was not yet ready to concede much. He immediately challenged portions of Wilson's proposal dealing with black political rights. On the evening of 5 December, he rejected Wilson's plan outright, exclaiming to a Salisbury crowd that "the fight goes on!" On the following day Wilson dispatched his Foreign Secretary, George Brown, to the UN to request selective mandatory sanctions. Brown did so on 8 December.[34]

The British initiative to transform the voluntary sanctions into mandatory ones prompted public criticism in the United States, as had earlier maneuvers against Southern Rhodesia. Constituent John East expressed his indignation to his senator, Sam Ervin (D-N.C.), even before the British officially announced their proposal in New York. Ervin promised to do what he could to prevent the imposition of mandatory sanctions.[35] Smith's most famous champion in the United States, Dean Acheson, spoke out against the British effort. In the 11 December issue of the *Washington Post*, he contended that further sanctions were entirely inappropriate for dealing with internal problems of Southern Rhodesia, which he deemed a sovereign state.[36]

The objections of Acheson and others had no impact on the Johnson Administration, and Goldberg seconded the British proposal in New York. On 16 December 1966, the UN Security Council passed resolution 232 (1966). Resolution 232 declared UDI a "threat to international peace and security" and ordered mandatory sanctions. The sanctions prohibited any member state from purchasing Southern Rhodesian products, including sugar, tobacco, and chrome. They also prohibited member states from selling weapons and oil, among other things, to Southern Rhodesia.[37] Senator Harry F. Byrd, Jr. (D-Va.) condemned the resolution on familiar grounds. Byrd suggested that if Johnson signed an executive order banning trade with Southern Rhodesia, he should call for similar sanctions against North Vietnam. He criticized punishing "peaceful" Southern Rhodesia economically, while "agressor" North Vietnam traded extensively with U.S. allies.[38]

Following the UN vote for mandatory sanctions, the Johnson Administration suspended the 1967 quota on Southern Rhodesian sugar, for the third straight year. Rostow explained to Johnson that prohibiting the importation of about 6.5 thousand tons of sugar was "one of the few small measures we can take to show our good faith to the black Africans on the Rhodesian question."[39] Then, on 5 January 1967, Johnson issued an executive order requiring that American citizens and corporations adhere to the mandatory sanctions against Southern Rhodesia.[40] American companies, for the most part, already had been respecting sanctions on the key items like oil, tobacco, and chrome. Johnson's order removed any choice in the matter, but it also drew criticism.

Representative H.R. Gross (R-Iowa) decried U.S. punishment of "friendly" Rhodesia, and requested that Johnson expose the "treacherous" British assistance to North Vietnam.[41] Gross basically parroted Senator Byrd's earlier reaction to the UN vote, but Representative James Utt (R-Cal.) utilized different reasoning when introducing a resolution to nullify the sanctions on 10 January 1967. He argued that sanctions by executive order were unconstitutional and urged Congress to reassert control of foreign affairs.[42] Utt persisted in his efforts to get a joint resolution pulling the United States out of the sanctions program but ultimately failed.[43]

Virginia's Harry Byrd orated further against Johnson's Southern Rhodesian policy on the Senate floor late in January, criticizing Goldberg and advocating sanctions against Hanoi. Byrd would eventually succeed in lifting the sanctions with the 1971 Byrd Amendment, most often discussed in regards to chrome. In early 1967, however, Byrd received the greatest pressure to lift sanctions from American tobacco companies whose holdings in Southern Rhodesia were damaged.[44] In general, though, the Vietnam issue provided the grist for the critics' mill. The emphasis on Vietnam by Byrd, Utt, Gross, and others in Congress had captured the attention of Johnson and his advisers as they convened an NSC meeting on 25 January.

Johnson asked Rusk to give an overview of U.S. policy towards Southern Rhodesia. Rusk predicted increased domestic criticism and the ongoing failure of sanctions to unseat Smith, reiterating that using British or American troops was not an option. The only hope was to get the British to renew negotiations, and then the

United States could "exert our influence behind the scenes." Goldberg emphasized that an active Rhodesian lobby was causing "difficulties with domestic public opinion and with Congress." He attributed U.S. support for sanctions at the UN to concern over the outlook of African Americans and black Africans, but added that the American role was "a moderating one."[45]

Johnson wondered what the British intended to do if Smith, aided by South African circumvention of sanctions, held out indefinitely. He added: "How are we going to work out of this black/white African problem: (a) without drifting into a situation involving the use of force; (b) upholding the UN; (c) maintaining our good relations with the UK; (d) avoiding a showdown with South Africa; and (e) retaining our influence in black Africa?" Rusk responded that if sanctions did not cause Smith to cave in, the only feasible action was to encourage the British to resume negotiations.[46]

Nicholas Katzenbach, who had replaced George Ball as undersecretary late in 1966, led the charge against the critics on Capitol Hill. Katzenbach countered their objections, particularly on the issue of trade with North Vietnam and on the legality of sanctions. He convinced Johnson to explain the sanctions in letters to the leaders of both chambers. Furthermore, he arranged numerous consultations between dissenting politicians and Goldberg. Katzenbach also arbitrated any appeals on what items should or should not be prohibited by the sanctions during the first part of 1967, with episodes of the *I Love Lucy* show among the items in question.[47]

While Katzenbach championed the Administration's position in Washington, Assistant Secretary Palmer joined Goldberg in taking the case to the public. Palmer challenged the critics on several counts. To those who praised the Smith regime for its orderly rule and anticommunism, Palmer argued that minority rule and white supremacy actually guaranteed long-term instability and would open the door to communist influence in southern Africa. Palmer also scolded those who thought the United States should pull out of the UN sanctions program, since it was the duty of the United States to support the international body it had been so instrumental in forming.[48]

While the advocacy of Goldberg, Katzenbach, and Palmer generated relatively little public ardor, leading African Americans did support the Administration's policy. Andrew Young, Martin Luther King's executive assistant, believed a nonviolent solution in Southern Rhodesia was a must, since Smith was well-equipped to quell any violent opposition.[49] King had offered his blessing for the sanctions from the first, and his words were generally given wide coverage throughout Africa.[50] King belonged to the most active group on the Administration's side regarding Southern Rhodesian policy, the American Committee on Africa (ACOA), which lobbied Congress in support of sanctions. The ACOA's chairman, A. Philip Randolph, lauded sanctions as "a genuine effort to solve the problem without violence."[51]

WITHSTANDING PUBLIC CRITICISM

Although support from the likes of Randolph encouraged the administration, public criticism for Johnson's policy far outweighed public backing. Dean Acheson's written and spoken critiques provided most of the tenets for the opposition, but he received written support from several journalists and scholars in 1967.[52] The speeches of Senator Byrd also garnered piles of favorable constituent letters and editorial praise from papers in Charleston, Miami, Nashville, Richmond, and Sturgis (So. Dakota). Most editors and constituents agreed specifically with Byrd's claim that the United States was cooperating in isolating Smith, while the British still dealt with Ho Chi Minh; a point illustrated by a *Chicago Tribune* cartoon.[53] Regardless of whether or not they agreed with this particular point, concerned citizens from Maine to California supported Smith.[54]

In addition, a number of organizations labored against Johnson's policy in 1967, including the Southern States Industrial Council and the American African Affairs Association (AAAA). Both of these groups sent investigatory teams to Southern Rhodesia and subsequently issued reports to members of Congress. They generally seconded the views of Acheson and Byrd, although the AAAA contributed its observation that "primitive" blacks in Southern Rhodesia were not ready for self-government.[55] These groups' endeavors against sanctions manifested the pro-Smith spirit among the American populace.

The best proof of the success of Acheson, Byrd, and the Rhodesian Information Office, however, was the existence of American citizen groups whose sole purpose was to lobby for Ian Smith and Southern Rhodesian independence. Some clubs were local, such as the Pro-Rhodesia Committee of Virginia, but most active Smith supporters belonged to chapters of the Friends of Rhodesia (FOR). A national umbrella organization, FOR comprised 122 branches with over 25,000 members in 1967.[56] Members of FOR provided the vast majority of the mail to Washington demanding an end to sanctions.

Former Chrysler Corporation president L.L. "Tex" Colbert attracted more White House attention to Ian Smith in 1967, however, than any of the Friends of Rhodesia. While on safari, Colbert met personally with Smith. Smith told Colbert that he feared the power of the United States far more than that of Great Britain, and therefore hoped to send a representative to speak privately with Johnson. Smith believed that if Johnson knew the "truth" about Southern Rhodesia, he would not approve of current U.S. policy. According to Smith, Johnson was a "great man," but he did not understand the circumstances. Colbert relayed Smith's views to Walt Rostow, the new National Security Adviser, during a 22 April meeting.[57] The administration, rejecting Smith's suggestion that his representative meet with Johnson, held firm on sanctions and took no further action on Southern Rhodesia for the remainder of 1967.[58]

Most activity took place in Congress, where members on each side of the debate fired off rhetorical volleys. Representative Jonathan Bingham (D-N.Y.), who had befriended Joshua Nkomo in the early 1960s while working at the UN, sponsored a resolution praising sanctions and affirming the principle of "no independence before majority rule." Randolph and the ACOA lobbied in support of Bingham's resolution, but it evidently fizzled out. On the two-year anniversary of UDI, Senator Strom Thurmond (R-S.C.) chastised the Johnson Administration for its Southern Rhodesia policy that necessitated American reliance on Soviet chrome, which he considered a "grand absurdity."[60]

HUMPHREY TO AFRICA

While Johnson took no substantive actions specifically towards Southern Rhodesia in the second half of 1967, he did respond to Congressional criticism that his policy towards Africa was stale. On 22 August Senator Eugene McCarthy (D-Minn.), chair of the Foreign Relations Sub-Committee on Africa, demanded a new comprehensive policy towards Africa that would do more than just react to crises. He advocated an emphasis in foreign aid programs on research and development for the long term.[61] Johnson disliked being portrayed as less interested in Africa than John Kennedy had been. In analyzing McCarthy's speech, NSC staffer Ed Hamilton concluded that "no matter how one cuts the numbers on visits by African heads of government, the totals for the last four years aren't as impressive as those for 1961-63."[62]

To "demonstrate the continuing concern of the United States and the American people with the African continent," Johnson decided to send Vice President Humphrey to Africa. Between 30 December 1967 and 11 January 1968, Humphrey and an entourage that included Justice Thurgood Marshall and Maurice Tempelsman visited nine African countries. Humphrey invited several leaders to visit Washington and offered financial assistance for projects in the Ivory Coast, Ghana, and Somalia. Most significantly for U.S. relations with Southern Rhodesia, he spoke before the Organization of African Unity (OAU) in Ethiopia and met with Kenneth Kaunda in Zambia.[63]

On 5 January Humphrey explained to Kaunda that the United States continued to support Zambia in its struggle to get on its feet. In light of the ongoing hardship caused by UDI, the United States would upgrade a 300-mile stretch of the crucial Great North Road that linked Zambia to Tanzania.[64] The next day at an OAU gathering, Humphrey reviewed the Johnson Administration's Africa policy, with particular attention to UDI. Humphrey said: "We strongly condemned that action, refused to recognize the regime and joined with others in the imposition of voluntary sanctions. When stronger measures were required, we gave full support to the UN policy of mandatory economic sanctions against the illegal regime in Salisbury.... In the long run, such reactionary behavior cannot succeed."[65]

When George Ball and others had initially approved sanctions in December 1965, they had just such occasions in mind, and Humphrey milked U.S. participation in sanctions for all of its propaganda value. As for new concrete actions, Humphrey's visit served to confirm U.S. intention to upgrade a 300-mile section of the Great North Road linking Zambia's copper mines to the sea, at a cost of $1.5 million. Rather than a great gesture, this was really only a feeble attempt to make up for refusing to finance the Tan-Zam railroad, which the Chinese were constructing instead.[66]

Furthermore, upgrading the road fell far short of several other remarkable requests Kaunda recently had made. In September 1967, he asked Johnson if the U.S. could construct a weapons factory in Zambia; moreover, he even asked if the U.S. could supply Zambia with nuclear weapons! Compared to such proposals, road improvements were minor projects indeed.[67] Nonetheless, Humphrey's trip accomplished basically what Johnson intended; demonstrating to black Africans that the United States had not forgotten them.[68]

While the Johnson Administration maintained its moderate opposition to UDI, the white regime in Salisbury held firm. To meet with his Congressional allies and present his case to the American public, Smith wanted to visit the United States. The University of Virginia Law School had invited him to speak in 1967, but State had denied him a visa. In February 1968 Southern Rhodesian officials revived the issue of Smith speaking at the university. They pointed out that even Robert Kennedy believed Smith should get a chance to present his case in person. An American diplomat observed that such a visit raised "obvious difficulties," however, and once again State stymied the proposal.[69]

Meanwhile, ZANU and ZAPU forces battled on with virtually no success. In mid-March, about 100 guerrillas in Zambia tried to cross Kariba Lake into Southern Rhodesia. Smith's security forces nailed them in the process of crossing, killing 11. The remainder fled, but would not get far. The security forces meticulously combed the countryside in helicopters and threw the captives into detention camps. In the White House, newly appointed NSC staffer Roger Morris concluded that since the episode was neither a major guerrilla offensive nor a massacre, it presented "no immediate problem" for Johnson. The small scale of the liberation struggle in Southern Rhodesia was yet another reason that the United States refrained from any substantive initiatives during the last three years of his presidency.[70]

ONE LAST SANCTIONS ADJUSTMENT

Supporting a relatively meaningless British initiative, the Johnson Administration did approve one final tightening of the sanctions. In March the Smith government hanged five prisoners who had been convicted of murder. The Afro-Asian bloc at the UN responded in April by proposing the use of force to dislodge Smith. The British countered with a proposal that would extend the mandatory sanctions from selected products to all products—in other words, comprehensive mandatory sanctions. The Security Council passed the resolution on 29 May. Johnson issued an executive order in July banning American importation of "any commodities or products originating in Southern Rhodesia."[71]

Since selective sanctions already prohibited the importation of important items such as tobacco and chrome, the change to mandatory sanctions made no significant difference. The UN resolution did rekindle the public debate, however. Earlier that spring former Undersecretary George Ball provided more ammunition for Smith's supporters in his book *The Discipline of Power*, where he dismissed the santions as a "romantic delusion."[72] By no means did he express support for Smith, but his disparagment of sanctions was used by the Rhodesian Information Office in their propaganda campaign anyway.[73] Newspaper editorials called for recognition of Southern Rhodesia, stimulating another wave of constituent mail to members of Congress.[74]

Dean Acheson continued to generate public sympathy for Smith. He also supported Smith privately, through Roy Welensky, the former leader of the Rhodesian Federation. Acheson explained to Welensky: "Our attitude toward Rhodesia is unnecessary to appease our blacks and liberals, who have very little choice beyond the Democratic party." Acheson felt Johnson's policy was gaining nothing in domestic politics, and he decried sanctions as immoral and illegal. He concluded that U.S. policy was "totally contrary to our national interest." He believed friendly relations with South Africa and Portugal were much more important than with black African nations.[75]

Acheson provided the Smith regime with some moral support, but his views could have no effect on the Johnson Administration's relations with Southern Rhodesia in mid-1968. American policy was set in stone, and Southern Rhodesia had slipped steadily down the priority list since the first few months after UDI. The Tet Offensive in Vietnam, the assassination of Martin Luther King and ensuing riots, his own decision not to run for re-election, and Robert Kennedy's assassination dominated the President's time in the first half of 1968. Even within the realm of U.S. relations with Great Britain, Southern Rhodesia no longer warranted consideration. When discussing British concerns, Johnson and his advisers focused almost exclusively on monetary policy and to a lesser extent on British withdrawal from Asia and the Mediterranean region.[76]

JOHNSON'S POLICY ASSESSED

During Johnson's last six months in office, his efforts regarding Vietnam and the presidential election did not succeed. His policy towards Southern Rhodesia also failed in its highest objective, which was to oust Smith. In October, on board the HMS Fearless, Wilson and Smith met once again. Smith, buoyed by new chrome discoveries and facing no white political opposition at home, rejected Wilson's offers.[77] Although the Johnson Administration's diplomatic and economic maneuvers did not unseat Smith, they were successful in other ways. The policy of nonrecognition and sanctions had gained respect among black Africans, African Americans, and liberals.[78]

In applying and enforcing sanctions, the United States at times acted more aggressively than Great Britain. Indeed, while the Johnson Administration has generally been perceived as simply seconding the British in regards to Southern Rhodesia, it actually pushed the British into a tougher stand during the months following UDI. Furthermore, by pressing the British to negotiate, enforcing sanctions themselves, and challenging domestic critics of sanctions, the Johnson Administration carried out an active policy in hopes that a nonviolent solution would be reached. The policy fell far short of ending the rebellion, however. Therefore, Lyndon Johnson passed on the problem of Ian Smith's UDI to Richard Nixon and his National Security Adviser Henry Kissinger.

NIXON'S POLICY: INDIFFERENCE

Of course, Nixon and Kissinger also inherited the horrible circumstances in Vietnam as they took office in January 1969. Their efforts to "save face" in Southeast Asia, along with initiatives towards the Soviet Union, China, and the Middle East monopolized White House foreign policy efforts over the next five years. Concentration on these high priority areas in diplomacy, combined with the increasingly time-consuming problems of Watergate, guaranteed that Africa would get very little Oval Office attention during the Nixon presidency. That alone would not have necessarily been so different from Johnson's Southern Rhodesia policy. However, when Congress mounted serious challenges to the most important aspect of U.S. policy—chrome sanctions—Nixon refrained from any action in defense of sanctions. Nixon's indifference on Southern Rhodesia allowed Congress to overturn the Johnson Administration's policy with the 1971 Byrd Amendment.

The tone was set during Nixon's first months in office. During Nixon's initial year in office, some of the few signals that did emanate from the White House regarding Southern Rhodesia cheered Ian Smith's supporters. In March 1969, Dean Acheson sat by a roaring fire in the Oval Office and discussed foreign policy with the President and the national security adviser. After covering Vietnam and NATO issues in depth, Acheson condemned U.S. policy towards Southern Rhodesia over the previous eight years for wrongly punishing an ally because of its internal affairs. To Acheson's great pleasure, Nixon concurred that the internal affairs of southern African nations were no business of the United States or the UN. He promised to give the matter his personal attention.[79]

Nixon carried out his promise by requesting the National Security Council (NSC) to review U.S. policy towards southern Africa, considering "the full range of basic strategies and policy options open to the United States."[80] Shortly after Kissinger initiated the process, Acheson contributed a position paper espousing a complete abandonment of current policy towards Southern Rhodesia. Kissinger averred that the paper would be "cranked into the NSC review of Southern Africa."[81] The review would not be completed until the fall and finally discussed by the NSC in December.

EXCEPTIONS TO SANCTIONS?

In re-evaluating policy towards Southern Rhodesia, the most significant question involved chrome ore. In May, Union Carbide officials asked White House aide Patrick Buchanan to speak with Nixon concerning 150,000 tons of the metal. They had purchased it late in 1966, before Johnson's executive order imposing mandatory sanctions, and hoped Nixon would grant them a hardship exception and allow its importation. Buchanan had been "deeply involved" with questions involving Southern Rhodesian chrome since January and gladly broached the subject with the President.[82]

Although Nixon approved Buchanan's suggestion that Union Carbide be allowed to import the ore, nothing was done. Kissinger opposed the exception for Union Carbide, arguing that it would not solve any long-term problems and would be publicized as a breach of sanctions. He recommended delaying implementation of Nixon's decision until after the NSC reviewed Africa.[83] Buchanan prodded Chief of Staff H.R. Haldeman, who promptly informed Buchanan that any decision must await the NSC meeting.[84] So, although Buchanan successfully advocated Union Carbide's proposal to Nixon, Haldeman and Kissinger stonewalled it until the NSC's Africa session, which finally occured in December.[85]

At approximately the same time as Union Carbide approached Buchanan for help, the company sought similar succor from Senator Gale McGee (D-Wy.), who chaired the Foreign Relations African Sub-Committee.[86] After McGee spoke in May at a Union Carbide meeting, the company's vice president asked McGee about importing the infamous chrome ore purchased before the executive order. McGee replied that while he had some reservations about the wisdom of U.S. policy towards Southern Rhodesia, he could give Union Carbide no "grounds for hope that the situation will change."[87]

Union Carbide's wishes would not be satisfied in the near future, but it did have proof that its ore was purchased before the executive order, and therefore had a reasonable chance of eventual success. Two other companies that requested exceptions in 1969 had no such prospects. The Foote Mineral Company desired 57,000 tons of chrome ore that had been mined from its operations in Southern Rhodesia, but not before the deadline. The third company, Corning Glass, wanted to continue purchasing Southern Rhodesian petalite, a crucial component in ceramic stove tops and space ship parts. Despite the fact that Corning's president was Nixon's personal friend and a member of the transition team, his request was denied.[88]

Petalite never became a public issue, but chrome certainly did. Joining Foote and Union Carbide in seeking chrome imports were American manufacturers of stainless steel, because sanctions forced them to buy more expensive Soviet chrome. A steel industry lobbyist, glossing over the fact that Foote's chrome ore had not been purchased before the 1967 executive order, requested that the Nixon Administration grant exceptions for the entire 207,000 tons of Southern Rhodesian chrome ore owned by American companies. A committee consisting of 16 specialty steel producers made the exact same request, also neglecting to admit that Foote's 57,000 tons did not qualify by any stretch of the imagination.[89] Kissinger notified both groups that the decision on chrome would be made after the ongoing review of southern Africa policy was completed.[90]

The lobbyists convinced several members of Congress that their cause was just, and the congressmen in turn contacted various members of the Nixon Administration regarding renewal of chrome imports. In general the congress was told that the United States could not violate UN sanctions, particularly since it was the world's leading importer of chrome ore and doing so would entirely undermine the effort. Moreover, any hardship exceptions hinged on the NSC review.[91] California Republican state legislator Dick Barnes, who had visited Rhodesia in 1967 and claimed to be an old acquaintance of Nixon, also pushed for an end to chrome sanctions.[92]

A variety of corporations and politicians verbalized their opposition to sanctions and their support for Smith during Nixon's first half year in office. While few American critics of Smith spoke out loudly late in 1969, a small group of congressmen kept up the fight. Chief among them was Representative Charles Diggs (D-Mich.), the first black elected to Congress from Michigan. Since taking office in 1955, Diggs had been involved in civil rights issues, and increasingly active in American relations with Africa. He visited Nigeria early in 1969, the year he also became chair of the Foreign Affairs Subcommittee on Africa.[93]

In September Diggs received some support from *The New York Times*, which chastised Nixon for not developing a policy towards

Southern Rhodesia yet. The thrust of the newspaper piece was that it was time to make some decisions, most importantly regarding the U.S. consulate, which the British wanted closed.[94] Hoping to prod the White House into concluding their policy study, and with the specific goal of getting the consulate closed, Diggs directed hearings on Southern Rhodesia in October and November. His own desire to oust Smith was obvious, and it was strongly seconded by George Houser of the American Committee on Africa (ACOA). Acheson, who remained quite active in his opposition to U.S. policy throughout the year, testified in favor of Southern Rhodesian independence.[95] David Newsom, the new head of the African Bureau, spoke on behalf of the Nixon Administration, and explained that the NSC review of African policy was dealing with the situation.[96]

DELAY PATTERN ESTABLISHED

By the fall of 1969, a basic pattern was clear. A few members of the Nixon Administration applauded the Smith regime, most notably Patrick Buchanan. The vast majority, however, including Nixon and Kissinger, viewed Southern Rhodesia as an extremely low priority. While Nixon had acquiesced to Buchanan in May, i.e., approving the exception for Union Carbide, the President did not press for the exception to actually take effect in the following months. Kissinger opposed Buchanan's proposal, but did not feel strongly enough to eliminate it permanently. High officials in the Nixon Administration seemed quite content to stall on any decisions regarding Southern Rhodesia, and did so for almost a full year after inauguration.

Finally, on 17 December 1969, the NSC discussed the review of U.S. policy towards southern Africa that Kissinger had instigated in April. Supposedly, this meeting would answer the questions posed by supporters and opponents of current U.S. policy, including exceptions on chrome and whether or not to close the consulate. Instead, it demonstrated beyond a shadow of a doubt that the majority of high-level officials on the Nixon foreign policy team were indifferent or ignorant about events in Southern Rhodesia. Roger Morris, the NSC staffer in charge of Africa, had labored for eight months preparing the study under consideration. He described the December session as boring, filled with errors, free from any mention of national security or communism, and marked most strongly by the loathing many of the men felt for each other. Kissinger, he recalled, remained mostly silent and neutral.

As for discussion specifically about Southern Rhodesia, the first issue to arise was the status of the U.S. consulate in Salisbury. Secretary of State William Rogers favored closing it, while CIA Director Richard Helms wanted it to remain open because it was a useful source of intelligence regarding South Africa. No final decision was reached. Near the end of the meeting, Vice President Spiro "Ted" Agnew advocated importation of chrome. He rambled on, comparing slavery in the early United States to race relations in Southern Rhodesia. He erroneously compared "South Africa's (sic) 1965 UDI" to the Declaration of Independence. Nixon corrected Agnew: "You mean Rhodesia, don't you Ted?" Embarrassed, Agnew said no more on chrome, and the NSC failed to decide on the exceptions.[97]

The general point of the meeting was to weigh the options proposed in the NSC review of southern Africa policy, and Kissinger decided to choose option 2. This option advocated a lower profile at the UN, less pressure on Portugal, less criticism of South Africa, and a $5 million increase in aid to black African nations. Regarding chrome, it laid out the pros and cons of allowing exceptions for Union Carbide and Foote, but reached no conclusion. Kissinger questioned the efficacy of the Africa policy inherited from Johnson, and viewed option 2 as a more effective way to guard U.S. interests.[98] While the choice has been nick-named the "Tar Baby" option and criticized as racist, in fact it instigated virtually no change in U.S. relations with Southern Rhodesia.[99] In the short term, Kissinger's selection of option 2 resolved none of the key disputes. The decisions on the consulate and the chrome exceptions were simply prorogued pending further study.

In an effort to enlighten the American people on his overall foreign policy strategy, on February 18, Nixon sent a comprehensive report to Congress. While most of the report dealt with Europe, the Soviet Union, China, and Vietnam, it did include a section on Africa. The Nixon Administration praised the great progress of freedom that had taken place in Africa in the 1960s, but regretted the strife in the Congo and Nigeria and "the establishment of white minority rule in Southern Rhodesia." Under Nixon, there was "no question of the United States condoning, or acquiescing in, the racial policies of the white-ruled regimes." The primary goals of U.S. policy towards Africa were to encourage peaceful reforms and increase economic development.[100]

THE CONSULATE DECISION

One way the Nixon Administration could demonstrate that it did not condone the racial policies of the white regimes in southern Africa would be to close the consulate in Salisbury. The British had closed theirs in July 1969, requesting that the United States follow suit. Acheson and his allies, not surprisingly, countered that closing the consulate would be disastrous.[101] The New York Times, Diggs, and numerous others disagreed.[102] By February 1970, moreover, Secretary Rogers ranked among those espousing closure. Rogers returned from a tour of Africa at the end of the month and pressed Nixon to shut down the consulate.[103]

On 2 March, Ian Smith formally declared Southern Rhodesia a republic, no longer subject to the Queen of England. The American Committee on Africa subsequently led a renewed push to get the Nixon Administration to close the consulate. They urged Diggs to issue a statement calling for such action, and he complied on 6 March. The letter to Nixon advocating the consulate's removal was signed by 32 members of Congress, including black representatives Louis Stokes (D-Ohio) and Shirley Chisholm (D-N.Y.). Johnson had always been responsive to the concerns of moderate civil rights leaders, for both moral and political reasons. Nixon never displayed similar inclinations while president.[104]

That the letter from Congress had any influence on Nixon seems unlikely, then, but simultaneous action by British Foreign Secretary Michael Stewart evidently turned the trick. Stewart met with the American ambassador in London on 5 March, informing him that if the United States did not withdraw its consulate, the British would formally revoke the exequatur - legal permission for the consulate's existence. Given this ultimatum, Nixon finally conceded on an issue that he had put off for nearly a year. On 9 March 1970, Rogers announced that the consulate in Salisbury would shut its doors the following week.

The decision did not receive much attention in the American press, but drew headlines in England. In Salisbury, the press and public reacted angrily, but Smith denied that it would have any impact. In fact, the decision removed any hope by the rebel regime for international recognition of its republic.[105] Supporters of Smith in the United States condemned the closing, with Senator Eastland describing it as "absolutely preposterous." He added: "Once again we are dancing to the tune of Whitehall's Pied Piper in a game of follow-the-leader diplomacy."[106] Senator Thurmond and Representative Gross, other staunch allies of Smith, echoed Eastland's response.[107]

Many nongovernmental organizations continued to support Smith, often with not-so-subtly racist reasoning. The Southern States Industrial Council characterized the closing as irrational and decried punishing one of the few "civilized" nations in Africa because of pressure from black African "savages."[108] Kenneth Kaunda, who was probably a lot more "civilized" than anyone on the Southern States Industrial Council (SSIC), applauded the closing.

Julius Nyerere, another African leader who was as erudite and dignified as any SSIC member or official in the Smith's regime, requested that Nixon pay more heed to southern African problems. While the closing had symbolic importance, Nyerere knew full well that it would not be sufficient to bring down the Smith regime. In replying to Kaunda and Nyerere, Nixon reiterated U.S. support for peaceful transition to majority rule, pointing to his recent message to Congress and to ongoing U.S. participation in the sanctions.[109]

With the consulate decision made, sanctions returned to the center of the debate. In April, with support from Thurmond, Eastland introduced a resolution to end the "economically and militarily disastrous policy of economic sanctions against Rhodesia."[110] Fifty-two members of Congress petitioned the new British Prime Minister, Edward Heath, to terminate British sanctions against Southern Rhodesia.[111] These efforts in the Senate and in the House to end sanctions in the summer of 1970 came to naught, but by the fall it seemed that the climate was more propitious for a more aggressive challenge.

EXCEPTION REQUESTS DECIDED

In August the Nixon Administration at long last decided on the status of the exception requests that Foote and Union Carbide advanced. The most significant case was Carbide's 150,000 tons of chrome, and they received a positive answer. This immediately attracted criticism from Diggs et al., and has since been cited as proof that the Nixon Administration favored business over morality, and that Nixon forcefully enacted the "tar baby" policy. This explanation, nevertheless, is far too simplistic. An examination of the debate behind the Carbide decision, the August 1970 rejection of Foote's application, and the earlier rejection of Corning's request reveals a much more complex picture.

Corning Glass Works, of Corning, New York, presented a compelling case for importing Southern Rhodesian petalite. Corning utilized petalite, a rare lithium-bearing mineral, in the production of numerous items: laboratory bench tops, ceramic tops for electric stoves, spacecraft antenna windows, and gas turbine heat exchangers. About 4,000 employees in 12 American plants manufactured these specialty products, and they were in jeopardy of losing their jobs if Corning's access to petalite remained blocked. Corning chemists experimented in hopes of discovering substitutes for petalite, but as of 1969 had had no luck.

Corning's dependence on Southern Rhodesian petalite dated back to the early 1950s, when a tremendous deposit was discovered there. Corning had hoped to avoid reliance on a source over 6,000 miles away, but global search for comparable deposits of petalite had proven unsuccessful. In 1958, the firm signed a ten-year contract with the Southern Rhodesian petalite mine and had been in the process of extending the contract for five years when comprehensive mandatory sanctions were imposed in 1968. Corning stockpiled some petalite before the sanctions, but by 1969 the supply was dwindling rapidly so it requested that the Nixon Administration grant an exception.[112]

Corning needed petalite for its production of a number of important technical products, including some involved in the space program. Four thousand American jobs hinged on this aspect of operations. Furthermore, Corning Chairman Robert Murphy was a personal friend of the President. Murphy directed the foreign policy transition after Nixon's election, and Kissinger informed him in late 1969 that he "had a lot of credit" in the White House. Evidently, however, he did not have enough credit to get the petalite. Despite Murphy's link to Nixon and the powerful case for an exception, Corning's request was denied, without becoming part of the NSC review of southern Africa policy.[113]

The requests by Foote and Carbide to import Southern Rhodesian chrome ore, however, received considerable attention during the course of the NSC review and beyond. The final report differentiated between the two cases, specifying that Foote's 57,000 tons of chrome ore in SR did not meet any of the criterion for an exception.[114] Nevertheless, Foote could present a convincing argument. Foote's president, H.G. "Tony" Bliss, did not have Corning's direct ties to the Oval Office, but he was certainly a well-connected and respected businessman. Earning a BA and MA from Rutgers, he had taught chemistry there for a few years before joining Foote in 1933. Subsequently, he facilitated the development of several important advances in military technology, including the first nuclear submarines, and life-support equipment for astronauts. If Nixon was looking for patriotic American capitalists to support, he could find no better specimen than Tony Bliss.

Bliss pleaded Foote's case for importation of chrome before the House Subcommittee on Africa in October 1969. He emphasized the unique qualities of Southern Rhodesian ore and its holdings of about three-fourths of all the chrome ore outside of the Soviet Union. Banning imports of Southern Rhodesian chrome necessitated the purchase of expensive Soviet chrome, sparking inflation. It had also led to release of some of the chrome stockpile, which, in Bliss's view, jeopardized the national security. Bliss held that these sanctions were a bad idea in general. Moreover, sanctions punished Foote in particular, since they had lost control of their mines in Southern Rhodesia and paid about $1 million for 57,000 tons of ore that they could not retrieve.[115]

In July 1970, Bliss met with several officials from the Office of Economic Planning, reiterating the reasons why Foote should be allowed to import their 57,000 tons. A week later he appealed to Nixon, complaining that Foote had been "stripped of our assets by our own government, without any recourse or redress."[116] The NSC discussed the issue on 7 August, and Nixon decided to deny Foote's request for an exception.[117] Margaret Schwartz, a Treasury Department official, informed Bliss that "after reconsideration your application to import 57,000 tons of chrome ore of Rhodesian origin... is denied." Schwartz added, however, that Foote could go ahead and sell its assets in Southern Rhodesia.[118]

So Robert Murphy and Tony Bliss, leaders of two important American corporations, failed in their bids to attain exceptions from the Nixon Administration regarding imports from Southern Rhodesia. Murphy had connections in the White House, and he and Bliss both argued impressively how exceptions for their companies would benefit the U.S. economy. Yet, neither could muster any proof that the minerals they sought had been purchased before the January 1967 Excecutive Order. That was where Union Carbide's case for an exception differed from the others, as Carbide possessed proof that it had purchased 150,000 tons before the order.

Union Carbide, of course, had long been a powerful U.S. corporation. Carbide's activities in Southern Rhodesia had begun in 1923, and by 1969 the company had invested about $17 million in chrome mines there. Carbide controlled almost 80 percent of the chrome extracted from Southern Rhodesia in 1965. About half of what Carbide exported had gone to the United States before the sanctions, and its specialty steel mills in the United States had depended on the high quality Southern Rhodesian chrome. Like Foote, Carbide suffered from having to pay high prices for Soviet chrome and made the same general arguments against chrome sanctions.[119] Furthermore, a former Carbide executive, Kenneth Rush, was appointed U.S. ambassador to West Germany in 1969. Though the motivation and potential for him to pull strings for Carbide existed, he evidently had no impact on Nixon's August 1970 decision.[120]

The decision instead resulted from the fact that Carbide had purchased the ore in question before Johnson's 1967 order. Carbide transferred some $3 million to affiliates in South Africa in November and December 1966, which in turn paid for 150,000 tons of chrome on 21 December.[121] The NSC review of southern Africa conducted in 1969 acknowledged that Carbide had paid before the order, but it did not advocate an exception.[122] An interdepartmental debate raged throughout the spring and summer of 1970, with State opposed to granting an exception to Carbide, but with Treasury, Justice, Defense, and Commerce all in favor. After a 7 August NSC meeting, Nixon approved Carbide's request, that is, if they could convince Treasury of the date of purchase. Carbide manifested that they had paid for the ore in time, and on 18 September Treasury informed Carbide of the good news.[123]

The decision to allow Carbide to import 150,000 tons of chrome prompted an immediate cry of "foul" from Congressman Diggs, and the United Auto-Workers (UAW) registered a similar complaint. In responses to both, Kissinger denied that the United States was backing down from its solid support for the sanctions. To the UAW, he justified the exception for Carbide convincingly: "On legal grounds, there was no basis for refusing to permit this transaction.... On practical grounds, it is difficult to see how the Ian Smith regime would be hurt by permitting it to keep both the money and the chrome ore."[124]

One scholar of U.S. relations with southern Africa, William Minter, concluded that the exception for Carbide exemplified the Nixon Administration's preference for American corporations over international justice. Minter insinuated that Kenneth Rush assisted in obtaining special treatment for Carbide.[125] When the complete picture of the Carbide case is examined, however, it does not appear to be a situation of playing corporate favorites against the struggle for justice. If the Nixon Administration was set on helping Southern Rhodesian whites and American corporations, it would have granted exceptions to Foote and Corning as well. Of the three, Corning was probably best-positioned to receive a special favor from the White House.

Corning and Foote's failure to obtain help from Nixon and Kissinger, and the 15-month delay between Buchanan's initial approach to Nixon on behalf of Carbide and the final decision, illustrated Nixon and Kissinger's indifference on African issues. The lack of any administration demand for timely preparation of the NSC review, and the pathetic NSC discussion in December 1969, further highlighted their indifference. This lack of interest in Southern Rhodesia or any part of Africa opened the door for a much more serious blow to the sanctions, delivered in 1971 by Senator Harry F. Byrd (I-Va.).

THE BYRD AMENDMENT

Section 503 of the 1971 Defense Procurement Bill, commonly referred to as the Byrd Amendment, allowed for the importation into the United States of any strategic mineral being imported from a communist country. As an upshot of the amendment, which Nixon signed into law on 17 November, American firms renewed shipments of Southern Rhodesian chrome, nickel, and several other materials. The United States, therefore, joined South Africa and Portugal as the major culprits in violating the sanctions. The United States became the first country to vote for UN sanctions and then pass a law that violated them. The United States continued to participate in the sanctions, but no longer applied them to the one product that it had historically imported from Southern Rhodesia in the greatest quantity—chrome.

How and why did this happen? Since 1971, historians and other observers have posited a wide range of explanations for the passage of the Byrd Amendment. Some place the blame squarely on the Nixon Administration, seeing the amendment as a direct result of the "Tar Baby" policy adopted late in 1969.[126] Others commend the Nixon Administration for attempting to block the legislation and hold Congress responsible.[127] Variations on the "blame Congress" view credit corporate lobbyists for passing the Byrd Amendment.[128] Another view argues that Nixon and Kissinger were partly to blame because of their indifference.[129]

Except for the most extreme views—that Nixon either agressively supported or actively opposed the Byrd Amendment - all of the above points have merit. Congress initiated the amendment, corporate lobbyists advocated it, and Nixon and Kissinger ignored the debate in the months before its passage. These are all components of the complete explanation. However, none were new elements in the chemistry that produced the legislation in 1971. Smith's allies on Capitol Hill had introduced many antisanctions resolutions; Foote and Carbide had been lobbying since before 1969; and Nixon and Kissinger consistently ignored Africa during 1969-71. The catalyst, in fact, was the strategic and tactical skill of Senator Harry Byrd and his supporters in Congress.[130]

When lobbyists and members of Congress began their annual assualts on sanctions early in 1971, the pattern resembled that of previous years. Ten bills were introduced that would allow chrome to be imported in violation of the sanctions, and none got out of committee. In late February, however, a crucial new aspect of their strategy emerged. Representative James Collins (R-Tex.) presented a bill with unprecedented wording. Amending the 1945 UN Participation Act, the bill lifted bans on imports of any strategic material that could legally be imported from a communist country. Without mentioning Southern Rhodesia, chrome, or sanctions, Collin's bill would allow the United States to import Southern Rhodesian chrome. While the House Foreign Affairs Committee debated Collin's bill, Byrd proposed a nearly identical bill to the Senate Foreign Relations Committee.[131]

Byrd convinced Senator J. William Fulbright (D-Ark.) to have McGee convene the Africa Subcommittee for hearings on his bill, and the House Subcommittee on International Organizations agreed to consider Collin's bill. In preparing for the summer debate, Byrd and his subordinates gathered background information and met with officials from the Defense Department. Byrd's top aid discovered that chrome was essential for the production of jet engines, nuclear submarines, and Minuteman missiles. He concluded that "any action which even would appear to jeopardize our ability to produce these items would be suspect."[132] Byrd was building his case that relying on Soviet chrome threatened national security.

Tony Bliss of Foote Minerals simultaneously pressed the national security angle. In May he rounded up more allies for the cause, including George Bush, the U.S. Representative at the UN. After talking with Bliss, Bush opined that "if his data are correct, we are indeed faced with a very serious strategic mineral problem which could dictate a change in our policy." Bush recommended that Nixon's Assistant for International Economic Affairs meet with Bliss to hear his case. General Alexander Haig of the NSC also felt someone should talk with Bliss.[133]

Whether or not Bliss met with anyone at the White House is unclear, but he did testify before Congress in June. He reiterated that sanctions on Southern Rhodesian chrome had brought a drastic price rise; moreover, he stressed national security issues, particularly the depletion of the chrome stockpile. He pointed out that chrome was needed for jets and subs, and he cited Albert Speer, regarding the devestating effect of chrome shortages on the Nazi war machine.[134] In the Senate hearings, Dean Acheson made his final public appearance, pleading one last time on behalf of Ian Smith.[135]

In spite of the new emphasis on national security, the antisanctions group did not succeed in this round. In the Senate, McGee remained firmly opposed to chrome imports, and Byrd's bill died in the Africa Subcommittee. As the House debated Collin's similar bill, the State Department refuted the national security argument. The American supply of chrome was not dangerously low, State contended. Supporters of sanctions in the House such as Charles Diggs, with this help from the State Department, killed Collin's proposal.[136] The efforts by Byrd and Collins, like previous attacks on the sanctions, had fallen short. This time, however, Byrd did not quit.

Well before the Senate Subcommittee on Africa rejected Byrd's first 1971 chrome bill, he began solidifying the necessary support for his second attempt. In early June, Senators Margaret Chase Smith (R-Me.) and John Tower (D-Tex.) pledged support for Byrd's efforts. A few days later, subordinates for Senators Barry Goldwater (R-Ariz.) and Sam Ervin phoned with their backing. Byrd also contacted Senator Peter Dominick (R-Col.), who shared one crucial characteristic with the other four—he belonged to the Committee on Armed Services.[137] Byrd himself was a member of the Armed Services Committee, as was his staunch ally Strom Thurmond. Byrd had found the right committee for his next attempt.

As Byrd expected, the Foreign Relations Committee formally squashed his first bill on 5 August. Shortly thereafter he made his next move, as Armed Services debated the Military Procurement Act, which had already passed the House. Waiting until a point in the meeting when three liberal members were absent, Byrd proposed an amendment to the act. This amendment, section 503, was a near replica of his first 1971 chrome bill. The subsequent discussion revolved around the national security and anticommunism aspects of the bill. The committee approved section 503 by a vote of 13 to 0, and the Byrd Amendment had cleared the first hurdle.[138]

Byrd had succeeded in getting an antisanctions measure considered as part of legislation in the main Senate chamber, but that was not all. He had entrusted its passage to one of the largest "whales," in a Senate made up of whales and minnows, John Stennis (D-Miss.). As the Senate debated the bill, Byrd gained other powerful allies, most importantly Democratic Senator Robert Byrd of West Virginia. Furthermore, he had attached it to a major piece of legislation which would undoubtedly pass in some form. The $21 billion Military Procurement Act included so many high priority programs, moreover, that most criticism would be aimed at sections other than the Byrd Amendment.[139]

There were a few direct challenges before the amendment passed the Senate. The first was mounted by Senator McGee, who reminded his colleagues that an earlier version had been rejected by the Foreign Relations Committee and questioned the national security argument. He pointed to the fact that the Office of Economic Planning had recently recommended the release of significant amounts of chrome from the stockpile. Further, McGee explained how the amendment would put the United States in violation of treaty obligations at the UN and would harm relations with all of black Africa. Representative Diggs also impressed upon members of the Senate that the amendment would hinder relations with Africa.[140] McGee proposed an amendment that would negate the Byrd Amendment, but his proposal was defeated 46 to 36 on September 23.[141]

The following day, Senator Fulbright moved to reconsider the bill. Robert Byrd, notoriously knowledgeable on the rules of the Senate, outflanked Fulbright, and the motion was denied. Byrd's ploy forced Fulbright to draft a new amendment, with wording different from McGee's. Diggs and the newly formed Congressional Black Caucus urged Nixon to speak out against the Byrd Amendment and requested that senators support Fulbright's measure.[142] Nixon made no such announcement, and yet the new version (Fulbright's) passed the Senate 45 to 43 at 6 PM on 30 September. Several Byrd opponents left the chambers, confident that the amendment had been erased, but its supporters stayed late. Robert Byrd again spearheaded the counterattack, and succeeded in getting a re-vote on Fulbright's amendment scheduled for 6 October.[143]

At the White House, the NSC debated the best course of action. The new African expert, Marshall Wright, warned Kissinger that Diggs was misrepresenting Nixon's stand on the Byrd Amendment. Diggs had suggested to all senators that Nixon would support Fulbright's Amendment to negate Byrd's. Wright evidently believed that Nixon intended no such active support. Wright wanted to inform Nixon of developments, but Kissinger interceded with a simple scribbled note: "Forget it." If nothing else, Kissinger's note symbolized the administration's passive role in the entire debate. For whatever reason, Kissinger prevented any presidential action.[144]

A few members of the broadcast media played important roles at this juncture. Radio commentator Fulton Lewis, a long-time opponent of the Southern Rhodesian sanctions, regularly spoke on the air about the dangers of relying on Soviet chrome. His long diatribe at the end of September stirred up many constituents in support of the Byrd Amendment. During the debates over chrome, moreover, he met with at least six members of Congress and made it clear to them that opposing Byrd would damage them in their home districts.[145] Jesse Helms, vice president of a TV station in North Carolina, harped on the national security risk of depending on the Soviets for chrome.[146]

On 6 October, the Senate reconsidered Fulbright's challenge to Byrd, and defeated it 44 to 38. Therefore, the Byrd Amendment had passed the Senate, relying very heavily on southern Democrats.[147] Noteworthy among Byrd's Republican allies were Margaret Chase Smith and Bob Dole of Kansas. Neither had vested interests in stainless steel or ties to Southern opposition to civil rights. Smith evidently accepted the national security argument.[148] Dole, then chair of the Republican National Committee, had checked with the White House for guidance on the Byrd Amendment. Informed that the White House was "sitting it out" on this one, he concluded that Nixon was neutral and opted to support Byrd. Dole advised other Republicans of Nixon's neutrality and told them they were on their own.[149]

After a successful Senate amendment to a bill already passed in the House, legislation must be approved by a Conference Committee from both chambers. The chair of the group was Representative F. Edward Hebert of Louisiana. Back in September, Byrd first breeched the subject of section 503 going to Conference with Hebert. Representative W.C. Daniel of Virginia, Hebert's colleague on the House Armed Services Committee, reiterated Byrd's case to Hebert in mid-October. Hebert was sympathetic, and the amendment sailed through the Conference session. The Conference reported favorably on November 5, emphasizing national security.[150]

Despite a last-minute move to delete section 503 by Diggs and Donald Fraser (D-Minn.), the House approved the amended bill on 10 November, 251 to 100. The Senate did likewise the following day, 65 to 19. The next morning Byrd could brag: "last evening the Senate passed and sent to the White House for the President's signature, the Military Procurement Bill which incorporated my legislation on Rhodesian chrome."[151] The Byrd Amendment had cleared all congressional hurdles.

Before Nixon took action, *The New York Times* condemned Congress for undermining American participation in the sanctions that had begun with Johnson's executive order back in 1967. *The Times* editors credited the "Rhodesian lobby" for exploiting Congressional anticommunism and racism, as well as appealing to importers of expensive Soviet chrome. They blasted Byrd: "It was no accident that the Senate champion of white minority rule in Rhodesia was Harry F. Byrd Jr., a relic of the diehard fight for preservation of white domination in Virginia." The *Times* concluded that White House passivity was also to blame and wondered if it was an example of Nixon's "Southern Strategy" for re-election.[152]

Despite the *Times* pronouncement and another plea from Diggs, Nixon remained silent on the amendment.[153] The editorial had suggested that the Nixon Administration was pandering to the southern Senators for political gain, and that may well have been part of the story.[154] The most compelling reason for Nixon to avoid alienating Byrd and other southerners in the fall of 1971, however, was related to the Vietnam War. Senator Mike Mansfield was trying to force Nixon to remove all American troops from Vietnam, and Nixon needed help staving him off. Like so many other issues, then, the sanctions fell prey to Nixon's obsession with punishing the Vietnamese.[155] On 17 November 1971, Nixon signed the Military Procurement Act, with no comment on section 503.

Byrd's skill and dedication thus lifted the ban on imports of Southern Rhodesian chrome, and the United States joined South Africa and Portugal as the only admitted violators of the sanctions. The Byrd Amendment eliminated the one truly significant portion of U.S. opposition to Ian Smith. Why did Byrd do it? There is no doubt that he was influenced by Foote's Tony Bliss and the stainless steel industry's lobbyist, Tom Shannon.[156] However, a more fundamental reason lay beneath Byrd's efforts. Byrd's father, the former senator from Virginia, had been one of the most outspoken adversaries of integration and the civil rights movement. He had been the "Dixiecrat" candidate for president in 1952, 1956, and 1960. Harry Byrd, Jr., descended from one of the arch segregationists of U.S. history. Several of his allies in the fight had similar pedigrees, particularly Strom Thurmond, himself a "Dixiecrat" presidential nominee in 1948. These men, who had battled integration in the American South, identified with Ian Smith and his similar struggle for white supremacy in southern Africa.[157]

Benefitting from southern senators' sympathy for Smith and Nixon's pre-occupation with Vietnam, then, the Byrd Amendment went into effect on 1 January 1972. Foote unloaded its first shipment of chrome since 1966 in March, and Carbide received some in April.[158] The United States imported Southern Rhodesian chrome, in violation of the sanctions, until 1977. The economic effect on Southern Rhodesia of the amendment is difficult to measure, as it seems that Southern Rhodesia had not really had any trouble selling its chrome to other sources between 1967 and 1971. Ironically, American stainless steel manufacturers would be hurt by the amendment, because it allowed for importation of stainless steel as well as chrome. The impact on security was dubious, furthermore, as the United States continued to import Soviet chrome.

There was no doubt about the psychological boost for Smith, however, even before the amendment passed. Ian Smith's Minister of Foreign Affairs personally thanked Byrd for his "valiant and tenacious fight," promising a warm reception if Byrd ever visited Southern Rhodesia.[159]

Reaction from the other side of the struggle was equally strong. From prison in Southern Rhodesia, Zimbabwe African National Union leader Ndabaningi Sithole blasted the Byrd Amendment. The United States, by declaring war on sanctions, was acting as a world bully. While the United States had repeatedly claimed to support nonviolent means of solving the dispute, it had undermined the principal nonviolent method. Sithole exclaimed: "The action of the USA to resume chrome imports from Rhodesia under the present circumstances only goes to show that she cares more for metals than for justice and peace in southern Africa."[160] The developments that made Sithole's words ring true had occurred because Nixon and Kissinger, from 1969 to 1971, simply did not care about events in southern Africa.

NOTES

1. Dean Rusk to U.S. Embassy in London, 4 December 1965, drafted by William Rogers, etal., "U.K. Cables, 10/65-1/66," Box 209, National Security File - Country (hereafter NSF-CO), Lyndon B. Johnson Library, Austin, TX (hereafter LBJ).

2. Stainless steel is any alloy of iron containing at least 11 percent chrome, and it is valued for its resistance to temperature, corrosion, and oxidation.

3. Statement of J. Clayton Stephenson, 31 October 1969, in U.S. Congress. House. Committee on Foreign Affairs. Subcommittee on Africa. Rhodesia and United States Foreign Policy. Hearings, 91st Cong., 1st sess. Oct.17, 31; Nov.7, and 19, 1969. (Washington: US Government Printing Office, 1969), 31-32.

4. Rick Haynes to McGeorge Bundy, "Situation Report: Rhodesian Crisis," 13 December 1965, "Rhodesia - Memos, 12/63-1/66," Box 97, NSF-CO, LBJ.

5. *The Financial Times of London*, 24 February 1966, "Rhodesian News and Developments," enclosed in letter from Charles A. Bott of the Rhodesian Mining Enterprises, Salisbury, SR, to Senator Harry F. Byrd, Jr., 7 March 1966, "Rhodesia," Box 160, Accession #10320, Harry F. Byrd, Jr. Papers, Alderman Library Special Collections, University of Virginia, Charlottesville, VA (hereafter HB). The 20 January Order in Council is also mentioned in Harry R. Strack, *Sanctions: The Case of Rhodesia* (Syracuse: Syracuse University Press, 1978), 18.

6. G. Mennen Williams, *Africa for the Africans* (Grand Rapids: William B. Eerdmans, 1969), 116.

7. Anthony Solomon Oral History, LBJ, 14.

8. Memorandum of Conversation, Mann and Sir Patrick Dean, British Ambassador to the US, 23 December 1965, "U.K. Memos, 10/65-1/66," Box 209, NSF-CO, LBJ.

9. However, the contention by some supporters of Smith that he was an ally in the U.S. war against Vietnam was false. In a 6 October 1970 letter to Congressman John Schmitz, who had made such an assertion, Henry Kissinger explained that "no Rhodesian offer to help us militarily in Vietnam has ever in fact been received by the United States Government." Letter in "CO 124 9/1/70 -," Box 63, White House Central File-Countries, Richard Nixon Presidential Papers Project, National Archives II, College Park, MD.

10. Anthony Lake, *The "Tar Baby" Option: American Policy Toward Southern Rhodesia* (New York: Columbia University Press, 1976), 104.

11. Memorandum of Conversation, Haynes and Rowan, 16 February 1966, "Haynes Memos," Box 3, NSF- Name File, LBJ. Haynes and Rowan, two of the most influential African Americans regarding U.S. policy towards Africa in the 1960s, met over drinks for about an hour at the Mayflower Hotel. Rowan questioned the sincerity of the U.S. efforts to bring majority rule, while Haynes defended the Administration's actions, particularly the airlift into Zambia.

12. Memo marked "Secret," Komer to Bundy, 17 February 1966, "Komer Memos, V.2," Box 6, NSF-Name, LBJ.

13. Memorandum, Komer to the President, 17 February 1966, "Rhodesia, V.2," Box 97, NSF-CO, LBJ. This insightful memo by Komer was declassified on 11 January 1996.

14. Representative James C. Cleveland (NH) to President Johnson, 14 January 1966, and reply to Cleveland from Douglas MacArthur II, State's Assistant Secretary for Congressional Relations, 9 February 1966, "CO 250 1/6/66 -," Box 65, White House Central File - Country (hereafter WHCF-CO), LBJ.

15. Rose B. Shields, Secretary, North Dakota Chapter of the American Friends for Rhodesia, to Senator Milton Young (ND), 1 March 1966, "CO 250 1/6/66 -," Box 65, WHCF-CO, LBJ. See also Theodore Blackington, Government Teacher at Sumner High School, East Sullivan, ME, to Senator Edmund S. Muskie, 14 April 1966, and Dennis McGuckian, Norwich University, Northfield, VT, to Muskie, 6 April 1966, Folder 1, Box 647, Series 1, Edmund S. Muskie Collection, Edmund S. Muskie Archives, Bates College, Lewiston, ME (hereafter ESM).

16. Muskie to Theodore Blackington, 2 May 1966, Folder 1, Box 647, ESM.

17. Raymond W. Copson, *Executive-Legislative Consultation on Foreign Policy: Sanctions Against Rhodesia*, Congress and Foreign Policy Series, No.6 (Washington: U.S. Government Printing Office, 1982), 16.

18. Ottis Snipes, Jr., Commander, Mississippi Division, Sons of Confederate Veterans, to the Honorable Lyndon B. Johnson, 21 June 1966, "CO 250 1/6/66 -," Box 65, WHCF-CO, LBJ.

19. For an excellent discussion of Acheson's efforts to end the sanctions against SR between 1966 and 1971, see Douglas Brinkley, *Dean Acheson: The Cold War Years, 1953-1971* (New Haven: Yale University Press, 1992), 315-327.

20. The Acheson/Goldberg exchange is discussed in Lake, *"Tar Baby" Option*, 112-116.

21. On Fraser's suggestion that the U.S. issue a strong statement in support of ongoing sanctions, see memorandum, Walt Rostow to Johnson, 18 May 1966, "Rhodesia, V.2," Box 97, NSF-CO, LBJ. In this memo, Rostow explained to Johnson that the U.S. had a "gentleman's agreement" not to comment on Southern Rhodesia while the British were negotiating. On Kenyatta's support for the British efforts see memorandum, Benjamin Read, State's Executive Secretary, to Walt Rostow, 21 May 1966, "Kenya - Kenyatta," Box 32, NSF - Special Head of State Correspondence, LBJ.

22. Palmer replaced Williams on 1 April 1966. He was a career Foreign Service Officer who supported the sanctions policy, though not as aggressively as G. Mennen Williams had. For Palmer's views see Joseph Palmer Oral History Interview, LBJ; Thomas Noer, *Cold War and Black Liberation: The United States and White Rule in Africa, 1948-1968* (Columbia: University of Missouri Press, 1985), 186-187; Lake, *"Tar Baby" Option*, 97-98. Telcon, Joseph Palmer and Ball, 10 May 1966, "Southern Rhodesia 10/2/65-5/10/66," Box 6, George Ball Papers, LBJ.

23. American consulate, Salisbury, to State, 11 February 1966, "Rhodesia, V.2," Box 97, NSF-CO, LBJ; memorandum, Robert Komer to the President, 17 February 1966, ibid.

24. Robin Renwick, *Economic Sanctions* (Cambridge: Harvard University Press, 1981), 30. For discussion of the various ways the oil embargo failed, see William Minter, *King Solomon's Mines Revisited: Western Interests and the Burdened History of Southern Africa* (New York: Basic Books, 1986), 209-211.

25. Smith's speech detailed in U.S. consulate to State, 16 April 1966, "Rhodesia, V.2," Box 97, NSF-CO, LBJ.

26. Roy Wilkins to President Johnson, 4 May 1966, and Joseph Palmer to Wilkins, 27 May 1966, "CO 250 1/6/66 -," Box 65, WHCF-CO, LBJ. For further discussion of Wilkins' views on Southern Rhodesia in 1966, see Michael Krenn, *Black Diplomacy: African Americans and the State Department, 1945-1969* (Armonk: M.E. Sharpe, 1999), 116.

27. April 28 is celebrated as Chimurenga Day in Zimbabwe. David Martin and Phyllis Johnson, *The Struggle for Zimbabwe: The Chimurenga War* (London: Faber and Faber, 1981), 9-10. On the Security Force's 1966 seizure of ZAPU weapons, which they had obtained from the Soviets, see Daniel Kempton, *Soviet Strategy*

Toward Southern Africa: The National Liberation Movement Connection (New York: Praeger, 1989), 98.

28. Johnson's speech, 26 May 1966, "President's Speech on 3rd Anniversary of the Organization for African Unity, in Washington, 5/26/66," Box 5, NSF-Speech File, LBJ.

29. Memorandum, Dean Rusk to the President, undated, "Rhodesia, V.2," Box 97, NSF-CO, LBJ. This enlightening memo was declassified on 11 January 1996. It appears from the content and context to be from sometime between 5 July and 1 December 1966. While it is not clear that LBJ saw it, it does exemplify the view at the highest level of the State Department that the U.S. should not support a British deal with Smith that would not virtually ensure majority rule.

30. Memorandum to the President, from special 13 member Congressional committee on Africa, 9 August 1966, "Africa, General," Box 1-3, NSF - Edward Hamilton File. A note attached to the letter says: "Taken from the Evening Reading for the President, August 11, 1966." Palmer believed that such pro-sanctions groups in Congress had much more influence than the pro-Smith group led by Byrd and Thurmond. See Palmer Oral History, LBJ, 20-21.

31. Memo, "Subject: African Scene during your vacation," Ed Hamilton to Walt Rostow, 27 August 1966, "Hamilton Memos," Box 3, NSF-Name, LBJ. Hamilton replaced Ulrich Haynes, who left government and joined Spencer Stuart and Associates in New York on 1 August. Haynes offered to serve as an outside consultant on Africa, but there is no evidence that he was ever called upon. See memo, Haynes to Rostow, 1 June 1966, "Haynes Memos," Box 3, NSF-Name, LBJ.

32. Austen Morgan, *Harold Wilson* (London: Pluto, 1992), 297; Strack, *Sanctions*, 19.

33. Kaunda's letter discussed in memorandum, Hamilton to Rostow, 16 October 1966, "Hamilton Memos," Box 3, NSF-Name, LBJ. For Kenyatta's ideas and Johnson's response, see Johnson to Kenyatta, 10 November 1966, "CO 250 Rhodesia-Nyasaland," Box 11, WHCF-Confidential, LBJ.

34. Smith quoted in Noer, *Cold War and Black Liberation*, 228. For details of Smith/Wilson meeting, see State Department paper, "Southern Rhodesia," discussed during 25 January NSC meeting, "CO 250 Rhodesia-Nyasaland," Box 11, WHCF-Confidential, LBJ; Renwick, *Economic Sanctions*, 34.

35. East's letter of 6 December and Ervin's views on SR detailed in Sam Ervin to Dr. John East, 12 December 1966, "CO 250 1/6/66-," Box 65, WHCF-CO, LBJ.

36. Brinkley, *Dean Acheson*, 317.

37. Strack, *Sanctions*, 20; Renwick, *Economic Sanctions*, 35.

38. Excerpts from Statement by Senator Harry F. Byrd, Jr., 21 December 1966, "Rhodesia: January 12-25, 1967," Box 159, HB. Byrd was appointed to the Senate on 12 November 1965 as a Democrat, to replace his father who had resigned. In 1970 and 1976, Byrd was re-elected as an Independent. For his discussion of the 1970 campaign, see Harry F. Byrd, Jr., *Defying the Odds: An Independent Senator's Historic Campaign* (Harrisonburg: Donnelley, 1998).

39. Due to a technicality, the State Department insisted that sugar be handled separately from all of the other items that would be covered by sanctions. See Rusk to Johnson, 27 December 1966, Rostow to Johnson, 3 January 1967, and Johnson to the Secretary of Agriculuture, 3 January 1967, "Rhodesia Memos, V.2," Box 97, NSF-CO, LBJ.

40. Lyndon Johnson, Executive Order 11322, "Relating to Trade and Other Transactions Involving Southern Rhodesia ," 5 January 1967, "CO 250 Rhodesia-Nyasaland," Box 11, WHCF-Confidential, LBJ. Copies of the order can also be found in "CO 250 Rhodesia," Box 65, WHCF-CO; "Rhodesia Memos, V.2," Box 97, NSF-CO; and it is printed in Lake, *"Tar Baby" Option*, 295-297.

41. Telegram, H.R. Gross to Johnson, 5 December 1967, "CO 250 Rhodesia," Box 65, WHCF-CO, LBJ. State's Assistant Secretary for Congressional Relations, Douglas MacArthur II, explained to Gross that British trade with North Vietnam was minimal and included no strategic items. See MacArthur to Gross, 31 January 1967, ibid.

42. Utt's effort is described in a press release, 12 January 1967, folder 2, box 747, ESM; Lake, *"Tar Baby" Option*, 116.

43. Kenneth Spilman, a University of Pennsylvania pastor, wrote to Senator Gale McGee (D-Wy.) requesting that he oppose Utt's resolution. See Spilman to McGee, 8 June 1967, Folder 8, Box 163, Series III, Gale McGee Collection, Acession #9800, American Heritage Center, Laramie, WY (hereafter GM).

44. Byrd's 23 January 1967 speech summarized in a news clipping in "Rhodesia, February 1967," Box 159, HB. See Thomas Miller, President, Miller Tobacco, to Byrd, 30 January 1967, and S.G. Christian, Vice President, Dibrell Brothers Tobacco, to Byrd, 18 January 1967, ibid.

45. Summary Notes of 567th NSC Meeting, 25 January 1967, 12:10 to 12:45 P.M., "NSC Meetings, 1/25/67 Southern Rhodesia," Box 2, NSF-NSC Meetings File, LBJ. One of the few other attendees to speak at this meeting was Deputy Defense Secretary Cyrus Vance,

who repeated Rusk's assertion that no U.S. troops were to be utilized.

46. *Ibid*, 2.
47. Memo, "Notification to Congress on Southern Rhodesia," Nicholas Katzenbach to Johnson, 14 February 1967, "Rhodesia, V.2," Box 97, NSF-CO, LBJ; memo, Joseph Califano to Johnson, 23 February 1967, "CO 250 Rhodesia-Nyasaland," Box 11, WHCF-Confidential, LBJ; Lake, *"Tar Baby" Option*, 102.
48. The 24-page text of Palmer's 28 February 1967 speech, entitled "Southern Rhodesia," is in "Rhodesia," Box 194, Charles Diggs Papers, Moorland-Spingarn Research Center, Howard University, Washington, DC (hereafter CD). Palmer delivered this speech at the California Institute of Technology in Pasadena.
49. Andrew Young to William van den Heuvel, 10 March 1967, Folder 38, Box 19, Southern Christian Leadership Conference Papers, Martin Luther King Library, Atlanta, GA. For a discussion of Young's philosophy at the time in general, see Andrew J. DeRoche, "A Cosmopolitan Christian: Andrew Young and the Southern Christian Leadership Conference, 1964-68," *The Journal of Religious Thought* 51, #1 (Summer-Fall 1994), 67-80.
50. King's popularity in black Africa was witnessed during a 3 month tour in early 1967 by W.D. Bayles, a former employee of Standard Oil. He added that Robert Kennedy and Arthur Goldberg were also frequently cited by black Africans. See Bayles to Senator Harry F. Byrd, Jr., 2 April 1967, "Rhodesia, 1967 Mar-Sep," Box 159, HB.
51. A. Philip Randolph, form letter to members of Congress, 4 April 1967, Folder 1, Box 647, ESM.
52. For example, see John Davenport, "The American Interest in Southern Africa," February 1967, an essay printed by the Free Society Association, Folder 8, Box 163, GM; or Charles Burton Marshall, *Crisis Over Rhodesia: A Skeptical View* (Washington: Johns Hopkins School of Advanced International Studies, 1967). Marshall was a friend of Acheson's, and his book was distributed to Congress members by the RIO. Marshall's book and a cover letter from RIO chief Kenneth Towsey to Senator Gale McGee are contained in folder 8, box 163, GM.
53. See clippings of February 1967 editorials praising Byrd's stance, in "1967 Feb Rhodesia," Box 159, HB; editorial sent to Byrd and passed on to the White House, 1 June 1967, "CO 250 1/6/66 -," Box 65, WHCF, LBJ.
54. For example, see Donald Gray, Blue Hill (ME), to Senator Muskie, 12 June 1967, and John Cornwell, San Diego, to Muskie, 4 May

1967, Folder 1, Box 647, ESM; Reuben Andersen, Pine Bluffs (WY), to Senator McGee, 20 January 1967, Folder 4, Box 162, GM; Spencer McCallie, Headmaster of the McCallie School in Chattanooga, to President Johnson, 9 January 1967, "CO 250 1/6/66 -," Box 65, WHCF-CO, LBJ.

55. J. Clifford Miller, Chairman, Legislative Committee, Southern States Industrial Council, to Senator Muskie, 18 January 1967, Folder 1, Box 647, ESM; memo to AAAA members with "Report on Rhodesia," 17 April 1967, folder 5, box 162, GM. Conservative columnist James Kilpatrick participated in the AAAA's mission to SR and helped prepare the report.

56. The Pro-Rhodesia Committee's resolution against sanctions is in "1967 Oct-Dec Rhodesia," Box 159, HB. The statistics on FOR are in Eshmael Mlambo, *Rhodesia: The Struggle for a Birthright* (London: Hurst, 1972), Note 15, 301.

57. Colbert's description to Rostow of his conversation with Smith is detailed in a memo, Rostow to Johnson, 22 April 1967, "Rhodesia Cables, 2/66-12/68," Box 97, NSF-CO, LBJ. For information on Colbert's futile efforts to meet with Johnson see a series of memos in "CO 250 Rhodesia," Box 65, WHCF-CO, LBJ. Colbert's escapades are discussed in Noer, *Cold War and Black Liberation*, 231, but not in depth because Rostow's memo to Johnson was not yet declassified.

58. The only NSC meeting devoted to Africa during the second half of 1967 gave less than a minute to Southern Rhodesia, when Katzenbach asserted that the U.S. must keep pressure on the British not to settle for an unacceptable deal with Smith. See Summary Notes of 572nd NSC Meeting, 13 July 1967, "NSC Meetings, 7/13/67. African Problems," Box 2, NSF-NSC Meetings File, LBJ.

59. See the resolution and memo, Bingham to Charles Diggs, 13 June 1967, and Randolph to Congress, in "Rhodesia," Box 194, CD.

60. Copson, *Sanctions Against Rhodesia*, 16. The view of Thurmond regarding the absurdity of importing chrome ore from the USSR was supported staunchly by Charles Thompson of McAllen (TX) who returned from a visit to Southern Rhodesia in December. See copy of Thompson's letter to Thurmond received by Senator Byrd, "Rhodesia 1967 Oct-Dec," Box 159, HB.

61. Press Release, "McCarthy Urges More Realistic Aid Programs for Africa," 22 August 1967, "Africa, General," Box 1-3, NSF-Edward Hamilton, LBJ.

62. Memorandum, Hamilton to Johnson, 22 August 1967, ibid.

63. Humphrey's report to Johnson, 12 January 1968, "Africa - VP's

Report on African Visit," Box 77, NSF-CO, LBJ, 1-3. The detailed report, declassified in 1995, is very insightful.

64. Hubert Humphrey, Official Statement to President Kaunda of Zambia, 5 January 1968, "Africa- VP's Report on African Visit," Box 77, NSF-CO, LBJ.

65. Remarks of Vice President Humphrey, OAU, Addis Ababa, Ethiopia, 6 January 1968, "Africa - VP's Report on African Visit," Box 77, NSF-CO, LBJ.

66. Humphrey's report to Johnson, 29; memorandum, "Great North Road (Zambia and Tanzania)," Hamilton to Rostow, 18 January 1968, "Hamilton Memos," Box 3, NSF-Name, LBJ.

67. Kenneth Kaunda to Lyndon Johnson, 27 September 1967, "Zambia, Presidential Correspondence," Box 61, NSF-Special Head of State Correspondence, LBJ. This incredible letter was declassified in January 1999.

68. Terrence Lyons dismissed Humphrey's visit as having "produced no momentum," but that is not what Johnson was after. See Lyons, "Keeping Africa off the Agenda," in Warren Cohen and Nancy Tucker, eds., *Lyndon Johnson Confronts the World: American Foreign Policy, 1963-1968* (Cambridge: Cambridge University Press, 1994), 272.

69. US Consulate in Salisbury to State, #619 and #648, February 1968, "Rhodesia, V.2," Box 97, NSF-CO, LBJ.

70. Memorandum, Roger Morris to Rostow, 19 March 1968, "Rhodesian Cables, 2/66-12/68," Box 97, NSF-CO, LBJ.

71. Memorandum and Status Report on Southern Rhodesia, Read to Rostow, 9 May 1968, "Rhodesia, V.2," Box 97, NSF-CO, LBJ; Executive Order 11419, "Relating to Trade and Other Transactions Involving Southern Rhodesia," 31 July 1968, "TA2/CO," Box 4, WHCF-Trade, LBJ. In November Rusk advised Johnson to inform Congress of the order with official letters, and Johnson complied on 7 January 1969. While such letters were strictly a formality, the delay underlined the unimportance of the whole exercise.

72. George Ball, *The Discipline of Power: Essentials of a Modern World Structure* (Boston: Little and Brown, 1968), 245.

73. See the RIO's "Rhodesian Viewpoint," 8 May 1968, Folder 5, Box 188, GM.

74. For approval of the *Bangor Daily News* editorial calling for recognition, see John Edmunds, Bridgewater, ME, to Senator Edmund Muskie, 11 June 1968, Folder 5, Box 855, ESM.

75. Dean Acheson to Roy Welensky, 11 July 1968, Folder 430, Box 33, #1087, Acheson Papers, Yale University, New Haven, CT (hereaf-

ter DA). Welensky expressed similar sentiments in a letter to SR's Foreign Minister, Angus Graham, on 23 July 1968, Folder 170, Box 13, DA. The letters are discussed in Brinkley, *Acheson*, 320.

76. Summary Notes of 587th NSC Meeting, "Current Issues Affecting US-UK Relations," 5 June 1968, "NSC Meetings, 6/5/68, US-UK Relations," Box 2, NSF-NSC Meetings, LBJ.

77. Renwick, *Economic Sanctions*, 40; Morgan, *Harold Wilson*, 299.

78. Noer, *Cold War and Black Liberation*, 237.

79. Memorandum of conversation between Acheson, Nixon, and Kissinger, 19 March 1969, Folder 173, Box 68, DA.

80. Henry Kissinger to Secretaries of State and Defense, and CIA Director, "National Security Study Memorandum 39: Southern Africa," 10 April 1969, microfiche #00379, *South Africa: The Making of US Policy, 1962-1989* (Washington: National Security Archive, 1991).

81. Dean Acheson, "US Policies Toward Southern Africa Require Change," 30 April 1969, Folder 173, Box 68, DA; Kissinger to Acheson, 7 May 1969, "CO 124 Rhodesia (1969-70)," Box 62, WHCF-CO, Nixon Project, NA2 (hereafter NP).

82. Memorandum, Pat Buchanan to Peter Flanigan, 19 June 1969, "CO 124 Rhodesia (1969-70)," Box 62, WHCF-CO, NP; Noer, *Cold War and Black Liberation*, 241.

83. Memorandum, John Brown to H.R. Haldeman, 19 May 1969, "Chairs-Coffee, 1969-70," Box 24, WHCF-Subject, Trade, NP.

84. Memorandum, H.R. Haldeman to Pat Buchanan, 20 May 1969, ibid.

85. Coincidentally, the *American Heritage Dictionary* (Houghton Mifflin, 1982) quoted Richard Nixon in its definition of "stonewall."

86. McGee began his history graduate studies at the University of Colorado in the late 1930s, then earned a Ph.D. in history from the University of Chicago in 1946. He joined the history faculty at the University of Wyoming that year, and in 1958 won a seat in the U.S. Senate. For a summary of his career, see "Chronology," 8, GM.

87. Fred Shanklin to Gale McGee, 19 May 1969, and McGee to Shanklin, 19 June 1969, Folder 6, Box 486, GM.

88. Lake, *"Tar Baby" Option*, 148-149; Tony Bliss, President of Foote Mineral Company to Tom Huston, White House staffer, 25 June 1969, "Carrots-Copper," Box 50, WHCF-Subject, Trade, NP; Henry Kissinger to Robert Murphy, Chairman of the Board, Corning Glass, 11 September 1969, "CO 124 Rhodesia Begin - 12/31/69," Box 63, WHCF-CO, NP.

89. John Roche, president of the American Iron and Steel Institute, to Kissinger, 12 June 1969, and Thomas Shannon, attorney for the Tool and Stainless Steel Industry Committee, to Kissinger, 23 June 1969, "Carrots-Copper," Box 50, WHCF-Subject, Trade, NP.

90. Kissinger to Shannon, 25 August 1969, Kissinger to Roche, 25 August 1969, and Roger Morris memorandum to Kissinger, "Letters on Rhodesian Chrome Embargo from American Iron and Steel Institute and Thomas Shannon," 7 August 1969, ibid.

91. For example, see Representative Thomas Morgan (R-Penn.) to Secretary of State William Rogers, 10 July 1969, and Kissinger to Morgan, 16 August 1969, "Carrots-Copper," Box 50, WHCF-Subject, Trade, NP. Other members of Congress making similar requests included Edward Garmatz and Edward Derwinski.

92. E. Richard Barnes to Nixon, 29 August 1969, "9/1/69-12/31/69," Box 1, WHCF-Subject, Foreign Affairs, NP. The White House staff debated over responding to such a conservative constituent, then sent a noncommital acknowledgement. Rosemary Woods asked Jim Keogh to look over Barnes' letter and the suggested reply, since she judged Barnes to be "an *extremely conservative* type." See memo, Woods to Keogh, 18 September 1969, ibid.

93. For a brief biography of Diggs see Maurine Christopher, *Black Americans in Congress* (New York: Thomas Crowell, 1976), 209-214.

94. Editorial, "Wanted: A Rhodesian Policy," *The New York Times*, 25 September 1969.

95. Acheson had recently submitted a long memo on Southern Rhodesia to the White House. See "Memorandum for Mr. Kissinger," 1 October 1969, Folder 173, Box 68, DA. In 1969 the RIO compiled several of Acheson's speeches and articles into a book, *Dean Acheson on the Rhodesian Question*, which was sent to members of Congress. Among other places the book can be found in Folder 6, Box 486, GM, Folder 13, Box 1080, ESM, or "Rhodesia - Pamphlets," box 312, CD. Acheson also met with Rogers on 12 December 1969 and urged him to allow the chrome ore owned by Union Carbide and Foote into the U.S. See Memcon, Folder 173, Box 68, DA.

96. Copson, *Executive-Legislative Consultation*, 17. Also see, U.S. Congress. House. Committee on Foreign Affairs. Subcommittee on Africa. Rhodesia and United States Foreign Policy. Hearings, 91st Cong., 1st sess. Oct.17, 31; Nov.7, and 19, 1969. Washington: U.S. Government Printing Office, 1969.

97. Roger Morris, *Uncertain Greatness: Henry Kissinger and American Foreign Policy* (New York: Harper and Row, 1977), 109-119.

98. National Security Council Interdepartmental Group for Africa, "Study in Response to National Security Study Memorandum 39: Southern Africa," fiche 00379, *South Africa: The Making of US Policy, 1962-1989*; Morris, *Uncertain Greatness*, 119-120.

99. Many authors have focused on the "Tar Baby" option in criticizing the Nixon policy towards southern Africa. They have a very strong case regarding Portugal and its colonies of Mozambique and Angola, but the evidence for Southern Rhodesia simply does not bear the weight of their censure. The most important example, which remains in many respects an outstanding work, is Anthony Lake's *"Tar Baby" Option*. For discussion of U.S. support for Portugal in its efforts to quell rebellion in Mozambique, see Iain Christie, *Samora Machel: A Biography* (London: Zed, 1989).

100. "First Annual Report to the Congress on United States Foreign Policy for the 1970's," 18 February 1970, *Public Papers of the Presidents of the United States, Richard Nixon, 1970* (Washington: US Government Printing Office, 1971), 158.

101. Dean Acheson to White House, "The US Consul General in Salisbury Should Not be Withdrawn," 7 July 1969, Folder 173, Box 68, DA. Also see Walter Robertson to Nixon, 29 October 1969, attached Kissinger memo, and Nixon reply to Robertson, "CO 124 Rhodesia (1969-70)," WHCF-CO, NP. Robertson was a friend of Nixon's and his points were "well-taken," according to Kissinger. However, Nixon's reply explained that these issues would be part of the NSC review and promised nothing.

102. *The New York Times*, 25 September 1969; House Subcommittee on Africa, "Rhodesia and United States Foreign Policy," October 1969. The American Committee on Africa and a group of 43 peace corps volunteers in Malawi also expressed the view that the consulate be closed. See ACOA to Gale McGee, 8 July 1969, Folder 3, Box 487, GM; Peace Corps volunteers to Nixon, 24 July 1969, "CO 124 Rhodesia, begin - 12/31/69," Box 63, WHCF-CO, NP.

103. Lake, *"Tar Baby" Option*, 142.

104. ACOA to Diggs, 3 March 1970, "Congressmen Urge Closing of US Consulate in Rhdesia," and letter from Diggs to Nixon, 6 March 1970, "SA Rhodesia," Box 191, CD. Lack of black influence over Nixon discussed in Alexander DeConde, *Ethnicity, Race, and American Foreign Policy: A History* (Boston: Northeastern University Press, 1992), 177-178. Shirley Chisholm was the first black woman elected to Congress, from Brooklyn in 1968. See Chisholm,

Unbought and Unbossed (Boston: Houghton Mifflin, 1970), 148-149.

105. Lake, *"Tar Baby" Option*, 142-143. For details of some of the intrigue by US and British officials in the months leading up to the closing, see ibid, 134-141.

106. Copson, *Executive-Legislative Consultation*, 18.

107. For March 11 and 12 White House acknowledgments to the messages from Gross and Thurmond, see "CO 124 1/1/70-4/30/70," Box 63, WHCF-CO, NP.

108. Thurman Sensing, Executive Vice President of the Southern States Industrial Council, "Sensing the News," 19 March 1970, Folder 13, Box 1080, ESM.

109. Nixon to Kaunda, in cable from State to US Embassy, Lusaka, April 1970, "CO 170 Zambia (1969-70)," Box 88; Nixon to Nyerere, 4 May 1970, "CO 124 Rhodesia (1969-70)," Box 62, WHCF-CO, NP.

110. Copson, *Executive-Legislative Consulatation*, 18.

111. The 52 Representatives' message prompted Diggs to mount a campaign for a letter to Heath supporting sanctions. See Diggs to Colleagues, 3 August 1970, attached copy of his proposed letter to Heath, and copy of the letter from the 52, "Rhodesia," Box 312, CD.

112. See statement of Thomas Wood, vice president of Corning, 31 October 1969, in U.S. Congress, "Rhodesia and United States Foreign Policy," hearings Before the Subcommittee on Africa, 37-40.

113. Kissinger to Murphy, 11 September 1969, "CO 124 Rhodesia Begin - 12/31/69," Box 63, WHCF-CO, NP. Lake, in *"Tar Baby" Option*, 148-149, describes Corning's request as easily dismissed, though the above details suggest otherwise.

114. See Annex 4, pp. A-8 to A-11, National Security Council Interdepartmental Group for Africa, "Study in Response to National Security Study Memorandum 39: Southern Africa," fiche 00379, *South Africa: The Making of US Policy, 1962-1989.*

115. Statements of Representative Willie Andersen (Tenn.) and H.G. Bliss, 31 October 1969, US Congress, "Rhodesia and US Foreign Policy," Hearings Before the Subcommittee on Africa, 21-27.

116. Memorandum of conversation between Bliss, Christopher Norred, OEP Planning Officer, etal., 7 July 1970; Bliss to Nixon, 15 July 1970, "Chairs-Coffee, 1969-70," Box 24, WHCF-Subject, Trade, NP.

117. Lake, *"Tar Baby" Option*, 149 and 155. Lake was unable to ascertain whether the Nixon Administration formally denied Foote's request.

118. Margaret Schwartz to Bliss, 11 August 1970, "Chairs-Coffee, 1969-70," Box 24, WHCF-Subject, Trade, NP. For a detailed explanation of the Nixon Administration's support for SR chrome sanctions, see David Newsom, Assistant Secretary for Africa, to Bliss, 4 August 1970, ibid. White House staffers debated sending Bliss a sympathetic message from Nixon, but after determining that he was "no great personal friend" of the President, opted against doing so. See memos, Rose Mary Woods to Al Haig, 13 August 1970, and Marshall Wright to Kissinger, 20 August 1970, ibid.

119. Statement of J. Clayton Stephenson, President, Mining and Metals Division, Union Carbide, 31 October 1969, U.S. Congress, "Rhodesia and United States Foreign Policy," Hearings Before the Subcommittee on Africa, 29-35.

120. One of Nixon's professors at Duke Law School, Rush received an annual pension of $50,000 from Carbide while serving the Nixon Administration, and owned over $1 million in Carbide stock. For details about Rush see Lake, *"Tar Baby"*, 150-151. In 1974 Rush assured Charles Diggs that he had not been involved in the SR sanctions issue while in government service. See Rush to Diggs, 19 August 1974, "Boycotts-Embargoes/Rhodesia," Box 4, WHCF-S, Gerald Ford Library, Ann Arbor, MI.

121. Statement of J. Clayton Stephenson, 31 October 1969, "Rhodesia and United States Foreign Policy," Hearings Before the Subcommittee on Africa, 36.

122. See Annex 4, pp. A-8 to A-11, National Security Council Interdepartmental Group for Africa, "Study in Response to National Security Study Memorandum 39: Southern Africa," fiche 00379, *South Africa: The Making of US Policy, 1962-1989*. In this part of the report Morris presented the pros (11) and cons (13) of allowing in the SR chrome desired by Foote and Carbide.

123. Lake, *"Tar Baby" Option*, 154-155.

124. Kissinger to Diggs, 14 October 1970, "CO 124 9/1/70 -," Box 63; Leonard Woodcock, UAW President, to Nixon, 6 November 1970, and Kissinger to Woodcock, 2 December 1970, "CO 170 Zambia (1969-70)," Box 88, WHCF-CO, NP.

125. Minter, *King Solomon's Mines Revisited*, 238.

126. For the most extreme version, which portrays Nixon as actively supporting the amendment, see Martin Meredith, *The Past Is Another Country: Rhodesia UDI to Zimbabwe* (London: Pan, 1980), 216-218. Depictions of the Nixon Administration as passive supporters are Gaddis Smith, *Morality, Reason, and Power: American*

Diplomacy in the Carter Years (New York: Hill and Wang, 1986), 139; Noer, *Cold War and Black Liberation*, 241-242.

127. Robin Renwick, *Economic Sanctions*, 44; G. Mennen Williams, Oral History Interview, LBJ, 18.

128. For the extreme position that Union Carbide and the RIO "imposed" the Byrd Amendment, see Minter, *King Solomon's Mines Revisited*, 238-239. Also see Mira Wilkins, *The Maturing of Multinational Enterprise: American Business Abroad from 1914 to 1970* (Cambridge: Harvard University Press, 1974), 548.

129. Morris, *Uncertain Greatness*, 119-120; Copson, *Executive-Legislative Consultation*, 19.

130. Byrd's skill is emphasized in the two most thorough studies of the amendment, Strack, *Sanctions*, 146-164; Lake, *"Tar Baby" Option*, 198-238. Also see Copson, *Executive-Legislative Consultation*, 20-21.

131. Lake, *"Tar Baby" Option*, 199-201. Lake explained that it was unclear whether Byrd's office, Collin's office, or lobbyists for Union Carbide and Foote came up with the crucial new language.

132. Memo to Senator Byrd, from his top aid Jack Brooks, "Meeting with Mr. Carr and Mr. Davis of the Defense Department," 24 May 1971, "Rhodesia: chrome, 1971 Apr-Sep," Box 161, HB.

133. Peterson jotted Bliss's phone number and a request that his secretary make an appointment for Bliss with his assistant on the letter. George Bush to Pete Peterson, Assistant to the President for International Economic Affairs, 26 May 1971. Haig, memo to Eugene Cowen, "Rhodesian Chrome," 20 May 1971, "CO 124 Rhodesia, 1/1/71 -," Box 62, WHCF-CO, NP.

134. Statement of L.G. Bliss, United States Congress. House. Economic Sanctions Against Rhodesia. Hearings Before the Subcommittee on International Organizations and Movements of the Committee on Foreign Affairs. Ninety-second Congress. First Session. June 17 and 22, 1971. (Washington: U.S. Government Printing Office, 1971), 68-72.

135. Brinkley, *Dean Acheson*, 327.

136. See the detailed letter to Foreign Affairs Committee Chair Thomas Morgan, from David Abshire, State's Assistant Secretary for Congressional Relations, 4 June 1971, "CO 124 Rhodesia 1/1/71-," Box 62, WHCF-CO, NP. Donald Fraser, Chair of the House Subcommittee considering the Collin's bill, included Abshire's letter in the record of the hearings.

137. Margaret C. Smith to Byrd, 4 June 1971; John Tower to Byrd, 4 June 1971; Jack Brooks memo to Byrd, 7 June 1971; Byrd memo

to self, 12 June 1971, "Rhodesia: Chrome, 1971 Apr-Sep," Box 161, HB.

138. Lake, *"Tar Baby" Option*, 204-205. For a slightly different version, but one that also emphasizes Byrd's skillful timing, see Strack, *Sanctions*, 147.

139. Stennis described as a Senate "whale" in Lake, *"Tar Baby" Option*, 205. For a positive analysis of Byrd's shift to the Armed Services Committee, see *Metals Week*, 27 September 1971, copy in "Rhodesia: chrome, 1971 Oct 21-Dec," Box 160, HB.

140. Gale McGee, Statement on Military Procurement Bill, and attached letter to colleagues, 16 September 1971, "Rhodesia: Chrome, 1971 Apr-Sep," Box 161, HB; Charles Diggs to all senators, 15 September 1971, "SA Rhod.," Box 191, CD.

141. On 24 September 1971, Byrd sent personalized thank you letters for helping defeat McGee's amendment to eight senators including Barry Goldwater, John Stennis, and Margaret Chase Smith. See "Rhodesia: Chrome, Apr-Sep.," Box 161, HB. Smith explained to a constituent that she did not think the U.S. should punish Southern Rhodesia for its treatment of blacks unless it punished the USSR for its treatment of Jews. See Margaret C. Smith to Esther Levy, Bangor, ME., 22 November 1971, Margaret Chase Smith Library, Skowhegan, ME.

142. Telegram, black caucus to Nixon, 29 September 1971, and Diggs to all senators, 29 September 1971, "SA Rhod.," Box 191, CD. For discussion of the Congressional Black Caucus' early efforts regarding Africa, see Herschelle Challenor, "The Influence of Black Americans on US Foreign Policy Toward Africa," in Abdul Aziz Said, ed., *Ethnicity and U.S. Foreign Policy* (New York: Praeger, 1981), 166-169; Steven Metz, "Congress, the Antiapartheid Movement, and Nixon," *Diplomatic History* 12 (Spring 1988), 170-177.

143. Lake, *"Tar Baby" Option*, 207-211.

144. Marshall Wright memo to Kissinger, "Diggs Misrepresents President's Position on Byrd Amendment," 30 September 1971, "CO Rhodesia 1/1/71-," Box 62, NP. Kissinger's note was scrawled on the bottom of this memo, with no date. Thus, it is impossible to conclude exactly what he meant. He may have liked the misrepresentation, or may have felt it to be an accurate depiction. On the other hand, it simply may have been after the 6 October vote and thus too late to bother.

145. See his 29 September 1971 address in "Rhodesia: Chrome, 1971 Apr-Sep.," Box 161, HB. His effect on Congress described in Lake, *"Tar Baby" Option*, 228-230. Lewis admitted in 1973 to taking

$1000 from the Rhodesian Information Office for a 1972 trip to Southern Rhodesia.

146. See thank you for the 1 October editorial from Byrd to Jesse Helms, Executive Vice President of WRAL-TV, Raleigh, NC, 11 October 1971, "Rhodesia: Chrome, 1971 Oct 11-20," Box 160, HB.

147. See the list of recipients of thank you notes from Byrd, in "Rhodesia: Chrome 1971 Oct 4-8," Box 160, HB. Key Southerners included Eastland, Long, Stennis, Thurmond, and Tower.

148. Throughout her twenty-four years in the Senate, Smith advocated a high defense budget in the interests of national security. For a discussion of her impact on foreign relations, see Rhodri Jeffreys-Jones, *Changing Differences: Women and the Shaping of American Foreign Policy, 1917-1994* (New Brunswick: Rutgers University Press, 1995), 105-130.

149. Lake, *"Tar Baby" Option*, 223. While there was no clear reason for Dole to support the interests of Union Carbide or Ian Smith, he remained an ally of Byrd on the issue of chrome for at least another year. See Dole to Byrd, 29 August 1972, "Rhodesia: Chrome, 1972 Jul-1973 Jan," Box 160, HB. In this message, shortly after Congress had rejected McGee's attempt to repeal the amendment, Dole wrote: "I am pleased our efforts to rectify this situation appear to have prevailed."

150. Byrd to Hebert, 24 September 1971, "Rhodesia: Chrome 1971 Apr-Sep," Box 161; Daniel to Hebert and memo to Byrd, 15 October 1971; Daniel to Byrd, 20 October 1971, "Rhodesia: Chrome 1971 Oct 11-20," Box 160, HB.

151. Byrd to Thomas Florence, Colonial Heights, VA., 12 November 1971, "Rhodesia: Chrome 1971 Oct 21-Dec," Box 160, HB.

152. Editorial, "U.S. Against the Charter," *The New York Times*, 12 November 1971, clipping in "Rhodesia: Chrome 1971 Oct 21-Dec," Box 160, HB. In a response to the *Times* on 13 November, Byrd noted the "bitter personal attack" made upon him, but focused on reminding them of the national security component of his argument.

153. Diggs asked Nixon to publicly oppose the amendment in a 23 October 1971 letter. The reply from Assistant Secretary Abshire came only on 16 November, and contended that it was too late to do anything. The letter and reply are in "SA Rhod.," Box 191, CD.

154. Buchanan and Haldeman evidently opposed any NSC efforts to get Nixon to fight the Byrd Amendment. They felt it particularly important to have Byrd's support, because he had been elected in 1970 as an Independent. See Lake, *"Tar Baby" Option*, 225.

155. See Strack, *Sanctions*, 151, 266. For his contention that Vietnam overshadowed the debate over the Byrd Amendment in the fall of 1971, Strack cited interviews with chief of the African Bureau David Newsome.

156. He remained in close contact with Bliss into 1972 and beyond. He also kept in touch with Tom Shannon, the chief lobbyist for the stainless steel industry. See Jack Brooks memo to Byrd about Bliss, 2 February 1972, "Rhodesia: Chrome 1972 Jan-May;" Shannon to Byrd 29 April 1972 and 5 June 1972; Byrd to Shannon, 6 June 1972, "Rhodesia: Chrome 1972 June," Box 160, HB. Shannon claimed to have introduced the idea of the amendment to Byrd in 1970. In any case, there is no doubt about the impact of his lobbying in general. See Lake, *"Tar Baby" Option*, 230-231.

157. Byrd's general sympathy with whites in Southern Rhodesia evidently was shared by his brother and sister-in-law, who visited there in 1972. Their visit mentioned in Isabel Eady, an American tourist in Salisbury, to Byrd, 38 March 1972, "Rhodesia: chrome, 1972 Jan-May," Box 160, HB.

158. Lake, *"Tar Baby" Option*, 214.

159. J.H. Howman, SR Foreign Affairs Minister, to Byrd, 11 January 1972, "Rhodesia: Chrome 1972 Jan-May," Box 160, HB. While his brother did visit, the author has found no evidence that Byrd did.

160. Sithole to Secretary Rogers, 10 October 1972, in Aquino de Braganca and Immanuel Wallerstein eds., *The African Liberation Reader: Volume 3, The Strategy of Liberation* (London: Zed, 1982), 78-80.

6

HENRY KISSINGER PURSUES THE
SOUTHERN RHODESIAN DRAGON

Between 1972 and 1975, most of the activity in the United States regarding Southern Rhodesia focused on overturning the Byrd Amendment. In 1972, Senator Gale McGee led the first such attempt to return the United States to compliance with UN sanctions. Partly because of Nixon's apathy, however, he failed. With support from Henry Kissinger, Senator Hubert Humphrey succeeded in repealing the Byrd Amendment in the Senate in 1973. Humphrey's initiative fizzled out the next year, however, because his allies in the House were unable to match his success. Upon replacing Nixon in 1974, President Gerald Ford officially supported repeal. Yet, he refrained from any substantive action, and another repeal attempt led by Representative Charles Diggs in 1975 also failed. The key actors in Congress then decided to delay their next effort until after the 1976 elections.

While Congress debated chrome between 1972 and 1975, the conflict in Southern Rhodesia escalated into a guerrilla war. Nationalist leader Robert Mugabe was released from prison and boosted the liberation struggle by recruiting youths to join him in Mozambique for training. In 1972 and 1973 the Nixon Administration remained aloof from the struggle, but events in Portugal in 1974 forever altered the calculus in southern Africa. The resulting independence of Angola and Mozambique sparked conflicts that attracted the attention of Secretary of State Henry Kissinger.

Kissinger initially sponsored American intervention in Angola, funneling $32 million in aid to oppose Soviet influence. When Congress terminated this funding in January 1976, Kissinger looked for a new strategy towards Africa.

The struggle in Southern Rhodesia intensified in early 1976, and when British Prime Minister James Callaghan proposed a plan for majority rule in March, it was greeted with skepticism. Kissinger praised the British plan, however, and decided to pursue a Southern Rhodesian solution. According to one former American diplomat, with the end of Kissinger's tenure approaching he was looking for another "dragon to slay."[1] In April, he visited southern Africa and delivered a remarkable speech in Lusaka, pledging a sincere U.S. effort to bring peace and majority rule to Southern Rhodesia. Over the summer, he and his subordinates laid the groundwork for an attempt to forge a settlement.

In September, Kissinger returned to southern Africa and practiced his shuttle diplomacy. He confronted Southern Rhodesian Prime Minister Ian Smith and forced him to accept the principle of majority rule.[2] While Kissinger failed to end the conflict in 1976, in many ways his effort broke new ground. Kissinger's personal intervention symbolized the high priority that Southern Rhodesia had attained in U.S. foreign relations by 1976 - an unprecedented position, which it would occupy until Zimbabwe's independence in 1980.

MCGEE AND DIGGS CHALLENGE
THE BYRD AMENDMENT

During 1972 Southern Rhodesian blacks rejected a proposed new constitution and began the armed liberation struggle that would eventually result in the formation of the independent nation of Zimbabwe. While the Nixon Administration took no direct part in these events, the issue of Southern Rhodesian chrome continued to attract attention in Washington. Members of Congress, led by Senator Gale McGee (D-Wy.) and Representative Charles Diggs (D-Mich.), attempted to overturn the Byrd Amendment and block the importation of Southern Rhodesian chrome ore.

Since 1972 was an election year, partisan politics fueled some of the assaults on the Byrd Amendment. Senator Edmund Muskie (D-Me.), a leading candidate for the Democratic nomination, strongly criticized the arrival of a shipment of chrome ore from Southern Rhodesia in March. He blamed the Nixon Administration for allowing transport of this "symbol of apparent American disregard for the black majority in Rhodesia, the opinion of most African nations, the rulings of the United Nations and the beliefs of many concerned Americans."[3] Muskie urged the Nixon Administration to make it clear that the chrome imports did not mean that the United States had abandoned the black majority in Southern Rhodesia.

In fact, the Nixon Administration publicly criticized the Byrd Amendment several times in early 1972. In February, President Nixon blamed it on Congressional disregard for the United Nations. In March, Secretary of State William Rogers reiterated that the administration opposed the Byrd Amendment.[4] In April, UN ambassador George Bush called the chrome shipments an "embarrassment."[5]

Encouraged by these statements and also by private reassurances of support from White House staffers, Senator McGee decided to attempt repeal of the Byrd Amendment. The American Committee on Africa and several church groups lobbied on his behalf. The State Department also contributed, when Acting Secretary of State John Irwin contended that "our international interests have suffered" because of the Byrd Amendment. As the vote approached, McGee realized that he needed to sway a few Republicans in order to succeed. He requested that the White House make 5 or 6 phone calls to GOP senators who indicated that a call from Nixon would put them in McGee's corner. Nixon made no calls, and McGee fell short in the 31 May vote 40 to 36.[6]

The specialty steel lobby helped defeat McGee's repeal attempt, which was not surprising since that group had been one of the organizations primarily responsible for passing the Byrd Amendment the previous fall.[7] Senator Robert Dole (R-Kan), GOP national chairman, evidently pressed several of his wavering colleagues to retain the Byrd Amendment.[8] According to McGee, however, the blame for the Byrd Amendment's survival ultimately rested on the shoulders of the President. The administration had pledged to support his repeal attempt, but when it came down to a vote Nixon did not make the phone calls that are typically made to win close fights. McGee asserted: "After all the high sounding rhetoric, the White House alone must bear the burden and the responsibility for the failure of legislative efforts to turn this country around on the issue of sanctions against Rhodesia."[9]

After McGee's failure, Congress refrained from any other legislative assaults on the Byrd Amendment in 1972. The battle was not being fought exclusively in Congress, however. Activists targeted corporations doing business in southern Africa. As part of this new strategy, Diggs had attended the Union Carbide stockholders meeting as a proxy in April. He expressed the displeasure of the Congressional Black Caucas with Carbide's importation of chrome from Southern Rhodesia. He added that growing numbers of African Americans opposed the imports. Most importantly, he explained that blacks in Southern Rhodesia supported sanctions, and therefore disagreed with Carbide's practices. According to Diggs: "Union Carbide is an international criminal profiting while the black majority of Rhodesia suffers."[10]

In addition to pressuring Carbide, Diggs, Shirley Chisholm, and the other members of the Congressional Black Caucus challenged the legality of the Byrd Amendment. They first took their case to the U.S. District Court for the District of Columbia, arguing that it violated treaty obligations to the United Nations. In June, Judge Aubrey Robinson rejected their case on the grounds that Congress had the legal right to abrogate treaties and that the judicial branch was not qualified to rule on issues of foreign policy.[11]

Emphasizing the fact that Judge Robinson was black, the press in Salisbury hailed the decision: "Negro Judge Turns Down Chrome Move."[12] Diggs and his allies next turned to the U.S. Court of Appeals, which, in October, also rejected their appeal. This strategy would fizzle for good when the Supreme Court refused to hear Digg's appeal early the following spring.[13] The Congressional Black Caucus fired one last shot in the war against chrome imports, writing to Nixon in December, but to no avail.[14]

RISING NATIONALISM IN SOUTHERN RHODESIA

While the dispute over chrome garnered significant attention in the United States, in Southern Rhodesia the debate revolved around a proposed new constitution. In late 1971, Prime Minister Ian Smith and British Foreign Secretary Alec Douglas-Home had agreed to the constitution which would gradually increase black voting. The

British required the approval of black Southern Rhodesians, though, and dispatched a commission headed by Edward Pearce to monitor public opinion early in 1972. The 20 members of the Pearce Commission were mostly conservative former British colonial officials, and Smith expected them to speak to a few chiefs and rubber stamp the constitution. The leader of the Zimbabwe African National Union, Ndabaningi Sithole, requested that Nixon actively oppose the proposed new constitution. The Nixon Administration, however, decided to withhold judgement on the proposed constitution until the Pearce Commission announced its findings.[15]

While leading nationalists in Southern Rhodesia such as Sithole and Joshua Nkomo hoped Pearce's final report would advise against the constitution, they could do little about it since they were in prison. The task of rallying sentiment against the constitution among blacks fell to Abel Muzorewa, a Protestant minister who had studied in Missouri and Tennessee and emerged as an activist by early 1972. Muzorewa took charge of a new grassroots organization, the African National Congress, which spread the word to oppose the constitution. In early February, he addressed large crowds in London, rallying British public opinion against the settlement. He then took his message to the UN in New York. Finally, he met with U.S. officials in Washington, but found the Nixon Administration disinterested.[16]

After talking with Muzorewa and substantial numbers of blacks across the country, the Pearce Commission concluded in May that the majority opposed the new constitution. Therefore, the British abandoned the proposed constitution as unworkable and suspended their efforts at negotiating a settlement. The fact that the Pearce Commission accepted the will of the black people in Southern Rhodesia represented a major turning point in the struggle that eventually brought independence to Zimbabwe.[17]

The efforts by Muzorewa and others to stir resistance to the proposed constitution had fostered a resurgence of nationalism among Southern Rhodesian blacks. In late 1972, the Zimbabwe African National Union decided to renew the Chimurenga (Shona for liberation war). Leaving their training grounds in Mozambique, 60 soldiers entered the northeastern corner of Southern Rhodesia in December. Their strategy was to increase political awareness among the peasants and wreak havoc, while avoiding open confrontations with Smith's deadly security forces. A squad of nine carried out the first action on 21 December, cutting the phone lines to a white-owned farm and laying landmines on the approach road. They retreated to the hills and watched the security forces respond. Smith's forces sped to the scene, and suffered 11 mine casualties.[18] The Chimurenga continued until 1979.

HUMPHREY THREATENS BYRD AMENDMENT
Early in 1973, Ian Smith downplayed the threat to stability posed by guerrillas. Indeed, the guerrilla activity was extremely limited at first and received little attention in the United States. The key issue of American relations with Southern Rhodesia continued to be the importation of chrome ore and chrome products. The opponents of the Byrd Amendment, rallied by the Washington Office on Africa, introduced a powerful new argument into the discourse. The importation of cheap ferrochrome from Southern Rhodesia, an unintended consequence of the Byrd Amendment, resulted in the closure of three ferrochrome plants in Ohio and the loss of over 1,000 jobs.[19]

Senator Hubert H. Humphrey (D-Minn.) took the lead in attempting to rally support for another repeal effort. In April, he and co-sponsors including McGee and Edward M. Kennedy (D-Mass.) presented their case against the Byrd Amendment to their colleagues. The Byrd Amendment harmed the economy (e.g., ferrochrome plant closures), embarrassed the United States at the UN, and provided moral support for Smith's minority regime. Contrary to Senator Harry F. Byrd's contention that his amendment would increase national secruity by reducing dependency on the Soviet Union for chrome, the United States imported just as much Soviet chrome in 1972 as it had before the amendment.[20]

On 22 May 1973, Humphrey introduced Senate Resolution 1868 and Representative Donald Fraser (D-Minn.) introduced House Resolution 8005. These identical bills would "amend the United Nations Participation Act of 1945 to halt the importation of Rhodesian chrome and... restore the United States to its position as a law-abiding member of the international community."[21] Three days later, a group of about 40 people met to plan a lobbying strategy to secure passage of the bill. The group included congressional staffers, representatives from labor unions, and the head of the Washington Office on Africa. They believed passage would be easier in the Senate and agreed to act there first.[22]

During the summer and fall of 1973, public support for repeal of the Byrd Amendment emanated from a variety of sources. Earl Warren, retired Chief Justice, blasted the U.S. government for violating international law by importing Southern Rhodesian chrome.[23] The study *Irony in Chrome*, financed by the Carnegie Endowment, argued that the imports of Southern Rhodesian ferrochrome had done more harm to the American economy in 1972 than the sanctions had done between 1965 and 1971.[24] Longshoremen in Baltimore refused to unload a cargo of chrome. A task force on corporate responsibilty in Buffalo offered to assist the repeal effort, as did the League of Women Voters.[25]

The Nixon Administration generated words in favor of repeal in the months leading up to the vote on Humphrey's bill, words more important than public support. On June 7, UN Ambassador John Scali urged Congress to re-impose the ban on Southern Rhodesian chrome. Later that month Peter Flanigan, Assistant to the President for International Economic Affairs, assured Diggs that Southern Rhodesian chrome was "not an important element in U.S. security or in our overall foreign economic policy."[26]

KISSINGER SUPPORTS REPEAL

At the end of the July the Senate Foreign Relations Committee considered Humphrey's bill and decided to delay action until the Africa subcommittee held hearings, which Humphrey directed on September 6. The next day, during the Senate's consideration of Henry Kissinger's nomination for Secretary of State, Kissinger said: "the Administration will support the repeal of the Byrd Amendment."[27] On 18 September, the Foreign Relations Committee favorably reported Humphrey's bill to the Senate floor unanimously, but debate was delayed until late November.[28]

In the meantime, Kissinger reaffirmed his support for the repeal efforts. The new secretary of state explained to Diggs that the Byrd Amendment "is not essential to our national security, brings us no real economic advantage, and is detrimental to the conduct of foreign relations." He added that it had not reduced the imports of Soviet chrome, but had "impaired our ability to obtain the understanding and support of many countries including such important African nations as Nigeria, a significant source of petroleum and a country where we have investments of nearly $1 billion."[29]

When the House Subcommittee on Africa convened on 5 October, they emphasized Kissinger's view. Diggs and his cohorts also presented a number of other key pieces of evidence that supported repeal from earlier in the year, including the June statements by Ambassador Scali and White House aide Flanigan, and Kissinger's September testimony. Their case was growing stronger, and their bill had accumulated 110 co-sponsors in the House, including freshman Representative Andrew Young (D-Ga.). Young, winning election in 1972 in a district that included Atlanta, became the first African-American congressman from the deep South since 1901. The subcommittee adjourned on 17 October, awaiting results from the Senate.[30]

That morning, a *Los Angeles Times* editorial strongly condemned the Byrd Amendment, citing Kissinger's assertions.[31] Ten days later William Timmons, a presidential assistant, reaffirmed the administration's backing of repeal and even attested to Nixon's role. Timmons wrote: "You may rest assured that the president fully supports this policy and will take action as appropriate as the legislation is considered by the Congress."[32] Humphrey attempted to get debate on his resolution opened in the main Senate chamber throughout October, but Byrd and his ally Strom Thurmond prevented action by threatening a filibuster.[33]

Finally, Senate Majority Leader Mike Mansfield (D-Mont.) decided that debate would begin on 20 November. In defending his amendment, Harry Byrd received the powerful support of Democratic Whip Robert Byrd (D-W.Va.). Robert Byrd refused to set a time limit on debate, necessitating a cloture motion approved by two-thirds of the Senate. Humphrey tried to get the required vote several times in late November and early December, but failed. With assistance from McGee and White House staffer Tom Korologos, however, Humphrey succeeded on 18 December. The Senate approved repeal of the Byrd Amendment, 63 to 26.[34]

REPEAL STALLS IN THE HOUSE

The debate over Southern Rhodesian chrome moved to the House of Representatives. Diggs led the 1974 fight in the House, and his staff corresponded with over 1,000 black groups throughout the country to garner support. Diggs pointed out the damage that the Byrd Amendment was doing to U.S. relations with Africa, especially oil-rich Nigeria. He emphasized Kissinger's October 1973 letter refuting the importance of Southern Rhodesian chrome for American national security. He also wanted to manifest to the public the link between the amendment and the conservative agenda of Harry Byrd, Jr.—but to do so "gently."[35]

Victory would not be easy, though. The leader of the Ford Motor Company, Henry Ford II, explained that he needed large quantities of high-quality chrome to produce catalytic converters in 1974. Environmental laws necessitated these new features, increasing the automobile industry's consumption of chrome. Higher chrome prices, therefore, would hurt the industry more than ever, so Ford opposed repeal. Furthermore, approximately 50 small businesses who utilized stainless steel expressed their opposition to Diggs' efforts, because the Byrd Amendment kept prices down.[36] Nonetheless, the repeal effort in the House cleared the first hurdle on 27 June, when the Committee on Foreign Affairs recommended S.1868 by a vote of 25 to 9.[37]

Winning a floor vote, however, would not be so easy. One poll of 166 Representatives in late July showed 104 opposed to repeal, 30 in favor, and 32 undecided.[38] Before risking a general vote in the face of such discouraging evidence, Diggs and Young appealed for more public support.[39] Nixon's resignation in early August ushered Gerald Ford into the Oval Office, and shortly thereafter some of Diggs' allies requested that he back the repeal effort.[40] On 20 August, Ford's press secretary announced that the President favored repeal.[41]

By early September, the repeal forces appeared to be gaining ground on the important industrial front. The United Automobile Workers and the AFL-CIO participated in the lobbying crusade against Byrd. Reversing his earlier position, Henry Ford II advocated repeal:

> Although we continue to be concerned about the availability of sufficient quantities of ferrochrome to meet vehicle emission requirements in the US, we have concluded that other national and international considerations must take

precedence at this time and our policy now is to support the enactment of S. 1868.[42]

Wayne Fredericks, a State Department official in the 1960s, was influential in convincing Ford to change his mind.[43] The Ford Motor Company's support greatly pleased Diggs, and he underlined it in his ongoing efforts to influence other members of the House. Support for retention of the Byrd Amendment remained formidable, however, through the fall of 1974. Four times the repeal forces scheduled a vote; but, fearful of defeat, each time at the last minute they backed down. On 19 December they gave up on passing S.1868, and opted to start over from scratch the following year.[44] The second major asssault on the Byrd Amendment, initiated early in 1973 by Hubert Humphrey, had failed.

Events in Southern Rhodesia in December 1974 added ammunition to the pro-Byrd arsenal. Ian Smith released nationalist leaders Joshua Nkomo, Ndabaningi Sithole, and Robert Mugabe from prison. Their freedom, according to Byrd supporters, indicated that a settlement was near. In that case, why should American companies break contracts with Southern Rhodesia, only to draw up new ones after the settlement? While the argument contained many holes, it did influence the decision in December to abandon the repeal bill in the House.[45]

THE PORTUGUESE COUP

The release of Nkomo and the others represented the culmination of a series of important developments regarding southern Africa in 1974. On 25 April, Portuguese armed forces toppled the government in Lisbon with a coup d'etat. The army's desire to terminate colonial wars in Angola and Mozambique, which had lasted thirteen years and killed almost eight thousand Portuguese, motivated the coup. The coup leaders immediately announced that they would pursue political settlements in Angola and Mozambique that would bring peace, but did not provide specific details. The guerrillas in Mozambique stepped up hostilities in July, prompting Lisbon to initiate earnest negotiations in August. At that point, the liberation forces' leader Samora Machel met with the Portuguese representatives in Tanzania. The following month in Zambia, they signed an agreement recognizing Mozambique's independence.[46]

The end of Portuguese rule in Mozambique drastically altered the calculus in southern Africa. Ian Smith lost a key ally, and his 764-mile border with Mozambique suddenly became a potential infiltration route for guerrillas. South African President John Vorster quickly grasped the significance of an independent Mozambique; therefore, he and Zambian President Kenneth Kaunda initiated a period of detente. Through discussions, they hoped to avert an escalation of violence in the region, particularly in Angola and Southern Rhodesia. With that in mind, they convinced Smith to allow Nkomo and other imprisoned nationalists to attend a November conference in Zambia.[47]

Smith's acquiescence reflected the increasing impact of the liberation struggle in Southern Rhodesia. By late 1974, fighting had claimed the lives of nearly 100 of his Security Forces. He knew that the guerrillas were getting support from the peasants, so his troops had begun forcing blacks into "protected villages." With Machel in charge of Mozambique, the military situation in Southern Rhodesia would only deteriorate. Furthermore, Mozambique's independence greatly increased Smith's reliance on South Africa for trade and aid. Thus, when Vorster suggested allowing Nkomo and the others to attend the November conference, Smith could not afford to refuse.[48]

Nkomo, as undisputed leader of the Zimbabwe African People's Union (ZAPU), attended the first meeting in Zambia. The Zimbabwe African National Union (ZANU), however, argued about whom to send. Sithole had fallen into disfavor with several of his colleagues in prison, and they voted to send Robert Mugabe. Kaunda, Machel, and Tanzania's Julius Nyerere basically refused to deal with Mugabe and demanded to see Sithole. This lack of unity among the Southern Rhodesian nationalists, among other factors, prevented any real progress towards a settlement. More important, perhaps, was the fact that Ian Smith was not yet prepared to negotiate a transfer of power. He did agree to extend the parole of Nkomo, Sithole, and Mugabe, and they were released from prison permanently in December. For Nkomo, the time in prison had been "a long ten years."[49]

RECRUITING A LIBERATION ARMY

The release of the nationalists in December 1974 contributed slightly to the debate over chrome in the U.S. House of Representatives. More importantly, though, it meant the nationalists could return to their positions as the leaders of the liberation struggle. Upon his release from prison, Mugabe began addressing small meetings around Salisbury. He explained to the people that ZANU was still fighting against Smith's government forces, and that they should join the liberation forces. A few of his colleagues who had been released simultaneously spread the same message to other areas of Southern Rhodesia.

During the first three months of 1975, moderate numbers of recruits crossed into Mozambique to join ZANU. At the end of March, Mugabe himself went to Mozambique in order to help organize the guerrillas. For the next two months he instructed small groups of recruits about the history of the struggle at secret locations, since the Portuguese forces had not entirely withdrawn and would inform Smith of any Mugabe rabble-rousing. In June, with the departure of the Portuguese, Mugabe and some 1,500 ZANU fighters convened at a large barracks for mass training.[50]

The exodus of youths prompted Smith to impose a curfew in a kilometer-wide zone along a 400-kilometer stretch of the border with Mozambique on 25 July. He met with various nationalist leaders through the summer to arrange an all-parties conference, which occurred in a railroad car on the bridge at Victoria Falls on 25 August. Smith sat down with Nkomo, Sithole, and Muzorewa, but the session lasted only a few hours and accomplished nothing. The ceasefire in the months leading up to the conference had allowed Smith to improve the position of his security forces, so from the nationalists' perspective the detente process initiated by Kaunda and Vorster had done as much harm as good. They resumed recruiting in earnest, and during September and October about 1,000 would-be guerrillas swarmed into Mozambique each week.[51]

The fight for an independent Zimbabwe under majority rule turned a corner in 1975, putting it on course for eventual triumph. The U.S. government stayed out of the struggle in 1975, despite the direct plea of Zambia's president during an 19 April banquet at the White House. Responding to Ford's toast, Kaunda praised the past American record against colonialism, but criticized recent policy as inactive. He asserted: "If we want peace we must end the era of inertia in Rhodesia... We call upon America to support our efforts in achieving majority rule in Rhodesia." Kaunda and 22 fellow Zambians performed a song, then he sang a duet with his wife while playing guitar. His behavior surprised some of the 120 in attendance, and his criticism of U.S. policy reportedly left Kissinger "furious."[52]

While he and Ford kept the United States out of the fighting in Southern Rhodesia in 1975, a private American citizen named Robert K. Brown advertised in several magazines calling for mercenaries to join Ian Smith's forces. Another U.S. citizen, retired General Chesley Peterson, attempted to aid Smith's cause by inviting his "friend" to visit him in Utah. The State Department informed Peterson that Smith would not be allowed a visa, and the White House concurred.[53]

A THIRD SHOT AT REPEALING BYRD

As in the previous several years, the vast majority of activity related to Southern Rhodesia in Washington in 1975 dealt with chrome. On Capitol Hill, Representative Fraser introduced a new bill on 14 January that would repeal the Byrd Amendment. Fraser's bill, co-sponsored by Diggs and John Buchanan (R-Ala.), went to the Foreign Affairs Committee for consideration. On 18 March the Subcommittee on International Organizations approved the bill, 4 to 1. However, Fraser added an amendment requiring that any imports containing chrome include certification that the chrome therein did not come from Southern Rhodesia.[54]

Fraser intended to prevent nations from buying cheap Southern Rhodesian chrome and undercutting the prices of American specialty steel producers, who would be forced by sanctions to use higher-priced Soviet chrome ore. The White House did not issue any high level statement regarding the amendment, but National Security Council staffers concluded that Ford's general position in favor of repeal still stood firm. Because of Fraser's amendment, the Foreign Affairs Committee sent the bill back to subcommittee for additional hearings on 19 June. Assistant Secretaries from Treasury, Commerce, and State advocated repealing the Byrd Amendment, but registered some reservations about Fraser's amendment.[55]

Nonetheless, in July the Foreign Affairs Committee recommended the bill, 17 to 8. The Armed Services Committee, however, opposed its passage 29 to 7. As this third attempt to repeal the Byrd Amendment staggered towards a floor vote, very few legislators paid it close attention. Senator McGee contended that because black nationalists would eventually triumph, long-term access to Southern Rhodesian chrome would best be guaranteed by repealing the Byrd Amendment and supporting the sanctions against Smith. A similar point could be made that supporting sanctions against Smith helped relations with Nigeria, who supplied 20 percent of American crude petroluem imports.[56]

Had the President taken up the cause and pushed the argument that supporting sanctions would serve long-term U.S. interests, the Byrd Amendment may have been overturned in 1975. Ford never joined the battle, however. His staff repeatedly postponed his meetings with legislators on both sides of the debate. Fraser and McGee tried to meet with him before the vote in order to get him to agitate for repeal, but they were not accomodated. There is no evidence of Ford knowingly avoiding them, however, and he similarly postponed meetings with Byrd Amendment supporters. He made no personal attempt to sway legislators either way. Ford himself never addressed the chrome issue publicly, and his press secretary simply reiterated the basic position favoring repeal. On 25 September the House rejected Fraser and Digg's bill 209 to 187.[57]

Ford finally met with several key actors in the chrome debate on 4 November. After reviewing the breakdown of the 25 September vote, he talked with one of the leading defenders of the Byrd Amendment in the House, Edward Derwinski (R-Ill.). Derwinski credited the White House for blocking repeal, which certainly exaggerated Ford's effectively neutral stance.[58] Indeed, later that day Ford received McGee, Fraser, and John Buchanan to strategize about future repeal efforts, and they concluded that a check should be run to determine which opponents of repeal might switch their votes. Ford requested a report on the matter within a week.[59]

Presidential aides conducted the check of representatives, and concluded that only four Republicans would consider changing votes. They discovered "the very mention of renewing this issue to be a red flag among Republican Members." They predicted that "a new bill would meet the same fate as the last one." Ford perused their report, then asked them to inform Fraser and his co-sponsors that it would be best to give up on the repeal effort until 1976. He emphasized: "Better explain this to John Buchanan and Fraser."[60] Thus, in the only significant area of direct U.S. relations with Southern Rhodesia in 1975, the Byrd Amendment survived, chrome imports continued, and the United States violated the UN sanctions for another year.

KISSINGER TAKES NOTE OF AFRICA

The Ford Administration played no direct part in the fighting between Ian Smith and the black nationalists in 1975, but it did contribute significantly to the struggle in Angola. The 1974 coup in Lisbon led to a withdrawal of the Portuguese from Angola, and the Popular Movement for the Liberation of Angola (MPLA) seemed assured of victory. Agostino Neto led the MPLA, receiving support from the Soviets, the Cubans, and Nigeria. In January 1975, Kissinger decided to back a rival group, the National Union for the Total Independence of Angola (UNITA), led by Jonas Savimbi. The CIA began channeling money and weapons to Savimbi's forces, who were receiving massive assistance from South Africa. The Soviets stepped up their support of the MPLA, the United States did likewise for UNITA, and by November Kissinger had allotted $32 million in covert aid to the Angolan war.[61]

The CIA operation in Angola drew fire from many quarters, including the U.S. Congress. Senators Dick Clark (D.-Iowa) and John Tunney (D.-Cal.) proposed an amendment to a foreign aid bill blocking future covert funds for Angola, and the Senate approved it on 19 December. The House did likewise in January 1976 by a resounding 323 to 29.[62] Rebuffed by Congress, Kissinger tried a different angle. As the Organization of African Unity met to discuss Angola early in 1976, the secretary of state attempted to rally African support for Savimbi's UNITA. Furious that the United States had sided with South Africa, the Nigerian president attacked Kissinger and Ford in the newspapers. Headlines screamed "To Hell with America," and Nigerian students stoned the U.S. embassy. In a final reaction to the U.S. policy in Angola, Nigeria banned Kissinger from future visits.[63]

With his hands tied by Congress and his policy lambasted by Nigeria, Kissinger sought a new strategy for southern Africa. Unable to fight the Soviets and the Cubans militarily, he would instead try to remove potential battlefields. Thus his attention turned in the spring of 1976 to Southern Rhodesia, where the intensifying conflict offered ripe ground for Soviet influence. By negotiating a settlement between Smith and the nationalists, Kissinger could head off the Soviets.[64]

Kissinger's decision to stride onto the southern African stage reflected many factors in addition to his desire to limit Soviet influence. The escalating conflict in Southern Rhodesia threatened to damage irreparably the already poor U.S. relations with key nations like Nigeria. With its allies Nigeria would call for armed intervention against Smith's regime, to which the United States would never agree. The dispute would cause the United States severe headaches at the UN. Even if the Soviets had not been supplying arms to the black nationalists, the above considerations would have probably prodded the American government into a more direct role in the conflict in 1976.[65]

In the wake of Kissinger's aborted effort in Angola, Democrats amplified their criticism of the Ford Administration's policy towards southern Africa. In January, Senator Clark testified that American policy there should strive for human rights and racial equality. In March, Congressman Diggs espoused a "total reassessment of US policy toward Africa." Diggs argued that CIA actions in Angola, which had in fact placed the United States on the same side as South Africa in the conflict, typified U.S. support for the interests of the white minority regimes. He strongly suggested that the United States should stop supporting the white governments, but not only for moral reasons. He pointed out that since blacks would certainly control Southern Rhodesia someday, it was in the best interests of the United States to stop supporting the whites as soon as possible.[66]

As Kissinger first pondered the SR situation in early 1976, this sort of "foreseeing the inevitable" probably affected his thinking more than a desire to fight for racial justice. Of course, couching American policy in terms of racial justice could be an effective tactic against the Soviets. Furthermore, such a stance might gain some liberal support for Ford in his bid for election in the fall. However, Kissinger realized that a diplomatic initiative towards the conflict could also damage Ford, particularly with the conservative wing of the Republican party who supported Ronald Reagan. Kissinger's motives in deciding to visit Africa were convoluted. Perhaps the key reason was the simplest - with the end of Vietnam negotiations he needed a new challenge and was looking for "another dragon to slay."[67]

Meanwhile, the war against the Smith regime resumed in January of 1976. With logistical support from Nyerere and more arms from China and Machel's stock, approximately 700 ZANU soldiers infiltrated Southern Rhodesia from Mozambique. In February, Machel decided to close the border and thereby significantly tighten the sanctions against the Smith regime, which moved about 50 percent of its exports and imports through Mozambique. Machel officially shut off this traffic on 3 March. The move would cost Mozambique upwards of $100 million in revenue annually, but would also damage Southern Rhodesia considerably. Three months of negotiations featuring thirteen meetings between Smith and Nkomo fizzled in March. The intransigent Smith proclaimed on British television: "I don't believe in majority rule ever in Rhodesia—not in a thousand years."[68]

In Parliament on 21 March, a few days after the Smith/Nkomo talks terminated, British Prime Minister James Callaghan delineated a plan for resolving the crisis. If Smith would agree to four conditions, the British would oversee a constitutional convention to plan Southern Rhodesia's independence. The four requirements Smith had to accept were: (1) the principle of majority rule, (2) elections including the black majority within two years, (3) no independence before majority rule, (4) timely negotiations. Callaghan hoped Smith would seize the opportunity to avert further bloodshed, but he was not particularly optimistic. As things turned out, he had initiated the diplomatic process that would culminate in an independent Zimbabwe four years later.[69]

KISSINGER'S FIRST VISIT TO AFRICA

Not surprisingly, Smith rejected Callaghan's terms outright. Kissinger, though, praised them as a "most constructive approach." He pledged a major effort "to help all parties to return to the negotiating table."[70] Indeed, it would be Kissinger who took the lead in the international mediation effort regarding Southern Rhodesia, using Callaghan's proposals as a springboard. By mid-April he had decided to visit Zambia and spell out a new American policy towards southern Africa in a major speech.

The State Department began feverishly arranging the logistics of Kissinger's trip. Kissinger wanted to meet with Nkomo and Muzorewa and also sought advice from Kaunda and Nyerere as to whether he should see any other nationalists. Nyerere felt that Nkomo and Muzorewa were the people that Kissinger should see, because when the time came to negotiate a settlement, "Joshua and the Bishop will be there." Muzorewa, however, had a prior engagement in North Africa and thus would miss Kissinger. American diplomats in Zambia urged him to see the secretary, because Kissinger hoped to foster unity in the liberation movement by seeing multiple leaders. Muzorewa insisted that his prior engagement took precedence and refused to meet with Kissinger. American diplomats had better luck with Nkomo, who agreed to see the secretary. When Nkomo expressed reservations about transportation, the American ambassador in Zambia offered to arrange a flight for him.[71]

As Kissinger departed for Africa on 23 April, he announced that the new U.S. policy sought a transition from white rule in Southern Rhodesia to a majority-ruled Zimbabwe.[72] The "doctor of diplomacy" reached Lusaka on 26 April and met with President Kaunda that evening. After the two had talked for a while, Nkomo was ushered into the room. Nkomo later described the encounter as follows:

> I spent about seven minutes with Kissinger. He spoke in short sentences in a dull, flat voice, like a businessman doing a quick deal. It was more like talking to a robot than to a person. First he would say something, then withdraw it and say something else, then add a further point to that, so by the end I only knew that whatever he wanted it was not what I wanted. He struck me as clever, of course, but unpleasant and untrustworthy.[73]

Evidently, Kissinger did not intend to befriend Nkomo, or deal with him as an equal in negotiations. He had no interest in hearing Nkomo's ideas about how to reach a settlement and hoped to orchestrate a solution himself. Still, members of his staff worried that meeting with only Nkomo, and not Smith, would bring charges that the United States was taking sides. Such concern was unwarranted since the meeting never received any publicity in the United States, but Kissinger's speech the following day certainly did. State insisted that Kaunda hold the luncheon in Lusaka instead of Livingstone, in order to guarantee a large press turnout.[74]

Kissinger opened his remarkable speech by espousing three broad, long-term goals for Africa—peace, economic development, and racial justice. He added that the United States supported African solutions for African problems and desired unity among and within African nations. He pointed to American history as an example of the possibility of achieving racial justice. Citing Jefferson, Kissinger reaffirmed the U.S. Government's committment to the Declaration of Independence. Sounding a lot like Woodrow Wilson, he concluded his introduction: "We support self-determination, majority rule, equal rights and human dignity for all the peoples of southern Africa—in the name of moral principle, international law and world peace."[75]

Focusing specifically on the conflict in Southern Rhodesia, Kissinger praised Zambia and Mozambique for selflessly closing their borders and thus tightening the sanctions. He began a description of the new American policy towards Southern Rhodesia by seconding the plan pronounced by British Foreign Secretary Callaghan - majority rule within two years, then independence. As for a U.S. role, it would refrain from providing the Smith regime with any support whatsoever and would urge Smith to negotiate a majority-rule settlement rapidly. Moreover, Kissinger promised that the Ford Administration would push Congress to repeal the Byrd Amendment.

In the short run, the United States would financially assist Mozambique and other neighbors of Southern Rhodesia that bore the burdens of war. In the long run, the independent nation of Zimbabwe would receive American aid. Furthermore, the United States would strive to protect the rights of the white minority after majority rule took effect. In order to carry out this ambitious policy, Kissinger intended to cooperate closely with the presidents of the Frontline States - Zambia, Tanzania, Mozambique, and Botswana. In addition, Kissinger called on the government of South Africa to use its "influence in Salisbury to promote a rapid negotiated settlement for majority rule in Rhodesia."[76]

In his Lusaka address, Kissinger intimated a significant American role in facilitating the transition from Southern Rhodesia to Zimbabwe. This represented a dramatic departure from the basic American policy, dating back to Eisenhower, of supporting British efforts. For the first time, a U.S. secretary of state made Southern Rhodesia a high priority. Kissinger's expression of this new policy drew fire from all sides. Smith complained that Kissinger had not given the Southern Rhodesian government a chance to explain its position. The Soviet paper *Izvestia* derided his plan as an attempt to undermine the liberation movements, and Soviet Foreign Minister Andrei Gromyko characterized it as a combination of "political gimmickry and financial handouts."[77]

Campaigning for the Georgia primary, Ronald Reagan suggested that Kissinger's criticism of Smith's regime could lead to a "massacre." In Texas a few days later he added that Kissinger's actions "undercut the possibility for a just and orderly settlement."[78] In a *New York Times* column, George Kennan questioned whether majority rule in Southern Rhodesia would be beneficial, pointing to the chaos which resulted from independence in other African states. Columnist and former Nixon aide Patrick Buchanan excoriated Kissinger's new policy for putting "the moral authority of the United States behind the militant Marxist regime of Mozambique, and against the beleaguered pro-Western Government of Rhodesia." White House staffers feared that Reagan would utilize ammunition provided by Buchanan to assault Ford in the ongoing primaries. They prepared rebuttals for Ford and his spokesmen that emphasized how the new policy would prevent Soviet influence in southern Africa.[79]

Senator Harry Byrd took umbrage at Kissinger's statement in Lusaka that he would pursue repeal of the Byrd Amendment. On 13 May at a meeting of the Senate Foreign Relations Committee, Byrd confronted Kissinger face to face. He suggested that Kissinger was a hypocrite for supporting sanctions against Southern Rhodesia but not against South Africa. He emphasized that stopping imports from Southern Rhodesia necessitated reliance on the Soviets. He accused Kissinger of putting "great trust in the Soviet Union" and "embracing communist Russia with great vigor," to which

Kissinger objected strongly. Kissinger responded that since blacks would inevitably gain control in an independent Zimbabwe, long-term U.S. interests were best served by his new policy, even if it required increasing imports of Soviet chrome temporarily.[80]

LAYING THE FOUNDATIONS FOR NEGOTIATIONS

Despite the criticism from conservatives like Byrd, Buchanan, and Reagan, Kissinger charged ahead with his intervention in the struggle. In May he held preliminary talks with the South African ambassador to the United States, Pik Botha. In late June in the Bavarian mountains of West Germany, Kissinger discussed Southern Rhodesia with Prime Minister Vorster. They went over the spectrum of issues, including the establishment of a specific fund to assist whites. Kissinger discovered that Vorster was willing to pull the plug on Smith, partly to take some of the international heat off his own regime. Kissinger's primary question had been answered satisfactorily.[81]

While the effort by Kissinger reaped some positive results by the summer of 1976, leading nationalists in Southern Rhodesia publicly questioned the secretary's intentions. Abel Muzorewa accused Kissinger of getting involved in order to consolidate his "Tar Baby" policy, by which he would support the white regime in Salisbury. Muzorewa pointed to the 200 or so mercenaries from the United States who had joined Smith's forces in May, insinuating that the Ford Administration at least indirectly supported their presence. Ndabaningi Sithole, though not suggesting U.S. government complicity, also emphasized the rising number of American mercenaries in the struggle. By the end of 1976, approximately 1,200 foreign volunteers battled against the liberation forces, and most of them came from the United States or England. Several hundred Americans flocked to Southern Rhodesia, encouraged by the efforts of Robert K. Brown. His newly founded *Soldier of Fortune* magazine provided subscribers with a Southern Rhodesian recruitment poster as a gimmick that year.[82]

Evidently, the Ford Administration played no role in sending mercenaries. Members of Congress refrained from any such accusations, but did express concern about the possibility of U.S. military involvement on Smith's side—particularly if Cuban troops joined the liberation forces. Representative Andrew Young, while visiting South Africa in 1974 with Arthur Ashe, had befriended jailed nationalist Robert Sobukwe. In 1975 two of Sobukwe's children moved into Young's home, where they remained for several years while they attended school.[83] Young emerged as a leading activist in the fight against the white regimes in southern Africa. He sought clear policy statements from the White House on ten separate points, including the American reaction to future Cuban involvement in Southern Rhodesia. National Security Council staffer Jeanne Davis responded that while Cuban involvement certainly would prompt an American response, military involvement was not an option. Davis outlined Ford Administration policy by reiterating Kissinger's basic plan: (1) support the British blueprint for majority rule, (2) get South Africa to lean on Smith, (3) consult with black Front Line leaders, and (4) repeal the Byrd Amendment.[84] Young must have been pleased by the response, for he later facilitated the success of this very policy as a member of the Jimmy Carter Administration.

For the rest of 1976 Young and his allies in Congress withheld any initiatives on Southern Rhodesia, postponing their next assault on the Byrd Amendment until after the fall elections. The White House also remained inert. President Ford was aware of the debate, especially the questions about the fate of whites. National Security Adviser Brent Scowcroft perused statistics regarding white migration to and from Southern Rhodesia. While they displayed some curiousity, Ford and Scowcroft took no significant action as the elections approached, content to leave that to Kissinger and his subordinates at State.[85]

In early August, American diplomats in southern Africa began arranging details for an upcoming visit by William Schaufele and William Rogers, Assistant Secretary for African Affairs and Undersecretary for Economic Affairs, respectively. Kissinger informed Nyerere and Kaunda that Schaufele and Rogers were coming to share the latest developments in U.S. talks with Great Britain, as well as to hear the Front Line leaders' latest views.[86] Meanwhile, Smith's Security Forces struck a brutal blow. Just after dawn on August 9, they swooped down on a camp of unarmed refugees at Nyadzonia, in Mozambique. Wearing Mozambique army uniforms and black face paint, Smith's men took the refugees utterly by surprise. Using anti-tank guns, they cut down at least 675 people, then dumped the bodies into ten mass graves.[87]

The Nyadzonia massacre, to say the least, decreased the likelihood for productive negotiations between Smith and the nationalists in the near future. Progress also faced the stumbling block of on-going quarrels among the nationalist leaders. During the last week of August, Rogers and Schaufele discussed this problem at length with Nyerere and Kaunda. Both presidents believed that the lack of unity in the liberation movement precluded a settlement in Southern Rhodesia, and that it would be better to focus on the dispute in Namibia. Schaufele responded that while Kissinger appreciated the challenges inherent in the situation, he hoped that the Front Line presidents could weld sufficient unity among the liberation forces to make transition to majority rule possible. Kissinger intended to meet with Vorster again; then, if Kaunda and Nyerere indicated that there was a reasonable possibility of reaching a settlement, he would fly to southern Africa.[88]

The new American ambassador to Zambia, Stephen Low, met personally with Nkomo on September 4 and highlighted the need for unity. Nkomo countered that the transition to Zimbabwe must be brought about by Zimbabweans, and that it could not be imposed from outside. Low appreciated Nkomo's view, but suggested he travel to Dar Es Salaam and talk with the other nationalists anyway.[89] Nkomo complied, and for four long days he haggled with Mugabe and Muzorewa. Nyerere, who had convened the summit, energetically re-enacted the proceedings for the U.S. ambassador: "Muzorewa says he will participate if Nkomo does first. Nkomo wants to get rid of Muzorewa... Mugabe has still another confused position." Nyerere believed an agreement possible if these three could get together, but he did not think that was imminent. He feared that Kissinger might be expecting to perform a miracle by returning to the region and felt such hopes were premature even for the master of shuttle diplomacy.[90]

While the nationalists argued in Dar, Kissinger rendez-voused with Vorster in Zurich. In the aftermath of the Nyadzonia massacre, the conflict seemed increasingly likely to escalate. If the fighting spread, it could draw in more outsiders. Cuban involvement, for example, might radicalize the liberation movement beyond a level with which the United States would be willing to work. Therefore, Kissinger hoped that Vorster could push Smith into a settlement before the future Zimbabwe was lost to extreme Marxism. Vorster and his advisers, for their part, seemed most concerned with the fate of whites after the transition to Zimbabwe. They advocated significant financial guarantees for whites who stayed, and also those who emigrated. Kissinger and Vorster did not exactly share the same priorities; nevertheless, they adjourned the meetings, agreeing that Vorster would lean harder on Smith, and that Kissinger would return to Africa later in the month.[91]

KISSINGER'S SECOND TRIP TO AFRICA

State's planning for the secretary's second Africa trip revealed much about Kissinger's strategy towards the dispute. He very much desired a success in the form of a signed agreement. He emphasized that he would therefore need to revisit Vorster: "If the present negotiations are to have a successful outcome, I will have to meet again with the South African Prime Minister." He would then meet with Nyerere or Kaunda, and he specified that whoever it was "should be mandated to conclude negotiations." As for the nationalists, he hoped to talk with Nkomo. He would consider speaking with others if they happened to be in his vicinity, but made it clear that American officials should not invite any except Nkomo. The secretary wanted his meeting with Nkomo to occur after he had met with the Front Line presidents and Vorster.[92] Kissinger's strategy, then, placed relatively little emphasis on learning the views of ZANU or ZAPU; instead it would utilize balance of power diplomacy to reach a rapid settlement, thus enhancing the secretary's image.

Kissinger departed from Washington on 13 September, and stopped first in Tanzania. Nyerere expressed his skepticism about working with Vorster and Smith. He suggested that if there were some miraculous breakthrough, Kissinger should just get an agreement on the principle of majority rule, leaving the details to the British. However, he predicted that Kissinger's chances of convincing Smith to accept majority rule were "nil." Kissinger, on the other hand, optimistically believed that the South African prime minister was "putting the screws on Rhodesia." Indeed, Smith and Vorster met in Pretoria on 14 September. As one of Smith's aids recalled: "Vorster started applying maximum pressure on Smith."[93]

At this point, Vorster began elucidating the writing on the wall for the stubborn Smith, who returned to Salisbury to ask the Parliament for a mandate to negotiate with Kissinger. They complied. Kissinger journeyed from Tanzania to Zambia on 16 September, discussing the situation briefly with Kaunda upon arrival. Kaunda underlined how much he wanted peace, and stressed the importance of getting Smith to accept the principle of majority rule. Late that night, Kissinger and several American and British diplomats gathered at the Intercontinental Hotel for an hour and assessed the prospects for a settlement. They knew from BBC reports that Smith had received a mandate from Parliament to "negotiate on the future of his country." Kissinger intended to meet with Smith in South Africa, but only if Vorster assured him that Smith had accepted majority rule. He joked that if this effort failed, he alone would "get the blame." He admitted that he was not sure how Vorster would get Smith to that point, adding: "I don't know what we will do if the South Africans don't produce him."[94]

The next morning, September 17, Kissinger and Kaunda talked extensively. They displayed mutual respect, at times speaking seriously and at other times jokingly. They agreed that a settlement would be difficult, but that they should maintain optimism. Kissinger admitted knowing little about the nationalists, adding that he liked Nkomo but neither he nor his colleagues knew Mugabe. Kaunda then spoke at length about the liberation movement, emphasizing his friendship with Nkomo and lack of knowledge about Mugabe.

At the most significant juncture, Kissinger outlined his proposals for the meetings in South Africa. He would only require the acceptance of the principle of majority rule, leaving arrangements of the details of the transition to Zimbabwe for a conference that would include the Salisbury regime and the nationalist groups. Such a strategy was exactly what Kaunda wanted and what Nyerere advocated. Ambassador Low, who attended the meeting, recalled that Kaunda was "impressed by Kissinger." Kaunda had no reason to doubt that the secretary would pursue the strategy of obtaining a general agreement only, and assured Kissinger that "you have our prayers."[95]

After the meeting concluded on this upbeat note, the secretary and his entourage flew to Pretoria and started another round of talks with the South African prime minister. Discussions between Kissinger and Vorster continued during the morning of the 18 September, as Smith was arriving from Salisbury. Smith and Vorster lunched, then attended a rugby match in the afternoon.[96] Vorster joined Kissinger for a late dinner at the U.S. Ambassador's residence that night. They discussed a Kissinger/Smith meeting proposed for the next morning, and the secretary stressed his desire for concrete results: "It cannot be that a meeting with him is without consequence."[97]

It had been agreed earlier that Vorster would call Smith with the logistics of a Kissinger/Smith meeting. The American Ambassador, William Bowdler, remarked that Smith was staying so close that Vorster could simply yell to him out the window. Kissinger quipped: "It would make a good news story!" Instead, Vorster and Smith talked by phone for about two minutes and agreed to a meeting the next morning. Afterwards, Vorster explained to Kissinger that Smith accepted the need for a settlement in principle, "but he wishes to raise certain issues with you."[98]

KISSINGER CONFRONTS SMITH

At 10 A.M. on Sunday morning, 19 September, Ian Smith encountered Henry Kissinger. Before full discussions, the two spoke privately for about 20 minutes. Reportedly, Kissinger laid down the law with Smith:

"Your reputation as a devious lying twister is even worse than mine. But let me warn you not to try any funny stuff with me because this time you will have met your match." Whether or not those were his exact words, there is no doubt that Kissinger rattled Smith. One of the Southern Rhodesian delegates observed: "I don't know what was said but Smith was far more pliable when we assembled than I had ever known him to be."[99]

After the delegations assembled, Kissinger lectured Smith and his cohorts on their grim predicament. He displayed an impressive knowledge of the military situation, pointing out that the dire economic picture would only worsen. He predicted that Smith could only last another three months in the face of the mounting crisis. After thus emphasizing the urgency of reaching a settlement, the secretary unveiled a five-point plan. The plan, designed mostly by the British, consisted of: (1) majority rule within two years, (2) immediate establishment of an interim government, with a half black and half white executive council, (3) British legislation allowing majority rule and independence, (4) termination of sanctions and guerrilla activities, and (5) foreign economic support.[100]

Smith read over the point proposing majority rule within two years and remarked: "You want me to sign my own suicide note." After this dramatic appeal for sympathy, he began his counter-offensive. He requested that the minister of defense and the minister of law and order both be white, for the duration of the interim government. Kissinger responded that it would be easier to get acceptance from the nationalists to a plan whereby one of those ministers was white, the other black. Smith agreed, but contended that his Parliament would only approve a settlement if both posts were reserved for whites.

They next considered the make-up of the interim government's executive council. Smith desired that the black members be approved by his Parliament. Kissinger challenged that point and opined that Kaunda would insist on a spot on the council for Nkomo. He added that Nyerere would want a ZANU leader on the council. Assistant Secretary Schaufele specified that Nyerere would probably want Mugabe on the council. Kissinger concluded that, in any case, the Front Line presidents and nationalist leaders must choose the black members of the council. After an intense four hours, the meeting broke up at 2 P.M.[101]

During the recess, the Southern Rhodesian negotiating team weighed their options. Smith felt that they had to accept the proposals laid out by Kissinger. He and his advisers agreed to fight for the clause guaranteeing that the Defense Department and the Law and Order Department would be headed by whites. They spoke with Vorster, who erased any doubts they may have had about the necessity of accepting the proposal. Kissinger, meanwhile, updated the press on the day's events. He characterized the chief results of the first meeting as "clarification."[102]

At 6 o'clock that evening, Vorster, Kissinger, and his entourage gathered to hear Smith's decision. First, however, Nancy Kissinger strolled into the room and gave Ian Smith, one of her "heroes," a hug. After Smith recovered from this unusual breech of diplomatic protocol, he got down to business. He accepted the five-point plan for majority rule; however, this was under the condition that Kissinger get the Front Line presidents' approval for his crucial amendment, that the ministers of defense and law/order be white for the duration of the interim government. If that stipulation was agreeable to Kissinger, then Smith would "recommend the package to his government."[103]

After three hours, the second and final Kissinger/Smith encounter concluded. Smith flew back to Salisbury to present the proposals to his government. Kissinger announced the developments to the press, with guarded optimism. He remained in Pretoria that night, conversing with Vorster about Southern Rhodesia one last time. Rogers and Schaufele, Kissinger's two top assistants on this project, informed him that they would continue to discuss economic components of the settlement with Smith's assistants. Kissinger expressed confidence that the Southern Rhodesians' questions should all be answered satisfactorily. Kissinger and Vorster both hoped that, by the end of the week, Smith would announce his acceptance of the five-point proposal.[104]

FRONT LINE AND NATIONALIST REACTION

Kissinger shuttled up to Zambia the following morning and talked with Kaunda and his advisers for over two hours in the afternoon. While most of the conversation focused on serious details regarding Southern Rhodesia, Kissinger at one point kidded with Kaunda: "I was criticized less on my first trip to Africa, when I did nothing.... Maybe I should go back to my original position." During another of the lighter moments, the secretary joked: "I'm going to blame you, Mr. President, for whatever happens. You were the first African president to insist that I come here." Kaunda promptly replied: "Forgive me for my sins."[105]

Kissinger described the five-point plan that he had proposed to Smith, beginning with majority rule within two years. He explained that Smith would probably accept the plan and announce it on Friday, but that Kaunda and Nyerere had to approve it first. Kaunda asked to examine Kissinger's notes on the proposal and wondered how the settlement was to be enforced. Kissinger responded that the provisional government in Salisbury during the interim period would be an unprecedented step towards majority rule, and that the Americans, British, and South Africans would monitor the proceedings.

Then, almost as an afterthought, Kissinger dropped the bomb: "There is one other thing they've asked for. They want to keep the Defense and Law and Order ministers for this two-year period." Kaunda paused, then commented: "Well, Mr. Secretary of State, I cannot say much at this juncture. I'll have to discuss this with my colleagues." Obviously, Kaunda was troubled by this clause that would keep real power in white hands. Kaunda's Home Affairs Minister, Aaron Milner, and his top adviser, Mark Chona, echoed his concern. Chona wondered whether Smith would be satisfied if one of those key ministers were white, the other black. Kissinger responded that Smith insisted both be white, in order to prevent the type of chaos that had occurred in Angola a few years before.[106] The secretary attempted to put the proposals into perspective:

> When you get a black government, a black Prime Minister, a fixed date for independence, and a suspended constitution, it is a new situation. You have to weigh this against the uncertain prospect, and continued fighting, of which you would have a major burden. This is what I want you to think about. We aren't pushing you; it's your decision.[107]

Kissinger claimed not to be pushing the President. Kaunda countered that in fact he was being pushed, since Smith was expected to make an announcement about the proposals in four days. The lengthy talks ended a little later with some more friendly banter, but it was clear that Kaunda was not optimistic about reaching a successful settlement based on Kissinger's proposals. Nonetheless, Kissinger informed Vorster that the talk with Kaunda had been "generally encouraging." He acknowledged that the Zambians had reacted unfavorably to Smith's clause but concluded that the reaction was "not unduly hostile." He seemed to think a solution could be reached, as long as Smith did not make any additional changes to the plan they had agreed to in Pretoria.[108]

The hope for any real long-term settlement based on that five-point plan received a serious setback the following day. Kissinger and Nkomo met briefly, and Nkomo examined the agreement that Smith was expected to announce. He objected to Kissinger having negotiated the make-up of the interim government. He concluded that the proposals had "very serious flaws." Later, he recalled that

"Kissinger's southern Africa proposals were not really concerned with African problems at all, but with super-power politics.... His ideas were of no interest to us."[109] There was the rub. Kissinger had not cleared the plan with the ZANU or ZAPU leaders before offering it to Smith; as it turned out, they rejected it outright.

Another problem with Kissinger's approach, at least from the perspective of many blacks in Africa and the United States, was his close cooperation with Vorster. As the negotiations took place, rioting raged across South Africa in the wake of a June police crackdown on students at Soweto. Concern about Kissinger's tactics in southern Africa prompted intense discussions during a Congressional Black Caucus conference in September. Many leading African Americans wanted to form a group to lobby for progressive policies towards Africa. As a result, Diggs and Young laid the foundation for TransAfrica.[110]

Unaware of these developments and undaunted by reality, Kissinger visited Nyerere in Tanzania on Wednesday, 22 September. Accounts vary about what he told the Front Line chair, and no memorandum of the conversation is available. There is no doubt, however, about what he did afterwards. He lied. He informed Vorster that both Kaunda and Nyerere found the proposals an "acceptable basis for settlement of the Rhodesian question." Even if by some chicanery Kissinger had been able to get Nyerere's approval for the plan, by no means had Kaunda agreed to it. Nkomo, furthermore, had rejected it, and that suggested that the more radical ZANU leaders in Mozambique would do the same. Nevertheless, the message that the proposals had been approved by the Front Line was passed on to Smith.[111]

Smith cajoled his cabinet and a 50-member parliamentary caucus into advocating the proposals. At 8 P.M. on Friday, 24 September, Smith spelled out the plan on Southern Rhodesian television. He explained that Southern Rhodesia would make the transition to majority rule within two years; however, he emphasized that sanctions and fighting would terminate, and that the Defense and Law/Order ministries would be in white hands. He couched the announcement in terms that would assuage white worries. Still, it was a remarkable speech from a man who had predicted earlier in the year that majority rule would not occur for a thousand years.

The State Department immediately circulated a statement by President Ford, which welcomed Smith's speech as "an act of realism" that represented the first step towards establishing the multiracial and independent nation of Zimbabwe. Ford praised the key contributions of the British, the South Africans, and the Front Line rulers. Not surprisingly, he made no mention of Nkomo or any other nationalists, since Kissinger's approach had ignored their views. In a separate message, Ford specifically thanked Vorster for his help regarding Southern Rhodesia and his kindness towards Kissinger.[112]

The day after Smith's address, the Front Line presidents convened in Zambia. They agreed that it was a positive step for the Salisbury regime to embrace a transition to majority rule. However, they decried just about all of the details of the plan. They espoused an all-parties conference outside of Southern Rhodesia, chaired by the British, to start from scratch on the arrangements for the transition to majority rule. The State Department praised the Front Line presidents' statement, emphasizing that majority rule was the main hurdle and that the details could be worked out at a conference. State's reaction cheered Nyerere, who did not want to seem ungrateful for what Kissinger had done. He explained that he and the other presidents simply did not trust Smith, fearing that he intended to maintain the traditional power structure under a facade of majority rule.[113]

Kissinger responded to the concerns of the Front Line presidents in detail a few days later. He reiterated his faith that an acceptable solution could be based on the five-point proposals. He asserted: "There is no possibility that, under the proposals, Smith can run the show. Indeed, once the interim government is formed, the present structure in Salisbury would disappear."[114] While Smith may not have been allowed to "run the show" during the transition period, it was disingenuous for Kissinger to claim that the present structure would disappear. Since the late 1950s, Southern Rhodesia had been virtually a police state. With the military and police under white control, the old structure would surely not change.

Details such as this were major stumbling blocks to a rapid settlement, but Kissinger did not come to grips with the facts. He urged the Front Line leaders to get the representatives of ZANU and ZAPU to the conference table with Smith. He argued that a breakdown would only bring an escalation in violence. He warned: "A decision not to accept the opportunity now offered would be a serious one. The opportunity now presented will not return." In truth, only the opportunity for Kissinger to get credit for a settlement would soon be gone and not return.[115] He realized that the approaching elections would probably end his tenure in government and any chance for him to receive lasting credit.

The liberation forces had a very different timetable. Kissinger had fundamentally misjudged their willingness to continue the war in order to get a truly acceptable settlement. For them, a settlement based on Kissinger's proposals was no settlement at all. They believed that more fighting would lead to opportunities for much better solutions in the future. At the urging of the Front Line, though, they agreed to attend a conference in October in Geneva. A few weeks before the gathering, Nkomo and Mugabe formed a loose coalition called the Patriotic Front.[116]

THE GENEVA CONFERENCE AND FORD'S DEFEAT
The Geneva Conference opened on 28 October, chaired by a former British ambassador to the UN, Ivor Richards. Nkomo, Mugabe, and Muzorewa entered the negotiations viewing the Kissinger proposals as only the most general starting point, while Smith claimed that they were a done deal, the approval of which was only a formality. Over the next seven weeks, the two sides never bridged the gap between their positions, dealing unsuccessfully with two main issues.[117]

First, they tackled the challenge of setting a specific date for independence. Nkomo and Mugabe wanted an early date, whereas Smith hoped for the maximum of two years stipulated under the Kissinger plan. The British advocated a compromise to the nationalists but then equivocated to the media. By late November, even Nyerere had lost faith that the British were earnestly pursuing an acceptable settlement in Geneva. Discussing the British obfuscation of the independence date, Nyerere exclaimed: "Tell Kissinger they are making us look like damn fools!"[118]

With Nyerere's loss of optimism, Nkomo and Mugabe felt little reason to negotiate. Discussions turned to the issue of whether or not whites should be guaranteed control of the Defense and Law/ Order Ministries during the transition. There was even less hope for compromise on this point than on the independence date, and no breakthrough occurred. The Geneva Conference disbanded on 14 December, with the only significant achievement being the formation of a loose coalition between Nkomo and Mugabe. Known as the Patriotic Front, this coalition functioned throughout the subsequent three years of negotiations.[119]

The Geneva Conference failed to end the conflict in Southern Rhodesia for many reasons. One important shortcoming of the conference was the absence of top-level involvement by the British or the U.S. Had Foreign Minister Anthony Crosland or Kissinger himself orchestrated the events, progress may have been achieved. That was unlikely, however, considering the inflexibility of the two sides. In the words of former ambassador Steve Low, there was no "hurting stalemate" at Geneva. Low elaborated: "Put another way, each side believed it had more to gain by continuing the warfare than making the compromises asked of it."[120]

Low, then, suggested that even direct involvement by Kissinger at Geneva would not have made a difference. If he had, moreover, it would have been with decreased leverage. Shortly after the conference opened, Jimmy Carter triumphed over Ford, making Kissinger a lameduck. The loss came as no surprise to the secretary; in fact, he referred to the possibility of defeat throughout 1976, and was always well aware of impending elections.[121] Critics of Kissinger at the time and afterwards accused him of seeking majority rule in Southern Rhodesia in hopes of gaining liberal support for Ford's re-election, suggesting that Kissinger desired a quick solution to help Ford win in November.[122]

Kissinger rejected their view as "palpable poppycock." He added: "President Ford put his nomination at risk in launching and sustaining this effort." The secretary had a point. While it would be difficult to measure, it seems that Kissinger's trip to Africa in April boosted Ronald Reagan's challenge for the nomination more than his diplomacy helped Ford in November. The criticism that Kissinger conducted the September negotiations in Africa rapidly, at the expense of details, certainly was accurate. He repeatedly stressed the urgency of reaching a settlement quickly.[123] But the contention that he hoped to thereby help Ford remain in office misses the mark. He expected to be out of office shortly and did not think a Southern Rhodesian settlement would help much anyway. Achieving a solution quickly, however, would associate his name with it and add one more notch in his belt. It wasn't to be. Geneva fizzled, Ford lost, and the challenge of mediating the dispute was passed on to the administration of Jimmy Carter.

CONCLUSION

What can we conclude about Henry Kissinger's foray into African affairs in 1976? On one level, his efforts regarding Southern Rhodesia were a failure, reinforcing scholarly conclusions about his personal flaws. The war raged for three more years, during which Smith and his Rhodesian Front party retained control of the power structure to a great extent. Kissinger's unsuccessful effort resulted from many of the characteristics for which scholars generally criticize him: (1) a desire for individual glory, (2) a willingness to distort the truth, (3) a tendency to ignore the circumstances within a nation in favor of global balance of power considerations, and (4) a disregard for crucial details.[124] Kissinger's tactical mistakes, especially deceiving the Front Line and ignoring the views of Nkomo and Mugabe, foiled any hope of a settlement in 1976.

On the other hand, in some ways Kissinger succeeded. A consensus exists regarding the importance of Kissinger's coercing Smith to accept majority rule, which was the first step towards an independent Zimbabwe. After Smith endorsed it on television, there was no going back.[125] Kissinger's prestige was an important factor in wringing this concession from Smith.[126] Success or failure aside, personal mediation in the dispute by an American official at so high a level as secretary of state set a precedent. Kissinger's activity in 1976 represented a dramatic departure from his earlier indifference to Southern Rhodesia, and that of his predecessors. Kissinger's successor, Cyrus Vance, carried on the 1976 policy of personal diplomacy, with assistance from Andrew Young and President Carter himself. Kissinger deserves some credit, then, for initiating the high-level U.S. mediation that would eventually contribute to the formation of Zimbabwe. He had not "slain the dragon," but he had led the Carter Administration to the dragon's lair.

NOTES

1. Former U.S. ambassador to Zambia Steve Low offered this explanation for Henry Kissinger's 1976 interest in Southern Rhodesia in an interview with the author on 11 November 1995 .

2. Kissinger's diplomacy in 1976 is treated in great detail in Walter Isaacson, *Kissinger: A Biography* (New York: Simon and Schuster, 1992), 685-692; David Martin and Phyllis Johnson, *The Struggle for Zimbabwe: The Chimurenga War* (Boston: Faber and Faber, 1981), 215-263; and Martin Meredith, *The Past Is Another Country: Rhodesia UDI to Zimbabwe* (London: Pan, 1980), 50, 221-222, 251-260. None of these works utilized unpublished primary documents. This chapter is based significantly on such material obtained from archives and from the State Department via the Freedom of Information Act.

3. Press Release, "Muskie Deplores Racist Policy," 14 March 1972, Folder 3, Box 1889, U.S. Senate: Senate Office Series, Edmund S. Muskie Collection, Edmund S. Muskie Archives, Bates College, Lewiston, ME (hereafter ESM).

4. Rogers and Nixon cited in John Copson, *Executive-Legislative Consultation on Foreign Policy: Sanctions Against Rhodesia, Foreign Affairs Committee Print, Congress and Foreign Policy Series, No. 6* (Washington: U.S. Government Printing Office, 1982), 26.

5. Bush speech at Tulane University quoted in 23 April 1972 *Washington Star*, clipping in "1972 Jan-May Rhodesia: Chrome," Box 160, Accession #10320, Harry F. Byrd, Jr. Papers, Special Collections Department, Alderman Library, University of Virginia, Charlottesville, VA (hereafter HB).

6. For McGee's explanation of the the events leading up to the vote see "Sanctions as as Instrumentality of the United Nations - Rhodesia as a Case Study," Hearings Before the Subcommittee on International Organizations and Movements of the Committee on House Foreign Affairs, House of Representatives, Ninety Second Congress, Second Session, June 13, 15, and 19, 1972, 131-134. For ACOA and church support for repeal see joint letter to Senators, 15 May 1972, Folder 17, Box 1647, ESM.

7. James F. Collins, Senior Vice President, American Iron and Steel Institute, to Senators, 28 April 1972, copy and cover-memo in "1972 Jan-May Rhodesia: Chrome," Box 160, HB.

8. An unnamed congressional aid described Dole's actions in William Raspberry, "McGee Feels Let Down," *Washington Post*, 5 June

1972, clipping in "Rhodesian Chrome," Box 191, Charles Diggs Papers, Moorland-Spingarn Research Center, Howard University Archives, Washington, DC (hereafter CD).

9. See McGee's 19 June testimony, Hearings Before the Subcommittee on International Organizations and Movements of the Committee on House Foreign Affairs, 131-134. A copy of the testimony can also be found in "Rhodesian Chrome-Nickel," Box 191, CD.

10. Diggs statement at Union Carbide Stockholders Meeting, 18 April 1972, "Rhodesian Chrome," Box 191, CD. For an insightful discussion of activists' early efforts to influence corporations, see Robert Massie, *Loosing the Bonds: The United States and South Africa in the Apartheid Years* (New York: Doubleday, 1997), 263-332.

11. United States District Court for the District of Columbia, Civil Action No. 773-72, *Charles Coles Diggs, Shirley Anita Chisholm, et al., Plaintiffs, v. John B. Connally, Secretary of the Treasury of the United States, et al., Defendants*, Filed by Clerk James F. Davey, 19 June 1972, copy in "1972 June Rhodesia: Chrome," Box 160, HB. Among those joining the Caucus in bringing the suit were Gore Vidal, whose books were banned in Southern Rhodesia.

12. See *Rhodesia Herald*, 22 April 1972, clipping, ibid.

13. Harry R. Strack, *Sanctions: The Case of Rhodesia* (Syracuse: Syracuse University Press, 1978), 148-149.

14. Louis Stokes, chair, and ten other CBC members, to Nixon, 13 December 1972, "CO 124 Rhodesia 1/1/73 - ," Box 62, White House Central Files - Countries (hereafter WHCF-CO), Nixon Presidential Materials, National Archives II, College Park, MD (hereafter NP).

15. Sithole to Nixon, enclosed in Cable, U.S. Embassy, Lusaka, Zambia to State Department, 22 January 1972, "CO 170 Zambia 1/1/71," Box 88; Nixon to Julius Nyerere, President of Tanzania, 28 December 1971, "CO 124 Rhodesia 1/1/71-," Box 62, WHCF-CO, NP.

16. For a thorough discussion of these events, see Abel Muzorewa, *Rise Up and Walk: An Autobiography* (London: Evans Brothers, 1978), 92-117.

17. The significance of the Pearce Commission is emphasized in James Scarritt, "Zimbabwe: Revolutionary Violence Resulting in Reform," in Jack Goldstone, ed. *Revolutions of the Late Twentieth Century* (Boulder: Westview Press, 1991), 249-250.

18. Martin and Johnson, *Struggle for Zimbabwe*, xiv, 73-74, and 90-91. The incredible efforts of Samora Machel, leader of the rebels in

Mozambique, to assist the ZANU guerrillas is described in Iain Christie, *Samora Machel: A Biography* (London: Zed, 1989), 79.

19.   The Washington Office on Africa (WOA) monitored legislation regarding U.S. policy towards Africa. It was supported by a number of churches and the American Committee on Africa. For information on the closing of ferrochrome plants, see WOA memo, 25 January 1973; Edgar Lockwood, WOA chair, to Diggs, 8 February 1973; and Lockwood to Senator Edward Kennedy, 6 February 1973, "Zim/Rhod: Byrd Amendment," Box 192, CD.

20.   Humphrey and 5 co-sponsors to "Dear Colleague," 27 April 1973, Folder 7, Box 1998, ESM. Henry Kissinger, then National Security Adviser, indicated to Representative Donald Fraser in a 29 March 1973 meeting of the House Foreign Affairs Committee that he was concerned about the Byrd Amendment's negative impact on U.S. foreign relations. He offered to call Senator Humphrey to discuss repeal, but it is not clear whether or not he did. See Fraser to Kissinger, 9 April 1973, "CO 124 Rhodesia 1/1/73-," Box 62, WHCF-CO, NP.

21.   Hearings Before the Subcommittee on Africa of the Committee on Foreign Affairs, House of Representatives, Ninety-third Congress, First Session, October 5 and 17, 1973, "The Repeal of the Rhodesian Chrome Amendment" (Washington: U.S.G.P., 1974), 1.

22.   Anthony Lake, *The "Tar Baby" Option: American Policy Toward Southern Rhodesia* (New York: Columbia University Press, 1976), 270-271.

23.   Text of Warren's speech before the Ralph Bunche Development Committee, Chicago, Il., 16 June 1973, copy in "Zim/Rhod: Sanctions," Box 192, CD. Warren's argument appealed strongly to Diggs, as his attached handwritten note attests: "Plug *intl law* violation (half Congr are lawyers)."

24.   Diane Polan, *Irony in Chrome* (New York: Carnegie Endowment, 1973), in Folder 7, Box 1998, ESM. Anthony Lake directed the larger project of which Polan's 37 page booklet was a part. He included a revised version in his *"Tar Baby" Option*, 239-269.

25.   Diggs to Mr. E. Gleason, International Longshoremen's Association, New York, NY, 18 June 1973, "Zim/Rhod: Sanctions;" Walter Simpson, Western New York Peace Center, Buffalo, to Diggs, 28 July 1973; Lucy Wilson Benson, President, League of Women Voters, to Diggs, 5 October 1973, "Zim/Rhod: Byrd Amendment," Box 192, CD.

26.   Digg's staffer rejoiced at receiving word from the White House at "long last," and Diggs entered the letter into the Congressional

Record. Flanigan to Diggs, 26 June 1973; attached memo from Barbara (Digg's staffer) to Diggs and Digg's handwritten note, 27 June 1973; attached draft of item for Congressional Record, "Zim/Rhod: Sanctions," Box 192, CD.

27. U.S. Congress. Senate. Committee on Foreign Relations. Nomination of Henry A. Kissinger. Hearings, 93d Cong., 1st sess., Sept.7, 10, 11, and 14, 1973. (Washington: U.S.G.P.O., 1973), 48.

28. For details about the Senate Foreign Relations Committee's handling of Humphrey's bill, see Lake, *"Tar Baby" Option*, 272-273.

29. Kissinger to Diggs, 3 October 1973, original copy in "Zim/Rhod: Sanctions," Box 192, CD. A press release by the UPI on 5 October summarized the letter. See "Rhodesia," Box 124, Ron Nessen Papers, Gerald R. Ford Library, Ann Arbor, MI (hereafter GF).

30. House Subcommittee on Africa. Repeal of the Rhodesian Chrome Amendment. October 5 and 17, 1973, 1-5.

31. "US, Rhodesia and a World of Law," *Los Angeles Times*, 17 October 1973, clipping in "Zim/Rhod: Sanctions," Box 192, CD.

32. Timmons to Joan Neil, Chair, Peace and International Relations Committee, Illinois Conference of the United Church of Christ, 27 October 1973, "CO 124 Rhodesia 1/1/73-," Box 62, WHCF-CO, NP.

33. Digg's handwritten note attached to a copy of the Congressional Record for 3 October 1973, in "Zim/Rhod: Sanctions," Box 192, CD.

34. Korologos to McGee, 27 December 1973, "CO 124 Rhodesia 1/1/73-," Box 62, WHCF-CO, NP. For details of the efforts by Robert Byrd and other events surrounding the 18 December vote, see Lake, *"Tar Baby" Option*, 273-274.

35. Typed notes, *Meeting Re: Byrd Amendment*, Diggs and staffers, 26 February 1974, "Zim/Rhod: Byrd Amendment," Box 192, CD. The leader of the NAACP, among others, offered to help. See Roy Wilkins to Diggs, 22 February 1974, "Byrd Amend - Gen," Box 110, CD.

36. Telegram, Ford to Diggs, 4 January 1974; letters to Diggs from various companies, February 1974, in "Zim/Rhod: Byrd Amend," Box 192, CD.

37. Strack, *Sanctions*, 150. For an enthusiastic response to the committee's vote, see Siteke Mwale, Zambian Ambassador, to Diggs, 18 July 1974, "Byrd Amend - Gen," Box 110, CD. Representative Bella Abzug (D-N.Y.) expressed her support for repeal in a 9 July 1974 letter to the Washington Office on Africa, cited in Rhodri Jeffreys-Jones, *Changing Differences: Women and the Shap-*

ing of American Foreign Policy, 1917-1994 (New Brunswick: Rutgers University Press, 1995), 147.

38. Whip Poll Results on S.1868, 29 July 1974, "Rhodesian Chrome," Box 15, Freidersdorf Files, GF.

39. Young to "Dear Friend," 19 July 1974; Diggs to "Dear Friend," 6 August 1974, "Byrd Amend - Gen," Box 110, CD.

40. Charles Rangel of the Congressional Black Caucus and Donald Fraser, two of Diggs' staunch allies, cabled Ford on 14 August and 15 August, respectively. See White House acknowledgments, 19 August 1974, "CO 124: Rhodesia, 8/9/74-5/31/76," Box 43, WHCF-CO, GF.

41. Jerald terHorst, press secretary to Harry Byrd, 28 August 1974, ibid.

42. Andrew Biemiller, Director of the AFL-CIO legislation department, to Diggs, 16 August 1974; Jack Beidler, UAW Legislative Director, to "Dear Representative," 23 July 1974; telegram, Ford to Diggs, 12 September 1974, "Byrd Amend - Gen," Box 110, CD.

43. Massie, *Loosing the Bonds*, 389-390.

44. Diggs to over 200 corporations, 22 November 1974, "Byrd Amend - Gen," Box 110, CD. For decisions not to hold votes, see Strack, *Sanctions*, 150 and Lake, *"Tar Baby" Option*, 275. When the chairman of Knight Newspapers, James Knight, visited Ian Smith during the summer of 1974, Smith proposed that the Ford Motor Company sell his country 10,000 cars. Knight relayed the idea to Henry Ford II, but nothing evidently came of it. See Knight to Harry Byrd, 15 November 1974, "Foreign Relations: Rhodesia, 1973-75," Box 283, HB.

45. Lake, *"Tar Baby" Option*, 275.

46. Martin and Johnson, *The Struggle for Zimbabwe*, 115-121; Christie, *Samora Machel*, 85.

47. Carol Thompson, *Challenge to Imperialism: The Frontline States in the Liberation of Zimbabwe* (Boulder: Westview Press, 1985), 12-14; Stephen Chan, *Kaunda and Southern Africa: Image and Reality in Foreign Policy* (London: British Academic, 1992), 78-79.

48. Martin and Johnson, *The Struggle for Zimbabwe*, 145-147. In July 1974 Smith's security forces moved 44,000 blacks into 21 protected villages. This mirrored U.S. and French strategy in Vietnam. See Meredith, *The Past Is Another Country*, 136.

49. Martin and Johnson, *The Struggle for Zimbabwe*, 148-157; Nkomo, *Nkomo: The Story of My Life* (London: Methuen, 1984), 119.

50. Martin and Johnson, *The Struggle for Zimbabwe*, 204-207; Christie, *Samora Machel*, 95; Xan Smiley, "Zimbabwe, Southern Africa and the Rise of Robert Mugabe," *Foreign Affairs* 58, #5 (Summer 1980), 1060-1083, at 1062. Christie wrote that Mugabe crossed into Mozambique in March, Smiley wrote that it was in April.

51. Thompson, *Challenge to Imperialism*, 26 and 50; Martin and Johnson, *Struggle for Zimbabwe*, 205.

52. Kenneth Kaunda, "Response to a Toast," 19 April 1975, "Zambia," Box 192, CD; Meredith, *Past Is Another Country*, 218-219.

53. Discussion of Brown's activities in notes for Press Conference, 24 June 1975, "Rhodesia," Box 124, Ron Nessen Papers; Chesley Peterson to Gerald Ford, 24 November 1975, and Roland Elliott, director of White House correspondence, to Peterson, 31 December 1975, "CO 124 Rhodesia 8/9/74-5/31/76," Box 43, WHCF-Subject, GF.

54. H.R. 1287, "A Bill to Amend the United States Participation Act of 1945 to Halt the Importation of Rhodesian Chrome," Committee Print, 18 March 1975, "6/19/75 Hearings on Rhodesian Chrome (2)," Box 18, David Macdonald Papers (hereafter DM), GF. Memo, "H.R. 1287, Rhodesian Chrome," Vern Loen to Brent Scowcroft, 18 March 1975, "Rhodesian Chrome," Freidersdorf Files, Box 15, GF. Buchanan had supported the Byrd Amendment until 1973, but observing proceedings at the United Nations that year convinced him that it should be repealed. See Lake, *"Tar Baby" Option*, 274.

55. Memo, "Max Friedersdorf's request for guidance on H.R. 1287 - Rhodesian Chrome," 3 April 1975, "Co 124: Rhodesia, 8/9/74-5/ 31/76," Box 43, WHCF-Sub, GF. Fraser to William Simon, Secretary of Treasury, 17 June 1975; Fraser's opening statement on Certificate of Origin Amendment, 19 June 1975; Statement of David Macdonald, Assistant Secretary of the Treasury, released 22 June 1975, "6/19/75 Hearings on Rhodesian Chrome (1)," Box 18, DM, GF.

56. Strack, *Sanctions*, 150. McGee to Perry Wilson, Chairmen of the Board of Union Carbide, 15 September 1975, Folder 3, Box 542, Series III, Gale McGee Collection, Accession #9800, American Heritage Center, Laramie, WY (hereafter GM). Central Intelligence Agency, "United States: Imports from Sub-Saharan Africa, by Major Product, 1975," attached to memo, Rick Inderfurth to Zbigniew Brzezinski, 5 April 1977, "Southern Africa (3/77-4/77)," Box 14, Brzezinski Donated Papers, Jimmy Carter Library, Atlanta, GA (hereafter JCL).

57. Press Conference notes, "President's Position on Byrd Amendment," 28 August 1975; and "Rhodesian Embargo," 26 September 1975, "Rhodesia," Box 124, Ron Nessen Papers, GF.

58. Memo, Freidersdorf to Ford, "Representative Edward J. Derwinski," 3 November 1975, "CO 124 Rhodesia, 8/9/74-5/31/76," Box 43, WHCF-Sub; Memo, "House vote on H.R. 1287," 4 November 1975, "Countries-Rhodesia, Box 7, Presidential Handwriting Files, GF. Both memos are marked "The President has seen."

59. Confidential White House Memo, "Meeting with Senator Gale McGee and Congressmen Donald M. Fraser and John Buchanan," with attached handwritten notes, 4 November 1975, "Rhodesian Chrome," Box 15, Freidersdorf Files, GF.

60. James Connor memo to Max Friedersdorf, "Rhodesian Chrome," 19 November 1975; Friedersdorf memo to Ford, "Rhodesian Chrome," 15 November 1975, with attached handwritten note from Ford to "Max;" Vern Loen memo to Friedersdorf, "Rhodesian Chrome bill," 14 November 1975, "Countries - Rhodesia," Box 7, Presidential Handwriting File, GF.

61. Thomas Noer, *Cold War and Black Liberation: The United States and White Rule in Africa, 1948-1968* (Columbia: University of Missouri Press, 1985), 242-244; Robert Shepard, *Nigeria, Africa, and the United States: From Kennedy to Reagan* (Bloomington: Indiana University Press, 1991), 84-88; Isaacson, *Kissinger*, 675-685.

62. Robert D. Schulzinger, *Henry Kissinger: Doctor of Diplomacy* (New York: Columbia University Press, 1989), 222-224.

63. Sheperd, *Nigeria, Africa, and the United States*, 88-89.

64. For the view that the blocking of funds for Angola by Congress convinced Kissinger to try diplomacy regarding Southern Rhodesia, see Jeffrey Davidow, *A Peace in Southern Africa: The Lancaster House Conference on Rhodesia, 1979* (Boulder: Westview Press, 1984), 20.

65. Stephen Low, "The Zimbabwe Settlement, 1976-1979," in Saadia Tauval and I. William Zartman, eds., *International Mediation in Theory and Practice* (Boulder: Westview Press, 1985), 96-98.

66. Statement by Charles Diggs at National Black Political Assembly, Cincinnati, March 18-20, 1976, in "Democratic Party Foreign Affairs," Box 110, CD. Digg's arguments drew upon the resolutions of the Democratic Foreign Affairs Task Force's Study Group on Africa, which included future Carter Administration officials Anthony Lake and Donald McHenry. The resolutions and the list of Task Force members are attached to Digg's statement.

67. Clark' view and Talleyrand's "foreseeing the inevitable" in Isaacson, *Kissinger*, 685-686. Possibility of liberal support for Ford noted in Noer, *Cold War and Black Liberation*, 244. "Dragon to slay" phrase used by Stephen Low in interview with the author, 13 November 1995.

68. Martin and Johnson, *Struggle for Zimbabwe*, 222-226. Smith quoted in George Houser, *No One Can Stop the Rain: Glimpses of Africa's Liberation Struggle* (New York: Pilgrim Press, 1989), 329.

69. Appendix, "The Road to Geneva," in Christopher Nyangoni and Gideon Nyandoro, eds., *Zimbabwe Independence Movements: Select Documents* (New York: Harper Row, 1979), 450-451. Martin and Johnson, *Struggle for Zimbabwe*, 229; Low, "Zimbabwe Settlement," 91. Low emphasized that the Callaghan's basic formula remained throughout the ensuing four years of negotiations.

70. Excerpts from Kissinger's 22 March speech in Dallas included in "Kissinger on U.S. Intentions on Rhodesia and Cuba," 23 March 1976, in "Rhodesia," Box 124, Ron Nessen Papers, GF.

71. Confidential Telegrams, State Department to U.S. Embassy in Lusaka, Zambia, 13 April 1976; State to Lusaka, 16 April 1976; U.S. Embassy in Dar Es Salaam, Tanzania to State, 16 April 1976; Lusaka to State, 18 April 1976; Lusaka to State, 19 April 1976; and State to Lusaka, 19 April 1976. These six telegrams are on microfiche in possession of the author, received from the State Department through the Freedom of Information Act (FIA). Documents from those fiche will hereafter be identified by "FIA 8802541."

72. Isaacson, *Kissinger*, 687.

73. Nkomo, *Nkomo*, 171.

74. Talking points for press conference on "Rhodesian Dispute," with handwritten note concluding that the U.S. had taken sides against Smith, in "Kissinger Trip to Africa," Box 16, Michael Raoul-Duval Papers, GF; Lusaka to State, 18 April 1976, FIA 8802541.

75. Henry Kissinger, "Address at a Luncheon in the Secretary's Honor," State House, Lusaka, Zambia, 27 April 1976, 1-2, in "Kissinger Trip to Africa," Box 16, Michael Raoul-Duval Papers, GF.

76. *Ibid*, 3-6.

77. Smith quoted in Meredith, *Past Is Another Country*, 222; Daniel Kempton, *Soviet Strategy Toward Southern Africa: The National Liberation Movement Connection* (New York: Praeger, 1989), 117.

78. Reagan quoted in Jon Nordheimer, "Reagan Attacks Kissinger for His Stand on Rhodesia," *The New York Times*, 1 May 1976.

79. George Kennan, "Surfacing Doubts about Black Rule," *The New York Times*, 2 May 1976, in Folder 7, Box 550, GM; Patrick

Buchanan, "Pie in the Sky Over Nairobi," released by *The New York Times* special features, 11 May 1976, in "Kissinger Trip to Africa," Box 16, Raoul-Duval Papers, GF. For staffers' efforts, see handwritten note to Duval from Dick Cheney, 12 May 1976; memos from Duval to Cheney and Warren Hendricks with attached talking points, 12 and 14 May, 1976, in "Kissinger Trip to Africa," Box 16, Raoul-Duval Papers, GF.

80.   Harry F. Byrd, Jr., "Rhodesian Chrome: The President's Options," speech in the Senate, 6 May 1976; notes of conversation between Byrd and Kissinger at meeting of Senate Foreign Relations Committee, 13 May 1976, in "1976 May 1-13 For Rel Rhod," Box 284, HB.

81.   Martin and Johnson, *Struggle for Zimbabwe*, 239; Nyangoni and Nyandoro, *Zimbabwe Independence Movements*, 451; talking points for press conference, "HAK-Vorster Meeting," 24 June 1976, "Rhodesia," Box 124, Ron Nessen Papers, GF.

82.   Muzorewa speech in Dar Es Salaam, 31 May 1976, and Sithole speech at UN, 8 June 1976, in Nyangoni and Nyandoro, *Zimbabwe Independence Movements*, 410, 422-423. Meredith, *Past Is Another Country*, 231. William Minter, *King Solomon's Mines Revisited: Western Interests and the Burdened History of Southern Africa* (New York: Basic Books, 1986), 276. The author's uncle Don Feeney, a Vietnam veteran, vividly recalls the widespread attempts to recruit mercenaries for Southern Rhodesia in the mid-1970s.

83.   Benjamin Pogrund, *Sobukwe and Apartheid* (New Brunswick: Rutgers University Press, 1991), 325-326; Massie, *Loosing the Bonds*, 407.

84.   Jeanne Davis, NSC Staff Secretary, to Young, 22 June 1976, and "Answers to Questions posed by Congressman Young;" Young to Davis, 19 May 1976, with list of ten questions, in "CO 124: Rhodesia (2) 6/1/76-1/20/77," Box 43, WHCF-Subject, GF.

85.   Ford highlighted a 20 July 1976 *New York Times* article about a guarantee plan for whites, and asked Scowcroft for his reaction. See the article and handwritten note in "Countries - Rhodesia," Presidential Handwriting Files, GF. Scowcroft received statistics from Richard Sykes of the British Foreign Office, a friend with whom he had dined at George and Barbara Bush's house. See Scowcroft to Sykes, 5 July 1976, and attachments, in "CO 124: Rhodesia (2), 6/1/76-1/20/77," Box 43, WHCF-Subject, GF.

86.   Kissinger to Nyerere, 11 August 1976; Kissinger to Kaunda, 11 August 1976; and U.S. Embassy Lusaka to State, 11 August 1976, in the microfiche collection *South Africa: The Making of U.S. Policy,*

1962-1989 (Washington: National Security Archive, 1991), documents 606, 607, and 608.

87. Martin and Johnson, *Struggle for Zimbabwe*, 240-242.

88. Schaufele to Kissinger, 28 August 1976; Kissinger to Nyerere, drafted by Schaufele and Rogers, 31 August 1976; and similar message from Kissinger to Kaunda, 1 September 1976, in *South Africa: The Making of U.S. Policy, 1962-1989*, documents 615, 617, and 619.

89. Low to State, 4 September 1976, FIA 8802541. The key role played by Low in U.S. relations with Zimbabwe was first brought to the author's attention by former ambassador Donald McHenry in a phone conversation on 17 July 1995.

90. Martin and Johnson, *Struggle for Zimbabwe*, 244-245. Spain, U.S. Ambassador in Dar, to State, 9 and 11 September 1976, FIA 8802541.

91. Kissinger to British Foreign Secretary Anthony Crosland, sent from Kissinger's plane, 14 September 1976, FIA 8802541.

92. Quotations from Kissinger to Embassies in Dar and Lusaka, and Kissinger to Dar, "The Secretary's Africa Trip," 10 September 1976, FIA 8802541. Discussion of meeting Nkomo but no other nationalists in Kissinger to Lusaka, 12 September 1976; Stephen Low to State, 13 September 1976; Low to Dar for Kissinger, 15 September 1976; and Kissinger to Low, 16 September 1976, ibid.

93. Meredith, *Past Is Another Country*, 251-257; Thompson, *Challenge to Imperialism*, 30; quotations from Martin and Johnson, *Struggle for Zimbabwe*, 248-249. Smith later strongly condemned Vorster for his overall policy towards Southern Rhodesia in 1976. See Ian Smith, *The Great Betrayal: The Memoirs of Africa's Most Controversial Leader* (London: Blake Publishing, 1997).

94. Peter Rodman, NSC Staffer, memorandum of conversation among Kissinger, Rogers, Schaufele, Low, and British diplomats Patrick Miles and Richard Samuel, 16 September 1976, FIA 8802541.

95. Rodman, memo of conversation among Kaunda, his special assistant Mark Chona, Kissinger, Rogers, Schaufele, and Low, 17 September 1976, Lusaka, FIA 8802541. Quotation by Low from Low to the author, 17 July 1995. Low, in an interview with the author on 13 November 1995, remembered Kaunda's joking about American official protocol, among other things.

96. Meredith, *Past Is Another Country*, 253. Evidently, Vorster forced Smith to sit in a separate section at the match. See Smith, *The Great Betrayal*, 201.

97. Rodman, memo of conversation among Vorster, Foreign Affairs Secretary Brad Fourie, Kissinger, Rogers, Schaufele, and U.S. Ambassador to South Africa William Bowdler, 18 September 1976, FIA 8802541.

98. *Ibid.*

99. "Lying twister" quote in Meredith, *Past Is Another Country*, 50. Comment by Smith's aide in Martin and Johnson, *Struggle for Zimbabwe*, 250. Smith recalled the events somewhat differently. He praised Kissinger's tone and intentions, and placed all blame on Vorster. See Smith, *The Great Betrayal*, 201-208.

100. Meredith, *Past Is Another Country*, 254; Thompson, *Challenge to Imperialism*, 30-31.

101. "Suicide note" quotation in Meredith, *Past Is Another Country*, 254. Discussion about ministers and council in Martin and Johnson, *Struggle for Zimbabwe*, 250-251.

102. Martin and Johnson, *Struggle for Zimbabwe*, 251. The key role of Vorster is discussed in a 1987 BBC interview by Ian Smith, in Michael Charlton, *The Last Colony in Africa: Diplomacy and the Independence of Rhodesia* (London: Basil Blackwell, 1990), 3. Kissinger's afternoon press statement enclosed in telegram from Pretoria to State, 19 September 1976, FIA 8802541.

103. Martin and Johnson, *Struggle for Zimbabwe*, 252. Martin and Johnson got these descriptions of the meetings in a 1980 interview with a member of Smith's delegation. Smith recalled the meeting with the "pleasant" Nancy Kissinger, wishing it could have lasted longer. See Smith, *The Great Betrayal*, 206.

104. Kissinger's evening press statement in telegram from Pretoria to State, 19 September 1976. Rodman memorandum of conversation among Vorster, Muller, Botha, Kissinger, Rogers, and Schaufele, 19 September 1976, Pretoria, FIA 8802541.

105. Rodman memorandum of conversation among Kissinger, Schaufele, Kaunda, Chona, and Aaron Milner, Zambian Minister of Home Affairs, 20 September 1976, Lusaka, FIA 8802541, pg. 6.

106. *Ibid.*, 4, 12, and 13.

107. *Ibid.*, 14.

108. Kissinger message to Vorster, in telegram from Lusaka to Pretoria, 20 September 1976, FIA 8802541.

109. "Serious flaws" quotation in Zambia *Daily Mail*, 23 September 1976, cited in Martin and Johnson, *Struggle for Zimbabwe*, 253. Kissinger/Nkomo meeting in Meredith, *Past Is Another Country*, 258. Description of Kissinger's proposals in Nkomo, *Nkomo*, 11.

110. Randall Robinson, *Defending the Spirit: A Black Life in America* (New York: Penguin, 1998), 96-97.

111. Martin and Johnson, *Struggle for Zimbabwe*, 253; Meredith, *Past Is Another Country*, 259. Message from Kissinger to Vorster, in telegram from Dar Es Salaam to Pretoria, 22 September 1976, FIA 8802541. For another analysis that condemns Kissinger's dishonesty, see Stephen Stedman, *Peacemaking in Civil War: International Mediation in Zimbabwe, 1974-1980* (Boulder: Lynn Reiner, 1991), 120.

112. Statement by Ford, 24 September 1976, in telegram from Kissinger to U.S. embassies in Africa. Message from Ford to Vorster, in telegram from State to Pretoria, 25 September 1976, FIA 8802541.

113. Front Line presidents' Lusaka statement summarized in Thompson, *Challenge to Imperialism*, 31. State response in telegram to all U.S. embassies in Africa, 26 September 1976. Summary of Nyerere's conversation with U.S. ambassador in Tanzania, James Spain, in telegram from Dar to State, 27 September 1976, FIA 8802541.

114. Kissinger message for Machel, in telegram from New York to Maputo, 29 September 1976, FIA 8802541, 2.

115. *Ibid.*, 3.

116. Meredith, *Past Is Another Country*, 268. Although Mugabe formed the Patriotic Front with Nkomo in October and attended the Geneva Conference, he had not yet entirely seized the leadership of ZANU. Many guerrillas still looked to Muzorewa, who had recruited them. Machel did not formally support Mugabe until December. See Christie, *Machel*, 96; Smiley, "The Rise of Robert Mugabe," 1062-1063.

117. Martin and Johnson, *Struggle for Zimbabwe*, 260; Nyangoni and Nyandoro, *Zimbabwe Independence Movements*, 452; Meredith, *Past Is Another Country*, 274-286; Muzorewa, *Rise Up and Walk*, 218.

118. Memorandum of conversation between Nyerere and Congressman Charles Diggs, Dar Es Salaam, 23 November 1976, untitled folder, box 81, CD. Diggs was on a fact-finding tour that had visited Geneva and Zambia and was going to Mozambique and South Africa.

119. Hasu Patel and H.K. Bhila, "The Last Becomes the First: The Transfer of Power in Zimbabwe," in Prosser Gifford and Wm. Roger Louis, eds., *Decolonization and African Independence: The Transfers of Power, 1960-1980* (New Haven: Yale University Press, 1988), 453.

120. Low, "The Zimbabwe Settlement," 92. Low identified the absence of Crosland as significant, but not critical. For the view that

Kissinger's absence was crucial, see Wellington Nyangoni, *African Nationalism in Zimbabwe* (Washington: University Press, 1978), 116.

121. Lameduck status was emphasized by Low in an interview with the author, 13 November 1995. The importance of election cycles in Kissinger's diplomacy, particularly regarding Vietnam, is discussed in Robert Schulzinger, "How Long, Oh Lord, How Long?" in *Peace and Change* (April 1995), 226-236.

122. The possibility that Kissinger would help Ford in the election by settling the dispute is noted in Noer, *Cold War and Black Liberation*, 244. For the charge that Kissinger was rushing the negotiations as fall approached, see Charle Diggs and Yvonne Burke to Kissinger, 2 September 1976, FIA 8802541.

123. Kissinger to Diggs, 3 September 1976, FIA 8802541. For an example of Kissinger's emphasis on a speedy settlement, see Kissinger telegram from Lusaka to Dakar, 17 September 1976, ibid.

124. These Kissingerian habits are discussed in Schulzinger, *Doctor of Diplomacy*, 3, 239, and 242. Smith, perhaps not surprisingly, later described Kissinger's efforts as "straightforward" and sincere. See Smith, *The Great Betrayal*, 206.

125. The importance of Kissinger's achievement is acknowledged in virtually all sources, including those from perspectives as far apart as former State official Steve Low, journalist Martin Meredith, and Zimbabwean scholars David Martin and Phyllis Johnson. See Low, "The Zimbabwe Settlement," 92; Meredith, *Past Is Another Country*, 270; and Martin and Johnson, *Struggle for Zimbabwe*, 263.

126. Kissinger's prestige is noted by Low in "The Zimbabwe Settlement," 104; and also by Jeffrey Davidow, another State official, in his *Dealing with International Crises: Lessons from Zimbabwe* (Muscatine: Stanley Foundation, 1983

7

THE CARTER ADMINISTRATION AND THE TRANSFORMATION OF SOUTHERN RHODESIA INTO ZIMBABWE

In April 1980, Southern Rhodesia officially became the independent nation of Zimbabwe. Robert Mugabe, Zimbabwe's first Prime Minister, visited the White House in August. He thanked President Jimmy Carter for U.S. support in Zimbabwe's struggle for peace and justice. Carter pronounced that he was proud of having taken a greater interest in Africa than his predecessors. He emphasized that Andrew Young and certain members of Congress had made it possible for his administration to carry out a policy that helped transform Southern Rhodesia into Zimbabwe.

Indeed, Young and other members of Carter's foreign policy team eagerly sought a settlement of the Southern Rhodesian conflict upon taking office. They began by repealing the Byrd Amendment, an action that helped gain the trust of black Africans. They then joined the British in advancing Anglo-American proposals, which ultimately fizzled but kept the negotiating process alive. Young's informal diplomacy at Malta, in particular, helped form a bond with Mugabe.

When Ian Smith attempted to achieve independence through an internal settlement with Abel Muzorewa, Carter himself asserted control of U.S. policy. He took the strongest stand on Southern Rhodesia ever taken by an American president, refusing to recognize Muzorewa or lift sanctions. He benefited from strong support from Representative Stephen Solarz (D-N.Y.), and from a new constituency on U.S./African relations. Carter's stand helped convince the government of Margaret Thatcher to arrange an all-parties conference at Lancaster House in 1979. The Americans played a supporting role to the British and African lead players during the conference, but the Carter Administration facilitated the final settlement. Between 1977 and 1979, the actions of Carter and key supporters contributed to the resolution of the conflict, which finally lead to peace and an independent Zimbabwe in 1980.

CARTER'S ELECTION AND FOREIGN POLICY TEAM

During his tenure as Governor of Georgia, Jimmy Carter gained some insights about foreign policy as a member of the Trilateral Commisssion. This informal group advocated economic cooperation, particularly among the United States, Japan, and western Europe. At Trilateral meetings, Carter met Columbia University scholar Zbigniew Brzezinski. The two discussed foreign policy issues as the 1976 election drew near, and Carter decided, should he gain the presidency, to name Brzezinski national security adviser. The first decision on which Carter turned to him for advice was naming a secretary of state.

In October 1976, Carter was considering three candidates for the position: Paul Warnke, George Ball, and Cyrus Vance. These three lawyers all had extensive international experience and strong ties to the Democratic party and the eastern establishment. Brzezinski favored Vance, who advocated arms control, more emphasis on economic and environmental concerns, and more attention to the southern half of the globe.[1] He identified Southern Rhodesia as one of the key spots, and suggested that Carter modify the approach taken by Henry Kissinger, crafting a policy that was "more acceptable to the Africans."[2]

The discussions would have amounted to nothing, of course, if Carter did not become president. He earned a narrow victory in the electoral college by winning every southern state except Virginia. While the majority of whites in several southern states supported Ford, black voters backed Carter. African Americans turned the tide in Louisiana, North and South Carolina, and most remarkably,

Mississippi. Upon hearing that Carter won Mississippi, Congress-man Andrew Young (D-Ga.) remarked: "the hands that picked cot-ton finally picked the president."[3] Carter's election signalled a re-markable rise of black influence not only in the Democratic party, but on foreign policy as well.

On 30 November Carter chose Vance as secretary of state. Hav-ing selected Brzezinski and Vance, Carter next looked to fill the position of U.S. ambassador to the United Nations. He intended to work more closely with the UN than had his predecessors and to use it as an avenue for improving relations with less-developed nations. In mid-December Carter offered the job to Andrew Young, who had been one of his staunch supporters during the election. Young later recalled another factor:

> Carter asked me to be ambassador because he wanted people
> to take human rights seriously, and he said that the fact I
> was associated with Martin Luther King would help people
> take human rights seriously.

Hoping to take King's nonviolent approach onto the international stage, Young accepted.[4]

Carter, Brzezinski, Vance, and Young all agreed that the United States should help the British negotiate a settlement in Southern Rhodesia that would end the war. Vance and Young, in particular, shared strong feelings on the subject and worked closely from the start of the new administration.[5] They both believed that facilitat-ing the transition to an independent, majority-ruled Zimbabwe was right in principle. They also felt it was in the best interests of the United States, since it would undermine Soviet influence with black Africans and improve U.S. relations with Nigeria.[6]

REPEALING THE BYRD AMENDMENT

Vance and Young concurred that a good first step for the Carter Administration would be to repeal the Byrd Amendment, thereby shutting off imports of Southern Rhodesian chrome. On 11 Janu-ary 1977, Young introduced H.R. 1746 - "a bill to amend the United Nations Participation Act of 1945 to halt the importation of Rho-desian chrome."[7] Representative Charles Diggs (D - Mich.) co-sponsored the bill, but refused to join the battle in earnest until the White House demonstrated a sincere desire to help get it passed.

After Young's confirmation, Carter announced that he would be a member of the cabinet. The assumption of a cabinet post by one of the leading congressional advocates for repeal of the Byrd Amendment suggested that a strong measure of executive support would be forthcoming. Before tackling the amendment, however, Carter wanted to canvas the opinions of black African leaders regarding the best course of action for achieving a settlement in Southern Rhodesia. Young recalls that on the day he was sworn in, Carter "handed me a note saying I should go to Africa, and get some sense of what African leadership expected."[8]

By sending Young to gather their input, Carter hoped to regain the trust of black African leaders. While Kissinger had made Southern Rhodesia a high priority and forced some concessions from Ian Smith, he had alienated leaders in important states like Nigeria. Young, it was hoped, would do a better job of listening to the Africans than Kissinger.[9] His ten-day trip began on 4 February in Tanzania, where President Julius Nyerere emphasized the importance of repealing the Byrd Amendment.[10] During his crucial stop in Nigeria, he convinced General Olusegun Obasanjo, the head of state, that Carter was sincere. Young undid much of the damage that Kissinger had done to U.S./Nigerian relations.[11] Overall, Young met with 17 African heads of state in the course of the visit, and many of them urged him to repeal the amendment.[12] Young relayed their views to the President, who assessed the Africa trip as "an extraordinarily good job."[13]

In the meantime, the move to repeal the Byrd Amendment had begun. One key legislator, Representative John Dent (D-Pa.), switched his position. Dent had supported chrome imports in the past, but upon learning that technological advances had eliminated the steel industry's reliance on high-grade Southern Rhodesian chrome ore, he supported sanctions.[14] The key point that had converted Dent, that the United States no longer needed Southern Rhodesian chrome, was reiterated in Senate hearings by E.F. Andrews, President of Allegheny Ludlum Industries. Andrews had lobbied tirelessly for continuing SR chrome imports since 1967.[15] His testimony that imports were no longer required, therefore, carried a lot of weight with previous Byrd supporters.

In addition to the strong technical argument provided by Dent and Andrews, the Carter Administration wheeled in some heavy artillery for the repeal battle. Testifying before a Senate subcommittee, Vance described sanctions against Southern Rhodesia as crucial for reaching a settlement. He assured the subcommittee that the President wanted to return the United States to compliance with sanctions. The best way to broker peace was to stand by the British, and repealing the Byrd Amendment would be a good start.[16]

Young had become something of a celebrity, and according to one of his associates at the UN, "Andy was often greeted as if he was one of the Beatles."[17] His former colleagues in Congress may not have been quite that ecstatic, but did express their pleasure that he had been appointed, and welcomed him back to testify. Young characterized repeal as a "kind of referendum on American racism," which would demonstrate that the United States did not support Ian Smith. Furthermore, the measure would smooth relations with black African nations such as Nigeria, who ranked among the leading suppliers of oil to the United States.[18]

Almost immediately after entering office, then, the Carter Administration requested that Congress repeal the Byrd Amendment. The amendment's author, Senator Harry Byrd, Jr. (I-Va.), tried to hold his ground. However, he faced an uphill battle in light of the administration's effort and the technical argument that American industries no longer needed high-grade chrome ore. He received some support, particularly from PPG Industries of Pittsburgh, which imported Southern Rhodesian chrome to produce industrial chemicals.[19] An SR farmer, John Trevelyan, argued that sanctions hurt local blacks who worked in the mines, and therefore applauded Byrd's stand.[20]

Despite such correspondence and the assistance from PPG industries, Byrd could not fend off the assault on his amendment. On 14 March the House passed H.R. 1746, and the Senate approved the bill the following day.[21] President Carter hosted a signing ceremony, inviting a large contingent that featured long-time repeal activists Young, Diggs, Hubert Humphrey (D-Minn.), and former Senator Gale McGee.[22] Upon signing the bill Carter proclaimed:

> This legislation probably has as high a symbolic importance in international affairs as anything that I will do this

year.... I think it puts us on the side of what is right and proper.... This puts us back on the side of support with the United Nations. It puts us in strategic position to help with the resolution of the Rhodesian question.[23]

With significant help from Congress, the Carter Administration succeeded in blocking Southern Rhodesian chrome imports, thereby accomplishing a first step in its policy of assisting the British to negotiate a settlement.[24] Carter joined Young at the UN, where the delegates enthusiastically applauded the announcement of repeal.[25] The editors of the *The New York Times*, however, reacted with less enthusiasm. A 20 March 1977 editorial condemned Carter as hypocritical for claiming to be on the side of justice in repealing Byrd, while simultaneously aiding the corrupt government of Zaire in its crushing of the Shaba rebellion.[26]

While *The Times* criticism of Carter's policy towards Zaire may have had some merit, Carter Administration officials strongly disagree with the charge that reimposing the sanctions against chrome had no real effect. Stephen Low, Ambassador to Zambia from 1976 to 1979, recently explained that the impact of repealing the Byrd Amendment took many forms. Its greatest impact was probably domestic, because it forced Congress to debate the issues and stirred up public opinion. Low added that sanctions did take a toll on the Southern Rhodesian economy, putting pressure on Smith to reach a settlement. Sanctions, according to Low, were an important part of the formula that produced an independent Zimbabwe.[27] In Young's view, repealing the BA contributed to an atmosphere of trust among the United States, Great Britain, and black African leaders. He opined that this atmosphere was crucial in the eventual success of negotiations.[28]

THE ANGLO-AMERICAN INITIATIVE

The repeal encouraged the British, and Prime Minister James Callaghan visited Washington in March. He and Carter agreed that Southern Rhodesia should be a high priority, and they assigned that policy to their chief diplomats. Vance met with the new British Foreign Secretary, David Owen, a 38-year-old neurologist, who intended to take some chances in pursuit of a settlement. Owen and Vance decided that the United States and Great Britain should sponsor an all-parties conference.[29] Failure of the previous year's Geneva Conference, escalating warfare, and visits to southern Africa by communist leaders convinced them of the urgent need for a redoubled effort.[30] Owen presented their plan for a conference to Ian Smith in April, and left Africa optimistic about convening major talks within a few months.[31]

The leaders of the Patriotic Front (PF), Robert Mugabe and Joshua Nkomo, objected to an all-parties conference at which the United States would play a major role. Vance and Owen concluded that the PF's view precluded a conference, and instead formed the Anglo-American consultative group. Consisting of Johnny Graham, an experienced Foreign Office diplomat, and Stephen Low, the consultative group's task was to shuttle around southern Africa and determine the terms for an acceptable settlement. Graham and Low developed a close friendship, which facilitated their endeavors to bring about peace.[32]

Before the consultative group began shuttling, Young attended a UN conference on southern African crises at Maputo, Mozambique. He explained to the participants that the United States hoped for a rapid resolution in Southern Rhodesia. He condemned recent military strikes into Mozambique by Smith's forces. The circumstances would not allow an easy solution, Young admitted, but he pledged the best efforts of the United States in consultations aimed at crafting a settlement.[33] Frontline leaders Samora Machel of Mozambique and Kenneth Kaunda of Zambia insisted that the armed struggle continue, but promised Young that they would support the Anglo-American negotiations as a "second legitimate form of struggle."[34]

In the wake of the Maputo Conference, Graham and Low began their mission, meeting with Ian Smith in late May. They informed him that the British defined majority rule as "one man - one vote," and this was a necessary condition for the transition to an independent Zimbabwe. Initially, Smith rejected universal suffrage, but Graham and Low argued that expanding the suffrage could be in his best interests. If he allowed only a few well-educated blacks to vote, most of them would probably be nationalists and Smith opponents. However, broadening the electorate could generate some popular support among blacks.[35]

Graham and Low presented this case to Smith, but he showed no change of heart regarding the recent military strikes into Mozambique and continued to threaten similar manuevers into Zambia. The May round of consultations by Low and Graham did not accomplish any major breakthrough, but the State Department judged it a step in the right direction that was "reasonably encouraging."[36] In early June, Low briefed officials from State and the National Security Council (NSC) on the first round of consultations. One NSC staffer characterized Low's reports as "most helpful to our thinking."[37]

In mid-1977 approximately three thousand soldiers of Mugabe's Zimbabwe African National Union (ZANU) roamed the countryside, as did a smaller number of fighters from Nkomo's Zimbabwe African People's Union (ZAPU). June marked the beginning of an upsurge in guerrilla warfare, and Smith's security forces continued their extreme measures to quell it.[38] In a strategy similar to that of the U.S. forces in Vietnam, Smith's forces moved about a half-million black peasants into "protective villages."[39]

Once soldiers infiltrated Southern Rhodesia from either Mozambique or Zambia, it was extremely difficult to identify them among the rural population. Therefore, Smith's forces launched raids into those neighboring states.[40] The dramatic raids may have temporarily raised the morale of some whites in Salisbury, but they angered the Carter Administration. At the end of June, Young denounced "the folly of the Rhodesian regime in lashing out against its neighbors." The incursions would "only lead to more death, to intensified hatred, to even more bitter armed conflict and even greater ruin in southern Africa."[41]

While publicly criticizing Smith's tactics, the Carter Administration continued to cooperate in the British pursuit of a negotiated settlement. In early July, Graham and Low presented a draft plan to Smith and the PF. It stipulated that the British would govern during the transition, the ceasefire would be monitored by an international force, and the security force and the guerrilla forces would be integrated to form the new national army. Mugabe objected strongly because the draft ignored the crucial question of who would actually be in power during the transition. He demanded to know what army would be in charge, raising an issue that would remain a sticking point until the final settlement over two years later.[42]

This second round of consultations by Graham and Low, while not very encouraging, at least had determined for certain what issues needed to be resolved. Later, in July, they joined their superiors for a meeting in the White House about how to proceed. Carter hosted Vance, Owen, and several subordinates from State and the Foreign Office.[43] Owen, evidently frustrated by Mugabe's intransigence, proposed orchestrating a settlement that included Nkomo but not Mugabe. He wondered if they could get Nkomo to accept UN-supervised elections, a new Constitution, and financial guarantees for whites.[44] Anthony Lake and Richard Moose from State opposed the idea of a settlement without Mugabe.[45] They predicted that such a maneuver would damage relations with the Frontline presidents, and would not stop the fighting. Vance agreed, since Mugabe's guerrilla force was much larger than Nkomo's.[46]

Moose and Lake put a damper on Owen's suggestion, because they believed both factions of the PF needed to be involved in a settlement in order for it to endure. These two had joined Young in what critics perceived as the Carter Administration's pro-PF group, which supposedly was pushing Carter to help the PF take power. On 4 August Julius Nyerere, President of Tanzania and a key member of the Frontline group, arrived in Washington for a state visit.[47] Even "extremists" like Moose would be shocked by the development precipitated by Carter.

During two days of meetings, Nyerere conversed with Carter about Southern Rhodesia. Nyerere advocated removing the Smith regime, dismantling the security force, and replacing it with an army "based on the liberation forces." To the astonishment of Nyerere, Carter agreed with his plan. Moose was dismayed. He relayed the news to Vance—then in the Middle East—and to Low. When Low informed his British counterparts, they were "livid."[48]

Carter, in his talk with Nyerere on 4 August, had seemingly undermined the consultations which Low, Graham, and the other British negotiators had been conducting since May. Conceding Nyerere's point that the new army of Zimbabwe should be "based on the liberation forces" altered the equation to a point where Smith would surely reject it.[49] Nonetheless, an agreement between presidents could not simply be ignored, and any further talks would have to try to iron out the wrinkles Carter had caused. Young and Owen, referred to as the "terrible twins" because of their youthful energy, headed for Africa in late August to propose a settlement.[50]

First, they stopped in Nigeria and discussed their proposal with General Obasanjo. Next, Owen laid out for the PF and Frontline leaders the main points of a blueprint that he intended to announce on 1 September. This Anglo-American Plan replaced the previous year's Kissinger Plan, incorporating modifications resulting from the recent consultations, particularly one man—one vote. However, the plan did not specify that the new army of Zimbabwe would be "based on the liberation forces." Some representatives of the PF and Frontline reacted harshly, disappointed that Owen had reverted to what they considered an unacceptable position.[51]

Young, a veteran of many difficult negotiating sessions during the civil rights movement, remained optimistic and remarked: "In an armed struggle, you have battle after battle after battle. But you never expect a single battle to win the entire war." During an afternoon session, Nyerere conceded that the Anglo-American Plan did represent the gist of what he and Carter had discussed earlier in the month. The Frontline leaders agreed that Owen and Young should carry on with their efforts and present the plan to South African president John Vorster.[52] The next morning, Young and Owen talked again with PF leaders Mugabe and Nkomo. They seemed willing to join Smith in negotiations, with British and UN mediation. Young believed such a step to be crucial in heading off an "internal settlement," whereby Smith would finagle a deal that did not include the PF.[53]

In the afternoon, Young and Kaunda reviewed key details of the proposal, particularly the issue of the armed forces during and after the transition period. Young believed that after an end to the fighting Smith's forces would gradually disintegrate: the white draftees would quickly go home, the mercenaries would disappear, and most soldiers guilty of atrocities would make themselves scarce. The new army would combine some remaining elements of Smith's forces with the guerrilla armies and appointment of all officers would be subject to the approval of the new government.

If the plan were accepted, therefore, the Carter/Nyerere agreement that the army be "based on the liberation forces" would emerge over time. In order to make acceptance palatable for Smith, however, the published Anglo-American Plan would include "only a vague reference to this matter." Although Owen was insisting on extremely cautious language in public so as not to alienate whites and sabotage the agreement, Young concluded that the army would ultimately be controlled by the PF. Carter and Callahan had both agreed to this result, and the Anglo-American Plan was intended to bring it about.[54] After thus reassuring Kaunda, Young took off for South Africa.

In the past, Young had condemned the South African government as illegal.[55] The potential for a clash with Vorster loomed large, and upon arrival at the airport in Pretoria the press asked Young if he planned to raise the issue of human rights. Young answered: "I'm here in support of the British initiative on Rhodesia, and I think that if we can make any headway on that, that's really all I'll have time for on this visit."[56] Along the road from the airport into Pretoria, protesters waved signs exhorting Young to go home. However, Vorster cordially shook hands with Young when they met face-to-face for the first time.[57]

Owen and Young discussed the Anglo-American Plan with Vorster for three hours on the morning of 29 August. Vorster warned that since the draft did not guarantee the integrity of the Southern Rhodesian security forces, Smith would reject it. Furthermore, Vorster would not use his leverage on Smith, so any effort to sway Smith would be the responsibility of Owen and Young.[58] Reconvening in the afternoon, the diplomats focused exclusively on the issue of a new army of Zimbabwe "based on the liberation forces." Vorster expressed absolute certainty that when Smith heard that phrase, negotiations would cease.[59]

While in South Africa, Young learned that Nyerere had asked for some clarification on the composition of the Zimbabwean army. Young decided to fly up and explain to Nyerere that the phrase "based on the liberation forces" would prompt Smith to derail the negotiations. Young hoped he, Owen, and Nyerere could agree on language that was less explicit but still preserved the key principles. If they could craft such a proposal, they might keep the Frontline on board and prevent Smith from rejecting it out-of-hand.[60]

Owen, Young, and Moose conferred with Nyerere for about two hours on 30 August, but could not agree on revisions. Instead, they opted to go forward with the publication of the original Anglo-

American Plan, which did not specify the makeup of the Zimba-bwean army. Also on 1 September, Owen would announce his ex-pectation that the new army would be "based on the liberation forces" as well as "acceptable elements" of Smith's forces. Owen and Young hoped that the separate statement would be enough to satisfy the Frontline and the PF.[61]

On the eve of announcing the Anglo-American Plan, Young assessed the situation realistically. If negotiations ceased, Young feared an "internal settlement" engineered by Smith, which would not include Mugabe and Nkomo. Young elaborated: "We have got to keep this package together or we face serious problems from an internal solution. We meet Ian Smith today and he will probably reject our views. It is important that he be isolated in the interna-tional community."[62] Young's concerns were well-founded, as Smith was laying the foundation for an internal settlement. He called for an election in hopes of rallying white support and isolating the extreme faction. If he could once again get a strong mandate from the white electorate, he would gradually pursue a settlement with black leaders who were not in the PF, such as Abel Muzorewa and Ndabaningi Sithole.[63]

Election results rolled in during the morning of 1 September, and Smith's Rhodesian Front party triumphed in a landslide, gain-ing 85 percent of the vote (all voters were white). Smith announced that he would now work to finalize an internal settlement, which he had been considering for quite some time. Smith added that the vote of confidence would "strengthen his hand" in his talks with Owen and Young later that morning.[64] After a sleepless night, the British and Americans flew into Salisbury and commenced a meet-ing with Smith, who had been up all night himself listening to the election returns. The circumstances, to say the least, were less than ideal for productive negotiations.[65]

After Owen presented the White Paper detailing the Anglo-American Plan, Smith launched into a diatribe about Britain's bro-ken promises. He and his advisers rejected the idea of international supervision of the transition period. In fact, they made it clear that they were not committed to anything in the plan, including elec-tions based on "one man—one vote." After listening patiently to Smith and Owen trade accusations, Young finally interjected:

"Where I come from we have a saying that there isn't any point crying over spilt milk." Smith smiled for the first time all day.[66] Young and Owen pointed out the economic benefits of an internationally recognized settlement: an end to sanctions, and the establisment by the United States and Britain of the Zimbabwe Development Fund. Young concluded that although Smith had not rejected the proposal, he probably would continue to seek an internal solution.[67]

Owen, Young, and Moose next met with Muzorewa and then with Sithole. Both had been given copies of the White Paper to look over beforehand. Muzorewa and Sithole expressed approval at the plan's espousal of universal suffrage, but had some reservations about their roles in a transition. Owen and Young explained to both that they strongly opposed an internal settlement and discussed the dangers of pursuing such a course. After the meetings Muzorewa announced his support for the plan, but Sithole was more cautious.[68]

Following these meetings, at 4:30 PM on 1 September, the Anglo-American Plan was published simultaneously in Salisbury, London, and New York.[69] As had been promised to Nyerere, Owen also released a separate Law and Order statement regarding the make-up of the future national army of Zimbabwe. It would be "based on the liberation forces." While Owen was presenting this statement to the media, Graham and Low held a second session with representatives from Smith's regime.

The meeting proceeded relatively smoothly until Graham distributed the Law and Order statement. This was the first time Smith's representatives saw the statement. According to Low: "The Rhodesians did not disguise their surprise and dismay at the contents of the statement, particularly the phrase that the independence army would be based upon liberation forces." They believed that the announcement of this idea would spark a white exodus. The 2-hour meeting convinced Low that the Southern Rhodesians were willing to negotiate over the details of the Anglo-American Plan itself but not the Law and Order statement.[70] The hectic week of diplomacy in southern Africa was over. None of the principals in the conflict had completely accepted the package, but none had entirely rejected it either.

As the efforts to find a settlement in Southern Rhodesia stumbled forward, circumstances in South Africa went from bad to worse. The Carter Administration had opted against trying to impose economic sanctions on the Pretoria regime, instead supporting the Sullivan Principles.[71] Still, activists such as newly incorporated TransAfrica lobbied for economic measures against apartheid. Their cries intensified in September as rioting and repression again escalated in South Africa, sparked by the 12 September death of Stephen Biko, a popular, 30-year-old black resistance leader, who died in custody after police officers beat him with a hose and slammed his head against a wall. At the time, Police Minister James Kruger denied that his officers caused the death, thereby increasing the resulting international demand for justice.[72]

That demand was indeed widespread. In the streets of New York, demonstrators marched behind a banner that read: "Avenge the Murder of Stephen Biko." In Congress, forty representatives and two senators founded an ad hoc group to monitor events in South Africa. At the United Nations in October, forty-nine African nations requested that the Security Council consider imposing sanctions against South Africa. Young announced on 24 October that he personally favored sanctions, but added: "The president and secretary of state will have to decide what sanctions are appropriate."[73]

Three resolutions were considered in October: the first would ban foreign investment, the second would end nuclear cooperation, and the third would stop internal arms production in South Africa. Following instructions from Washington, Young joined the representatives from Great Britain and France in vetoing all three. He did vote for a less comprehensive measure that passed on 4 November, making the voluntary arms embargo from 1963 a mandatory embargo.[74] The embargo prohibited "the sale or tansfer of weapons and ammunition, military vehicles and equipment, paramilitary police supplies, and even spare parts." It was the first time the UN imposed mandatory sanctions against a member state.[75]

The arms embargo came as no surprise to leaders in Pretoria like Foreign Minister Botha, who had been expecting such a vote since Biko's death.[76] South African whites probably breathed a sigh of relief that economic sanctions were not imposed in the fall of 1977. As it turned out, that was the closest they came to being implemented during the Carter Administration. After 1977, top American officials toned down their rhetoric regarding apartheid. From 1978 to 1981, the Carter Administration initiated no real concrete challenge to apartheid. This was partly due to their hopes of achieving a settlement in Southern Rhodesia first. It also reflected the lack of a really strong anti-apartheid movement in Congress. Although Diggs kept up his fight for sanctions, there remained a general apathy on the hill. In such a climate it would have been difficult for Carter to have done much more. Young later opined: "I think we pushed the South African Government about as far as we could in the Carter Administration."[77]

MALTA CONFERENCE

The Americans and British sought an all-parties conference in order to negotiate a settlement for SR based on the Anglo-American Plan. Signs throughout the fall were not encouraging, however. Nkomo and Mugabe believed they stood to gain more by continuing the guerrilla war. On 23 November, Smith's Security Forces launched their largest attack of the war into Mozambique. The three days of fighting killed over one thousand people, including about one hundred children. Some mass graves of women were later discovered.[78]

The PF was more determined than ever to fight, and Smith was gradually progressing towards an internal settlement with Sithole and Muzorewa. In the midst of these discouraging developments, Low and Graham returned to Salisbury in hopes of arranging an all-parties conference in London. Smith did not intend to take part in an all-parties conference, since he felt an internal settlement was imminent.[79] At the end of 1977, it seemed that the Anglo-American Plan would not be given a chance.

In Washington, the first hints of Congressional support for an internal settlement emerged. Senator Robert Dole (R-Kan.) criticized the Carter Administration for refusing to give the negotiations between Smith, Muzorewa, and Sithole a chance. According to Dole, certain members of the administration (undoubtedly he meant Young and Moose) would not be satisfied unless Mugabe and Nkomo assumed control of an independent Zimbabwe. Dole concluded: "The negotiations in Salisbury are moving ahead.... We cannot afford to be the stumbling block on the road to peace in Rhodesia."[80]

While Dole contended that Smith's effort towards an internal settlement was "moving ahead," Moose believed that they would bog down. In his view, the circumstances were ripe for a meeting with the PF. The looming threat of an internal deal forced the PF to take the Anglo-American Plan more seriously. If the British and Americans could make some progress with the PF and Smith's effort did stall, then Owen could possibly obtain South African support and broker a settlement.[81] It was agreed that talks with the PF should be arranged, so Owen requested them to meet with him and Young. On 19 January, Mugabe and Nkomo accepted Owen's invitation to meet later in the month on the island of Malta.[82]

The British and the Americans intended to focus on the details of the transition period, having received some helpful suggestions along those lines from Machel.[83] Low and Moose concluded that the talks would proceed more smoothly without a formal agenda, and both felt it imperative that the PF have some say regarding modifications to the Anglo-American Plan.[84] As the final logistics for Malta were being arranged, Young insisted that he stay in the Dragonara Hotel with the PF, to allow for "in depth discussions."[85]

The conference opened on the morning of 30 January, with Owen reiterating his goal to pursue a settlement based on the Anglo-American Plan. In the first two days of formal sessions, the PF manifested their desire for a "dominant role" during the transition period between ceasefire and elections. The sessions afforded both sides a good opportunity to lay out their ideas in depth, the first time Owen and Young talked at length with Nkomo and Mugabe. Reporting on the first two days, British radio announced that the PF had agreed to a policing role for the UN. This report was premature and drove Nkomo to distraction. Young succeeded in calming him down, and Nkomo "clearly felt himself in the presence of a friend in Andy Young."[86]

Indeed, much of the progress at Malta resulted from Young's informal personal interactions with the PF. During the initial coffee break, a gigantic PF aide in military fatigues accosted Young: "I need to talk to you." Young, caught off guard and slightly intimidated by the large man, followed him to the corner. The Zimbabwean inquired: "What happened to the Oakland Raiders?" He had earned a Ph.D at Berkeley and wondered how the Raiders' season ended up. This exchange reinforced Young's generally positive view of the PF delegation, which included several men with Ph.D.s from American and British universities. He established a relationship of mutual respect with many of them, swimming in the hotel pool or jogging. He drank beer with Nkomo and drank orange soda with teetotaler Mugabe during a latenight conversation.[87]

Remarkably, Young orchestrated talks over lunch between the PF and British Field Marshal Richard Carver, who would be Resident Commissioner if a settlement were reached. Carver had served heroically in World War II, then commanded the force that crushed the Mau Mau rebellion in Kenya in the 1950s. During a lowpoint at the start of the Malta Conference, a PF aide accused Young of bringing the "Mau Mau crusher" to quell the Zimbabwe liberation movement. After Young gained the trust of the PF, however, its leaders were willing to talk over military details even with Carver.[88]

Informal talks facilitated two of the key areas of progress at Malta. Partly because of the atmosphere Young created, the PF agreed to active roles in the transition for the Resident Commissioner and a United Nations force. Overall, though, the substantive results of the conference were negligible. It would be wrong to condemn Malta too harshly, however, since no settlement could have been reached without Smith anyway. Furthermore, because the Americans and the British were entirely unwilling to become directly involved in the war or to extend sanctions to South Africa, the PF could not be expected to make too many concessions to them while fighting continued. Young realized that Soviet promises of weapons also limited the leverage of the United States and Great Britain.[89]

Despite the lack of a major substantive breakthrough at Malta, the PF wanted to continue talks with Owen and the Americans.[90] Young concluded that Malta was only a "minimal success," but had "succeeded in keeping a negotiated settlement alive."[91] Low underlined the unprecedented opportunity for detailed discussion with Nkomo and Mugabe.[92] Both he and Vance later described Malta as having made "some progress," and several scholars have seconded that conclusion.[93] By keeping the negotiating process going, the Malta Conference resuscitated a middle course between war and Smith's internal settlement.

THE INTERNAL SETTLEMENT

Americans who had participated at Malta argued vigorously for subsequent actions to maintain the momentum. Young and Moose suggested meetings with the Frontline presidents, to enlist them to pressure the PF into remaining involved with the Anglo-American effort. Young and Moose agreed that the internal settlement would not stop the fighting, and therefore should not be supported by the Carter Administration. According to Young, "U.S. interest lies in the ability to bring peace to an independent majority-ruled Zimbabwe without resultant civil strife." In his mind, only an agreement inclusive of the PF could do that.[94]

While Young, Moose, and others in the Carter Administration opposed an internal settlement, support mounted in Congress. A group of 24 representatives led by Edward Derwinski (R-Ill.) praised the Smith/Muzorewa negotiations as "peaceful and constructive endeavors," which would lead to elections based on universal adult suffrage. The representatives requested that the President support Smith's efforts. They desired that he "terminate immediately" the U.S. participation in the Anglo-American initiative, which was designed to benefit only the "Marxist" and "terrorist" faction.[95]

Early in 1978, a faction gradually formed in Congress that opposed the Carter Administration's Southern Rhodesia policy. The debate intensified suddenly on 15 February, when Smith, Muzorewa, and Sithole signed a preliminary pact, agreeing on the principles for an internal settlement. Smith characterized the achievement as a "victory for moderation." The British government opposed the plan. Johnny Graham asserted that the Anglo-American Plan remained the standard against which any settlement had to be measured. The British would only support a settlement that actually transferred power, and which was internationally acceptable.[96] Smith's preliminary announcement certainly did not indicate that these conditions would be met.

The day after Smith's announcement, Young vehemently decried the preliminary deal as unacceptable, because it would not bring peace. Young did not think that it addressed the issues "for which some 40,000 guerrillas are fighting." Excluding the PF would probably result in a situation like Angola, with blacks fighting blacks in a bloody civil war. State Department spokesman Ken Brown concurred, explaining that Smith's package did not meet the requirements of the Anglo-American Plan, mainly because it did not include the PF.[97] A few days later, in a detailed and nuanced analysis of the possible ramifications of Smith's tentative settlement, Low supported Brown and Young's basic view.

From the first days of the Carter Administration, Young occasionally had made controversial statements without thinking them through carefully. Low, on the other hand, was a classic diplomat - cautious and balanced in his reports and statements. After having negotiated considerably with the Frontline, the PF, and Smith for almost two years, he understood the circumstances as well as any American. Like Young, Low feared that Smith's deal would exacerbate the conflict, and that the PF would step up the guerrilla fighting and obtain more assistance from the Soviets and the Cubans. Moderate elements of the PF would lose out to extremists and increasingly radicalized military commanders could wind up in charge. According to Low, the agreement between Smith and Muzorewa was not in the best interests of the United States, or of southern Africa in general.[98]

Thus, Low provided a very reasoned argument in support of Young's denounciation of the tentative internal settlement. His secret telegram was not presented to the public or to the Congress, the latter subjecting Young's view to harsh criticism. John Laverge, chairman of Richmond's Universal Tobacco Company, hoped that the State Department would "take a more constructive and positive attitude towards the events in Rhodesia." In a congratulatory telegram to Smith he claimed that despite the "lukewarm" reaction by the U.S. government, the majority of Americans supported the settlement.[99]

In fact, the majority of Americans probably paid no attention to the developments in Southern Rhodesia, or to the reactions by the State Department and Andrew Young. Senators Bob Dole and Orrin Hatch (R-Utah), however, applauded the tentative settlement and attacked the views of State and Young as "irresponsible and inflammatory." They requested that Carter give Smith's plan a chance, and let the people of Southern Rhodesia solve their own problems.

They specifically believed that "Ambassador Young should keep out of these negotiations." They questioned the extent to which Young was accurately representing the American people and reiterated that his views were "inflammatory."[100]

On 3 March, members of Congress critical of Young and supportive of the tentative internal settlement welcomed the news: Smith, Muzorewa, and Sithole signed a final agreement. The package, known as the "Salisbury Plan," called for elections after a one-year transition, during which whites would retain control of the police and military. Smith's army would enforce martial law during the elections. Of the one hundred seats in parliament, twenty-eight would be reserved for whites. Followers of the PF would not be allowed to vote, unless they renounced the guerrilla struggle. Nkomo and Mugabe rejected the Salisbury Plan outright.

Senator Harry Byrd urged the Carter Administration to give the Salisbury Plan a chance. According to Byrd: "There is every indication that settlement signed today by Prime Minister Smith and Black Rhodesian leaders can lead to a rapid transition to majority rule within a constitutional framework." He believed the plan deserved U.S. encouragement. Furthermore, if the UN considered a proposal condemning the plan, Byrd hoped the Carter Administration would vote against it. Such a resolution, in his view, would only give comfort to "terrorists."[102] Dole declared that the Salisbury Plan warranted "the support of the American people and the U.S. Government."[103]

On 8 March, Muzorewa met with Vance, Lake, and Moose at the State Department. The Americans feared that under the internal settlement, power would remain in white hands and the war would escalate. Muzorewa attempted to dispel their fears, but to no avail. Despite Muzorewa's pleas, the U.S. officials intended to continue working for a deal that included the PF.[104] In the afternoon, Vance joined Carter and Owen for a discussion on Southern Rhodesia. Afterwards they informed the media: "There was full agreement that the two governments will jointly continue their efforts to facilitate a settlement among all the parties."[105]

The Congressional Black Caucus, which had grown to 16 members, advocated a strong public denunciation of the Salisbury Plan by the president himself. Carter, in turn, characterized the internal settlement as "inadequate."[106] This was not the strong statement for which the Black Caucus hoped, but instead reflected the moderate course Carter was following. Because of the fierce criticism that members of Congress heaped on Young and the State Department in February, Carter insisted that Young and Vance refrain from either condemning or supporting the internal settlement.[107]

Mid-March tested the Carter Administration's views on the Salisbury Plan. African delegates to the UN tabled a resolution for a Security Council vote, decrying Salisbury as "illegal and unacceptable." Following directions from the State Department, Young abstained.[108] In defense of the abstention, Young delineated the past actions and future goals of the United States, underlining that the Carter Administration still supported the Anglo-American Plan. He credited Muzorewa and Sithole with wanting independence for Zimbabwe and equality for Zimbabweans as much as the PF did. However, the deal they signed with Smith would not allow participation by all parties in the transition or election. For those and other reasons, Young concluded that the Salisbury Plan would "prolong violence rather than end it." He advocated an all-parties conference to revisit the Anglo-American Plan.[109]

Considering Young's propensity for speaking from the heart, his handling of the African resolution was quite moderate. Congressional opponents failed to acknowledge this moderation, however, and continued working for a recognition of the internal settlement. The Frontline and the PF, meanwhile, excoriated the United States and Great Britain's abstention. Mugabe pointed to the abstention as proof of "the duplicity of the western countries in regard to the Rhodesian question." The ZANU leader repudiated the Salisbury Plan as illegal, since Smith was an illegal prime minister. He would not meet with the Salisbury signatories; instead he wanted to resume the Malta talks with the British and Americans.[110]

DAR ES SALAAM CONFERENCE

Jack Gaylard, the secretary of Smith's cabinet, informed U.S. and British diplomats that Smith would not attend an all-parties conference. Nonetheless, the Carter Administration's dedication to peace received strong support from a House quintet led by Cardiss Collins (D-Ill.) and Paul Tsongas (D-Mass.). Young, with Nyerere, pondered what to do next. Nyerere indicated that the PF was prepared to reach an agreement with the Americans and British, so planning for a top-level initiative began.[111]

Before that effort took place, Carter paid the first visit to sub-Saharan Africa by a U.S. president. He stopped in Liberia and Nigeria. During five days in Lagos, he and General Obasanjo discussed the Southern Rhodesia situation in depth. Obasanjo urged Carter not to support the internal settlement, and Carter agreed. In a public speech Carter cited Martin Luther King, saying that Nigeria would soon be able to proclaim: "Free at last." This represented the highpoint of U.S. relations with Nigeria, which would soon deteriorate.[112]

Two weeks later Owen, Vance, and Young - "the most powerful diplomatic team ever assembled to tackle the Rhodesian issue"— tried to arrange a meeting of all the principals. On 14 and 15 April the Anglo-American contingent sat down in Dar Es Salaam with Nkomo and Mugabe to pick up where the Malta talks left off.[113] To the chagrin of the Anglo-American team, Nkomo and Mugabe insisted that they must control the executive council during the transition period. Owen and Vance reminded them that the Anglo-American Plan called for a neutral government during transition, and so their desire to run the executive council was unaccepatable.[114]

Although some progress was made on other details, the disagreement over control of the executive council precluded any comprehensive agreement at Dar. The PF would make no more concessions until Smith could be brought to the table.[115] In a move of great importance, Owen promised the PF that Great Britain would not recognize any government in Salisbury until an all-parties conference occurred.[116] Clearly, resolution of the SR crisis hinged on arranging such an event.

Following the trail blazed by Kissinger in 1976, Owen and Vance flew to Pretoria in hopes of getting Vorster to push Smith into an all-parties conference. The South Africans would not commit to such a role, although they did admit that any lasting settlement must be accepted internationally.[117] After the talks, Vorster indicated his general disappointment with the policies towards Africa of the Carter Administration. He derided the United States for "the lukewarm way in which they welcomed the internal settlement. I think they were wrong in taking up that attitude."[118]

Finding Vorster in no mood to facilitate their plans, Owen and Vance explained to Smith and Muzorewa that they could not support the internal settlement, and that they wanted to hammer out a deal acceptable to everyone at a roundtable. Smith and Muzorewa contended that participating in such meetings with the PF would detract from their primary responsibilities of running the country. Owen and Vance reiterated that the internal settlement simply was not acceptable, because it was not "beneficial to the people of Rhodesia as a whole," and insisted on an all-parties conference. Smith and Muzorewa agreed to consider attending such a roundtable, but refrained from giving a definite answer.[119]

Thus, the unprecedented collection of American and British diplomats who toured southern Africa in April failed to arrange a conference among the principals. However, they successfully manifested their policy towards the ongoing conflict. They would not recognize the Salisbury Agreement, and would endeavor to get the internalists and the PF together to negotiate a better package. The press accused the Anglo-Americans of playing favorites, and holding out for victory by Mugabe or Nkomo.[120]

In reality, it was not a matter of favoring either Mugabe or Nkomo over Muzorewa. It was nothing personal. The simple fact of the matter was that the internal settlement would not end the war, and a plan agreed to by the PF was a prerequisite for peace. Yet, that did not rule out a role in the future government for Muzorewa. Low, the key American diplomat on the ground in southern Africa from 1976 to 1979, believed it important to maintain contact with Muzorewa. When the internal settlement disintegrated, he could be brought into negotiations for a better solution.[121]

Events in Zaire once again impaired progress in the Southern Rhodesia negotiations. Rebels hoping to overthrow General Mobutu invaded Zaire from Angola and Zambia on the 13 May. On 18 May, the Carter Administration provided 18 transport planes for Belgian and French operations against the rebels. Within a few weeks, the rebels retreated, after limited fighting. The U.S. role did not go unnoticed by the Frontline leaders. Nyerere impugned the American logistic support for neocolonialism in Zaire, and the incident contributed to the breakdown of the Anglo-American initiative.[122]

THE CASE-JAVITS AMENDMENT

The Carter Administration's policy of withholding recognition of the internal settlement faced direct challenges in Washington, moreover. Senators Jesse Helms (R-N.C.) and S.I. Hayakawa (R-Cal.) emerged as the administration's most formidable opponents. Hayakawa won a Senate seat in 1976, with substantial monetary aid from the South African government.[123] Helms had supported the Byrd Amendment in 1971, while still a television commentator in North Carolina. Earlier, he had opposed the civil rights movement as an editorialist and city politician throughout the 1950s and 1960s. Often, he had emphasized that the civil rights movement was controlled by communists, and his most severe attacks were aimed at Martin Luther King.[124] So, it was not surprising that Helms would criticize Carter's policy, for at least three reasons: (1), It was championed by Young, King's former assistant; (2), it seemed to favor Nkomo and Mugabe whom he perceived as communists; and (3), it had reinstated sanctions.

So, Helms crafted an amendment to the State Department authorization bill that would lift sanctions against Southern Rhodesia in order to give the internal settlement a chance. In a 28 June vote that was too close for the comfort of the Carter Administration, the Senate tabled the Helms amendment.[125] Undaunted by defeat, Helms decided to reintroduce his sanctions-lifting legislation as an amendment to the International Assistance Security Bill. As his plans became known in early July, the State Department began working with allies on Senate staffs to derail Helm's attempt. The Washington Office on Africa orchestrated a planning session for various lobbyists interested in opposing Helms and preserving sanctions.[126] In a conversation with Senate Majority Leader Robert Byrd (D-W.Va.), Warren Christopher outlined the damaging effects on overall U.S. policy in Africa that lifting the sanctions would have.[127]

Bishop Muzorewa, at Helm's invitation, arrived in Washington on 16 July. The next day he lunched with *Washington Post* editors, accompanied by Helms' staffer John Carbaugh. The stoic Muzorewa impressed many in his clerical attire, and Carbaugh attempted to arrange a meeting between Muzorewa and Brzezinski. Furthermore, Carbaugh threatened that if the Carter Administration refused to compromise on lifting sanctions to some extent,

Helms had enough support to get his amendment passed. After the meeting, White House aides debated about who, if anyone, should meet with Muzorewa. Officials at State, meanwhile, began secretly drafting a compromise as an alternative to the Helms Amendment.[128]

The NSC staff informed Carter of Muzorewa's visit and Helms' proposed amendment. It warned: "Suspension of sanctions would be a godsend to the Internal Settlement regime, which is floundering badly and is rapidly coming to the conclusion that it will fail.... The Patriotic Front, on the other hand, would see suspension of sanctions as clear evidence that the United States was not to be trusted." It added that because ending sanctions would strengthen Smith, the PF would be tempted to seek additional support from the Soviets or Cubans. The Helms Amendment, therefore, could result in an escalation of fighting with more communist involvement. The public debate, unfortunately, had degenerated into a simple case of the "Marxist" PF versus the "democratic" Internal Settlement.[129]

At a 19 July breakfast meeting with 20 undecided Senators, Carter mentioned the importance of maintaining the administration's policy towards Southern Rhodesia. Although they realized that even more personal meetings with smaller groups would be most effective, White House staffers concluded that drastic measures were needed to block Helms. On 20 July, the administration hosted some one hundred Senate staffers in the White House family theater. Delays and hot weather created a tense atmosphere, exacerbated by the late arrival of the primary speaker, Anthony Lake. After Lake's presentation, a hostile audience member dominated the question period, and the session deteriorated into a shouting match.[130]

As the vote approached, both sides stepped up their lobbying. Prosanctions activists like Vernon Jordan, President of the National Urban League, labored against the Helms Amendment. Jordan argued that the amendment would "place this country in the position of forfeiting the cooperation of the front line states, betraying its pledge to the United Nations, and retarding efforts to achieve a successful compromise among the Rhodesian Parties."[131] Randall Robinson of TransAfrica, which had finally raised enough money to open an office in Washington, joined in the fight to keep sanctions. On 26 July, as a result of the administration's effort and the assistance of lobbyists like Jordan and Robinson, Helm's second attempt at lifting sanctions was defeated in the Senate.

Also on 26 July, however, the Senate approved an amendment to the Security Assistance Authorization Bill, which amounted to a compromise between the two positions. Senators Clifford Case (D-N.J.) and Jacob Javits (R-N.Y.) drafted the amendment, with help from Christopher. The Case-Javits amendment would lift sanctions after 31 December 1978, if Carter determined the following: (1) the Southern Rhodesian regime demonstrated its intention to negotiate in good faith at an all-parties conference, and (2) all political and population groups in Southern Rhodesia participated in a free election witnessed by impartial observers.[133] The Carter Administration, therefore, succeeded in the summer of 1978 in blocking Helms and also in defending two key points: an all-parties conference and elections that included the PF.

SMITH VISITS WASHINGTON

Meanwhile, in southern Africa peace seemed further away than ever. Black refugees, many of them potential soldiers, continued to stream into Zambia and Mozambique. Hundreds of whites emigrated from Southern Rhodesia each week, as tourism further declined and casualties mounted. In July and August, Low and Graham shuttled between Salisbury, Lusaka, and Dar Es Salaam in hopes of arranging an all-parties conference, but to no avail.[134] On 4 September Nkomo's ZAPU forces shot down a jet carrying vacationers near Lake Kariba. The crash killed thirty-eight, and of the eighteen survivors, ten were shot as they fled the wreckage.

This incident prompted outrage among whites in Southern Rhodesia, and also reverberated in the United States. The downing of the jet and massacre of some survivors added grist for the mill of those who portrayed the PF as terrorists. Constituents mailed members of Congress postcards depicting Nkomo as a "communist" and recounting the jet incident.[135] Of sixty-seven editorials in major newspapers between June and mid-September, nearly three-fourths supported the internal settlement. The few that did support U.S. policy and oppose the internal settlement still condemned PF terrorism.[136]

Hayakawa and twenty-six other senators invited Smith and the executive council to visit Washington, in hopes of rallying American enthusiasm for the internal settlement. Those inviting Smith included an all-star cast of conservatives: Harry Byrd, Barry Goldwater, Jesse Helms, Bob Dole, and Strom Thurmond, among others. Hayakawa requested that Carter facilitate the process of getting a visa for Smith, who had accepted the invitation. Smith agreed that Congress needed to hear the "full facts of the Rhodesian situation," and hoped to arrive in Washington before Congress adjourned in mid-October.[137]

Influential African Americans, including Representative Parren Mitchell (D-Md.), notified the White House that they opposed Smith's visit and hoped he would not be granted a visa.[138] TransAfrica coordinated protests against Smith at consulates across the country. State initiated a high-level review of Smith's request, and Vance certainly would have preferred to block the visit, if circumstances allowed. However, he believed that doing so would give Hayakawa and his allies more leverage to terminate sanctions. Vance later observed that by fall 1978, the Carter Administration was "on the defensive regarding the internal settlement."[139] Hayakawa and Helms pressed State to stop delaying, and on 4 October Vance approved a visa for Smith.[140]

At that point, Brzezinski and Vance disagreed about the future course of American policy towards Africa. Brzezinski argued that the United States should confront the Soviets about their activity in Africa, or decrease U.S. activity in Africa. Basically, he wanted to return to viewing Africa through a Cold War lens. Vance, on the other hand, favored a continuation of the current policy of seeking African solutions to African problems, outside of the U.S./Soviet rivalry. Vance and Young agreed, moreover, that alleviating racial, political, and economic problems in southern Africa would be the best way to prevent Soviet influence.[141] Dealing best with Southern Rhodesia meant arranging an all-parties conference to negotiate an alternative to the internal settlement.

Ian Smith and his delegation arrived in Washington on 7 October, and two days later met with Vance and Peter Jay, British Ambassador to the United States. Jay and Vance requested that Smith meet with the PF. Smith rejected the idea, arguing that he and the rest of the executive council were too busy carrying out the internal plan. On 12 October, however, Smith and Sithole reversed their position. They agreed to participate in a conference with the PF, as long as there were no preconditions.[142]

Smith and his delegation stopped next in New York, where the American-Rhodesian Association hosted a lavish banquet for them. From there it was on to California for three days. Smith met with Governor Ronald Reagan and was impressed with his views on Southern Rhodesia. The Los Angeles World Affairs Council provided a feast for Smith and twelve hundred supporters, including Senator S.I. Hayakawa. For fun, Smith visited the San Diego zoo and Disneyland. He later recalled that the home of Mickey Mouse "provided us with some of our happiest moments of the trip." It was then on to Palm Springs to talk with Gerald Ford, who expressed his regret that Carter was not living up to Kissinger's promises to Smith and blamed it on the American voters. After this discussion Smith's entourage visited Houston, returning to Washington on 18 October.[143]

Carter still had no interest in meeting with Smith. For Harry Byrd, the administration's treatment of Smith was a disappointment. The Virginia senator met three times with Smith, and staunchly advocated the internal solution. He contended that Carter should have hosted Smith at the White House to hear Smith's side of the story. In Byrd's opinion such a meeting never occurred because "at the urging of UN Ambassador Andrew Young, the President has made the proterrorist position the policy of our government."[144] Byrd hinted that if Carter could break free from Young's influence, he would see that Smith was a reasonable man, and possibly decide to give the internal solution a chance.

Byrd and other supporters of the internal settlement suggested that the PF forces were the "terrorists," and that the actions of the Smith regime's security forces were prompted by guerrilla insurgency and thus justifiable. Events on 18 October cast serious doubts on their interpretation. Smith's forces bombed a refugee camp in Zambia, just a few miles from Lusaka. Hundreds of young men were wounded, and about two hundred were killed. George Houser of the American Committee on Africa had just visited this location, one of ZAPU's "boys victory camps," and described it as "not military."[145]

Another raid a few days later killed mostly young women in a second refugee camp. These camps, partly funded by the United States, provided education and medicine for young refugees. When military officials realized that they had hit the wrong target and killed so many girls, they staged a cover-up operation. Meanwhile, commandos destroyed Nkomo's house in Lusaka and began supplying poisoned clothes to the refugee camps.[146] In these instances, clearly, the Southern Rhodesian security forces' actions merited the label "terrorism."

In Washington, State officials received confirmation from Smith that he would attend an all-parties conference, but the bloodshed in Zambia suggested that he was in no hurry to reach an agreement with the PF. According to Moose: "Such actions only increase the distrust that divides the parties and make all the more difficult the task of engaging the parties in serious negotiations aimed at ending the conflict."[147] The raids into Zambia and subsequent attacks on ZANU bases in Mozambique, in fact, virtually guaranteed that Nkomo and Mugabe would refuse to attend an all-parties conference in the foreseeable future.

Smith's visit to the United States had failed to generate a noticable increase in support from Americans, but nonetheless had infuriated the PF and its allies. By December it was clear that the Anglo-American initiative towards SR had bogged down. Smith was pressing ahead with plans for an election based on the internal plan, and his security forces continued their brutal punishment of PF guerrillas and civilian refugees alike. Seeing no other viable response to the raids, the PF decided to escalate their struggle against Smith and his executive council. Among their Frontline supporters, even pacifist Kaunda concluded that it would be impossible to get the Anglo-American plan back on track, and that a "military solution" was the only answer. One last attempt by Low and the British to arrange a conference in December failed, and the Anglo-American Plan was practically aborted.[148]

MUZOREWA'S ELECTION

Before the House of Commons in January, Prime Minister Callaghan stated that he would not hold an all-parties conference in the near future. This announcement encouraged Southern Rhodesian officials to seek support for the internal settlement, since the Anglo-American plan obviously would not succeed in the short run. They targeted the U.S. Senate as a likely ally and hoped that the Senate would force the Carter Administration to lift sanctions.[149] Carter did not want to lift sanctions, but Southern Rhodesia was not his top priority for 1979. The debates over Panama and the Strategic Arms Limitation Talks (SALT) were much more important. In response to a query from Brzezinski, NSC staffer Madeleine Albright explained: "Although we will have to be involved in some defensive action on lifting Rhodesian sanctions, the issue is pretty low on the President's legislative agenda. His schedule will be filled with SALT, MTN, and Panama Canal legislation."[150]

While the President could not devote much time to the issue, Vance and Young continued to work for a settlement that would be acceptable to leading black Africans and the British. In early February, Young maintained his faith in the Anglo-American Plan. He hoped that by continued diplomacy, the United States could help the British negotiate a "genuine transfer of power" and thereby "bring the human suffering there to an end." Young concluded: "To those who say that our diplomatic initiatives have failed, I remind them that the military solution has failed as well. Certainly, diplomatic initiatives deserve as much time and patience as military solutions."[151]

Young acknowledged, however, that circumstances looked very bleak for a settlement that would include the PF and thus end the war. Fighting still raged in February, with Nkomo's forces downing a second passenger jet. Smith scheduled the internal elections for mid-April, throwing another monkey wrench into the works. Under the Case-Javits Amendment from 1978, Carter would be forced to lift sanctions if the SR government agreed to attend a conference and if free and fair elections took place. So, it would be necessary to determine if the April elections were free and fair. After talking with members of TransAfrica, Vance advised Carter that the administration should not send observers to the elections, because that would legitimize the internal settlement. Doing so would anger African leaders and undermine any future negotiations. If the Congress decided to send observers, Vance believed that the administration should remain neutral.[152]

On 1 March, Senators Hayakawa and George McGovern (D-S.D.) proposed that Congress sponsor a team of observers.

McGovern supported the Carter policy, but feared that without sponsoring observers Congress would get information biased towards the internal regime. During hearings to consider the McGovern/Hayakawa proposal, Jesse Jackson strongly opposed the idea of sending observers. Randall Robinson seconded Jackson's position. According to Robinson, sending obervers would have multiple negative effects: "This course will give Mr. Smith hope. The war will be extended. More lives will be lost. The credibility of our foreign policy in Africa will be devastated."[153]

Jackson and Robinson both spoke for an emerging interest group in the United States, which actively opposed American support for the white regimes in southern Africa. Young later identified this "new constituency for U.S.-African affairs" as a key element behind the Carter Administration's policy towards the conflict. In addition to civil rights leaders like Jackson and lobbyists like Robinson, it included many of the new black politicians in Congress and in city governments. Some whites also participated, particularly those who had opposed the war in Vietnam.[154]

In part responding to the views of this "new constituency," the Carter Administration decided not to send observers to the Southern Rhodesian elections.[155] Moose testified that doing so would seriously harm the international reputation of the United States and hinder future attempts at negotiating.[156] Vance reiterated that the Carter Administration would not send observers. The administration did not support the internal settlement, because it could not bring peace.[157] Despite the administration's stance, the Senate overwhelmingly approved the proposal to send a team.[158]

Meanwhile, the House had begun debating a similar resolution. Representative Stephen Solarz (D-N.Y.) led the fight against it. As chair of the House Foreign Affairs Committee's subcommitee on Africa, he orchestrated extensive hearings to provide Congress with detailed background on the situation in Southern Rhodesia.[159] Anthony Lake summarized U.S. policy from 1965 to 1976. Moose again explained the Carter Administration's decision against observers. In early April, the Africa subcommittee defeated the resolution unanimously, guaranteeing that the full Foreign Affairs Committee would not consider it. Thus, Solarz blocked the Senate's effort to send a team sponsored by Congress.[160]

Debate in London echoed that in Washington, as Prime Minister Callaghan fought the Conservative cry for observers. On 1 April the Parliament voiced "no confidence" in Callaghan, and Margaret Thatcher emerged as the leading candidate to replace him. In mid-April, Thatcher sent five observers to Southern Rhodesia. Expectations rose that after her expected election in May, she would recognize the internal regime if the elections were judged "free and fair".[161]

Preparations for the elections moved ahead. The two candidates would be Muzorewa and Sithole, and everyone except Sithole expected Muzorewa to win easily. The Security Forces visited the villages and strongly encouraged the peasants to vote. According to Low, it would be virtually impossible for outside observers to accurately judge whether or not the elections were "free and fair," because so much intimidation would already have occurred before they arrived. Low concluded that after the elections, the war would probably worsen.[162]

The PF leaders, in fact, pledged to carry on the war. Nkomo contended that the elections could not be fair with about 95 percent of the country under martial law in 1979. He announced that any government resulting from the vote would be illegitimate, and the guerrillas would oppose it. He decried the United States and Britain for their ambivalence towards the elections and accused them of "collaborating and conniving at Smith's gimmick and gamble."[163] Mugabe also condemned the vote and pledged that his forces would fight on until victory.[164]

Despite the opposition of ZAPU and ZANU, over 60 percent of eligible blacks voted between 17 and 20 April. They selected candidates from Muzorewa's party for 51 of 72 black seats in parliament, thus designating him the first black prime minister of Southern Rhodesia. The turnout seemed impressive, but Low argued that it was misleading. It reflected the intimidation by the Security Forces, as well as the armies of Muzorewa and Sithole. Nkomo and Mugabe judged it a sham.[165] Nevertheless, Muzorewa would become the leader in Salisbury at the end of May, and this intensified the debates in Washington and London about lifting sanctions and recognizing the internal regime.

On 25 April, the *MacNeil/Lehrer Report* examined the results of the elections. Young appeared in defense of the administration's policy. He compared the elections to pre-1965 elections in the southern United States, when blacks were influenced and intimidated. He argued that recognizing Muzorewa would only guarantee continued fighting, which would eventually bring about greater Soviet involvement on the side of the PF. He pointed out that if the United States lifted sanctions, it would lose credibility with the PF and Frontline and also lose any remaining leverage for getting Muzorewa to an all-parties conference.[166]

Representative Robert Bauman (R-Md.), who chaired the American Conservative Union, presented the position that the elections were "free and fair." He questioned the current U.S. policy that supported "terrorists" and argued that the Carter Administration should lift sanctions. If Carter refused to lift sanctions, moreover, he predicted that the Congress would override him. He warned: "The tide has turned in the House, as it has in the Senate, and I think that if the President fails to act, it will be at his own political peril."[167]

CARTER'S DETERMINATION

Carter manifested his position to the press on 27 April. He characterized the elections as a "step in the right direction." However, under the provisions of the Case-Javits Amendment, he was required to wait until Muzorewa was officially installed as prime minister and then determine whether the elections had been "free and fair." Muzorewa's inauguration was scheduled for 31 May, so until then Carter would not make a final decision. Also, he asked Senate Majority Leader Robert Byrd to withhold support for any measure that preempted Case-Javits and tried to force an end to sanctions before Carter had made his determination.[168]

Although Representative Bauman opined that the "tide had turned" in the House regarding Southern Rhodesia, that was not necessarily the case. Representative Solarz mounted a major offensive against the attempts to lift sanctions and recognize Muzorewa. He organized a "Rhodesia Strategy Group," which included some 60 assistants and staffers. They targeted a list of 93 uncommitted "swing" votes. In late April, the group began encouraging concerned citizens to write to these Congressman. The Congressional Black Caucus joined Solarz in his fight, urging Carter to work for a "peaceful and fair settlement in Zimbabwe" by not lifting sanctions prematurely. The Black Caucus, having grown to sixteen with the addition of William Gray (D-Pa.), added that maintaining sanctions was a "major issue" for the African-American community.[169]

While Solarz and his allies worked hard in defense of sanctions, opponents of sanctions did little lobbying.[170] The pro-Muzorewa forces did not think they needed much lobbying, however, since they expected a great boost from London. On 4 May, Margaret Thatcher was elected prime minister. Thatcher represented the Conservative Party, which had been very critical of the Southern Rhodesia policy of Labour's Foreign Secretary David Owen. Thatcher was impressed with the results of the internal settlement and by Muzorewa and had no use for Mugabe or Nkomo. A Conservative Party team of observers judged the election "free and fair." Yet, in Thatcher's view, all of that was outweighed by a need to stop the fighting. As she later recalled: "I was well aware that what the people of Rhodesia needed above all was peace and stability."[171]

With that in mind, she relied heavily on the advice of her foreign secretary, Peter Carrington. He suggested that they not recognize Muzorewa hastily, but instead proceed cautiously. Carrington emphasized the need for a settlement that was broadly accepted around the world. They decided to consult with the Carter Administration, whose views Thatcher considered to be "of vital importance." During discussions in Washington, Vance urged Carrington to seek an all-parties conference and to maintain sanctions.[172] Thatcher's exact plans for Southern Rhodesia were not clear, but she and Carrington definitely wanted a settlement that would bring peace. Therefore, to the disappointment of Helms and other supporters of Muzorewa, Thatcher refrained from recognizing the internal settlement in May.

Focus shifted back to the U.S. Senate where Harry Byrd, Hayakawa, and Helms pushed for a prompt decision from the President. When the decision was not forthcoming, Helms proposed an amendment that would require an end to sanctions. Carter refrained from active participation in the Senate debate, having put his faith in Robert Byrd. Byrd initially intended to support a resolution that would give Carter two weeks after Muzorewa's inauguration to make a determination. However, fearing passage of Helms' amendment, Byrd realized that a compromise was necessary. The resulting amendment to the State Department Authorization bill expressed the "sense of the Senate" that the President should lift sanctions, and passed by a landslide on 15 May.[173]

The Carter Administration held its ground, though, since the amendment was nonbinding. Carter would make his decision after Muzorewa took office. In the meantime, Vance visited Thatcher and her new Foreign Secretary Peter Carrington, on whom she depended heavily regarding foreign policy. Carrington had considerable experience, having served as Lord of the Admiralty from 1959 to 1963 and Defense Secretary from 1970 to 1974. He also understood the circumstances in Southern Rhodesia quite well, having visited as a board member for a mining company. Upon rejoining the government in early May 1979, he announced that he would "settle" the conflict.[174] The challenge for Carrington, as it had been for his predecessors back to 1965, was how to settle it.

On 21 May Carrington met with Vance, who explained that Carter had very specific requirements in mind before he would lift sanctions: revising the constitution, an all-parties conference, and an internationally supervised election. Carrington responded that he would prefer more general criterion, since he would need some flexibility to stem the tide calling for recognition in Parliament. Carrington warned that Thatcher would not fight to maintain sanctions. He realized, though, that recognition of Muzorewa would damage British relations with the United States and black Africa. He did not know when Thatcher would make a decision, and was only certain that it would be before November, since that was when British sanctions would expire if no further action was taken.[175]

The meeting, while inconclusive, was informative and somewhat encouraging. Carrington indicated that he and Thatcher planned to take the lead on Southern Rhodesia, giving the United States less of a role than they had played with Owen and Callaghan. Yet, he also manifested his intention to proceed carefully, weighing the opinions of the United States and African nations like Nigeria. On 30 May, Vance convinced Carter that more general guidelines for recognition would give Carrington the necessary flexibility to make progress towards a solution.[176] The following day saw the inauguration of Muzorewa, which meant that Carter had to make his determination.

Throughout May and early June, Carter received messages from African-American leaders encouraging him to maintain sanctions. Jesse Jackson, Corretta Scott King, Maynard Jackson, and Richard Hatcher (President of the National Conference of Black Mayors) all opposed lifting sanctions. Another plea to keep sanctions, circulated by TransAfrica, was signed by one hundred eighty-five prominent African Americans. White House aide Louis Martin, a black himself, emphasized to Carter the importance of these leaders' views on Southern Rhodesia. George Meany, President of the AFL-CIO, indicated that his powerful labor union agreed with the black leadership.[177]

While Congressional staffers belonging to the Rhodesia Strategy Group rallied support from influential citizens around the nation, members of Congress lobbied Carter directly. The Black Caucus strongly opposed recognition of Muzorewa.[178] By far the most active member of Congress on the issue in May and June, however, was Stephen Solarz, who had visited Southern Rhodesia and the Frontline States in April.

Solarz, summarizing his conclusions in a report for Carter, argued that Muzorewa was no more democratic than the PF leaders. He emphasized that there really was little difference between Mugabe, Nkomo, Muzorewa, and Sithole. In his view: "Our real interest in Rhodesia, therefore, is not so much in who wins the war but in ending the war." Muzorewa's triumph would not end the war, and the longer it continued the more the Soviets would become involved. Solarz concluded:

> The only way to bring the war to an end in the relatively near future... is through an agreement on the part of all the parties involved to shift the struggle from the battlefield to the negotiating table. Unfortunately, if we were to recognized the internal settlement and lift sanctions at this time, this possibility would go down the diplomatic drain.[179]

Solarz admitted that if the President decided to maintain sanctions, opponents of the policy would mount a serious effort to overturn the decision. He believed that as long as Carter was willing to actively assist him, however, he could block the opposition in the House. In order to further underline his position, Solarz met with Vice President Walter Mondale in early June.[180] Solarz had prevented Congress-sponsored observers of the elections, organized the Rhodesia Strategy Group, traveled across southern Africa, submitted a detailed report to Carter, and met with Mondale. He rested his case and awaited the President's determination. According to Steve Low, the efforts by Solarz were heroic and led to a "turning point" in U.S. relations with Southern Rhodesia.[181]

That turning point came on 7 June when Carter announced his decision. Carter forcefully asserted the following: "First, I am absolutely convinced that the best interests of the United States would not be served by lifting the sanctions. Second, I am equally convinced that the best interests of the people of Zimbabwe-Rhodesia would not be served by lifting of the sanctions." Carter discussed the shortcomings in the constitution and the prevalence of martial law during the elections. He remarked, "I cannot conclude that the elections were either free or fair."[182]

Carter, then, had decided to maintain sanctions against the Muzorewa government. His announcement, and Vance's subsequent discussion with reporters, elucidated the general reasons for the decision: the elections were not free and fair, and the Southern Rhodesian government had not yet agreed to confer on all relevant issues. Carter and Vance did not specify when they might lift sanctions, only calling for progress towards "genuine majority rule." They made it clear, however, that all-party negotiations would be needed in order to sufficiently modify the constitution, and that such a conference would have to be arranged by the British.[183]

Carter acknowledged that he did not "have a majority of support in the United States Senate." However, he believed the sanctions were a matter of principle for him and the nation. He felt that lifting them would harm U.S. standing across Africa, would violate U.S. pledges going back to Lyndon Johnson's presidency, and would not help the people of the United States or Southern Rhodesia. For these reasons Carter wanted to maintain sanctions, and he pledged to "do everything I can within my power to prevail in this situation."[184] Thus, Carter intended to fight the Senate in defense of his administration's policy. By making this decision, Carter took the firmest stance on Southern Rhodesia ever taken by a American president.

Carter's defiance of the Senate earned him public praise from columnist Vernon Jordan and private congratulations from David Owen, who opined that "it is good to see principles upheld."[185] As the President had expected, however, his decision was assaulted in the Senate. Senators Helms and Harry Byrd proposed an amendment to the Defense Authorization Bill that would overturn Carter's decision and require an end of sanctions. Vance testified on the administration's behalf, but the amendment passed in the Senate on 12 June by a solid margin.[186] The Senate, as expected, was mounting a serious threat to overturn Carter's decision through the Defense Bill, which would be considered by a House-Senate committee in September.

Meanwhile, the House debated a sanctions amendment to the State Authorization Bill. Solarz championed the resolution, which would leave the decision over when to lift sanctions to Carter. The administration joined Solarz in an impressive effort to sway undecided representatives: Young, Brzezinski, Moose, and Lake phoned several, and Mondale hosted a breakfast for one hundred. Cardiss Collins (D-Ill.) spoke eloquently in favor of the Solarz Amendment during the final debates on 28 June, and it passed convincingly.[187] The House upheld Carter's decision, at least until the bicameral conference on the Defense Authorization Bill, which would not occur until September. The House vote reflected Solarz and the Rhodesia Strategy Group's hard work, but also demonstrated the high priority that the White House gave to Southern Rhodesia in 1979. On Carter's list of important leglislative battles, only Panama and SALT II ranked ahead of defending Southern Rhodesia policy.[188]

Carter's stance disappointed Smith and Muzorewa, who had hoped for U.S. recognition. Smith later criticized Carter's decision to maintain sanctions, and accused him of "hypocrisy and rank dishonesty" in pursuit of black votes. Muzorewa, at Helms' invitation, visited Washington to plead his case. Appearing on *Good Morning America*, Muzorewa blasted the President's position, blaming it on Andrew Young. He contended that the sanctions were actually exacerbating the fighting, by encouraging the PF.[189] At

Camp David on 11 July, Carter informed Muzorewa that he would not lift sanctions, because doing so would not contribute to a lasting solution or an end to the fighting.[190]

LUSAKA AND LANCASTER

By holding firm in the face of Muzorewa's pleading, and by fighting with the Senate, Carter demonstrated his resolve to the British. The U.S. policy influenced Foreign Minister Carrington's thinking as he weighed British options in July 1979. He realized that the British could not lift sanctions and grant independence to the Muzorewa regime, in part because the United States would not recognize its legitimacy. Carrington later recalled that "the Muzorewa election was not really a proposition which anybody would have agreed to.... Certainly not the Americans." More importantly, though, Carrington did not think that Muzorewa could end the war. If it continued, the Soviets and the Chinese would get more involved and the crisis would be prolonged indefinitely.[191]

The primary factor that motivated the British to seek a new solution in mid-1979, then, was the fact that the fighting was escalating. In July, over twenty thousand PF soldiers roamed approximately two-thirds of rural Southern Rhodesia, where the people continued to support them.[192] The war cost the Muzorewa government over $1 million per day, and soldiers and civilians suffered casualties at a rapidly increasing rate. Mozambique and Zambia bore the costs of about two hundred thousand refugees between them, as well as destruction from Security Force raids. The war hurt everyone in southern Africa, and since Muzorewa could not end it, Carrington decided not to support him.[193]

On 1 August, the annual Commonwealth Conference opened in Lusaka. Thatcher had not yet backed off from her election pledges to recognize Muzorewa. On the eve of the conference, Nigeria nationalized the holdings of British Petroleum, which only added to the hostility in the air. The stage was set for a bitter confrontation at Lusaka. Yet Machel, tiring of the war, opted not to pick a fight with Thatcher. Kaunda chaired the conference, and he wisely waited until the third day to discuss Southern Rhodesia. At that point, Nyerere took over and gave a very diplomatic speech in which he acknowledged progress, but he called for a new constitution, internationally supervised elections, and all-parties negotiations.[194]

The major breakthroughs came over the weekend, when Thatcher and Nyerere compared their positions and found significant common ground. Due in large part to the skill of Kaunda, the leaders hammered out a compromise agreement. The primary elements were: (1) elections monitored by Great Britain, (2) a new constitution, and (3) a ceasefire during the election. With some prodding from Carrington, moreover, Thatcher agreed to bring all of the parties together in London. The Lusaka summit concluded on 6 August, and shortly thereafter Thatcher sent invitations to the Muzorewa government and the PF to attend a conference at Lancaster House.[195]

Meanwhile back in the United States, two series of events transpired that affected the Carter Administration's role: one involved sanctions, and the other involved Andrew Young. On 26 July, Young talked with Zehdi Terzi, the Palestinian Liberation Organization's UN observer. Receiving a tip that Young had met with a PLO representative, a *Newsweek* reporter asked the State Department about it the following day, and Assistant Secretary William Maynes queried Young.[196] After initially denying that anything substantial had been discussed, Young informed the Israeli government that he and Terzi had conversed about a UN resolution on Palestinian rights. Israel filed a formal protest against Young for violating the agreement not to meet with PLO representatives. In a private meeting on 15 August, Vance told Young that he should resign. Young then talked at length to Carter, who offered no alternative, so Young quit.[197]

As the Young saga unfolded, members of the House and the Senate conferred on the State Authorization Bill. The Senate version included the nonbinding resolution advising Carter to lift sanctions immediately. Solarz and Helms compromised, and the final version left the decision to Carter, stipulating that he make another determination no later than 15 November.[198] On the day that Young resigned, 15 August, Carter signed the bill into law and thereby agreed to make a second decision on sanctions by 15 November.

Carter hoped that a settlement might be reached in London before that date, although it was still unclear whether or not the Lancaster House conference would take place. Smith and Muzorewa decided to attend, since they were not getting international recognition and perceived that their chances for a profitable settlement were best with Conservatives in control of Great Britain. Mugabe and Nkomo did not want to go to Lancaster, feeling that they could still gain more by fighting. At a meeting of non-aligned states in Cuba, Mugabe denounced the Lusaka agreement and the proposed Lancaster conference. The Frontline leaders confronted him and Nkomo, however, and insisted that they participate at Lancaster. Machel, in particular, forced Mugabe to concede by threatening to end Mozambique's support for the war.[199] So, grudgingly and with little hope for success, all the parties gathered at Lancaster House on 10 September.

In mid-September on Capitol Hill, conferees began haggling over another relevant piece of legislation, the Defense Authorization Bill. The Senate version featured Harry Byrd's proposal, which mandated an immediate end to sanctions. The majority of the conferees, including Byrd himself, had voted consistently to end sanctions. The Carter Administration faced a tough fight and focused its efforts on the chair of the Armed Services Committee, Senator John Stennis (D-Miss.). With help from Solarz, administration officials urged Stennis to delete the Byrd Amendment. TransAfrica's leaders joined the fray, urging the conferees not to lift sanctions, but they were not optimistic.[200]

Carter himself turned the tide, though, when he met with Stennis on 24 September to discuss the Defense Bill. The bill included a second controversial amendment, which funded a new nuclear aircraft carrier. Evidently, Carter hinted that if Stennis deleted the Byrd Amendment, he would approve the Defense Bill with the nuclear carrier amendment.[201] Whether or not such a quid pro quo occurred, there is no doubt that Carter pledged to veto the Defense Bill if it lifted the sanctions against Southern Rhodesia.[202]

Carter, as he had in June, took a stronger stand on Southern Rhodesia than any of his predecessors. As a result, Stennis prevailed on the conferees, and the final version of the Defense Bill did not lift sanctions. The fight over the Defense Bill represented a major triumph for the Carter Administration and its allies in Congress, and many of the key players celebrated at the home of Solarz afterwards.[203] As a result of their victory, the decision on sanctions remained the President's and would depend on the progress at Lancaster.

The United States did not officially participate at Lancaster, where Carrington was clearly in charge. To the consternation of the Carter Administration and the British, Helms tried to influence the proceedings. Two of Helms' staffers indicated to Smith and Muzorewa that if they held out long enough, the Senate would force Carter to lift sanctions. Carrington informed Vance of this activity, and the secretary forced Helms to recall his aides.[204] During the Lancaster negotiations the American ambassador to Great Britain, Kingman Brewster, maintained contact with all sides. Through Brewster, the United States insisted that everyone be treated equally during the ceasefire, a condition that was crucial for gaining Mugabe's support for the final settlement. The Carter Administration's pledge to seek financial aid for an independent Zimbabwe also helped keep Mugabe on board.[205]

While the American role was significant, the cooptation of Mugabe at Lancaster owed much more to the impressive efforts of Carrington. Mugabe arrived at Lancaster in a confident and stubborn mood, finally in charge of the ZANU forces who were doing the majority of the fighting. Carrington laid down the law from the outset, however, and firmly controlled the agenda. He decided to tackle one issue at a time and began with the constitution. After forging an agreement that reserved seats for twenty whites, Carrington turned to the issue of elections. He doggedly persevered, and it was agreed that the British would supervise. In early November, Carrington brought up the final major issue—the groundrules for the ceasefire.[206]

At this critical point, the British sanctions were due to expire. Carrington fought off one last attempt from the right wing of the Conservative party to recognize Muzorewa and lift sanctions, and Thatcher agreed to extend them for a month.[207] Carter was also required to make a determination on sanctions by the middle of November. At a 14 November meeting with African-American leaders the President announced that it was "in the national interest of the United States to continue sanctions against Zimbabwe-Rhodesia." While progress had been made at Lancaster no settlement had been signed and lifting sanctions could jeopardize a final agreement. Carter added that he would lift sanctions after the British Governor assumed authority in Salisbury and initiated the process leading to elections.[208]

Carter's decision probably had relatively little impact at Lancaster, where the talks had bogged down over the ceasefire issue. Mugabe resisted the Carrington proposal that all PF guerrillas be rounded up in observation points during the period leading up to elections. He considered giving up on the Lancaster negotiations, but Machel convinced him to return to the table. He remained opposed to the ceasefire arrangements, though, and the conference dragged on into December. In hopes of forcing the PF to accept the terms, Carrington sent Christopher Soames to Salisbury as governor.[209]

The British then asked the United States to lift sanctions as soon as Soames arrived in Salisbury on 12 December. TransAfrica opposed lifting sanctions at that point, fearing that U.S. corporations would supply massive funds for the re-election of Muzorewa. Carter was also unsure, and he wanted assurances that the process leading to free elections had begun. The British unhappily sought such assurances.[210] A few days later Robin Renwick, one of Carrington's top assistants, sent a "fervent plea" that Carter lift sanctions. Renwick characterized an announcement by Carter as "the key to forcing the PF to final settlement."[211] Carter complied on 16 December, issuing an executive order lifting sanctions. Hearing the news, Muzorewa exclaimed "hurrah for the lifting of sanctions."[212]

With some pressure from Machel, Mugabe and Nkomo finally initialed the package on 17 December. The White House rejoiced: "The world can celebrate a triumph of reason and an extraordinary diplomatic successs. A long, destructive and tragic conflict is ending."[213] At a ceremony on 21 December, all parties signed the Lancaster House accords. The ceasefire went into effect on 28 December. While fighting did not stop entirely overnight, the violence markedly diminished in January, and the ceasefire held. Carter watched the events unfold with hope. Thanking Solarz for his help maintaining sanctions, he praised Thatcher and Carrington for their wisdom and tenacity.[214]

ZIMBABWE'S FIRST PRIME MINISTER
Mugabe returned to his homeland on 27 January, after 16 years in prison or exile, and was greeted by very large crowds. Elections

took place one month later, and Mugabe won by a landslide. His party took fifty-seven seats in parliament, Nkomo's took twenty, and Muzorewa's only three. The results frightened the whites in Southern Rhodesia, surprised the British, and meant that Mugabe would be the first prime minister of the new nation of Zimbabwe. On 4 March he addressed the people in forgiving Biblical terms, asking them to turn swords into ploughshares.[215] When the news reached Washington, Vance praised the results of the election as "an historic breakthrough." Brzezinski congratulated Mugabe for his "moderate conciliatory pronouncements."[216]

Zimbabwe celebrated its Independence Day on 17 April 1980. Bob Marley and the Wailers played "Zimbabwe," written especially for the joyous occasion. Andrew Young and Averell Harriman led an impressive U.S. delegation that included Solarz, Moose, and Maynard Jackson.[217] Randall Robinson represented TransAfrica, and sat next to a South African woman who repeatedly remarked that she hoped to see a similar event in her country someday. Robinson assured her that she would.[218]

At midnight Prince Charles officially handed power to Mugabe, who faced the tremendous challenges of leading Zimbabwe to recovery. The war had killed about forty thousand, displaced over one million, and destroyed thousands of bridges, schools, and clinics.[219] The United States provided Mugabe about $25 million in aid during his first year, only enough to make a dent in the rebuilding, so the onus of recovery fell on the people of Zimbabwe themselves.[220]

Taking the reins with confidence, Mugabe promulgated policies that appeased the fears of the whites, naming a white minister of agriculture and leaving the military under a white general. He dealt with the disappointed Nkomo by appointing him interior minister. He advocated educational reform and refrained from radical measures such as land reform. In August, he journeyed to the United States and was warmly received, first at the UN where he accepted membership for his newly independent state. He addressed the General Assembly, and then a large crowd in Harlem. He appeared on *Meet the Press* and the *MacNeil/Lehrer Report*. In Washington he dined with members of Congress and Secretary of State Edmund Muskie.[221]

During the afternoon of 27 August Carter met with Mugabe for about an hour, then presided over a reception for him in the East Room. Carter congratulated Mugabe on his country's independence, and his courage in making it possible. He praised Mugabe's leadership since his election as "a notable example of the alleviation of tension" fostering "confidence, unity, and hope." He pointed to the parallels between the United States and Zimbabwe regarding their struggles against racial injustice. He explained that his administration had placed a much higher priority on Africa than its predecessors in order to help Africans and Americans. He cited Martin Luther King's point that "injustice anywhere is a threat to justice everywhere."[222]

Carter discussed the struggle for human rights. He praised Andrew Young, who was in attendance, for his longstanding efforts in that struggle, joking that Young had "never let me forget" the struggle in Zimbabwe. He attributed much of the impetus for U.S. policy to Young and to members of Congress who had dared to make votes contrary to public opinion. The dedication of Young and these members of Congress allowed the United States to maintain sanctions and stand on the side of justice, against the forces of oppression in the Zimbabwe conflict. According to the President: "The peaceful transition of Zimbabwe to popular majority rule is the strongest affirmation of our own human rights policy."[223]

Mugabe responded by thanking Carter for his efforts on behalf of the people of Zimbabwe. He lauded Young for his efforts to negotiate a settlement, and praised the President for preventing the Senate from lifting sanctions and recognizing the internal settlement. In the case of U.S. relations with Zimbabwe, Carter had "stood firm on a matter of principle." Mugabe concluded: "We believe in the same democratic principles. May these continue to tie us together. But more than that, may the friendship that we have established continue to exist."[224]

CONCLUSIONS

Upon taking office in 1977, Carter and his leading foreign policy advisers, particularly Young and Vance, agreed that Southern Rhodesia policy would be a high priority. They hoped to assist the British in negotiating a settlement that would end the war and result in the formation of an independent nation based on the principle of one person, one vote. The 1979 Lancaster Accords and the 1980 election of Mugabe as the first leader of an independent Zimbabwe represented the realization of the primary goals of Carter's Southern Rhodesia policy, and reflected several important factors.

The success of the Carter Administration's policy owed much to the hard work of many State Department officials, from high-level figures such as Vance to lesser-known individuals like Moose and Low. Young's informal approach to diplomacy helped create a positive relationship with Mugabe and Nkomo. A new constituency for U.S. relations with Africa, including black politicians and lobbyists like TransAfrica, provided support for the administration. A few members of Congress, most notably Solarz, beat back an effort led by Helms to recognize the internal regime of Smith and Muzorewa. Carter himself took a firm stand in that debate on more than one occasion, maintaining sanctions until the last days of the Lancaster Conference.

Carter's commitment to sanctions represented the strongest stance regarding Southern Rhodesia ever taken by a U.S. president. Carter's personal role in resolving the conflict sets him apart from his predecessors. Eisenhower was never involved in any policy decision affecting Southern Rhodesia. Kennedy met with some of the principals and displayed potential as a mediator, but died before the crisis boiled over. Johnson supported some strong initiatives in support of the British reaction to Smith's 1965 unilateral declaration of independence, especially sanctions. However, Johnson himself never directly shaped U.S. policy. Nixon demonstrated thorough disinterest in Southern Rhodesia, thereby opening the door for Congressional conservatives to undermine the sanctions. While Kissinger set some remarkable precedents with his diplomacy in 1976, Ford refrained from any involvement.

So, Carter's concrete actions clearly broke new ground for a U.S. president - the content of his policy aside. More than that, however, when it came to Southern Rhodesia policy Carter displayed a real vision. He boldly agreed with Nyerere in 1977 that, after independence, the Zimbabwean army should include members of the guerrilla forces and the government security forces. He retained sanctions in 1978 while the public and Congress condemned the PF as Marxist terrorists. In 1979, he courageously refused to recognize Muzorewa, who was the first black prime minister of Southern Rhodesia and a Methodist bishop. Although Muzorewa's election did represent progress, Carter believed that a settlement involving all Zimbabweans and bringing peace was possible.

Beginning with the 1960s, doomsayers predicted horrible consequences if the armies of ZANU and ZAPU triumphed in Southern Rhodesia. Acheson and Byrd were among the first to assert that only Smith and his white supporters could maintain order, and that black rule would result in a bloodbath and chaos similar to the Congo. Many powerful senators such as Dole and Helms joined the chorus in the 1970s, predicting disaster if the Patriotic Front emerged victorious. They contended that Smith's internal settlement with Muzorewa was the best way to save Southern Rhodesia from ruin and preserve American interests in southern Africa.

These men would probably describe their position on Southern Rhodesia as "realistic," but perhaps it is more accurate to characterize them as pessimistic. They did not believe that the black liberation forces could possibly make peace with the white and black security forces, or that a multiracial Zimbabwe could ever be formed. Furthermore, they were certain that the black-ruled nation would ally itself with the Soviet Union, and that American interests in the region would be lost. As for the most powerful nation in that region, South Africa, undoubtedly the doomsayers had even less hope for any cooperation among blacks and whites there.

Carter's vision for southern Africa, however, was an optimistic one. He foresaw cooperation among the races in an independent Zimbabwe and believed such a nation would naturally seek the support and friendship of the United States, which had begun progressing in the 1960s towards a genuine multiracial democracy. Carter's own career owed much to the help he had received from African Americans, and his appointment of Young in part reflected his gratitude. Yet, he did not simply give Young a job as a reward for the black vote and leave it at that. He intended to work closely with Young to mediate disputes around the world. Young's influential role in the Carter Administration embodied the possibilities of racial cooperation in the United States.

Carter and Young shared a faith that people of different races could work together in America, the Middle East, and Africa. Their efforts to mediate between Arabs and Israelis had very different results in the short run, with Carter gaining praise and Young being forced to resign. In the long run both have been vindicated, though, as the Middle East peace process begun in the late 1970s at Camp David continued to gain ground through the 1990s. Events in southern Africa, moreover, have provided even more dramatic evidence of the wisdom of their vision.

●

NOTES

1. John Dumbrell, *The Carter Presidency: A Re-evaluation*, 2nd ed. (Manchester: Manchester University Press, 1995), 110-111.
2. Cyrus Vance, "Overview of Foreign Policy Issues and Positions," 24 October 1976, Appendix I, in Vance, *Hard Choices: Critical Years in America's Foreign Policy* (New York: Simon and Schuster, 1983), 451. David S. McLellan, *Cyrus Vance* (Totowa: Rowman and Allenheld, 1985), 26.
3. Dumbrell, *The Carter Presidency*, 88-89.
4. Young interview with author, 2 March 1994, Atlanta, GA. Bartlett C. Jones, *Flawed Triumphs: Andy Young at the United Nations* (Lanham: University Press of America, 1996), 2.
5. For example, Young hired his two key assistants, James Leonard and Donald McHenry, due to Vance's recommendations. On this point, see Seymour Maxwell Finger, "Andrew Young at the UN," *Foreign Service Journal* 57 (July/August 1980), 19. On the good relations between Young and Vance in general see Brian Urquhart, *A Life in Peace and War* (New York: Harper Row, 1987), 268-269.
6. Vance, *Hard Choices*, 257 and 261.
7. H.R. 1746, 11 January 1977, "TA 4-8 1/20/77-4/30/77," Box TA 18, White House Central File - Subject (hereafter WHCF-S), Jimmy Carter Library, Atlanta, GA (hereafter JCL).
8. Young interview with author, 2 March 1994. For the details of Young's confirmation, see Jones, *Flawed Triumphs*, 1-7.
9. Vance, *Hard Choices*, 256 and 261. When reporters asked Henry Kissinger's brother Walter why Henry had not lost his German accent, Walter explained that it was because Henry did not listen to others. See Robert D. Schulzinger, *Henry Kissinger: Doctor of Diplomacy* (New York: Columbia University Press, 1989), 9-10.

10. Statement by Cyrus Vance, 10 February 1977, in Hearings Before the Subcommittee on African Affairs of the Committee on Foreign Relations, United States Senate, Ninety-fifth Congress, First Session, On S.174, A Bill to Amend the United States Participation Act of 1945 to Halt the Importation of Rhodesian Chrome, February 9 and 10, 1977, "Rhodesian Sanctions," 57.

11. Robert Shepard, *Nigeria, Africa, and the United States: From Kennedy to Reagan* (Bloomington: Indiana University Press, 1991), 104.

12. Young's statement in Hearing Before the Subcommittees on Africa and International Organization of the Committee on International Relations, House of Representatives, Ninety-fifth Congress, First Session, on H.R. 1746, February 24, 1977, "The Rhodesian Sanctions Bill," 8 and 14.

13. Carter's praise for Young at a 14 February 1977 Cabinet meeting is recorded in the diary of Domestic Affairs Adviser Stuart Eizenstat, cited in Jones, *Flawed Triumphs*, 58.

14. Memo to Carter, "Meeting with Rep. John Dent," 4 February 1977, and attached statement by Dent in support of repeal, "TA 4-8 1/20/77 - 4/30/77," Box TA18, WHCF-S, JCL.

15. Statement of E.F. Andrews, 9 February 1977, Hearings Before the Subcommitee on African Affairs, "Rhodesian Sanctions," 13.

16. Vance testimony, 10 February 1977, Hearings Before the Subcommittee on African Affairs, "Rhodesian Sanctions," 55-66.

17. Urquhart, *A Life in Peace and War*, 277.

18. Young's testimony, 24 February 1977, Hearing Before the Subcommittees on Africa and International Organizations, "The Rhodesian Sanctions Bill," 7-22, quotation at 8.

19. See R.F. Sperring, PPG's vice president for supply, to Byrd, 23 February 1977, "Foreign Relations Rhodesia 1977 Jan-Feb," Box 284, Accession #10320-a, Harry F. Byrd, Jr. Papers, University of Virginia Library, Charlottesville, VA (hereafter HB). According to an attached note to Byrd, Sperring's letter was sent to some 30 senators and 60 representatives.

20. John Trevelyan to Byrd, 17 March 1977, "Foreign Relations, Rhodesia 1977 March 21-31," Box 284, HB. Trevelyan also described his experiences in Smith's Police Anti-Terrorist Unit, scouring the local villages unsuccessfully for "terrorists."

21. Harry R. Strack, *Sanctions: The Case of Rhodesia* (Syracuse: Syracuse University Press, 1978), 152.

22. Rick Hutcheson, White House Staff Secretary, Memo to staff, 16 March 1977, "TA 4-8 1/20/77-4/30/77," Box TA18, WHCF-S, JCL; Memo to Carter, "Bill Signing - H.R. 1746," 18 March 1977, ibid.

McGee, former Democratic Senator from Wyoming who had long supported sanctions, lost his bid for re-election in 1976.

23. "Remarks of the President Upon Signing H.R. 1746 Rhodesian Chrome Legislation," 18 March 1977, "Steel/Chrome <CF, O/A 24> <4>," Box 284, Staff Offices, Domestic Policy Staff, Eizenstat, JCL.

24. For a discussion of the factors resulting in repeal, see Raymond W. Copson, *Executive-Legislative Consultation on Foreign Policy: Sanctions Against Rhodesia* (Washington: U.S. Government Printing Office, 1982), 32-35. Copson concluded that the administration and Congress both deserved credit, as did the "honeymoon effect" early in Carter's term.

25. Carter to Young, 18 March 1977, "Name File: Young," JCL; Jones, *Flawed Triumphs*, 61.

26. "Rhetoric and Reality," *The New York Times*, 20 March 1977, copy in "3/18/77 Signing Rhodesian Chrome Embargo Bill," Box 3, Staff Offices, Speechwriters - Chron., JCL. For a discussion of Carter's policy towards Zaire, see Piero Gleijeses, "Truth or Credibility: Castro, Carter, and the Invasions of Shaba," *International History Review* 18 (February 1996), pp. 70-103.

27. Stephen Low interview with author, 13 November 1995, Denver, Colorado. In fact, the loss of the U.S. market caused the closure of a ferrochrome plant, laying off 900 black workers. See Robin Renwick, *Economic Sanctions* (Cambridge: Harvard University Press, 1981), 52.

28. Andrew Young, "The United States and Africa: Victory for Diplomacy," *Foreign Affairs* 59 (1981), 648-666, quotation at 649.

29. David Martin and Phyllis Johnson, *The Struggle for Zimbabwe: The Chimurenga War* (Boston: Faber and Faber, 1981), 266-267.

30. In late March, Fidel Castro toured southern Africa. Shortly after the chair of the Presidium of the Supreme Soviet, Nikolai Podgorny, visited Tanzania, Zambia, and Mozambique. Podgorny signed an arms deal with Samora Machel, and met with Josua Nkomo. For details of the visits, see Carol Thompson, *Challenge to Imperialism: The Frontline States in the Liberation of Zimbabwe* (Boulder: Westview Press, 1986), 33-34; Iain Christie, *Samora Machel: A Biography* (London: Zed, 1989), 101; Daniel Kempton, *Soviet Strategy Toward Southern Africa: The National Liberation Movement Connection* (New York: Praeger, 1989), 117.

31. Martin Meredith, *The Past Is Another Country: Rhodesia UDI to Zimbabwe* (London: Pan, 1980), 297-298.

32. Meredith, *Past Is Another Country*, 299; Vance, *Hard Choices*, 265; Low interview with author, 13 November 1995.

33. Young speech at Maputo, 19 May 1977, *American Foreign Policy: Basic Documents 1977-1980* (Washington: Department of State, 1983), 1167-1170.

34. Young to Carter, confidential memo, "Activities, May 25 to June 2," 3 June 1977, Mandatory Review document number (hereafter MR#) 91-078, JCL.

35. Stepen Low, "The Zimbabwe Settlement, 1976-1979," in Saadia Touval and I. William Zartman, eds., *International Mediation in Theory and Practice* (Boulder: Westview, 1985), 91-109, citation from 93. Low interview with author, 13 November 1995.

36. Statement of William Edmondson, Deputy Assistant Secretary of State for African Affairs, Hearing Before the Subcommittee on Africa of the Committee on International Relations, House of Representatives, Ninety-Fifth Congress, First Session, June 8, 1977, "United States Policy Toward Rhodesia," (Washington: U.S. Government Printing Office, 1978), 2-3.

37. Christine Dodson, NSC staffer, memo to Denis Clift, 8 June 1977, "FO2/CO178 1/20/77-1/20/81," Box FO12, WHCF-S, JCL.

38. William Minter, *King Solomon's Mines Revisited: Western Interests and the Burdened History of Southern Africa* (New York: Basic Books, 1986), 298; Thompson, *Challenge to Imperialism*, 33.

39. Smith claimed to be protecting the peasants from the guerrillas, when in fact many of the guerrillas were former peasants from the very same villages. As had been the case in Vietnam, the relocation policy probably did more harm to Smith's cause than good, pushing additional rural youth into the guerrilla forces. Testimony of Garfield Todd, former Prime Minister, 8 June 1977, Hearing Before the Subcommittee on Africa, "United States Policy Toward Rhodesia," 64.

40. Todd's testimony, ibid., 68. The NSC discussed the possibility of a meeting between Todd and Vice President Walter Mondale. One concern was that meeting with Todd, a close friend of Nkomo, would be perceived as U.S. favoritism for one faction of the PF over the other. See Dodson memo to Clift, 8 June 1977, "CO129 1/20/77-12/31/77," Box CO50, WHCF-S, JCL.

41. Young speech at UN, 30 June 1977, in Lee Clement, ed., *Andrew Young at the United Nations* (Salisbury: Documentary Publications, 1978), 49.

42. Low, "The Zimbabwe Settlement, 1976-1979," 102; Martin and Johnson, *Struggle for Zimbabwe*, 268; Meredith, *Past Is Another Country*, 300.

43. The participants in the 23 July 1977 meeting included Carter, Vance, Owen, Graham, Low, Richard Moose, and Anthony Lake. See Low's White House pass for the meeting, "Name File: S. Low," JCL.

44. Carter's handwritten notes from meeting with David Owen, "7/23/77," Box 39, Staff Secretary File, JCL.

45. Anthony Lake, who had resigned from the NSC in 1970 over the invasion of Cambodia, returned to government in the Carter Administration as head of the Policy Planning Staff. Richard Moose had replaced William Schaufele as Assistant Secretary for Africa in June.

46. Vance, *Hard Choices*, 269.

47. Preparations for Nyerere's visit described in memo from Peter Tarnoff, State's Executive Secretary, to Brzezinski, 9 July 1977, "CO 154: 1/20/77-1/20/81," Box CO55, WHCF-S, JCL. He was the first African head of state to visit during the Carter Administration and had last visited the U.S. in 1963.

48. Julius Nyerere, *Crusade for Liberation* (Dar Es Salaam: Oxford University Press, 1978), 8. Vance, *Hard Choices*, 269; Low interview with author, 13 November 1995.

49. For a critical analysis of Carter's agreement with Nyerere, see Stephen Stedman, *Peacemaking in Civil War: International Mediation in Zimbabwe, 1974-1980* (Boulder: Lynn Reiner, 1991), 135-136, 157, 219.

50. "Terrible Twins" from Urquhart, *A Life in Peace and War*, 279. They were labeled the "Hardy Boys" in the lead article in *Newsweek*, 5 September 1977, which came out on 29 August. The trip by Owen and Young received tremendous media coverage.

51. 27 August meeting in Zambia described in Low to State, Confidential Telegram, 27 August 1977, obtained on microfiche from State via Freedom of Information Act request number 8802626 (hereafter FIA 8802626.)

52. Jones, *Flawed Triumphs*, 61.

53. Confidential telegram, Young and Moose to State, 28 August 1977, FIA 8802626.

54. *Ibid.* The afternoon meeting on 28 August involved Kaunda, Young, Moose, and Low.

55. Young's past actions were discussed in a 22 August editorial in the *Magazine Zaire*, cited in a telegram from U.S. embassy in Kinshasa to State, 31 August 1977, FIA 8802626.

56. Young statement, press conference at Jan Smuts airport, detailed in telegram from U.S. Embassy in Pretoria to State, 28 August 1977, FIA 8802626.

57. Jones, *Flawed Triumphs*, 62.

58. Confidential telegram from William Bowdler, U.S. Ambassador in Pretoria, to State, 29 August 1977, FIA 8802626.

59. Report on meeting with Vorster from Young and Moose, enclosed in confidential telegram from Bowdler in Pretoria to State, 30 August 1977, FIA 8802626.

60. Young and Moose report, in Bowdler to State, 30 August 1977.

61. Confidential telegram from James Spain, U.S. ambassador in Dar Es Salaam, to State, 30 August 1977, FIA 8802626; Nyerere, *Crusade for Liberation*, 92. For a detailed report of the conversation with Nyerere, see Young and Moose telegram from Nairobi to State, 31 August 1977, FIA 8802626.

62. Message from Young to Nigerian President Obasanjo, in telegram from U.S. Embassy in Nairobi to U.S. Embassy Dar Es Salaam, 31 August 1977, FIA 8802626.

63. Martin and Johnson, *Struggle for Zimbabwe*, 270-271.

64. Smith's announcement reported by the South African Broadcasting Company and relayed to State in a classified telegram from Bowdler, 1 September 1977, from the microfiche collection *South Africa: The Making of U.S. Policy, 1962-1989* (Washington: National Security Archives, 1991), document number 780.

65. Low emphasized the fact that none of the negotiators had any sleep in an interview with the author, 13 November 1995.

66. Young "spilt milk" quotation in Meredith, *Past Is Another Country*, 313-314. Smith described the situation somewhat differently in his memoirs, recalling that Owen's attitude had prompted Young's words. See Ian Smith, *The Great Betrayal: The Memoirs of Africa's Most Controversial Leader* (London: Blake Publishing, 1997), 233.

67. Report of meeting by Young and Moose sent to State in confidential telegram from U.S. embassy in Nairobi, 2 September 1977, FIA 8802626.

68. Low report of talks in confidential telegram from U.S. embassy in Nairobi to State, 2 September 1977, FIA 8802626. After returning to Washington, Moose wrote to Sithole in hopes of convincing him to support the plan. His message was also in response to a message from Sithole to Carter. See Tarnoff memo to Brzezinski, 8 September 1977; Moose to Sithole, 7 September 1977; Sithole to Carter, 27 August 1977, "CO178 1/20/77-1/20/81," Box CO68, WHCF-Countries (hereafter CO), JCL.

69. For a detailed analysis of the Anglo-American Plan and the PF's objections, see Thompson, *Challenge to Imperialism*, 34-36.

70. Low's report of the meeting in his confidential telegram from Lusaka to State, 3 September 1977, FIA 8802626.

71. In March 1977, Secretary of State Cyrus Vance met with heads of American companies and black church leaders, to consider guidelines for U.S. businesses in South Africa. The resulting guidelines included: equal pay for blacks, desegregation of all facilities, training of blacks for supervisory positions, and more promotions of blacks. These became known as the Sullivan Principles, named after the head of the black church delegation, Leon Sullivan, a minister in Philadelphia. See Robert Massie, *Loosing the Bonds: The United States and South Africa in the Apartheid Years* (New York: Doubleday, 1997), 701.

72. For Biko's story, see Donald Woods, *Biko*, revised edition (New York: Henry Holt, 1987), or Richard Attenborough's film *Cry Freedom*. Many young people first learned about Biko's tragic death through Peter Gabriel's song "Biko," released in 1980. The policemen who killed Biko admitted the truth during conciliation trials in September 1997, twenty years after the murder. See *Rocky Mountain News*, 11 September 1997.

73. Demonstrators with Biko banner pictured in *Africa Report* (January-February 1980), 11. *Ad hoc* group mentioned in Stephen Weissman and Johnnie Carson, "Economic Sanctions Against Rhodesia," in John Spanier and Joseph Nogee, eds. *Congress, the Presidency and American Foreign Policy* (New York: Pergamon, 1981), 141. Young quoted in *The Washington Post*, 25 October 1977, A1.

74. Peter Schraeder, *United States Foreign Policy Towards Africa: Incrementalism, Crisis and Change*(Cambridge: Cambridge university Press, 1994), 218; Jones, *Flawed Triumphs,* 83-84.

75. Paul Gordon Lauren, *Power and Prejudice: The Politics and Diplomacy of Racial Discrimination*, 2nd ed. (Boulder: Westview, 1996), 282-283.

76. Jack Grobler, "Carter and Apartheid: Responses of South Africans to the Policies and Actions of the Carter Administration Regarding Their Country," Paper presented at the conference on The Carter Presidency, Atlanta, GA, 21 February 1997, 14. A copy of this paper is in the author's possession.

77. Schraeder, *U.S. Foreign Policy Towards Africa*, 219-220; May 22, 1985 testimony of Andrew Young in *U.S. Policy Toward South Africa*, Hearings Before The Committee On Foreign Relations, United States Senate, Ninety-ninth Congress, First Session, April 24, May 2 and 22, 1985 (Washington: USGPO, 1985), 312.

78. Minter, *King Solomon's Mines Revisited*, 298; Hasu Patel and H.K. Bhila, "The Last Becomes the First: The Transfer of Power in Zimbabwe," in Prosser Gifford and Wm. Roger Louis, eds., *Decolonization and African Independence: The Transfers of Power, 1960-1980* (New Haven: Yale University Press, 1988), 454-455; Martin and Johnson, *Struggle for Zimbabwe*, 288-290; Thompson, *Challenge to Imperialism*, 36.

79. Low, "The Zimbabwe Settlement, 1976-1979," 93.

80. Bob Dole letter to President Carter, 27 December 1977, "CO129 1/1/78-6/30/78," Box CO50, WHCF-S, JCL. Dole's letter is attached to several memos, and a lengthy 28 January 1978 reply to him from Acting Secretary Warren Christopher. Christopher disputed most of the main points in Dole's letter.

81. Moose, report of conversation in London between him, Low, Owen, etal., 16 January 1978, in telegram to State, FIA 8802607.

82. Confidential telegram from U.S. embassy in Maputo to State, and telegram from State to Secretary Vance's delegation enclosing President Carter's evening reading, 19 January 1978, FIA 8802607.

83. Confidential telegram from State to U.S. embassy in Dar Es Salaam, 21 January 1978, FIA 8802607.

84. Low to Moose, 24 January 1978; Moose to Low, 27 January 1978, FIA 8802607.

85. Telegram from State to U.S. embassy in Valleta, Malta, 25 January 1978; telegram from U.S. embassy in Valleta to State, 26 January 1978, FIA 8802607.

86. Confidential telegrams from Valleta to State, 30 and 31 January 1978; quotation about Young and Nkomo in Low report from Lusaka to State, 4 February 1978, FIA 8802607.

87. "The Survival of Andy Young," *Washington Post*, 8 August 1979, pp. E1 and E3, copy in "Andrew Young," Box 109, Staff Offices - Louis Martin, JCL. Hearings Before the Committee on Foreign Relations, United States Senate, Ninety-sixth Congress, First Session, March 5 and 7, 1979, "Rhodesia," U.S. Government Printing Office, Washington: 1979, 131.

88. Confidential telegram from Young in New York to State and to White House for Brzezinski, 4 February 1978, 8802607; Jones, *Flawed Triumphs*, 63.

89. Joshua Nkomo, *Nkomo: The Story of My Life* (London: Methuen, 1984), 188. Young expressed his view about the influence of Soviet promises in a cabinet meeting after Malta, noted in Stuart Eizenstat's manuscript diary, cited in Jones, *Flawed Triumphs*, 64.

90. Comments about Malta by ZANU official Edson Zvobgo in confidential telegram from U.S. embassy in Maputo to State, 17 February 1978, FIA 8802607.

91. Young to State and Brzezinski, 4 February 1978.

92. Low confidential telegram to State, 3 February 1978, FIA 8802607.

93. Low, "The Zimbabwe Settlement, 1976-1979," 94; Vance, *Hard Choices*, 285; Thompson, *Challenge to Imperialism*, 37; Martin and Johnson, *Struggle for Zimbabwe*, 291.

94. Report of Moose's conversation with the Zambian ambassador in Washington sent in confidential telegram from State to Lusaka, 9 February 1978; Young's report to Brzezinski and State, 4 February 1978, FIA 8802607.

95. Derwinski, et al., "Concurrent Resolution 475," House of Representatives, 9 February 1978, copy in untitled folder, Box 81, Charles Diggs Papers, Moorland-Spingarn Library, Howard University, Washington, DC (hereafter CD).

96. Announcement of settlement and Smith quotation in telegram from U.S. embassy in Pretoria to State, 15 February 1978; Graham's reaction in confidential telegram from U.S. embassy in London to State, 15 February 1978, FIA 8802607.

97. News reports in telegram from State to Lusaka, 16 February 1978, FIA 8802607.

98. Confidential telegram from Low to State and Young in New York, 20 February 1978, FIA 8802607.

99. John Laverge to Senator Harry Byrd with attached copy of telegram from Laverge to Smith, 16 February 1978, "1978 Jan-Sep For Rel: Rhodesia," Box 285, HB.

100. Dole and Hatch to Carter, 22 February 1978, attached memo from Tom Thornton to Brzezinski, 3 March 1978, and response from Brzezinski to Dole, 6 March 1978, "CO129 1/1/78-6/30/78," Box CO50, WHCF-S, JCL. The memo to Brzezinski is covered with handwritten comments by Rick Inderfurth and Dave Aaron (assistants to Brzezinski) about the outrageous nature of the personal attack on Young by Dole and Hatch. These NSC staffers concluded that it was best not to tell Young, since that would force him to respond "and he shouldn't."

101. Thompson, *Challenge to Imperialism*, 38-40; Martin and Johnson, *Struggle for Zimbabwe*, 293.

102. Byrd telegram to Carter, 3 March 1978, "CO129 1/1/78-6/30/78," Box CO50, WHCF-S, JCL. Same telegram also sent from Byrd to Vance, 3 March 1978, "1978 Jan-Sep For Rel Rhod," Box 285, HB.

103. Copson, *Executive-Legislative Consultation*, 39.
104. Report of 8 March conversation with Muzorewa in confidential telegram from State to London, 9 March 1978, FIA 8802611.
105. March 8 Statement in telegram from State to all African posts, 9 March 1978, FIA 8802611. While Owen and Vance publicly pledged to work for an all-parties settlement, there is some debate about whether or not they supported a secret attempt to draw Nkomo into the internal deal. For conflicting versions, see Vance, *Hard Choices*, 287; Jones, *Flawed Triumphs*, 65-66.
106. Chair of the Congressional Black Caucus Parren Mitchell (D-Md.), and Co-Chair Charles Diggs, to Carter, 9 March 1978, untitled folder, Box 81, CD; Jones, *Flawed Triumphs*, 66.
107. Vance, *Hard Choices*, 285-286.
108. Confidential memo from Moose and Charles Maynes, Assistant Secretary for International Organizations, to Vance, 14 March 1978, FIA 8802611; confidential memo to Carter from Young, 17 March 1978, MR 92-018, JCL.
109. Statement by Ambassador Andrew Young, 14 March 1978, untitled folder, Box 81, CD. The ten-page statement provides a very detailed comparison between the Salisbury and Anglo-American Plans.
110. Mugabe's 16 March press conference detailed in telegram from U.S. embassy in Maputo to State, 17 March 1978, untitled folder, Box 81, CD. The PF and Frontline reaction to the abstention also discussed in Vance, *Hard Choices*, 288.
111. Clipping from *The New York Times*, 18 March 1978, in untitled folder, Box 81, CD; Collins, Tsongas, and three others to Carter, 20 March 1978, "CO129 1/1/78-6/30/78," Box CO50, WHCF-S, JCL; Meredith, *Past Is Another Country*, 333.
112. Shepard, *Nigeria, Africa, and the United States*, 110.
113. "Most powerful" quotation from Meredith, *Past Is Another Country*, 333; Vance, *Hard Choices*, 288.
114. Summary of Dar talks in secret telegram from Christopher to Vance, 22 April 1978, FIA 8802611.
115. Low, "The Zimbabwe Settlement, 1976-1979," 94.
116. Nkomo, *Nkomo*, 188; Martin and Johnson, *Struggle for Zimbabwe*, 292.
117. Results of talks in Pretoria summarized in confidential telegram from Christopher to London, 21 April 1978, FIA 8802611.
118. Vorster's press conference after meeting with Owen and Vance in *Washington Post*, 21 April 1978, A23, copy in "Rhodesia 4/19/78-3/27/80," Box 26, Staff Offices, Speechwriters-Sub., JCL.

119. Owen and Vance conversation with Smith and Muzorewa detailed in Christopher to London, 21 April 1978, FIA 8802611; also summarized in Vance, *Hard Choices*, 289. Noteworthy in Smith's description of these sessions is his strong praise for Young's "honesty." See Smith, *The Great Betrayal*, 251-252.

120. See *Washington Star* editorial, 19 April 1978, copy attached to memo from Jim Fallows to Brzezinski, "Rhodesia 4/19/78-3/27/80," Box 26, Staff Office, Speechwriters, Sub., JCL.

121. Confidential telegram from Low to State, 26 April 1978, FIA 8802611. Low, "The Zimbabwe Settlement, 1976-1979," 99. Low interview with author, 13 November 1995.

122. Gleijeses, "Truth or Credibility: Castro, Carter, and the Invasions of Shaba," 84-85; Thompson, *Challenge to Imperialism*, 41.

123. Hayakawa's 1976 campaign against John Tunney, who had helped curtail U.S. intervention in Angola in 1975, benefitted from $200,000 from South Africa via a New York public relations firm. See Minter, *King Solomon's Mines Revisited*, 300.

124. Ernest Furgurson, *Hard Right: The Rise of Jesse Helms* (New York: Norton, 1986), 210-215, 225. In the 1980s, Helms led the opposition to the King holiday and to U.S. aid for Zimbabwe.

125. Copson, *Executive-Legislative Consultation on Foreign Policy: Sanctions Against Rhodesia*, 39.

126. Memo to Brzezinski from Peter Tarnoff, State Department Executive Secretary, 13 July 1978, "TA1/CO129 1/20/77-6/18/79," Box TA4, WHCF-Trade, JCL.

127. Christopher's efforts detailed in memo to Carter from Brzezinski, prepared by Madeleine Albright, 17 July 1978, "FO3-2/CO129 1/20/77-1/20/81," Box FO32, WHCF-For Affs, JCL.

128. Memo from Albright to David Aaron, assistant to Brzezinski, 17 July 1978, ibid.

129. Memo to Carter from Brzezinski, prepared by Albright, 17 July 1978, ibid.

130. Copson, *Executive-Legislative Consultation on Foreign Policy: Sanctions Against Rhodesia*, 41-42.

131. Vernon Jordan to Byrd, 24 July 1978, "1978 Jan-Sep For Rel Rho," Box 285, HB. Byrd was not swayed by Jordan's letter, and later received a thank you from the SR executive council for his efforts during the debate over the Helms Amendment. See Muzorewa, Sithole, and Smith to Byrd, 16 August 1978, ibid.

132. For discussion of TransAfrica's efforts against Helms, see Herschelle Challenor, "The Influence of Black Americans on U.S. Foreign Policy Toward Africa," in Abdul Aziz Said, ed., *Ethnicity and U.S.*

Foreign Policy (New York: Praeger, 1981), 170-175. For details on the early days on TransAfrica, see interview with Randall Robinson, *Africa Report* (January-February 1980), 9, and Randall Robinson, *Defending the Spirit: A Black Life in America* (New York: Penguin, 1998), 108-111.

133. Copson, *Executive-Legislative Consultation on Foreign Policy: Sanctions Against Rhodesia*, 39-40, and 43; Vance, *Hard Choices*, 290-291. Case-Javits made its way through the bicameral conferences and became law in September.

134. Martin and Johnson, *Struggle for Zimbabwe*, 295; Meredith, *Past Is Another Country*, 345-346.

135. Martin and Johnson, *Struggle for Zimbabwe*, 295; Kempton, *Soviet Strategy Toward Southern Africa*, 106. ZAPU shot down about 30 planes and choppers with Soviet missiles during the war. Senator Byrd received about 25 of the Nkomo postcards. See "1978 Oct-Dec For Rel Rhod," Box 284, HB.

136. For a fascinating analysis of the 67 editorials, see memo to Moose from Hodding Carter, 13 October 1978, "CO129 7/1/78-12/31/78," Box CO51, WHCF-S, JCL.

137. Letter to Sithole from Hayakawa and 26 others, 14 September 1978; Hayakawa to Carter, 15 September 1978; Sithole to Hayakawa, 21 September 1978, "CO129 7/1/78-12/31/78," Box CO51, WHCF-S, JCL.

138. Memo to Carter from Louis Martin about opposition to Smith's visit by Parren Mitchell and Richard Hatcher (Mayor of Gary, Indiana), 22 September 1978, "CO129 7/1/78-12/31/78," Box CO51, WHCF-S, JCL.

139. Vance, *Hard Choices*, 292.

140. Copson, *Executive-Legislative Consultation on Foreign Policy: Sanctions Against Rhodesia*, 43-45.

141. Vance, *Hard Choices*, 91-92.

142. Smith's shifting position described in Moose to Senator John Sparkman, Chair of the Foreign Relations Committee, 27 October 1978, "1978 Oct-Dec For Rel Rhod," Box 284, HB; Vance, *Hard Choices*, 292-293. Smith reiterated his willingness to participate in such talks privately to Robert Byrd, Senate Majority Leader. Byrd to Carter, 13 October 1978, "CO129 7/1/78-12/31/78," Box CO51, WHCF-S, JCL.

143. Smith, *The Great Betrayal*, 270-278, quotation at 276.

144. Byrd to Lee Brubaker, 13 October 1978, "1978 Oct-Dec For Rel Rhod," Box 284, HB.

145. Houser, *No One Can Stop the Rain*, 335; Martin and Johnson, *Struggle for Zimbabwe*, 296.

146. Houser, *No One Can Stop the Rain*, 331-332; Martin and Johnson, *Struggle for Zimbabwe*, 296; Patel and Bhila, "The Last Becomes the First," 454-455.

147. Moose to Sparkman, 27 October 1978. Smith's confirmation and the repurcussions of the raids also discussed in Vance, *Hard Choices*, 293.

148. Kaunda's view reported by Gilbert Cranberg in *The Des Moines Register*, apparently late November or early December 1978, but undated, in "Andrew Young Name File," Box CO4, WHCF-S, JCL. Last effort by the British and Low mentioned in Low, "The Zimbabwe Settlement, 1976-1979," 94.

149. Kingman Brewster, U.S. Ambassador to Great Britain, to State, 28 February 1979, FIA 8802656.

150. Memo from Albright to David Aaron, 26 January 1979, box CO4, WHCF-S, JCL. This was in response to a handwritten note on a 15 January memo to Brzezinski, "Madeleine - comment?" These and several other NSC memos dealt with a 5 January request by leaders of the African-American Institute to meet with Carter. While the NSC recognized the importance of working with constituents interested in Africa, they decided other issues should take precedence.

151. Young to Senator Edmund S. Muskie, 5 February 1979, "Foreign Relations - Rhodesia, #9" Box 2972, Edmund S. Muskie Collection, Edmund S. Muskie Archives, Bates College, Lewiston, ME (hereafter ESM).

152. Meeting between Vance and members of TransAfrica discussed in Robert Farrell, Los Angeles Councilman, to Vance, 27 February 1979; Vance to Carter, 1 March 1979, FIA 8802656.

153. See 5 March testimonies of Jackson and Robinson in Hearings Before the Committee on Foreign Relations, United States Senate, Ninety-sixth Congress, First Session, March 5 and 7, 1979, "Rhodesia," (Washington: U.S. Government Printing Office, 1979), 18-24, 46-51, quote at 50.

154. Andrew Young, "The United States and Africa," 651-653.

155. For an example of their views in addition to the testimonies of Robinson and Jesse Jackson, see Maynard Jackson, Mayor of Atlanta, to Vance, 5 March 1979, FIA 8802656.

156. Moose 7 March testimony, Hearings Before the Committee on Foreign Relations, "Rhodesia," 102. Young also testified during these hearings, arguing against lifting sanctions.

157. Vance's statement detailed in confidential telegram from Carter to President Nimeiri of the Sudan, 22 March 1979, FIA 8802656.

158. On 14 March the Foreign Relations Committee approved the McGovern/Hayakawa resolution 8 to 1. On 28 March the entire Senate approved it 66 to 27. See Stephen Weissman and Johnnie Carson, "Economic Sanctions Against Rhodesia," in John Spanier and Joseph Nogee, eds., *Congress, the Presidency and American Foreign Policy* (New York: Pergamon, 1981), 132-160. Weissman and Carson were staffers for the House Africa subcommittee.

159. Solarz became chair of the Africa subcommittee in January 1979. See Richard Deutsch, "A New Voice in the House," and accompanying interview with Solarz in *Africa Report* (March-April 1980), 39-46.

160. Of the nine members of the Africa subcommittee, three belonged to the black caucus and strongly supported Solarz: Diggs, Cardiss Collins (D-Ill.), and William Gray (D-Penn.). Of the other five, none were staunch conservatives. Nonetheless, the unanimous vote was a great achievement for Solarz. See Hearings Before the Subcommittee on Africa of the Committee on Foreign Affairs, House of Representatives, Ninety-sixth Congress, First Session, March 22, 27, and 29; April 2, 1979, "United States Policy Toward Rhodesia," (Washington: U.S. Government Printing Office, 1979), 54 and 151. Also see Copson, *Executive-Legislative Consultation on Foreign Policy: Sanctions Against Rhodesia*, 48-49; and Weissman and Carson, "Economic Sanctions Against Rhodesia," 139-140.

161. Martin and Johnson, *Struggle for Zimbabwe*, 300.

162. Message from Low, forwarded from State to London in secret telegram, 27 March 1979, FIA 8802656.

163. Nkomo's views from 29 March press conference in Lusaka, in telegram from Lusaka to State, 30 March 1979, FIA 8802656.

164. Mugabe's 11 April address on Zambian radio in Lusaka to State, 12 April 1979; his 13 April interview by *60 Minutes* at Lusaka airport in Lusaka to State, 14 April 1979, FIA 8802656. Mugabe's interview, along with one of Nkomo, aired on *60 Minutes* on 22 April.

165. Thompson, *Challenge to Imperialism*, 43; Confidential telegram from Low to State, 25 April 1979, FIA 8802656.

166. Transcript of 25 April *MacNeil/Lehrer Report*, attached to memo from Anne Holloway, Young's assistant, to Louis Martin, White House aide, in "Zimbabwe," Box 109, Staff Offices - Louis Martin, JCL.

167. *Ibid.*

168. Carter's 27 and 30 April statements detailed in telegram from Leonard at the UN to Young in Canberra, 30 April 1979, FIA 8802656. Carter to Byrd, 4 May 1979, "CO129 5/1/79-6/30/79," Box CO51, WHCF-S, JCL.

169. Efforts of Solarz and the Rhodesia Strategy Group detailed in Weissman and Carson, "Economic Sanctions Against Rhodesia," 145-146. Black Caucus position in Diggs, Collins, and Gray to Carter, 25 April 1979, "TA1/CO129 1/20/77-6/18/79," Box TA4, WHCF-Trade, JCL.

170. Weissman and Carson, "Economic Sanctions Against Rhodesia," 147.

171. Margaret Thatcher, *Margaret Thatcher: The Downing Street Years* (New York: HarperCollins, 1993), 72-73.

172. Paul Sharp, *Thatcher's Diplomacy: The Revival of British Foreign Policy* (New York: St. Martin's, 1997), 36-38; Robin Renwick, *Unconventional Diplomacy in Southern Africa* (New York: St. Martins, 1997), 22; Thatcher, *Margaret Thatcher*, 73.

173. The amendment was known as the Schweiker-DeConcini amendment, and it passed 75 to 19. For discussion of the debate in the Senate see Copson, *Executive-Legislative Consultation on Foreign Policy: Sanctions Against Rhodesia*, 52; Weissman and Carson, "Economics Sanctions Against Rhodesia," 143-145.

174. Michael Charlton, *The Last Colony in Africa: Diplomacy and the Independence of Rhodesia* (Oxford: Basil Blackwell, 1990), 5-6.

175. Vance, *Hard Choices*, 295-296.

176. *Ibid.*, 296-297. The Vance/Owen meeting is also discussed in Martin and Johnson, *Struggle for Zimbabwe*, 304; Jeffrey Davidow, *A Peace in Southern Africa* (Westview: Boulder, 1984), 28-29.

177. Richard Hatcher, Mayor of Gary, Indiana, to Carter, 15 May 1979; memo to Carter regarding phone call from Maynard Jackson, 23 May 1979; Corretta King to Carter, 25 May 1979; Louis Martin memo to Carter, 29 May 1979, "CO129 5/1/79-6/30/79," Box CO51, WHCF-S. Jesse Jackson to Carter, 6 June 1979, "Zimbabwe," Box 109, Staff Offices - Louis Martin. George Meany to Carter, 7 June 1979, "TA1/CO129 1/20/77-6/18/79," Box TA4, WHCF-Trade, JCL. The letter with 185 signatorees discussed in Ronald Walters, "African-American Influence on U.S. Foreign Policy Toward South Africa," in Mohammed Ahrari, ed., *Ethnic Groups and U.S. Foreign Policy* (New York: Greenwood Press, 1987), 74-75.

178. See letter from 34 members of Congress to Carter, 11 May 1979, "CO129 5/1/79-6/30/79," Box CO51, WHCF-Co, JCL. The letter urged Carter to maintain sanctions and was signed by Black Cau-

cus members like Diggs, Collins, and Shirley Chisholm, as well as by whites like Solarz and Jonathan Bingham (D-N.Y.).

179. Stephen Solarz, "Rhodesia: Where Do We Go from Here? A report of a Study Mission to Rhodesia, Mozambique, Zambia, Tanzania, Botswana, and South Africa from April 13-20, 1979," submitted to Carter with cover letter dated 23 May 1979, "TA1/CO129 1/20/77-6/18/79," Box TA4, WHCF-Trade, JCL, quotations at 12 and 13. Solarz report was also published for the House Foreign Affairs Committee in June 1979.

180. Talking points and background on Solarz with memo to Mondale from Christine Dodson, NSC staffer, 4 June 1979, Box CO4, WHCF-S, JCL.

181. Low interview with author, 13 November 1995.

182. "Remarks of the President in an Announcement on the Zimbabwe-Rhodesian Sanctions," 7 June 1979, "Zimbabwe," Box 109, Staff Offices- Louis Martin, JCL.

183. "Remarks of the President," 7 June 1979; transcript of Vance's answers following Carter's announcement, 7 June 1979, "Zimbabwe," Box 109, Staff Offices - Louis Martin, JCL.

184. "Remarks of the President," 7 June 1979, ibid.

185. Handwritten letter from Owen to Carter, 15 June 1979, attached to 2 July memo by Jerry Funk, "CO129 7/1/79-1/20/81;" excerpt from Jordan's 8 June speech at Baldwin Wallace College, "CO 129 5/1/79-6/30/79," Box CO51, WHCF-S, JCL.

186. The vote was 52 to 41 and is described in Weissman and Carson, "Economic Sanctions Against Rhodesia," 148-149. For a detailed explanation of Carter's decision to maintain sanctions, see testimony by Vance in Hearing Before the Committee on Foreign Relations, United States Senate, Ninety-sixth Congress, First Session, June 12, 1979, "Trade Sanctions Against Rhodesia," (Washington: U.S. Government Printing Office, 1979).

187. The vote was 242 to 147. The efforts leading up to it are detailed in Weissman and Carson, "Economic Sanctions Against Rhodesia," 148 to 151.

188. For an insightful and somewhat humorous look at Carter's legislative goals, see his handwritten P.S. on a 22 June 1979 note to Bob Beckel, "CO129 5/1/79-6/30/79," Box CO51, WHCF-S, JCL. Carter congratulated Beckel for helping to pass a Panama bill in the House in the note. In the P.S., he added: "Now how about SALT II, Zimbabwe-Rhodesia, Panama in the Senate, Namibia, Foreign Aid, the Taiwan Treaty, U-2 Overflights, MTN, Nicaragua and the problems around East Kazakhstan."

189. Smith, *The Great Betrayal*, 306; Jones, *Flawed Triumphs*, 72-73. Jones has conducted extensive research on Muzorewa.

190. Carter/Muzorewa meeting summarized in Carter to Representative Robert Duncan, 19 July 1979, "CO129 7/1/79-1/20/81," Box CO51, WHCF-S, JCL. Evidently Carter and Muzorewa also discussed the release of three CIA spies who had been captured by the security forces. See Smith, *The Great Berayal*, 308-310.

191. Interview with Carrington broadcast on BBC in 1988 printed in Charlton, *The Last Colony in Africa*, 47.

192. For the classic study of the role of the people in the war, see Terence Ranger, *Peasant Consciousness and Guerrilla War in Zimbabwe* (London: Cambridge University Press, 1985). For a direct challenge to Ranger's interpretation, see Norma Kriger, "The Zimbabwean War of Liberation: Struggles Within the Struggle," *Journal of Southern African Studies* 14 (1988), 304-322. For a view that seeks middle ground between Ranger and Kriger, see S. Robins, "Heroes, Heretics and Historians of the Zimbabwe Revolution: A Review Article of Norma Kriger's `Peasant Voices' (1992)," *Zambezia* 23 (1996), 73-91.

193. For discussion of the war and its impact in mid-1979, see Minter, *King Solomon's Mines Revisited*, 302-303; Martin and Johnson, *Struggle for Zimbabwe*, 309; Houser, *No One Can Stop the Rain*, 336; Thompson, *Challenge to Imperialism*, 43; Low, "The Zimbabwe Settlement," 94; and Peter Godwin and Ian Hancock, `Rhodesians Never Die': The Impact of War and Political Change on White Rhodesia, 1970-1980* (Oxford: Oxford University Press, 1993), 244-260.

194. Christie, *Samora Machel*, 107-108; Stephen Chan, *Kaunda and Southern Africa: Image and Reality in Foreign Policy* (London: British Academic, 1992), 95; Martin and Johnson, *Struggle for Zimbabwe*, 312-313.

195. Martin and Johnson, *Struggle for Zimbabwe*, 313-315; interview with Kaunda from 1988 published in Charlton, *Last Colony in Africa*, 55; Renwick, *Unconventional Diplomacy*, 24-29.

196. Jones, *Flawed Triumphs*, 130.

197. Jones, *Flawed Triumphs*, 131. See Young's 14 August 1979 letter of resignation to Carter; Carter's 15 August handwritten acceptance letter to Young; and Mondale's 15 August statement, in "Andrew Young," Box 109, Staff Offices - Louis Martin, JCL.

198. Weissman and Carson, "Economic Sanctions Against Rhodesia," 152.

199. Low, "The Zimbabwe Settlement," 105. Kaunda and Mugabe 1988 interviews discussing the 7 to 9 September 1979 Havana summit in Charlton, *Last Colony in Africa*, 67-71.

200. Randall Robinson and Richard Hatcher to Carter, 26 September 1979, "TA 1/CO 129 1/20/77-1/20/81," Box TA 4, WHCF-Trade, JCL.

201. Weissman and Carson, "Economic Sanctions Against Rhodesia," 153-154.

202. See 25 September 1979 memos from Albright to Brzezinski and Brzezinski to Carter; 25 September letter from Carter to Stennis; 28 September 1979 memos from Albright to Brzezinski and Brzezinski to Carter; and undated draft letter to Solarz, in "TA1/ CO129 6/19/79-1/20/81," Box TA4, WHCF-S, JCL.

203. Copson, *Executive-Legislative Consultation on Foreign Policy: Sanctions Against Rhodesia*, 62-64.

204. The actions of the aides, James Lucier and and John Carbaugh, are detailed in Vance, *Hard Choices*, 300; and Copson, *Executive-Legislative Consultation on Foreign Policy: Sanctions Against Rhodesia*, 64. According to Steve Low, Helms had previously sent staffers to Lusaka, where they told the Zambian government that after Carter was defeated in 1980, the CIA would aid Smith. Low interview with author, 13 November 1995.

205. Vance, *Hard Choices*, 299; Renwick, *Unconventional Diplomacy*, 41.

206. Low, "The Zimbabwe Settlement," 102; Xan Smiley, "Zimbabwe, Southern Africa, and the Rise of Robert Mugabe," *Foreign Affairs* 58 (Summer 1980), 1063-1064; Charlton, *Last Colony in Africa*, 123-128; Renwick, *Unconventional Diplomacy*, 30-43.

207. Martin and Johnson, *Struggle for Zimbabwe*, 315; Charlton, *Last Colony in Africa*, 127-128.

208. Jimmy Carter, "Presidential Determination No. 79," 14 November 1979, "Rhodesia 4/19/78-3/27/80," Box 26, Staff Offices, Speechwriters - Subject, JCL. Along with about 20 black leaders, Randall Robinson attended the meeting. See list of participants for 14 November 1979 Zimbabwe-Rhodesia Meeting, "CO 129 7/1/ 79-1/20/81," Box CO51, WHCF-Sub, JCL.

209. Charlton, *Last Colony in Africa*, 123-127, 131-133; Christie, *Samora Machel*, 108-109.

210. Robinson to Carter, 26 November 1979, "TA 1/CO129 1/20/77-1/ 20/81," Box TA4, WHCF-Trade, JCL. Vance, *Hard Choices*, 300-301.

211. Renwick's message summarized in memo from Jerry Funk to Brzezinski, "Lancaster House Up-date," 14 December 1979, "CO129 7/1/79-1/20/81," Box CO51, WHCF-S, JCL. Renwick also described the importance of the U.S. decision to lift sanctions in *Unconventional Diplomacy*, 59.

212. Executive Order #12183 Revoking Rhodesian Sanctions, 16 December 1979, "TA1/CO129 6/19/79-1/20/81," Box TA4, WHCF-Trade, JCL. Muzorewa to Byrd, 17 December 1979, "For Rel Rho, 1980-81," Box 285, HB.

213. Renwick, *Unconventional Diplomacy*, 60-61. The White House, press release, 17 December 1979, "Rhodesia 4/19/78-3/27/80," Box 26, Staff Offices, Speechwriters-Subject, JCL.

214. Carter to Solarz, 7 January 1980, "CO129 7/1/79-1/20/81," Box CO51, WHCF-S, JCL.

215. Mugabe's return in Meredith, *Past Is Another Country*, 401. Election results detailed in Martin and Johnson, *Struggle for Zimbabwe*, 330-335; Smiley, "Zimbabwe, Southern Africa and the Rise of Robert Mugabe," 1068-1071.

216. Vance statement before Senate Foreign Relations Committee in Appendix V, *Hard Choices*, 514. Brzezinski's view summarized in memo from Funk to Brzezinski, 18 March 1980, Box CO4, WHCF-S, JCL.

217. Video of Mugabe's swearing in and Marley's "Zimbabwe" on *Bob Marley: Time Will Tell* (Island Visual Arts, 1992). American delegation listed in White House press release, 14 April 1980, "Delegations (Zimbabwe), 4/14/80," Box 95, Chief of Staff - Butler. Harriman's report on Zimbabwe for Carter with 22 April 1980 letter to Brzezinski, "CO129 7/1/79-1/20/81," Box CO51, WHCF-S, JCL. Charles Diggs had been involved in U.S. relations with Zimbabwe since the 1950s but was not among the delegation, evidently because he was in court and about to begin a prison term for fraud.

218. Robinson, *Defending the Spirit*, 138-139.

219. Patel and Bhila, "The Last Becomes the First: The Transfer of Power in Zimbabwe," 459.

220. During 1980 the U.S. Economic Support Fund for Zimbabwe equaled $22.9 million and Public Law 480 shipments totalled $1.8 million. Total aid was $24.86 million. See Senate Hearings Before the Committee on Appropriations, Foreign Assistance and Related Programs, Fiscal Year 1982, 97th Congress, Ist Session, Part II (Washington: U.S. Government Printing Office, 1982), 267.

221. Mugabe's itinerary detailed in Carter, "Meeting With Prime Minister Robert Mugabe of Zimbabwe: Remarks at a White House Re-

ception," 27 August 1980, *Public Papers of the Presidents: Jimmy Carter 1980-81 Book II* (Washington: Government Printing Office, 1982), 1579-1580. Muskie replaced Vance on 28 April, after Vance resigned in protest of the attempted rescue mission for American hostages in Iran. See McLellan, *Cyrus Vance*, 158-161.

222. Remarks by Carter at reception for Mugabe, 27 August 1980, *Public Papers of the Presidents: Jimmy Carter*, 1580-1581.

223. *Ibid.*, 1581-1582.

224. Mugabe's remarks at the White House, 27 August 1980, ibid., 1582-1584.

8

THE U.S. AND SOUTHERN AFRICA:
1980-1994

In November 1980, Ronald Reagan soundly defeated Jimmy Carter
in the presidential election, winning all but six states and gaining
51 percent of the popular vote. During his two terms as president,
Reagan renewed aggressive relations against the Soviet Union,
returning to the rhetoric and confrontation of the early Cold War.
He sent troops to Grenada and arms to Nicaragua to oppose communism. However, his policy towards southern Africa was a bit
more complicated. While the Reagan Administration carried on
the Carter policy of supporting Zimbabwe and even supported
Mozambique, its policy toward South Africa became the subject
of heated debate not only in Washington but around the United
States.

As had been the case in Southern Rhodesia before it became
Zimbabwe, a small white minority ruled South Africa in the 1980s,
repressing the black majority under a notorious system known as
apartheid. Five million whites ruled 23 million blacks, who suffered forced relocation, received inferior education and housing,
and had no political representation.[1] According to Nelson Mandela,
the experience of a black person under apartheid was "circum-
scribed by racist laws and regulations that cripple his growth, dim
his potential, and stunt his life."[2]

In the 1980s, activists in the United States and around the world
waged an increasingly well-publicized campaign against apartheid.

The main goal of the activism was to convince governments to impose economic sanctions against South Africa in hopes of bringing a peaceful end to apartheid. The Reagan Administration opposed extensive sanctions, however, instead seeking reform by working with the South African government through a policy called constructive engagement. While a few members of Congress, most notably Representative Ronald Dellums (D-Cal.), fought for sanctions, the issue remained secondary for Reagan's first few years in office.

Opposition to Reagan's policy heated up in late 1984, however, in response to the brutal repression of blacks by the South African government. TransAfrica, an African-American lobbying group headed by Randall Robinson, orchestrated sit-ins at the South African embassy in Washington that lasted for nearly two years. TransAfrica's efforts encouraged grassroots efforts against apartheid around the country. In 1985, relations with South Africa became "one of the most prominent and divisive foreign policy debates of the Reagan period."[3]

By 1986, most members of Congress believed that the American people perceived sanctions against South Africa as an issue of human rights and an extension of the domestic civil rights movement. Thus, they passed the Comprehensive Anti-Apartheid Act in October 1986 over Reagan's veto. The legislation mandated a range of sanctions against South Africa, representing a watershed in U.S. foreign relations.[4] The act ultimately contributed to the dismantling of apartheid that started in 1990.[5] Furthermore, it was the first time a presidential veto related to foreign relations was overturned since Nixon's veto of the War Powers Act in 1973. The fact that Congress overrode the veto of a popular president demonstrated the unprecedented importance of race in American foreign relations, and influence of African Americans in U.S. politics. The Anti-Apartheid Act extended the chain that ultimately stretched from the civil rights movement of the 1960s, through relations with Zimbabwe during the Carter Administration, to the election of Nelson Mandela as South Africa's first black president in 1994.

POLICY DEBATE: 1980S

As Carter's presidency entered its fourth year in January 1980, Randall Robinson argued that the administration should be tougher on South Africa. He acknowledged the arms embargo and approved of the strong effort to renew and maintain sanctions against Southern Rhodesia, which was then in the process of becoming Zimbabwe. But in his view policy towards Pretoria needed a more aggressive stance. He explained: "Now if you ask what we would like to see changed, we would like to see serious United States support for comprehensive sanctions against South Africa."[6]

TransAfrica had been heavily involved in the fight over Southern Rhodesia sanctions in 1978 and 1979. Now that Zimbabwe was on the verge of independence, Robinson focused his concentration on South Africa. His constituency supported the new emphasis. For several days in late February and in early March 1980, over one thousand blacks from some three hundred national organizations gathered in Richmond, Virginia, and developed a national black agenda for the 1980s. The agenda espoused "the severance of all economic, diplomatic, political, and cultural relations with South Africa, a ban on new investment and U.S. support for mandatory sanctions against the Pretoria government."[7]

Under any circumstances, this was a very ambitious agenda. To make matters worse, black Americans who were interested in South Africa lost their most influential spokesperson in Congress during the summer of 1980. Having served 25 years in the House, Charles Diggs resigned his seat after appealing unsuccessfully to the Supreme Court. Convicted of mail fraud and payroll kickbacks, he would serve seven months in an Alabama prison. Without Diggs on the hill other members of the Congressional Black Caucus took up the fight, most notably Ronald Dellums. Dellums had been outspoken on South Africa since his election in 1970 but usually had been too extreme to be effective. In the 1980s, as a more experienced and powerful legislator, he would get a chance to lead the assault against apartheid. In carrying forward the legacy of Diggs, Dellums could count on the support of Robinson, who had worked on Diggs' staff in the mid-1970s.[8]

While the resignation of Diggs was a loss to the anti-apartheid movement, the triumph of Ronald Reagan in the fall of 1980 threatened to be a more serious blow. Although the Carter Administration may not have gone as far against Pretoria as activists like Robinson would have liked, things seemed likely to grow worse under Reagan's leadership. The chances of seeing economic sanctions imposed against South Africa in the 1980s lessened with Reagan's victory. Whomever he appointed to key positions in the State Department would probably be less sympathetic to sanctions than Cyrus Vance, Anthony Lake, and Richard Moose had been.

In the months after his election, Reagan began choosing his foreign policy team. Chester Crocker became a leading contender for the position of Assistant Secretary of State for Africa. He taught international relations and directed the African Studies center at Georgetown University. Early in 1981, Crocker laid out his views on U.S. policy towards South Africa in an article in *Foreign Affairs*. He delineated his strategy, which he referred to as "constructive engagement." The best way to facilitate lasting reform in South Africa, in Crocker's view, was to practice "sustained and nimble diplomacy." The situation was complex, and it required a complex policy. Reducing it to black versus white would not work. Isolating the Pretoria regime was also not productive. Interaction between top officials must increase, allowing real communication about ideas for reform.[9]

In particular, Crocker opposed economic sanctions against South Africa. He warned that such measures could result in major damage to the economy, long-lasting violence, and white flight. He believed that the current arms embargo should remain in place, but the "slippery terrain" of additional sanctions should be avoided. Mandatory economic sanctions would only serve to lessen American influence and limit its flexibility. Instead, the U.S. government should foster more contact between the American people and South Africa. He summmarized his outlook: "The skills, procedures and institutional clout of American foundations, unions, corporations, media, self-help organizations, professional groups, universities and cultural exchange bodies offer a vast potential as constructive agents of engagement in the U.S.-South African relationship."[10]

In the very next issue of *Foreign Affairs*, Andrew Young challenged Crocker's view on sanctions. Young contended that economic sanctions could serve a useful purpose by acting as a "scapegoat," as the U.S. Supreme Court had done during the process of overturning segregation in the American south. Young explained: "Sometimes external pressure can be quite helpful in producing results in areas where there is already general agreement but insufficient courage to move in the right direction."[11] In other words, economic sanctions would give whites an excuse to make changes that they already knew were right, but were afraid to risk on their own.

Young identified a recently formed coalition of American groups interested in achieving racial justice in Africa. The coalition included blacks, liberal whites, students, and church groups. They had fought successfully for sanctions against Southern Rhodesia during the Carter Administration, and applauded the transition to the majority-ruled nation of Zimbabwe. For the 1980s, Young predicted widespread demonstrations on college campuses and increasing pressure for American corporations to divest their South African holdings. He concluded: "This coalition is likely to respond to events in South Africa with an aggressive strategy calling for the severing of U.S. political and economic ties."[12] Thus, in the pages of *Foreign Affairs* in the spring of 1981, Crocker and Young foreshadowed the debate over sanctions against South Africa that would rage in the streets, boardrooms, and legislative halls of the United States in the 1980s.

CONSTRUCTIVE ENGAGEMENT BEGINS: 1981

In the short run, Crocker's position prevailed. In a 3 March interview with Walter Cronkite, President Reagan explained that the United States should not abandon its concerns about apartheid. However, instead of isolating the Pretoria regime, he preferred working with them. According to Reagan: "As long as there's a sincere and honest effort being made, based on our own experience in our own land, it seems to me that we should be trying to be helpful." In another interview later in the month he elaborated. Reagan characterized apartheid as "a repugnant thing." Yet, he added that "we had our own experience in this country with an apartheid that was just as ugly." The United States could be most helpful in ending apartheid by assisting reform efforts in South Africa, and not remaining "aloof and distant."[13]

Reagan's top advisers similarly embraced constructive engagement. His first secretary of state, Alexander Haig, laid out the administration's position, with some disclaimers. Haig explained to the Trilateral Commission: "First, let me assure you that there is no one in this Administration who would do anything but reject out of hand the concept of apartheid." Nevertheless, he disapproved of a policy towards South Africa of "hostility, antagonism, and isolation." He believed that "a relationship of confidence and cordiality" would have more impact on Pretoria.[14]

Reagan and Haig's support was important, of course, but the true quarterback carrying out constructive engagement would be Chester Crocker. Senate consideration of his nomination to lead the African bureau began in April. Crocker explained his plans to the Foreign Relations Committee. American policy should "encourage purposeful, evolutionary change in South Africa toward a nonracial society." It was the duty of the United States, as a multiracial democracy, to help Pretoria open the doors of opportunity to people of all races. Indeed, he emphasized that the United States should not "abandon" South Africa.[15]

Gradual reform of apartheid was only one of the reasons that Crocker intended to communicate with Pretoria. He also hoped to negotiate independence for Namibia. A mineral-rich territory in the southwestern corner of Africa, Namibia had been governed by South Africa beginning in 1915. Since the mid-1960s, Pretoria faced armed resistance in Namibia by the South West African People's Organization (SWAPO), which sought independence for Namibia. Efforts to resolve the dispute during the Carter Administration had made some progress, due especially to the work of Young's assistant and then successor at the UN, Donald McHenry. However, the peace talks disintegrated just as Carter left office. By forging closer ties with Pretoria, however, Crocker hoped to pick up the pieces and facilitate Namibian independence.[16]

As with Namibia, Crocker also planned to continue and expand Carter's policy towards Zimbabwe, which had achieved independence in April 1980 and was receiving $25 million in American aid during 1981. The Reagan Administration proposed increasing aid to Zimbabwe for 1982 to $75 million, and Crocker strongly supported this increase. He considered it a reward for Zimbabwe's progress towards a multiracial democracy under Robert Mugabe. By incorporating some capitalism into its economy, moreover, Zimbabwe exemplified a "winner" from which its neighbors should learn.[17]

Senator Jesse Helms grilled Crocker on Zimbabwe. He wondered if Crocker would have supported the settlement between Ian

Smith and Abel Muzorewa in 1979, which he and other senators had favored. He also wondered if Crocker believed the Lancaster Accords, which eventually brought Mugabe to power, were fair. Crocker responded to Helms that recognizing Muzorewa in 1979 would have been "very risky." Crocker judged the Lancaster settlement to be fair, and the resulting constitution democratic. Crocker's opinions on Zimbabwe were all the more significant, considering that his wife had grown up there and her family still resided there.[18]

Crocker's advocacy of aid to Zimbabwe displeased Helms, and he opposed Crocker's nomination. For perhaps the only time in history, this put Helms on the same side as TransAfrica, who opposed Crocker because of his plans not to isolate Pretoria.[19] Despite this bizarre convergence of Helms and TransAfrica, however, the Senate confirmed Crocker as Assistant Secretary of State for Africa on 9 June 1981. Beginning in mid-1981, he sculpted U.S. policy towards South Africa with a free hand, and he had no intention of applying economic sanctions.

In general, Crocker favored more communication between Americans and South Africans, instead of less. His constructive engagement did not prevent anti-apartheid activists from attempting to ostracize Pretoria however. Over one hundred groups joined in protest against a U.S. tour by the Springboks, a South African rugby team. As a result, matches in New York and Chicago were cancelled. Also in 1981, the Riverside Church of New York withdrew $6 million from Citibank, because it loaned money to South Africa. Entertainers including Stevie Wonder and the Jacksons joined the fledgling movement by announcing that they would not perform in South Africa. Such sentiment was relatively rare in 1981, however, and posed little threat to Crocker's policy.[20]

Attacks from the right also fizzled. Helms attempted in October to make aid to Zimbabwe contingent upon certification by the President that all North Korean advisers had been removed. Still disappointed that his support for Smith and Muzorewa had been thwarted by the Carter Administration, he hoped to get in one last jab at Mugabe. Despite support from pro-Smith stalwarts Strom Thurmond and Harry Byrd, the Senate rejected his amendment. In December, the Congress approved the proposed $75 million grant to Zimbabwe for 1982, and would continue providing major financial backing for Mugabe through 1986.[21]

CONSTRUCTIVE ENGAGEMENT ASSERTED: 1982

In February 1982, State Department representatives announced that controls on exports to South Africa of a number of items, including computers, would be relaxed. The State officials added that such nonsecurity items would not be used to enforce apartheid. When Secretary Haig testified before a Congressional subcommittee in March, Representative William Gray confronted him about these sales. Haig defended the action, reiterating that the Reagan Administration was "appalled" by apartheid. Gray questioned the administration's true committment to ending apartheid. He contended that computers would in fact be used by the South African bureau of labor to facilitate the enforcement of apartheid laws. Gray, an African-American minister first elected to the Congress in 1978, would eventually play a major role in imposing sanctions against South Africa. At this juncture, however, constructive engagement withstood his assault.[22]

Haig, however, would not be defending the policy for much longer. In June, he resigned as secretary of state. Reagan immediately announced that George Shultz would replace Haig. As Shultz flew from London to begin his new job, he pondered the international scene. Relations with the Soviet Union and China as well as unrest in the Middle East were among his top priorities. Yet, he believed the crises in Africa deserved ongoing attention. He supported the efforts to reach a settlement in Namibia and considered apartheid "abhorrent and oppressive."[23] As secretary he did not initiate a new strategy, however. Under Shultz, Crocker retained virtual autonomy to carry out constructive engagement.

Africa did receive some high-level attention in November, though, when Vice President George Bush spent about two weeks there. After stops in Senegal and Nigeria, he spent three days in Zimbabwe. In toasting Mugabe during a state dinner, Bush praised his "policy of reconciliation" and lauded Zimbabwe as "a noble experiment in a strife-torn region." Bush considered Zimbabwe's independence settlement to be a good model for Namibia, where the United States was focusing most of its energy. Bush thanked Mugabe for his help in the Namibian negotiations.[24]

From Zimbabwe, Bush flew to Zambia then on to Kenya. Speaking in Nairobi, the vice president explained how the United States was pursuing peace in southern Africa. Constructive engagement sought to build "bridges of communication" with all nations there, including South Africa. He then emphasized, however, that the United States considered apartheid to be wrong. The United States was committed to the idea of multiracial democracy and to every human's right to citizenship. Americans considered those principles to be a "sacred trust," which the Reagan Administration would not betray. Nonetheless, reality dictated that if peace was to be achieved in southern Africa, the Pretoria regime would have to be involved in the process.[25]

By explaining why isolating South Africa was not the answer, Bush was advocating Crocker's constructive engagement. He returned to this subject during a press conference two days later, just before departing from Kenya. A journalist asked if being friendly with Pretoria was not actually helping apartheid. Bush responded that dialogue with South Africa did not necessarily constitute approval of apartheid. On the contrary, the United States disliked apartheid and wanted to change it. With that in mind, Bush argued that "the worst thing that could happen... would be for the United States to withdraw or pull right back across the Atlantic Ocean and live comfortably."[26] Crocker could not have said it better himself.

Challenges to constructive engagement from both the right and the left gained some ground in 1982. Developments in Zimbabwe provided Helms with more ammunition with which to attack Crocker's regional strategy. Former soldiers who had deserted from Joshua Nkomo's army targeted government officials and white farmers in Matabeleland province. Mugabe sent in his new, Korean-trained 5th Brigade to quell the disturbance. They captured few of the dissidents. In the process, they killed some two thousand civilians and generally wreaked havoc.[27] One ramification of this tragedy was that Helms and his allies in the Senate could portray Mugabe as a repressive dictator in future debates over U.S. assistance to Zimbabwe.

From the other side of the political spectrum, anti-apartheid activists voiced support for the black opposition within South Africa. A group of thirty-three U.S. mayors signed an appeal to the Pretoria regime for the immediate release of Nelson Mandela. Mandela was a leading figure in the African National Congress, and he had been in prison since 1962. This petition for his release was one of the earliest manifestations of what would become a major international movement to free Mandela. On the labor front, the AFL-CIO began a program to train black South African union leaders to challenge apartheid from within.[28] These sort of actions, while a far cry from economic sanctions, threatened to provoke friction between American officials and the Pretoria regime. Such friction, in turn, could jeopardize constructive engagement.

Meanwhile, Crocker's policy faced more direct challenges at the United Nations. In December, the General Assembly passed a ten-part resolution condemning South Africa and requesting the Security Council to impose mandatory, comprehensive sanctions. The United States voted against every section of the resolution, registering the only "no" for three. The American alternative representative, Gordon Luce, explained the U.S. votes. He characterized the resolution as an attempt to punish and isolate South Africa, and opined that constructive engagement would be more productive. Luce added: "As for economic and cultural sanctions, there is no reason whatsoever to suppose they would have any practical effect... except perhaps to heighten tensions and make armed conflict more likely."[29]

CROCKER HOLDS ON: 1983

Appearing in February before the House Foreign Affairs Subcommittee on Africa, Crocker updated the legislators on events in southern Africa. The sticking point in the Namibian negotiations involved Cuban troops in Angola. In exchange for agreeing to a settlement on Namibia, South Africa wanted those troops withdrawn. Pretoria considered removal of the Cuban troops imperative for regional security. Since the United States was trying to pursue a nuanced policy that would bring peace to southern Africa, Crocker considered a quid pro quo on Cuban troops to be reasonable. At the same time, he believed the United States should continue its support for Zimbabwe, which could be a "keystone" in regional stability. Furthermore, the Reagan Administration should build similar bridges to Mozambique.[30]

Adding cooperation with Mozambique's Samora Machel to a strategy that already supported Zimbabwe's Robert Mugabe, while simultaneously communicating closely with the government in Pretoria, would represent a nuanced policy indeed. It amounted to a combination of the tactics of Henry Kissinger in 1976 and Andrew Young in 1977-78. From the very beginning of constructive engagement in 1981, its convoluted nature made it susceptible to criticism from both sides of the aisle in Congress. This criticism escalated in 1983, with the first strike coming from the right.

Senator Helms queried Crocker about whether he had any criticisms of the Mugabe government. Crocker responded that he and his superiors, including Vice President Bush, had indicated their displeasure about a variety of issues to Mugabe. As for recent reports of violent repression against civilians, Crocker explained that the United States would not condone such actions. Helms then wondered if the $75 million that State was requesting in aid to Zimbabwe for 1984 would "go to support a one-party Marxist system that Mr. Mugabe is building?" Crocker reminded Helms that the United States had pledged a three-year total of $225 million to Zimbabwe back in 1981. To some extent, then, this was a matter of the United States keeping its word. So far, the aid had reaped solid rewards. Mugabe's economy was a pragmatic mix of capitalism and socialism, and had succeeded in reassuring the private sector, which included many whites.[31] Despite Crocker's efforts, Congress approved only $40 million to Zimbabwe for 1984.[32]

While Helms challenged constructive engagement from the right, Representative Stephen Solarz initiated a strike from the left. He proposed an amendment to the State Department authorization bill that would apply a number of sanctions against South Africa. His amendment would require American firms in South Africa to comply with the Sullivan principles, prohibit new bank loans to South Africa, and block importation into America of the South African gold coin (the Krugerrand). Crocker's deputy, Frank Wisner, explained that the State Department opposed such sanctions. He and his colleagues believed that capitalism would "help to bring about the end of apartheid through a process of peaceful, evolutionary change." The Foreign Affairs Committee dropped the Solarz amendment.[33] The same sanctions would come up again later in the year, but Wisner had achieved a temporary victory.

However, challenges to constructive engagement from the left were not limited to just Washington. Grassroots activists around the country convinced state and city governments to apply various sanctions. The Massachusetts legislature overrode the governor's veto on a law requiring state divestment of all holdings in companies doing business in South Africa. The law effected $91 million worth of stocks and bonds in twenty-seven banks and corporations. Much of the lobbying had been done by the Boston branch of TranAfrica, whose strategy of spreading the movement around the country was beginning to pay off.[34]

During the summer of 1983, the anti-apartheid movement achieved results in other states as well. Philadelphia's city government prohibited the future investment of public employee pension funds in companies doing business in South Africa. New York followed suit. Protesters in both Denver and Pittsburgh convinced Pretoria to drop its plans for opening consulates. State governments in Michigan and Connecticut also started divesting. Students participated in rallies at many universities during 1983, but their really extensive involvement still lay in the future.[35] At the United Nations, Arthur Ashe and Tony Randall announced the formation of Artists and Athletes Against Apartheid. The group, whose leadership also included Harry Belafonte, would work to inform the public about apartheid and to support sanctions.

Back in Washington during September, Mugabe met with Reagan to discuss southern Africa. Mugabe requested that the United States put more pressure on Pretoria to get them to be less intransigent regarding Namibia and apartheid. Reagan, in turn, expressed his disappointment that Zimbabwe had abstained on a UN security council resolution which condemned the Soviet Union for shooting down a Korean passenger plane. In summing up their talks, Reagan admitted that they "didn't always agree." However, he pointed out the similarities between the United States and Zimbabwe: Both were multiracial societies born of revolution. He praised Zimbabwe for its ability to "serve as an inspiration in its part of the world."[36]

Mugabe thanked Reagan for his support. He concurred that the two nations shared the same goals for southern Africa, and also that there was some disagreement over tactics. According to Mugabe: "There might be some difference here and there in respect of the method of bringing about change."[37] Nonetheless, both nations wanted independence for Namibia and an end to apartheid. Moreover, in spite of their differences, the talks between the two leaders in September 1983 symbolized the fact that the Reagan Administration had carried on the support for Mugabe that had been initiated by Carter and Young. Admittedly, the support weakened significantly after 1983, but, in the context of Reagan's overall foreign policy, it was a remarkable exception to his staunch anti-communist policies, and demonstrated the influence of race in U.S. foreign relations.

In October, Representative Gray re-introduced the issue of sanctions against South Africa into the foreign policy debate in Congress. He and his primary ally Dellums, both members of the Congressional Black Caucus, hoped to attach an amendment to the Export Administration Act. Their amendment contained the same provisions as the amendment proposed in May by Solarz. Gray and Dellums succeeded in getting House approval in November. The Senate refused to take similar action, however, deciding that constructive engagement deserved a little more time to work. Dellums, who had been arguing for sanctions against South Africa since 1971, had again fallen short, but he was getting closer.[38]

A TURNING POINT: 1984

During the first half of 1984, State Department officials lobbied to maintain support for constructive engagement. Speaking at a Blair House luncheon for CEOs of firms with operations in South Africa, Secretary Shultz addressed the growing possibility of economic sanctions being enacted by Congress. While the Reagan Administration sought an end to apartheid, it still opposed sanctions as a means to achieve that end. According to Shultz: "We have persistently argued that proposals such as these, which seek to punish South Africa, are counterproductive. They hurt the very people we are trying to help." Enlightened leadership by American businesses, on the other hand, would be beneficial, so the United States should remained involved in South Africa.[39]

Appearing before a House subcommittee, Deputy Secretary for Africa Frank Wisner defended another component of constructive engagement—U.S. assistance to Zimbabwe. He acknowledged that the government of Zimbabwe had taken some actions in the previous few years with which the Reagan Administration disagreed. Nonetheless, he emphasized that Zimbabwe remained an important model for the rest of southern Africa, both politically and economically. Whites and blacks were working together in the government, and the private sector maintained significant autonomy despite Mugabe's socialist rhetoric. Wisner contended that other states in the region could learn from Zimbabwe's example, so the United States should continue aiding Mugabe's regime to promote stability. Later in the year, Congress approved $28 million in aid to Zimbabwe for 1985.[40]

The general goal for constructive engagement was peace throughout southern Africa. The most pressing specific goal was to negotiate independence for Namibia. In return for not isolating South Africa, the Reagan Administration desired cooperation towards these goals from Pretoria. By mid-1984, however, it was clear that Pretoria's policies towards Angola and Mozambique were detrimental to the goals of constructive engagement. South African troops occupied a portion of Angola, which prompted Cuba to send in more soldiers. Since Crocker had linked Namibian independence to the removal of Cuban troops, South African aggression precluded a settlement. Furthermore, Crocker's plans were also bedeviled by Pretoria's support for RENAMO, which caused increasing chaos and suffering in Mozambique.[41]

Events in South Africa itself, however, would be most instrumental in undermining constructive engagement. The United Democratic Front, formed in 1983, forged ties among over six hundred anti-apartheid groups across South Africa in 1984. As part of the United Democratic Front's nonviolent grassroots strategy, reminiscent of the U.S. civil rights movement, labor unions organized worker strikes and student groups boycotted schools. The United Democratic Front named Nelson Mandela as one of its patrons and worked to revive the ANC from a period of relative dormancy.[42]

In late August, the United Democratic Front (UDF) initiated protests against the first elections under South Africa's revised constitution. The new rules allowed Indians and mixed race "coloreds" to elect representatives to separate chambers of parliament, but continued to deny blacks any political rights. As a result of demonstrations during the first day of voting, 35 UDF leaders were arrested. During the second day of voting on 28 August, more protests occurred and more arrests followed. Real trouble began on 3 September, when mass protests erupted in the townships. Unrest spread and escalated into unprecedented popular uprisings. The security forces shot at crowds, occupied large areas, detained thousands, and clamped down on the press. In the United States, nightly news broadcasts showed South African police attacking unarmed demonstrators.[43]

It was becoming more difficult to defend constructive engagement, which featured cooperation with the very Pretoria regime responsible for such brutality. Assistant Secretary Crocker soon found himself in the unenviable position of trying to do just that, in a hearing before the Africa Subcommittee of the Senate Foreign Relations Committee. Crocker expressed the administration's regret about the recent bloodshed in South Africa, and also that the new constitution did not bring suffrage to the 73 percent of the population which was black. However, he reiterated his position that punitive sanctions would do more harm than good.[44]

Senator Paul Tsongas (D-Mass.) responded forcefully to Crocker's remarks. Tsongas, a former Peace Corps volunteer who had strongly supported the Carter Administration's sanctions against Southern Rhodesia, had not been critical of constructive engagement as of yet. However, the riots and repression of August and September 1984 had convinced him that it was time to speak out. He blasted the Reagan Administration for doing "nothing of any consequence" to pressure South Africa into ending apartheid. He slammed Crocker regarding cooperation with Pretoria: "I would be embarrassed to get up and give this testimony. We are in bed with them."[45]

In the view of Tsongas, no progress had taken place in South Africa during the three-and-a-half years of constructive engagement. He regretted remaining silent so long and pledged to join the fight for divestment and sanctions. The decision by Tsongas to work for sanctions signified the first rumblings of an earthquake in Congress that would accelerate in the last months of 1984, force Reagan into action in 1985, and ultimately overturn his veto in 1986. At the time, however, the spirited exchange between Crocker and Tsongas received little attention outside of the Senate meeting room.[46]

After Tsongas had spoken, subcommittee chair Nancy Kassebaum (R-Kans.) registered her view. While sharing Tsongas' outrage at the events in South Africa, Kassebaum did not yet support sanctions. She did, however, think that the Pretoria regime needed to take some concrete steps against apartheid in order to deserve continued cooperation from Washington. She suggested that the South African government set Nelson Mandela free. Kassebaum, whether she knew it or not, echoed the cry of many youths in England and the United States. Throughout 1984, young people danced to a top-ten song "Free Nelson Mandela," by a British rock group The Special AKA. It served as an anthem for the anti-apartheid movement on college campuses during the next few years.[47]

In October 1984, however, the majority of Americans still paid relatively little attention to South Africa. Public attention focused on the contest between Reagan and the Democratic challenger, former Vice President Walter Mondale. The most interesting thing about Mondale's candidacy was his choice of a woman, New York Representative Geraldine Ferraro, as his running mate. Despite this historic first, in the November voting Reagan won a forty-nine state landslide.[48] Reagan would be attempting to continue his foreign policy for another term. Any changes to constructive engagement would have to be initiated from outside the executive branch.

Reagan's re-election pushed Randall Robinson closer to a more radical strategy. When the UN approved a resolution condemning the crackdown against protestors in South Africa, the United States abstained. It was the last straw for Randall Robinson. He made plans with three fellow civil rights activists: Congressman Walter Fauntroy (a former assistant to Martin Luther King), Mary Frances Berry, and Eleanor Holmes Norton.[49]

On 21 November the group sat down in the South African embassy for a meeting. Eventually, Norton excused herself. A short time later a crowd gathered outside. Norton announced that Robinson, Fauntroy, and Berry would remain in the embassy until the South African government released all political prisoners. When the ambassador asked them to leave, they refused. Secret Service agents soon arrested them, and they all spent the night in jail. The story of the sit-in appeared on network news and in all major papers. TransAfrica's good timing and use of the sit-in tactics associated with Martin Luther King and the civil rights movement sparked considerable interest, and it was only the beginning.[50]

To coordinate ongoing demonstrations at the South African embassy and at other locations around the country, TransAfrica organized the Free South Africa Movement (FSAM), hoping to overthrow constructive engagement and to see comprehensive sanctions imposed. Long hours by Robinson and his dedicated young staff got the campaign off the ground. Protesters marched in Washington every day, and by early December similar actions were occurring in New York and Boston. Entertainers such as Tony Randall joined the picketers. High-profile arrests of members of Congress and leaders of organizations such as the National Organization of Women and the Southern Christian Leadership Conference kept the issue in the news.[51]

Civil disobedience, in order to protest apartheid and call for divestment and sanctions, spread across the nation. By February 1985, over two thousand people had been arrested. By October 1986, when Reagan's veto of the Comprehensive Anti-Apartheid Act would be overridden, some six thousand protesters went to jail. These included many noteworthy leaders such as Representative Patricia Schroeder (D-Col.) and Coretta Scott King.[52] The activism of the FSAM had a major impact on the debate over U.S. policy towards South Africa in the mid-1980s. Randall Robinson and TransAfrica deserve credit for overseeing the movement and for getting the ball rolling in November 1984.

Even Crocker, whose policy TransAfrica targeted, acknowledged Robinson's talents. Crocker later described his rival as "an articulate advocate, who knew how to frame the issues." Crocker believed that Robinson's chief goal was to attract attention for the cause, and in that he succeeded. However, Robinson probably could not have sparked such a movement without the help of the shocking images broadcast from South Africa. This crucial role of media in stirring public sympathy represented another similarity between the anti-apartheid movement of the 1980s and the civil rights movement of the 1960s. The government of South Africa, characterized by Crocker as "ministers of brutality, perversity, stupidity, and bad timing," followed in the footsteps of Bull Connor and George Wallace in undermining their own cause.[53]

Another key individual who stimulated the rising activism late in 1984 was Bishop Desmond Tutu. General Secretary of the South African Council of Churches, Tutu received the Nobel Peace Prize that year for his eloquent criticism of apartheid. He visited the

United States on his way to Norway and met with the President at the White House on 7 December. Reagan explained to Tutu that he felt there had been some progress in South Africa since 1981, and therefore intended to continue the strategy of "quiet diplomacy." After the meeting, Reagan defended constructive engagement and denigrated the protestors who called for sanctions, calling them "ignorant."[54]

During an appearance two days later on *This Week With David Brinkley*, Tutu took the offensive against Reagan. He questioned the efficacy of the Reagan Administration's diplomatic attempts to persuade Pretoria to change. Tutu explained: "I would say that the West has been trying to persuade the white South Africans since 1948. Isn't it time that they listened to the victims of apartheid? Isn't it time they said, we want to be friends with those who are going to be running this country.... Please for goodness sake, listen to our appeal."[55] Words such as these from Tutu, who was being compared frequently to Martin Luther King, boosted the efforts of Robinson, TransAfrica, and the FSAM as 1984 drew to a close.[56]

VIOLENCE ESCALATES: 1985

On 31 January 1985, South African President P.W. Botha offered Nelson Mandela his freedom if he "unconditionally rejected violence as a political instrument." On 10 February 1985, Mandela's daughter Zindzi read his response at Soweto's Jabulani stadium. He would not accept freedom unless the ban on the ANC was lifted and the apartheid system was repealed. He emphasized his commitment to the ANC and its leader Oliver Tambo, and placed the blame for violence in South Africa squarely on the shoulders of the white government.[57] Pretoria's security forces soon proved the truth of Mandela's assessment.

In mid-February, blacks in the shantytown of Crossroads outside of Capetown erected barricades to prevent forced removal to homelands. Security forces and some three thousand blacks exchanged rubber bullets and stones, then a real battle erupted. During the ensuing violence police suffered twenty-six injuries, while over two hundred fifty black civilians were wounded and eighteen killed. On 21 March about four thousand blacks gathered near the village of Uitenhage, outside of Port Elizabeth, to commemorate the 25th anniversary of Sharpeville and to celebrate the International Day of the Elimination of Racial Discrimination. Without provocation, police opened fire and killed nineteen. They then placed sticks in the hands of the dead, to make it look like less of a massacre, and instructed firemen to hose away the blood. Botha responded to the slaughter by banning twenty-nine more groups, thus placing all the blame for violence on demonstrators.[58]

During a televised press conference and then an interview, Reagan discussed the events in South Africa. He was asked if the Uitenhage massacre necessitated tougher measures by the United States against the Pretoria regime. He responded that the United States should not get tougher. Although the violence was tragic, he did not think the answer was to walk away and isolate South Africa. He explained that the bloodshed was not only the fault of the government: "I think to put it that way—that they were simply killed and that the violence was coming totally from the law and order side ignores the fact that there was a riot going on." He criticized factions within the South African black population who wanted to violently overthrow the government, instead of working for a peaceful solution.[59] Reagan intended to portray the situation in South Africa as a complicated one, which was certainly true. However, he came across as sympathetic to Botha and the security forces.

In hopes of elaborating on the administration's position and dispelling misperceptions, Secretary of State Shultz addressed the National Press Club in mid-April. He outlined U.S. policy towards southern Africa, emphasizing the importance of a peaceful end to apartheid. He explained that the Reagan Administration had been working to encourage reform in South Africa, and that things there had improved. According to Shultz: "We cannot have influence with people if we treat them as moral lepers, especially when they are themselves beginning to address the agenda of change." He recognized that there was a long way to go and also deplored the recent violence, nevertheless reiterating that constructive engagement had helped begin the reform process and concluding that emphasis on economic sanctions would do more harm than good.[60]

Meanwhile, a push for economic sanctions had begun in earnest in Congress. In March, Representatives Dellums and Gray had introduced House Resolution 1460 in order to: (1) prohibit new U.S. investment in South Africa, (2) prohibit American bank loans to the South African public sector, (3) ban sales of Kruggerands in the United States, and (4) stop American computer sales to the South African public sector. The Congressional Black Caucus, of which both Gray and Dellums were members, had grown to 20 people and was wielding more influence. Furthermore, 1985 saw Gray become the first black chair of the House Budget Committee, a position with considerable clout. Their sanctions bill would draw serious consideration in the House, and so would a companion bill introduced in the Senate by Edward Kennedy.[61]

In April and May, the Senate Foreign Relations Committee held extensive hearings. Fittingly Chester Crocker, the architect of constructive engagement, represented the administration. In response to charges that the U.S. government and Pretoria had a "cozy" relationship, he pointed to several measures: the Reagan Administration had adhered to the arms embargo, provided some $30 million for black South Africans' education, denounced violence, called for Mandela's release, and supported the Sullivan principles. This active policy had contributed to some progress, such as suffrage for Asians and Coloreds. Comprehensive economic sanctions, on the other hand, would reduce the ability of the United States to have any positive influence. Crocker emphasized that "walking away" from the problems in South Africa was not the answer.[62]

Randall Robinson and TransAfrica did not see the imposition of sanctions as walking away. In their view, removing American investment was the only way to force South African whites to make substantive changes. Their grassroots campaign was paying off in 1985, with 8 states, 37 cities, and 52 universities divesting funds from South Africa in that year alone. On 14 May, TransAfrica spearheaded an effort by the Free South Africa Movement to organize over five hundred groups that were lobbying Congress for sanctions. TransAfrica was in the lead of a national movement that was capturing the attention of all the legislators in Washington.[63]

Throughout May, debate continued in the Senate and the House over the sanctions bills. Robinson expressed TransAfrica's strong support for sanctions before the Foreign Relations Committee. He characterized the bill under consideration as not so tough that it would cause major economic dislocation in South Africa, but tough enough to clearly show the U.S. position. Robinson argued that imposing sanctions would help the United States maintain good relations with South Africa in the long run, "because black South Africans ultimately, inevitably are coming to power, and we certainly want to be perceived by them as having been responsive to their needs, to their hurts, to their sufferings." Since Tutu, Mandela, and the United Democratic Front supported sanctions, the United States should listen to their wishes.[64]

Andrew Young, then mayor of Atlanta, also presented prosanctions arguments on 22 May. Senator Kassebaum asked him if he thought the sanctions against Southern Rhodesia had worked, pointing out that they had caused the economy there to become more self-sufficient. He replied that the sanctions had worked, for a couple of reasons. First, they targeted particular items such as chrome. Second, they were part of a larger effort to resolve the conflict, which included military and diplomatic efforts. Unfocused sanctions on their own would not have achieved results in Southern Rhodesia, nor would they end apartheid. Sanctions could be a key piece in a larger puzzle however.[65]

Young also reinforced Robinson's point; that the U.S. government needed to make a forceful statement criticizing apartheid. He believed the Reagan Administration was against apartheid, but that constructive engagement was perceived as a friendly relationship with Pretoria. Overall U.S. policy towards Africa would benefit from concrete steps that refuted such misperceptions. He believed the legislation under consideration would do just that: "I think it is important for the U.S. Government to be on record in sending the kind of signal that I think the Kennedy bill sends... that we are not going to allow further bank loans, that we are not going to sell computer equipment to South Africa, and that there will be no further U.S. investment."[66]

Young then provided some insight into just how sanctions could facilitate change in South Africa. He believed that there were progressive elements among the white government who wanted to end apartheid, but for political reasons they were unable. Strong sanctions, however, would give them an excuse to do what they thought was right. Young recalled negotiations during the civil rights struggles in the U.S. South. He and white officials would agree on what changes needed to be made, but the officials were afraid to risk the next election by going public. So, both sides would quietly go to the courts and ask them to order the changes. Thus, segregation laws were overturned without undermining white political careers. Sanctions imposed by Congress could serve the same purpose in ending South African apartheid as court orders had served in ending segregation in the southern United States.[67]

Young elaborated on the principle:

> In difficult matters of social change, some outside idealistic authority is needed. I think the U.S. Senate in this case becomes that kind of authority, in an absence of moral authority within the South African political structure, to say to the people of South Africa that they must change and they must change quickly in order to avoid chaos and bloodshed.[68]

About ten days after the testimonies of Young and Robinson, the House approved its version of the sanctions bill, 295 to 127. Meanwhile, the South Africa government continued to defy world opinion. Botha ordered raids into Angola and Botswana and installed a new colonial government in Namibia. Responding on national television to a press query about these developments, Reagan once again seemed to be sympathizing with Pretoria: "There is no question about the violence of the ANC and their striking and their attacks on people and their murdering and so forth."[69] In other words, because the ANC used violent tactics, the United States should not punish Pretoria for its aggression.

The South African government was under pressure anyway. Domestic unrest continued into July, with the death toll since late 1984 surpassing 500, and Botha declared a national state of emergency. The ongoing conflict in South Africa reinforced the feeling among U.S. senators that they needed to take a stand. Despite efforts to filibuster by Jesse Helms, the Senate approved a sanctions bill on 11 July. This legislation, sponsored by Richard Lugar (R-Ind.) and Bob Dole, was somewhat weaker than the House version and the original Senate bill sponsored by Kennedy. A conference adopted it on 31 July, and the House approved it the next day.[70]

On 5 August, Reagan manifested his mixed feelings about the bill. He approved of parts of it, but disagreed with aspects that called for economic sanctions. He still did not think sanctions were an appropriate response to the state of emergency in South Africa. Once again he seemed to blame blacks: "We have seen the violence between blacks there, as well as from the law enforcement against riotous behavior. I think we have to recognize sometimes when actions are taken in an effort to curb violence."[71]

One of Ronald Reagan's great strengths was his ability to say what the vast majority of Americans wanted to hear. It was becoming clear by late 1985, though, that he was out of touch with public opinion on South Africa. The issue, as is usually the case, had become oversimplified. Divestment and economic sanctions were perceived as tough measures against apartheid, while opposition to such measures was considered to be support for apartheid. Crocker, Shultz, Bush, and other top advisers realized that it would be best to accept some limited economic sanctions in order to get Congress and the protestors off the administration's back. Reagan, instead, opted to fight it out. This choice reflected the advice of CIA director William Casey, Senate conservatives like Helms, and White House aide Patrick Buchanan.[72]

While Crocker and Schultz preferred some level of compromise with the prosanctions movement, polarizers like Buchanan wanted to confront them and beat them. According to Crocker, "Buchanan was helping to organize conservative and evangelical activist groups who might rally around the pro-South African views espoused by the Reverend Jerry Falwell."[73] The influence of Buchanan and his allies showed through in Reagan's public statements during the summer of 1985, when he tended to blame blacks for violence and empathize with the white government. Reagan's view, uncharacteristically, was getting further and further away from that of most Americans.

The distance between Reagan and public opinion, in fact, would peak the following year when his veto was overridden. Yet for the time being, with help from Dole and Lugar, the administration was able to stem the tide. Crocker and the Senate leaders agreed on a "finesse" move. As an alternative to the sanctions bill, Reagan issued Executive Order 12532 on 9 September. Reagan's order banned computer sales and bank loans to the South African government, and initiated a process of blocking the imports of Krugerrands into the United States. The measure also strongly encouraged American firms in South Africa to adhere to the Sullivan Principles and requested increases in funding for black South Africans' education. The major difference between Reagan's order and the sanctions bill before the Senate was that the order dropped the provision requiring a mandatory consideration of additional economic sanctions after one year, if the situation in South Africa had not improved.[74]

On one level, the order represented a concession to Congress. The issues of loans, computer sales, and Krugerrands had long been on the agendas of Congressional activists like Gray and Dellums. Other elements such as the emphasis on the Sullivan Principles and education for blacks re-affirmed constructive engagement. Furthermore, because the clause mandating consideration of additional economic sanctions after one year had been dropped, Reagan and Shultz claimed that they had held the line against sanctions. In fact, the order represented a compromise. Congress had forced the administration's hand, and several of the measures were certainly economic sanctions.

Still, the "finesse" move by Shultz, Crocker, Dole, and Lugar had saved face for the administration. Before the Senate could vote on the sanctions bill, Dole and Lugar snatched it from the table. Senator Kennedy blasted their manuever as "trickery." Undeterred, Dole and Lugar announced that Reagan's action constituted a strong enough statement against apartheid.[75] A showdown, which may well have resulted in a veto and then an override, was avoided. In principle, the President retained control of foreign policy. This was evidently due more to the work of advisers like Crocker than to Reagan himself however. During the 9 September press conference when he issued the order, the President was unable to explain clearly whether the order included sanctions. When reporters correctly pointed out that the order actually did include economic sanctions, Reagan dodged the questions.[76]

Despite the President's less-than-stellar performance and the concessions to Congress, Crocker's constructive engagement survived this round. Later in September, President Samora Machel of Mozambique met with Reagan in the White House. Machel amused Reagan with some jokes and impressed him with his sincerity.[77]

This friendly exchange boded well for Crocker's efforts to increase U.S. support for Machel's government and block South African aid to Machel's opposition, RENAMO. Backing the semisocialist Machel, like backing Mugabe in Zimbabwe, was part of Crocker's nuanced overall policy towards southern Africa. Crocker still hoped to connect Namibian independence with the withdrawal of Cuban troops from Angola. In support of Crocker's efforts to link Namibia and Angola, in November the United States vetoed a UN Security Council resolution calling for mandatory sanctions against South Africa unless they withdrew from Namibia.[78]

CONGRESS IMPOSES SANCTIONS: 1986

In early 1986, Crocker continued to pursue constructive engagement on several fronts. During January, he met with South African and Angolan representatives in Luanda, Angola. No breakthrough on the Namibian/Angolan linkage occurred, but he was determined to keep trying.[79] Crocker requested $15 million in aid for Machel's government in Mozambique, in order to promote regional stability. He criticized the South African government's support for RENAMO.[80] Assessing the situation within South Africa itself in March, he praised the government's decision to lift the state of emergency, while acknowledging that an end to apartheid was still a long way off. He believed Reagan's executive order was having a positive impact; however, he warned against imposing any additional sanctions, because they would bring "intransigence."[81]

In the Congress, Ronald Dellums once again introduced a tough sanctions bill, calling for total American divestment from South Africa and a complete ban on U.S. exports to South Africa. He pointed out that Bishop Tutu supported further sanctions, and surveys showed that 70 percent of black South Africans agreed. He cited Stephen Biko, who had contended that undermining the political economy of apartheid was worth short-term pain. He quoted Martin Luther King, who had observed that American and British investment made apartheid possible. Regarding the argument that sanctions would deprive blacks of jobs, Dellums compared apartheid to slavery. It would not have been logical to oppose emancipation because it might bring unemployment, and he felt the same thinking applied to ending apartheid.[82]

Dellums eloquently concluded:

> I believe that human rights is a journey upon which the entire world must embark and it has to start someplace. And it seems to me that as the pluralistic, multiracial society that we are in the United States, what better time, what better nation than us to lead the assault against the oppression and the immorality of apartheid in South Africa to the maximum extent possible?[83]

Crocker then presented the administration's position. While he did not question the motives of individuals like Dellums, he continued to oppose additional economic sanctions. He explained: "We don't believe in indiscriminate and blunt acts of economic punishment inflicted on the South African people and society and economy as a whole.... On the contrary, we think those are, in fact, dangerous courses of action that could, in effect, encourage even more intransigence on both sides."[84] The stage was set for another showdown over sanctions.

From February to May 1986, a commission appointed by the Commonwealth interviewed South Africans of all races and political persuasions in order to determine how much progress had been made. The very day the commission was scheduled to meet with Mandela, the Security Forces bombed and raided targets in Botswana, Zambia, and Zimbabwe.[85] These actions prompted the commission to depart abruptly, and stirred angry responses around the globe. The Reagan Administration condemned the raids and sent condolences to the victims.[86]

Concern about the ongoing crisis mounted in Congress, where Gray and Solarz introduced an alternative to Dellum's bill on 21 May. House Resolution 4868 blocked loans and new investments in South Africa, imports of South African uranium, and landing rights in the United States for South African airplanes. If Mandela was not free within one year, all computer sales to South Africa would be banned. Unlike Dellum's bill, however, HR 4868 provided funds for the education of black South Africans. Solarz prevailed over his colleague on the House Africa subcommittee, Dan Burton (R-Ind.), and the bill progressed to the entire Foreign Affairs Committee. Despite opposition to the legislation from Secretary Shultz and Crocker, the committee approved it on 10 June. Tough sanctions could soon pass in the House.[87]

Meanwhile, conflict escalated in South Africa. Over a million workers went on strike, protesting continuing repression by the government and its aggression against neighboring states. In response to the disturbances, police arrested hundreds of trade unionists, activists, and church leaders. President Botha feared that the tenth anniversary of the Soweto incident would spark total chaos. On 12 June he re-imposed a state of emergency and prohibited press coverage of racial unrest. He defied world opinion and exclaimed that South Africa was prepared to "go it alone."[88]

Botha evidently expected an international backlash, and indeed it was coming. The U.S. House of Representatives approved a tough anti-apartheid bill by voice vote on 18 June. Perhaps more surprisingly, Senator Kassebaum called Crocker the day after Botha's crackdown. Kassebaum urged Crocker to pressure the President to "get out front" on South Africa. If the administration did not act soon, Republicans in the Senate would take the initiative. Kassebaum suggested that Reagan express strong disgust for the developments in South Africa in a radio address. Crocker and Shultz reluctantly agreed to have Reagan deliver a major speech on South Africa, but worried that the final product would be influenced by Buchanan and other hardliners.[89] A speech that seemed sympathetic to Pretoria or antipathetic to the ANC would not satisfy Congress, where constructive engagement faced increasing challenges.

To make matters worse, as the struggle over the speech fermented, constructive engagement suffered another setback. During a July 4th reception at the U.S. embassy in Harare, Zimbabwe's Youth Minister, David Kariamazira, berated the United States for not imposing strict sanctions against South Africa. Former President Jimmy Carter and his family, honored guests at the reception, walked out in the middle of Kariamazira's tirade. In the short run the Reagan Administration suspended the remainder of Zimbabwe's 1986 aid package, blocking $13 million that had not yet been delivered. Mugabe apologized to Carter personally, acknowledging that Carter's Administration had been supportive of Zimbabwe, but he refused to apologize to the Reagan Administration. The July 4th speech was the last in a long line of diplomatic incidents between the two nations and proved very costly to Zimbabwe.[90]

Deteriorating relations with Zimbabwe damaged Crocker's regional strategy for southern Africa. However, Crocker could not focus on smoothing over the rift with Mugabe in July 1986, because a battle had been joined over the content of Reagan's approaching South Africa speech. On 8 July Crocker and Shultz submitted a draft to the National Security Council. Their version was a firm but moderate speech that stated reservations about sanctions but did not rule them out. On 13 July, Crocker received a version of the speech from the White House. It was identified as a "Buchanan/NSC" draft and basically ignored the draft that Shultz and Crocker had submitted. Crocker reported to Shultz that they "were in deep trouble."[91]

Chief of Staff Donald Regan had insisted that the National Security Council let Buchanan have free reign in drafting the speech, a decision which Crocker characterized as "obscene." Buchanan produced a "stridently polarizing message" that threatened to veto additional sanctions, spoke very briefly about the Pretoria regime's repressive tactics, and emphasized in great detail the terrorism of the ANC. For the next ten days, Crocker and Shultz fought to moderate the Buchanan draft. Shultz particularly hoped that Reagan would delineate some additional steps that the United States intended to take against apartheid. As Shultz and Crocker walked towards the East Room for the long-awaited oration, Buchanan and Casey emerged from an office. Reagan's "South Africa lobby" had been making last-minute changes.[92]

Reagan's message to the World Affairs Council on the afternoon of 22 July reflected Buchanan's influence, just as Crocker and Shultz had feared. Although Reagan did denounce apartheid and criticize Pretoria for renewing the state of emergency, he praised the progress that had ocurred under the Botha regime. He declared that he was still firmly opposed to economic sanctions, agreeing with Margaret Thatcher's description of sanctions as "immoral." He argued that if the United States abandoned South Africa, the Soviet Union would gladly fill the void and benefit from the abundant strategic minerals.[93]

Most damaging of all, however, was his depiction of the ANC. He decried the "calculated terror by elements of the African National Congress: the mining of roads, the bombings of public places." According to Reagan these actions were "designed to bring about further repression." Even when blasting Pretoria for its raids into neighboring states, Reagan castigated the "Soviet-armed guerrillas of the African National Congress" for perpetrating terrorism from bases in those states.[94] To a great extent, Reagan placed the blame for the violence on the ANC. Furthermore, by highlighting their ties to the Soviets, he suggested that the conflict was inspired by the Cold War's ideological battle rather than apartheid's oppression.

Once again, Reagan came across as sympathetic to the difficulties faced by the South African government. He indicated no intention of taking any concrete steps in response to the recent raids, arrests, and state of emergency. He did not signal any level of cooperation with Congressional efforts to impose additional sanctions. In Crocker's view, the "great communicator" had become the "great polarizer." He exacerbated a split among Senate Republicans, and formerly loyal leaders such as Dole, Lugar, and Kassebaum joined Democrats like Solarz and Gray in support of tougher anti-apartheid measures. Regarding the ultimate impact of the speech, Crocker dramatically concluded: "We lost the sanctions debate on July 22, 1986."[95]

While this may exaggerate the impact of one speech, there was no doubt that damage had been done. The next day, Shultz testified before the Senate Foreign Relations Committee and tried to salvage a compromise. He stood by much of what Reagan said, but indicated that the administration was willing to consider adjusting the measures that were already in place against Pretoria. He implied that some of the components of the legislation before Congress could be incorporated into another executive order. However, it was clear that he wanted control over U.S. policy to remain in the hands of the administration, and he warned against a "straitjacket of rigid legislation." He underlined his point: "Presidential discretion is necessary to introduce new measures if we conclude that they are necessary."[96]

Shultz pleaded the case for another "finesse" move by Lugar and Dole, similar to their actions in 1985 in support of Reagan's executive order, but in 1986 it was simply not to be. The grassroots anti-apartheid movement was too powerful to be ignored by Congress, especially in an election year. The activists, still led by Randall Robinson and TransAfrica, registered success after success in their campaign to get American money out of South Africa.

By the end of 1986, 19 states, 68 cities, and 131 colleges or universities divested $220 billion from companies doing business in South Africa. The message reached the masses through the media: *The New York Times* ran over one thousand stories on South Africa in 1986. Consumers boosted the cause: a fund-raising album by "Artists United Against Apartheid" netted $400 thousand for organizations such as the ANC and TransAfrica.[97]

Awareness of the ongoing crisis in South Africa, in and of itself, was certainly very significant. However, by late 1986 apartheid represented more than a foreign policy issue in the minds of voters and legislators. Americans equated the fight against Pretoria's institutionalized racism with the struggle for civil rights by African Americans in the 1960s. Americans perceived tougher sanctions not only as an alternative to the Reagan Administration's policy, but also as a rejection of racism. The vote over sanctions constituted a referendum on race. On 14 August, the Senate approved a tough bill by a staggering count of eighty-four to fourteen. Supporters included Republican leaders like Lugar and Dole. Dole, who had fiercely fought sanctions against Southern Rhodesia in the late 1970s, understood the critical racial dimension of the sanctions vote. He remarked: "This has now become a domestic civil rights issue."[98]

Dole had concluded that members of Congress could no longer stick by the President in opposing more sanctions, unless they wanted to be perceived as racist. As November elections approached, pressure from around the country mounted. On 25 August, the California state senate approved a measure requiring the divestment of over $11 billion in state pension and university funds from companies operating in South Africa. It was by far the largest victory for the divestment movement, amounting to more than triple the previous high for a state (New Jersey divested $3 billion).[99] Such a loud message from California, where Reagan had once ruled as governor, reverberated through the halls of Congress.

Meanwhile, the bicameral conference recommended the bill that had passed the Senate on 14 August. On 12 September the House approved it 308 to 77. They then sent what became known as the Comprehensive Anti-Apartheid Act (CAAA) to Reagan for his approval. Reagan waited two weeks before taking action. During that period, Crocker and Shultz argued for a creative response instead of a plain veto. They suggested announcing the appointment of an African American, Edward Perkins, as ambassador to South Africa. Furthermore, Reagan could unveil a plan to assist Zimbabwe, Mozambique, and black South Africans. Finally, a proposed visit to southern Africa by Shultz, during which he would meet with ANC leader Oliver Tambo, could also be revealed. They hoped that all of these moves, combined with another executive order incorporating parts of the CAAA, might prevent an override of Reagan's veto.[100]

As with the speech in July, however, the Buchanan/Casey influence again won out. On 26 September, Reagan vetoed the CAAA without proposing any initiatives that might assuage members of Congress. Not only that, in his explanation of the veto he even advocated increasing American investment in South Africa. Legislators immediately decried the veto. Edward Kennedy characterized Reagan's stand as putting "America on the side of racism in South Africa." Mickey Leland (D-Tex.), chair of the Congressional Black Caucus, described Reagan as "a thief in the night" who was trying to block a bill that the American people supported.[101]

Just three days after Reagan's veto, on Monday 29 September, the House voted 317-83 to override it. On 3 October the Senate made it official by a count of 78 to 21, despite an effort by Dole to prevent the override. Reagan lost the fight, and the Comprehensive Anti-Apartheid Act of 1986 became law. Content aside, the CAAA passage represented a significant event in the history of U.S. foreign relations. It was the first time since 1973, when Nixon's veto on the War Powers Act was overridden, that the President had been overridden on a foreign policy bill. In Crocker's view it was the worst possible outcome of the 1986 debate over South African policy. Shultz concurred, regretting the "true erosion of presidential control over foreign policy issues."[102] Leading scholars agree that the override was one of Reagan's worst foreign policy defeats.[103]

The passage of the CAAA, furthermore, reflected the growing presence of African Americans in politics. From 1970 to 1985, the number of blacks in the U.S. Congress doubled, from 10 to 20. Other figures were even more impressive: the number of state representatives shot up from 137 to 302, black mayors increased from 48 to 286, and total black elected officials went from 1,469 to

6,056.[104] African Americans around the country had helped enact divestment measures, which illuminated the writing on the wall for politicians at the national level. These black politicians in city and state governments carried out the anti-apartheid strategy of Robinson and TransAfrica and catalysed passage of the CAAA.

The content of the CAAA, moreover, was very significant. The act banned private loans, new investment, and computer sales by Americans to South Africa. It blocked imports of South African steel, uranium, and agricultural products into the United States, and withdrew landing rights in the United States for South African airlines. The sanctions imposed by the CAAA were "stronger than those adopted by any other of South Africa's former major trading partners."[105] Robert Mugabe believed that economic sanctions had helped end minority-rule in his own country and would do the same in South Africa. He praised the CAAA as the type of external pressure that was necessary to end apartheid.[106] Undoubtedly, the CAAA represented a "watershed in U.S.-South African relations," because henceforth the Pretoria regime would pay a concrete price for maintaining apartheid.[107]

APARTHEID CRUMBLES: 1987-1994

Early in 1987, the U.S. government took another step indicating that it had turned a corner in its relations with South Africa. On 28 January, Secretary Shultz conferred in Washington with ANC leader Oliver Tambo. They debated sanctions, and Shultz instructed Tambo to sever any ties to the Soviets. Despite the contentious tone of the meeting, it was extremely significant. Shultz had quelled the desire of conservatives to treat the ANC like the PLO and ostracize them. He knew that sooner or later, if it wanted to avoid complete catastrophe the Pretoria regime would be forced to negotiate with the ANC. His talk with Tambo helped pave the way. Regarding this meeting, Mandela later observed: "The Americans recognized the ANC as an indispensable element of any solution in South Africa."[108]

The United States could do a lot more than just meet with Oliver Tambo however. In mid-1987, the new Chairman of the Senate Foreign Relations SubCommittee on Africa, Paul Simon (D-Ill.), outlined his overall strategy for helping to bring peace to South

Africa. First, he felt the Congress needed to monitor closely the implementation of the CAAA. Also, he advocated renewed efforts to reach a settlement regarding Namibia. Finally, he espoused financial support for the Front Line states. According to Simon, Zimbabwe was "key to any effort to stabilize and strengthen southern Africa," and Mozambique was also very important.[109]

In effect, Simon proposed combining sanctions with several components of Crocker's constructive engagement. Mozambique came up first in June. When the Africa subcommittee haggled over whether to support the government of Mozambique or RENAMO, Simon's proposal to aid the government received a strong endorsement from Crocker. Randall Robinson seconded Crocker. The remarkable, albeit temporary, coalition of Simon, Crocker, and Robinson defeated Jesse Helm's attempts to aid RENAMO. In fact, Mozambique soon became the largest recipient of U.S. aid in sub-Saharan Africa.[110]

In response to changes in American policy such as the meeting with Tambo, the major aid to Mozambique, and the CAAA, the Pretoria regime launched a major offensive against Zimbabwe in September 1987.[111] Despite the increasing external pressure, moreover, the apartheid state retained its repressive hold over blacks in South Africa at the start of 1988. In March, Dellums introduced a measure that would tighten the sanctions. He acknowledged that the CAAA was good step, but argued that "only full and comprehensive sanctions, implemented internationally, will cause the South African government to change its policies." Dellums believed that as a multiracial nation, it was the duty of the United States to fight racial injustice abroad. To emphasize the link to the civil rights movement, he cited King. To refute the charges that further sanctions would hurt South African blacks, he quoted Biko.[112] All in all, it was another powerful presentation by Dellums.

Robinson testified in favor of Dellum's bill. He praised the comprehensive nature of the proposal, which he felt was a fitting response to the on-going violence and bannings in South Africa.[113] Robert Mugabe also advocated tougher sanctions by the United States. In an article in *Foreign Affairs*, which appeared about the time Dellums introduced his bill, Mugabe pressed American officials to take further action. While he was pleased by the CAAA, he hoped the United States would lean on other nations to impose similar measures. Like Dellums, he contended that black South Africans wanted tougher sanctions, citing Tutu as an example.[114]

The views of Mugabe, Robinson, and Dellums fell on deaf ears in 1988 however. The American public basically felt the crisis in South Africa was over. The widespread desire that the United States "do something" had been sated by the CAAA, and the public's attention had turned to other things. Therefore, the majority of Congress could also afford to sit tight on South Africa. Dellums was unable to pass his tougher bill. During the 1988 presidential campaign, moreover, both George Bush and Michael Dukakis refrained from making an issue of apartheid. Despite the wishes of activists like Robinson and Dellums, the CAAA would be the extent of U.S. punitive measures against Pretoria.

While there would be no toughening of sanctions, there were some positive developments in American foreign relations regarding the overall peace and stability of southern Africa in late 1988. On 1 September the State Department announced resumption of U.S. bilateral aid to Zimbabwe. While $5 million to facilitate commodity imports was quite a modest figure, the symbolic value of renewing good relations with Zimbabwe was far greater.[116] The decision was based partly on efforts by Mugabe to patch things up with Nkomo. Most importantly, early in 1988 he offered amnesty to any of Nkomo's "dissident" supporters. They surrendered, and a conflict that had plagued Zimbabwe since the early 1980s was virtually resolved. Mugabe had ridden the storm out, and even gotten back into the good graces of the United States. The positive developments in Zimbabwe had two main ramifications for South Africa: first, a staunchly anti-apartheid Mugabe would remain in control in Harare; second, by renewing support for Mugabe the United States again signaled to Pretoria its sympathy for multiracial democracy.[117]

While improved relations with Zimbabwe certainly pleased Crocker, he had even more cause for celebration regarding Namibia. In December 1988, after over seven years of shuttle diplomacy, he orchestrated a final settlement. In exchange for Namibian independence, the Cuban troops would depart from Angola. South African domination of Namibia, which dated back to World War I, would finally come to an end. (Namibia officially attained independence on 30 March 1990.) Crocker's achievement earned praise from old adversaries including Robinson, but conversely ended any chance for toughening the sanctions against South Africa.[118] Most importantly, Pretoria's willingness to resolve the Namibian conflict at the end of 1988 foreshadowed the remarkable developments of the next few years.

Preliminary discussions that would lead to the end of apartheid had begun. In May 1988, Mandela met with the government's secret working group. Talks started slowly, as representatives from Pretoria were very concerned about links between the ANC and communism. They informed Mandela that Prime Minister Botha hoped to speak with him in person before year's end. Mandela attributed Botha's desire to meet to the on-going pressure, from both inside and outside South Africa—including the "sweeping sanctions bill" passed by the United States two years earlier.[119]

In Washington, the George Bush administration quickly became involved in the South African drama. Secretary of State James Baker suggested to President Bush that he invite Albertina Sisulu to the White House. Sisulu was a leader of the United Democratic Front, and her husband Walter was imprisoned with Mandela. Bush agreed to invite her. In May, Baker met with South African Foreign Minister Pik Botha in Rome and urged him to set Mandela free. Botha explained that his government was working on that. Botha suggested that since Bush was going to meet with Mrs. Sisulu, he should also meet with F.W. de Klerk, who seemed likely to be the next president of South Africa. Baker left the meeting with a solid respect for Pik Botha, but he and Bush concluded that inviting de Klerk to the White House would do more harm than good in mid-1989.[120]

In July, Mandela and President Botha finally sat down together. They accomplished no substantive breakthrough, but they had "crossed the Rubicon." Weakened by a stroke, Botha resigned in August. His successor, F.W. de Klerk, announced in his inaugural that he sought peace and would negotiate with anyone who shared his goal. In December, Mandela met de Klerk, who displayed unprecedented sincerity. Mandela described the encouraging atmosphere: "From the first I noticed that Mr. de Klerk listened to what I had to say.... Mr. de Klerk seemed to be making an attempt to truly understand."[121] The receptiveness of de Klerk, reminiscent of how Jimmy Carter and Andrew Young worked with black African leaders in the late 1970s, constituted a key element in the ensuing negotiations.

On 2 February 1990, in the opening speech before Parliament, de Klerk began the process of dismantling apartheid. He ended the bans on the ANC and the Communist Party, freed many political prisoners, and lifted some restrictions imposed by the State of Emergency. A week later, he informed Mandela that he would be released the next day.[122] On 11 February 1990, after twenty-seven years, six months, and one week in prison, Mandela regained his freedom. Holding hands with his wife and raising his other arm boldly in the black nationalist salute, he slowly walked approximately seventy yards from the prison gates to a waiting vehicle. The walk resonated with powerful symbolism, since Mandela had been associated with the phrase "long walk to freedom" since the early 1960s.[123]

Around sundown that night, Mandela addressed a crowd of about twenty thousand in Cape Town. The speech was Mandela's first in public since his 1964 treason trial. He praised a variety of parties who had battled apartheid over the years, ranging from the ANC's military wing and the Communist Party to predominantly white groups of women and students. He encouraged his supporters to continue pressuring the Pretoria regime, and also requested the international community to maintain sanctions. He exclaimed: "Now is the time to intensify the struggle on all fronts."[124] There had been progress, but there was still a long ways to go.

Among other things, Mandela hoped the United States would not let up on Pretoria. In June he toured New York City, visiting Harlem and speaking at Yankee Stadium. He praised the strong support that black South Africans had received from African Americans, attributing it to great leaders like Martin Luther King. While attending a party at Robert DeNiro's loft, he joyously greeted Eddie Murphy, who had given twenty thousand dollars to the ANC. He explained to Murphy that his movies had provided great entertainment in prison. From New York, Mandela went on to Atlanta, where he laid a wreath on King's tomb.[125]

His last stop was Washington. There he thanked Congress for passing the CAAA. Aware that the Bush Administration was considering loosening sanctions, Mandela urged Congress not to do so yet. Later, Mandela and Bush discussed sanctions. While they disagreed on when sanctions should be lifted, Mandela respected Bush for his warmth and thoughtfulness. Bush, who had been the first world leader to telephone Mandela after his release, treated Mandela with great dignity and was "a man with whom one could disagree and then shake hands."[126]

Returning to South Africa, Mandela undertook a series of sessions with de Klerk, in which they hammered out a strategy for ending apartheid. The state of emergency, which dated back to 1986, was lifted completely in the fall of 1990. Partly as a reward for such actions, Bush hosted de Klerk at the White House in September. (De Klerk was originally scheduled to visit Washington in June before Mandela, but due to pressure from Randall Robinson and Jesse Jackson, members of Congress convinced de Klerk to postpone his trip.) After talking with de Klerk about recent events in South Africa, Bush characterized the progress away from apartheid as "irreversible."[127]

Indeed, the progress continued. The Group Areas Act and the Population Registration Act, the legal foundations of apartheid since 1950, were repealed in June 1991. As a result, on 11 July President Bush lifted major parts of the American sanctions against Pretoria. Hardline opponents of apartheid feared that Bush was moving too fast. Robert Mugabe, during a two-day visit to Washington later in July, urged Bush to keep the pressure on Pretoria until apartheid was completely overturned. Bush, who had visited Harare while vice president, praised the economic develpments initiated by Mugabe. The visit symbolized the ongoing improvement in U.S. relations with Zimbabwe, which received $40 million of American aid in 1991. Mugabe and Bush both judged their meeting a success and agreed that de Klerk was moving in the right direction.[128]

Back in South Africa, representatives from nineteen different parties convened in December to start formal plans for the transition to majority rule. The end of apartheid inched closer in 1992, but Bush would not be in office to see it. He was defeated in November by Bill Clinton, who then appointed an unprecedented number of blacks (three) to his original cabinet. Sixteen more African Americans also won seats in Congress in those elections, boosting the number in the Black Caucus to a record 40. That number included Carol Mosely Braun (D-Ill.), who became the first black woman ever elected to the Senate.[129]

These milestones for multiracial democracy in the United States came at a fitting time, as multiracial democracy was about to be born in South Africa. After difficult negotiations, the multiparty forum agreed in June 1993 that elections would be held in April 1994. Voters would chose 400 people to serve as a parliament and write a new constitution.[130]

After the elections were scheduled, Mandela returned to the United States for another visit. TransAfrica hosted a lunch so that some of the key African-American opponents of apartheid could meet Mandela. Ronald Dellums, who had sponsored sanctions legislation annually from 1971 until 1986, attended. So did boxer Sugar Ray Leonard, who had contributed $250 thousand to TransAfrica's program to educate South African blacks. Mandela, a former boxer himself, assumed his fighting stance when he saw Leonard, and the assembled luminaries roared.[131] Mandela was once again demonstrating the instincts of a great politician, which would shortly pay off.

During four days at the end of April 1994, millions of South African blacks cast their first votes in national elections. The ANC garnered 63 percent of the vote, which amounted to 252 seats in the first truly representative parliament in the history of South Africa. On 2 May de Klerk conceded victory to Mandela, who spoke at an ANC celebration that evening in the Carlton Hotel ballroom in downtown Johannesburg. Coretta Scott King attended the event, and Mandela honored her husband's memory: "I looked over to her as I made reference to her husband's immortal words.... we can loudly proclaim from the rooftops - Free at last! Free at last!"[132]

CONCLUSION

It was fitting that Corretta Scott King witnessed the triumph of racial justice in South Africa, for apartheid's end represented the final extension of her husband's vision onto the global stage.[133] King's vision of a multiracial democracy, relatively free of race-based revenge and retribution, took hold in the United States in the 1970s, in Zimbabwe in the 1980s, and in South Africa in the 1990s. Furthermore, American foreign policy helped extend King's vision not only by sharing his goals, but also by utilizing his methods. Willingness to negotiate with all sides, most notably including the ANC leaders, replicated the tactics of the civil rights movement. Similarly, the sanctions employed by the U.S. government resembled the economic boycotts by southern blacks in the 1960s.[134] American sanctions assisted the rise of Mugabe in 1980 and Mandela in 1994.

While important, American sanctions were certainly not the most important force in ending apartheid. Many other factors had helped convince de Klerk to take action in late 1989. Among the important ones was the end of communist rule in the Soviet Union, which effectively removed Pretoria's long-standing excuse for not dealing with the ANC. Also crucial was the realization by white leaders that maintaining apartheid was far too costly. With an economy based on such an inefficient system, South Africa could not continue to prosper. Part of the costliness, of course, was due to the additional "tax" imposed by international sanctions. White South Africans also resented compulsory military service, and worried about the widespread violence and general sense of uncertainty that increasingly characterized life under apartheid.[135]

The most important factor behind the relatively peaceful transition to majority rule in South Africa, however, was the courage and wisdom of black leaders like Stephen Biko, Desmond Tutu, and Nelson Mandela. They suffered imprisonment, beatings, and even death in order to bring justice to their native land. Moreover, their message was an inclusive one, which made it easier for de Klerk to finally accept. They had no intention of replacing white superiority with black superiority. In the tradition of Martin Luther King, they called for a society in which people of all races were equal. With important help from allies in many other nations including the United States and Zimbabwe, their dream materialized in 1994 with the triumph of multiracial democracy in South Africa.

The nonracial character of the new South African constitution, in turn, might help resuscitate King's vision in the United States.[136] Cooperation among blacks and whites characterized the civil rights struggles of the 1960s, which brought equal political participation for African Americans. By the 1990s, however, the on-going poverty and violence afflicting an inordinate number of blacks in the

United States suggested that King's dream had died. His humanistic vision of multiracial cooperation was too important to give up on, though. Americans must regain a sense of hope, and the best way to do that may be to look to South Africa. The incredible story of Mandela's triumph over apartheid should serve as an inspiration to all Americans and help renew King's vision in the land where it began.

NOTES

1. Paul Gordon Lauren, *Power and Prejudice: The Politics and Diplomacy of Racial Discrimination*, 2nd ed.(Boulder: Westview Press, 1996), 289-291.
2. Nelson Mandela, *Long Walk to Freedom: The Autobiography of Nelson Mandela* (Boston: Little, Brown, and Company, 1994), 83.
3. Pauline Baker, *The United States and South Africa: The Reagan Years* (New York: Ford Foundation, 1989), 4-5.
4. Peter J. Schraeder, *United States Foreign Policy Toward Africa: Incrementalism, Crisis and Change* (New York: Cambridge University Press, 1994), 190.
5. Robert Massie, *Loosing the Bonds: The United States and South Africa in the Apartheid Years* (New York: Doubleday, 1997), 620-671.
6. Randall Robinson, interviewed by Anthony J. Hughes, *Africa Report* (January-February 1980), 13-14.
7. Herschelle Challenor, "The Influence of Black Americans on U.S. Foreign Policy Towards Africa," in Abdul Aziz Said, ed., *Ethnicity and U.S. Foreign Policy* (New York: Praeger, 1981), 173. Challenor served on Diggs' staff from 1975 to 1978.
8. Details about Diggs and Dellums from Jack Salzman, et al., eds., *Encyclopedia of African-American Culture and History* (New York: Simon and Schuster, 1996), 742 and 766-767.
9. Chester A. Crocker, "South Africa: Strategy For Change," *Foreign Affairs* 59 (Winter 1980-81), 323-326, 345 and 350.
10. Crocker, "South Africa," 327, 346, and 350.
11. Andrew Young, "The United States and Africa: Victory for Diplomacy," *Foreign Affairs* 59 (Spring 1981), 662.
12. Young, "The United States and Africa," 653.
13. Extract of Reagan's 3 March 1981 interview with Walter Cronkite in Department of State, *American Foreign Policy Current Docu-*

ments 1981 (Washington: United States Government Printing Office, 1984), 1090. Extract of Reagan's 27 March 1981 interview with the *Washington Post* in *American Foreign Policy Current Domuments 1981* (hereafter *AFPCD 1981*), 1091-1092.

14. Extract of Haig's reply to a question after a 31 March 1981 speech before the Trilateral Commission, *AFPCD 1981*, 1094.

15. Crocker's 6 April 1981 statement before the Senate Committee on Foreign Relations in *AFPCD 1981*, 1071-1073.

16. For a detailed description of the negotiations over Namibia that lasted throughout the Reagan Administration, see Chester Crocker, *High Noon in Southern Africa: Making Peace in a Rough Neighborhood* (New York: Norton, 1992).

17. Extracts from Crocker's 6 April 1981 testimony before the Senate Foreign Relations Committee, *AFPCD 1981*, 1139-1140. The Reagan administration had announced on 24 March at a conference in Zimbabwe that it intended to provide $75 million per year in aid for three years, subject to congressional approval. See *AFPCD 1983*, 1200, Note 2.

18. Helms and Crocker exchange in ibid., 1140. Discussion of Crocker's wife Saone's background in Crocker, *High Noon*, 26.

19. Opposition by both TransAfrica and Helms noted in Baker, *The United States and South Africa*, 5.

20. Janice Love, *The U.S. Anti-Apartheid Movement: Local Activism in Global Politics* (New York: Praeger, 1985), 20-30.

21. U.S. aid to Zimbabwe totaled: $75 million in 1982, $60 million in 1983, $40 million in 1984, $28 million in 1985, and $28 million in 1986. See Appendix D in Alex Thomson, *Incomplete Engagement: U.S. Foreign Policy Towards the Repbulic of South Africa, 1981-1988* (Aldershot: Avebury, 1996), 334. Details on the failed Helms Amendment from a Senate Record Vote Analysis of the 22 October 1981 vote, compiled by the staff of the Republican Policy Committee, copy printed from the internet and in the author's possession.

22. Haig's exchange with Gray detailed in extracts from the 4 March 1982 hearings before the House Appropriations Committee's subcommittee on Foreign Operations, in the U.S. Department of State, *American Foreign Policy Current Documents 1982* (Washington: U.S. Government Printing Office, 1985), 1168-1169. Hereafter this volume will be referred to as *AFPCD 1982*.

23. Haig's resignation letter and Reagan's acceptance letter in *AFPCD 1982*, 48. Shultz describes his in-flight ponderings in George P. Shultz, *Turmoil and Triumph: My Years as Secretary of State* (New York: Charles Scribner's Sons, 1993), 6.

24. Toast by Bush in Harare, 16 November 1982, *AFPCD 1982*, 1232-1234.

25. Address by Bush before the Kenya Chamber of Commerce in Nairobi, 19 November 1982, in *AFPCD 1982*, 1162-1166.

26. Extracts from Bush's press conference at the Nairobi airport, 21 November 1982, *AFPCD 1982*, 1206-1208.

27. James R. Scarritt, "Zimbabwe: Revolutionary Violence Resulting in Reform," in Jack Goldstone, Ted Gurr, and Farrokh Moshiri, eds., *Revolutions of the Late Twentieth Century* (Boulder: Westview Press, 1991), 235-271, information on 1982 on 261.

28. Mayors' appeal in Love, *The U.S. Anti-Apartheid Movement*, 21; information on AFL-CIO from Thomson, *Incomplete Engagement*, 95-97; details about Mandela from Jack Grobler, *A Decisive Clash? A Short History of Black Protest Politics in South Africa, 1875-1976* (Pretoria: Acacia Books, 1988), 192-193.

29. Excerpts from the UN resolutions and statement by Luce, 9 December 1982, in *AFPCD 1982*, 1218-1224.

30. Extracts of Crocker's statement before the House Africa subcommittee, 15 February 1983, in U.S. Department of State, *American Foreign Policy Current Documents 1983* (Washington: U.S. Government Printing Office, 1985), 1140-1146. Hereafter this volume will be referred to as *AFPCD 1983*.

31. Exchange between Helms and Crocker in extracts from a 8 March 1983 hearing before the Senate Foreign Relations subcommittee on Africa, *AFPCD 1983*, 1199-1200.

32. State briefing, 21 December 1983, ibid., 1211.

33. Wisner's 3 May 1983 statement before the House Foreign Affairs subcommittee on International Operations, *AFPCD 1983*, 1149-1152.

34. Love, *The U.S. Anti-Apartheid Movement*, 41.

35. Thomson, *Incomplete Engagement*, 98; Love, *The U.S. Anti-Apartheid Movement*, 43-44. The anti-apartheid movement in Connecticut actually got rolling in 1980. For details, see Massie, *Loosing the Bonds*, 530-535.

36. Reagan's 13 September 1983 statement in the East Room prior to Mugabe's departure, in *AFPCD 1983*, 1208-1209. Their disagreements are outlined in extracts from a later press briefing by White House officials, ibid., 1210-1211.

37. Mugabe's 13 September 1983 statement in ibid., 1209-1210.

38. Efforts regarding sanctions in House and Senate summarized in Schraeder, *U.S. Foreign Policy Towards Africa*, 226. For details on Gray's amendment and the administration's opposition to it see

Crocker's 10 November 1983 address at Lawrence, KS, in *APFCD 1983*, 1127-1136, especially 1134.

39. George Shultz 29 March 1984 address to CEOs in Department of State, *American Foreign Policy: Current Documents 1984* (Washington: United States Government Printing Office, 1986), 816-819. Hereafter this volume will be referred to as *AFPCD: 1984*.

40. Excerpts from Wisner's 24 May 1984 testimony before the Africa Subcommittee of the House Foreign Affairs Committee, in *AFPCD: 1984*, 824-829. Aid amount from Thomson, *Incomplete Engagement*, 334.

41. Baker, *The United States and South Africa*, 17-21. For analysis of how South Africa's 1984 aggression in Angola and Mozambique represented a reaction to the 1980 election of Mugabe in Zimbabwe see James Barber and John Barratt, *South Africa's Foreign Policy: The Search for Status and Security, 1945-1988* (Cambridge: Cambridge University Press, 1990), 267-269.

42. Mandela, *Long Walk to Freedom*, 452.

43. Baker, *The United States and South Africa*, 27.

44. Crocker's testimony before the 26 September 1984 hearing of the Africa Subcommittee of the Senate Foreign Relations Committee, in *AFPCD: 1984*, 837-846.

45. Tsongas' response to Crocker in ibid., 843.

46. *Ibid.*, 844. The Crocker/Tsongas exchange is very interesting, as both men knew a lot about southern Africa but disagreed about what the U.S. should do.

47. Kassebaum's suggestion in ibid., 844. The author purchased the album "Free Nelson Mandela" in 1985 while a freshman at Princeton University and drove his roommates to distraction by playing it over and over. He purchased it again in 1997 on compact disc on "The Specials: The Singles Collection" and played it at his wedding.

48. Having just turned 18 in October 1984, the author cast his first vote that November, backing the Mondale/Ferraro ticket.

49. Randall Robinson, *Defending the Spirit: A Black Life in America* (New York: Penguin, 1998), 146-8. For an account that emphasizes the importance of Reagan's election, see Massie, *Loosing the Bonds*, 558. For details on Fauntroy's work for King in 1964, see Taylor Branch, *Pillar of Fire: America in the King Years, 1963-65* (New York: Simon and Schuster, 1998), 293-294.

50. TransAfrica's initial protest described in Robinson, *Defending the Spirit*, 151-154; Massie, *Loosing the Bonds*, 559-560; Ronald Walters, "African-American Influence on U.S. Foreign Policy To-

ward South Africa," in Mohammed Ahrari, ed., *Ethnic Groups and U.S. Foreign Policy* (New York: Greenwood Press, 1987), 75-82; Michael Cheers, "TransAfrica," *Ebony* (July 1987), 108-114.

51.   Juan Williams, "Black Leaders Find a Hot New Issue," a1 and a18; Michael Marriot, "TransAfrica in the Eye of the Storm," and "More Protesters Arrested," a19, *Washington Post* 12 December 1984.

52.   Walters, "African-American Influence," 75-82; Baker, *The United States and South Africa*, 27.

53.   Crocker, *High Noon in Southern Africa*, 258-259.

54.   Extracts from Reagan's 7 December 1984 remarks to the press, in *AFPCD: 1984*, 863-864.

55.   Extracts from the transcript of the 9 December 1984 interview with Tutu by Brinkley, in *AFPCD: 1984*, 865-866.

56.   On the comparisons between Tutu and King, see Massie, *Loosing the Bonds*, 556-557.

57.   Mandela, *Long Walk to Freedom*, 454-455.

58.   Lauren, *Power and Prejudice*, 292.

59.   Extracts from Reagan's 21 March 1985 press conference and excerpts from a 1 April interview with Reagan by *Washington Post* reporters, in Department of State, *American Foreign Policy Current Documents: 1985* (Washington: United States Government Printing Office, 1986), 827-828. This volume will hereafter be referred to as *AFPCD: 1985*.

60.   16 April speech by Shultz before the National Press Club, in *AFPCD: 1985*, 828-835, quotation at 830.

61.   Walters, "African-American Influence," 78; Baker, *The United States and South Africa*, 31-32; Schraeder, *U.S. Foreign Policy Towards South Africa*, 228.

62.   Extracts from 24 April and 2 May 1985 testimonies by Crocker before the Senate Foreign Relations Committee, in *AFPCD:1985*, 839-843.

63.   Williams, "African-American Influence," 77; Thomson, *Incomplete Engagement*, 333.

64.   22 May 1985 statement of Randall Robinson, Executive Director, TransAfrica, in *U.S. Policy Toward South Africa*, Hearings Before The Committee On Foreign Relations, United States Senate, Ninety-ninth Congress, First Session, April 24, May 2 and 22, 1985 (Washington: USGPO, 1985), 189.

65.   Young's testimony in ibid., 281-283 and 307-318, exchange with Kassebaum, 312-314. For an analysis of the effectiveness of the sanctions against Southern Rhodesia, which relies considerably on research in Zimbabwe, see William Minter and Elizabeth Schmidt,

"When Sanctions Worked: The Case of Rhodesia Reexamined," *African Affairs* 87 (April 1988), 207-237.

66. Young's testimony, ibid., 283.

67. *Ibid.*, 283.

68. *Ibid.*, 283.

69. House vote detailed in Schraeder, *U.S. Foreign Policy Towards Africa*, 228; South Africa actions in Lauren, *Power and Prejudice*, 293-294; excerpts from Reagan's 18 June 1985 remarks in *AFPCD:1985*, 844-845.

70. Schraeder, *U.S. Foreign Policy Towards Africa*, 228; State Department 12 July 1985 comments on the Lugar-Dole bill, in *AFPCD:1985*, 852.

71. Excerpts from Reagan's 5 August 1985 press conference in *AFPCD:1985*, 855-856.

72. Crocker, *High Noon in Southern Africa*, 271; Shultz, *Turmoil and Triumph*, 1115-1116.

73. Crocker, *High Noon in Southern Africa*, 271.

74. Reagan's 9 September 1985 announcement of the order and subsequent press conference; Executive Order 12532; message to Congress; and Shultz' press conference, in *AFPCD: 1985*, 861-871. Analysis of the difference between the order and the sanctions bill in Schraeder, *U.S. Foreign Policy Towards Africa*, 228-229.

75. Crocker, *High Noon in Southern Africa*, 277-278. Kennedy quote from Massie, *Loosing the Bonds*, 591.

76. Reagan's 9 September 1985 press conference, *AFPCD:1985*, 862-865.

77. The Reagan/Machel 19 September 1985 exchange described in Shultz, *Turmoil and Triumph*, 1117. Reagan's statement after the meeting in *AFPCD:1985*, 871-872.

78. Explanation of 15 November 1985 veto by the U.S. in *AFPCD:1985*, 875.

79. Extracts from Crocker's 28 January 1986 press conference in Department of State, *American Foreign Policy Current Documents: 1986* (Washington: U.S. Government Printing Office, 1987), 621-623. Hereafter this volume will be referred to as *AFPCD:1986*.

80. Extracts from 18 March 1986 written questions by Congressman David Obey and responses by Crocker, in *AFPCD:1986*, 639. A severe blow to Mozambique's development occurred on 19 October 1986, when Machel died in a plane crash. Shultz lamented it as a regrettable tragedy. See Shultz, *Turmoil and Triumph*, 1117.

81. Excerpts from Crocker's 12 March 1986 statement before the House Foreign Affairs Committee's subcommittee on Africa, in

AFPCD:1986, 631-635.

82. Dellum's 9 April 1986 statement in *Legislative Options And United States Policy Toward South Africa* Hearings and Markup Before the Committee on Foreign Affairs and Its Subcommittees on International Economic Policy and Trade and on Africa, House Of Representatives, Ninety-ninth Congress, Second Session on H.R. 997 and H.R. 4868, April 9, 16; June 4, 5 1986 (Washington: USGPO, 1987), 5-15.

83. Dellum's 9 April 1986 statement in *Legislative Options*, 11.

84. Crocker's 9 April 1986 statement in *Legislative Options*, 28.

85. The Emminent Persons Group included Olusegun Obasanjo and Malcolm Fraser, former leaders of Nigeria and Australia, respectively. See Mandela, *Long Walk to Freedom*, 459-461.

86. Deputy White House press secretary Larry Speakes' 19 May 1986 statement, in *AFPCD:1986*, 641.

87. Mark ups on 4 and 10 June 1986 of HR 4868 by Africa Subcommittee and Foreign Affairs Committee, in *Legislative Options*, 221-233 and 234-242.

88. Unrest and reaction described in Crocker, *High Noon in Southern Africa*, 305-306; Madela, *Long Walk to Freedom*, 461; Botha quotation from Lauren, *Power and Principle*, 294.

89. Crocker, *High Noon in Southern Africa*, 304-306.

90. In September, the Reagan Administration announced that it would provide no assistance to Zimbabwe in 1987. For details on the incident, see *The New York Times*, 10 July and 3 September 1986; State Department statements in *AFPCD:1986*, 647-649 and 667-668; and Douglas Brinkley, *The Unfinished Presidency: Jimmy Carter's Journey Beyond the White House* (New York: Viking, 1998), 194-196. On the overall deterioration of U.S. relations with Zimbabwe between 1983 and 1986, see Colin Stoneman and Lionel Cliffe, *Zimbabwe: Politics, Economics and Society* (New York: Pinter Publishers, 1989), 184-190.

91. Crocker, *High Noon in Southern Africa*, 319-321.

92. Shultz, *Turmoil and Triumph*, 1122; Crocker, *High Noon in Southern Africa*, 322-323.

93. Reagan's 22 July 1986 address, "U.S. Policy Toward South Africa," in *AFPCD:1986*, 652-657; Thatcher quotation from 653.

94. Reagan's address, *AFPCD:1986*, ANC quotations from 654-655.

95. Baker, *The United States and South Africa*, 43-44; Crocker, *High Noon in Southern Africa*, 323. Shultz was extremely disappointed with the speech. He blamed it on the backbiting by White House aides such as Buchanan. It was one of the factors that convinced

him to submit his resignation to Reagan on 5 August 1986. See Shultz, *Turmoil and Triumph*, 725.

96. Excerpts from 23 July 1997 statement before the Senate Foreign Relations Commmittee by George Shultz, in *AFPCD:1986*, 657-665.

97. Baker, *The United States and South Africa*, 31; Thomson, *Incomplete Engagement*, 206-208. *The New York Times* ran nearly 1,100 stories on South Africa in 1986, an average of 2.3 per day. See Massie, *Loosing the Bonds*, 606.

98. Importance of race in the debate and quotation from Dole in Pauline Baker, "The Sanctions Vote: A G.O.P. Milestone," *New York Times*, 26 August 1986. The civil rights aspect also emphasized in Crocker, *High Noon in Southern Africa*, 326.

99. Nicholas Kristof, "California Senate Passes Bill to Sell Pretoria-Linked Stock," *The New York Times* 26 August 1986, front page.

100. Crocker, *High Noon in Southern Africa*, 327-329. On 3 November, Perkins did become the first black U.S. ambassador to South Africa. See Schultz, *Turmoil and Triumph*, 1123; "Ambassador Perkins' Swearing in Ceremony," in *AFPCD:1986*, 677-679.

101. Buchanan and Casey's influence discussed in Crocker, *High Noon in Southern Africa*, 328-330. Reagan's 26 September 1986 message to the House explaining his veto in *AFPCD:1986*, 671-673. Congressional reaction to the veto in William Smith, "Eyeball to Eyeball: Reagan, Congress and a sanctions veto," *Time*, 6 October 1986, 36-37.

102. Crocker, *High Noon in Southern Africa*, 329-330; Shultz, *Turmoil and Triumph*, 1122-1123. Dole's efforts to defeat the override are bitterly recounted in Robinson, *Defending the Spirit*, 172.

103. Baker, *The United States and South Africa*, 44; Schraeder, *U.S. Foreign Policy Towards Africa*, 230.

104. John Hope Franklin and Alfred A. Moss, Jr., *From Slavery to Freedom: A History of African Americans*, 7th ed. (New York: McGraw-Hill, 1994), 555.

105. Schraeder, *U.S. Foreign Policy Towards Africa*, 230; quotation from Lauren, *Power and Prejudice*, 304.

106. Robert Mugabe, "Struggle for Southern Africa," *Foreign Affairs* 66 (Winter 1987/88), 311-327, especially 324-327.

107. Baker, *The United States and South Africa*, 46-47.

108. Shultz, *Turmoil and Triumph*, 1123; Mandela, *Long Walk to Freedom*, 477.

109. Paul Simon, "The Senate's New African Agenda," *Africa Report* (June 1987), 14-16, quote at 16.

110. Baker, *The United States and South Africa*, 57-58.

111. John Dzimba, *South Africa's Destabilization of Zimbabwe, 1980-1989* (New York: St. Martin's Press, 1998), 104-105.

112. Dellums 22 March 1988 statement in *Proposed Economic Sanctions Against South Africa* Hearings and Markup Before the Committee on Foreign Affairs and Its Subcommittees on International Economic Policy and Trade, and on Africa, House Of Representatives, One Hundredth Congress, Second Session On H.R. 1580, H.R. 1051, H.R. 2443, H.R. 3317, And H.R. 3328, March 22, 23; April 20, 28; and May 3, 1988 (Washington: USGPO, 1988), 40-47.

113. Robinson's 23 March 1988 testimony in ibid., 304-305.

114. Mugabe, "Struggle for Southern Africa," 323-326.

115. On the 1988 election, see Robert D. Schulzinger, *American Diplomacy in the Twentieth Century*, 3rd ed. (New York: Oxford University Press, 1994), 352-353. On the public's apathy, see Shraeder, *U.S. Foreign Policy Towards Africa*, 233-235.

116. "Resumption of US Aid to Zimbabwe," press briefing by Acting State spokeswoman Phyllis Oakley, 1 September 1988, in Department of State, *American Foreign Policy: Current Documents 1988* (Washington: U.S. Government Printing Office, 1989), 672. Eighteen self-help projects initiated by poor Zimbabweans also received American funding in 1988, from the African Development Foundation, a nonprofit organization formed by Congress in 1980. See Department of State, *American Foreign Policy: Current Documents 1989* (Washington: U.S. Government Printing Office, 1990), 609.

117. Mugabe's conciliation with Nkomo and ongoing effort against apartheid discussed in Scarritt, "Zimbabwe," 262 and 269. Reasons behind the renewal of aid mentioned in Baker, *The United States and South Africa*, 22.

118. Schulzinger, *American Diplomacy*, 353; Baker, *The United States and South Africa*, 70; Schraeder, *U.S. Foreign Policy Toward Africa*, 236.

119. Mandela, *Long Walk to Freedom*, 467, 469-470, and 479-480.

120. James Baker, *The Politics of Diplomacy: Revolution, War & Peace, 1989-1992* (New York: Putnam, 1995), 220-224.

121. Mandela, *Long Walk to Freedom*, 479-480, 483.

122. *Ibid.*, 484-485.

123. John Burns, "On Mandela's Walk, Hope and Violence," *The New York Times*, 12 February 1990, a1 and a14.

124. Christopher Wren, "Mandela, Freed, Urges Step-Up in Pressure to End White Rule," *The New York Times*, 12 February 1990, a1 and a14.

125. Massie, *Loosing the Bonds*, 665-668.

126. Mandela, *Long Walk to Freedom*, 508.

127. Effort by Robinson and Jackson described in Massie, *Loosing the Bonds*, 665. For details of de Klerk's September 1990 visit to Washington, see U.S. Department of State, *American Foreign Policy: Current Documents, 1990* (Washington: U.S. Government Printer, 1991), 794-799; quote at 795.

128. Lifting of sanctions in Baker, *The Politics of Diplomacy*, 228. Mugabe visit in "Mugabe Waxes Diplomatic on Bush's Sanctions Move," *Washington Post*, 25 July 1991.

129. Franklin, *From Slavery to Freedom*, 568-570. Coincidentally, in November 1992, due to the efforts of Bryant Gumbel, the *Today* show aired live from Harare, Zimbabwe for a week. This was a first for American television. See Robinson, *Defending the Spirit*, 273-274.

130. Lauren, *Power and Prejudice*, 308; Schraeder, *U.S. Foreign Policy toward Africa*, 44, 238-241; Mandela, *Long Walk to Freedom*, 531.

131. Robinson, *Defending the Spirit*, 180-182.

132. Mandela, *Long Walk to Freedom*, 538-540.

133. For an in-depth analysis of reactions to King's philosophy of nonviolence in South Africa from the 1950s to the 1990s, see Lewis Baldwin, *Toward the Beloved Community: Martin Luther King Jr. and South Africa* (Cleveland: Pilgrim Press, 1995).

134. My point here has also been made by George Fredrickson, *Black Liberation: A Comparative History of Black Ideologies in the United States and South Africa* (New York: Oxford University Press, 1995), 274-276.

135. For an emphasis on the importance of the Soviet Union's demise, see Lauren, *Power and Prejudice*, 307. The view that the economic costs and the "tax" of sanctions were key is put forth in Crocker, *High Noon in Southern Africa*, 485-492.

136. For an insightful analysis, comparing the conditions of blacks in America and South Africa in the 1990s, see the epilogue of Fredrickson's *Black Liberation*, 319-323

Epilogue

THE U.S. AND ZIMBABWE
AT MILLENIUM'S END

The spread of multiracial democracy to South Africa represented a great triumph for the people throughout southern Africa, but it by no means ended their problems. Nelson Mandela's leadership was widely acclaimed in the United States, yet many challenges remained. In neighboring Zimbabwe, in its second decade of multiracial democracy, the initial euphoria was long gone. Opposition to white rule had been a clear goal around which to unite, but beyond that it became more complex. Difficult questions, those regarding the economy, remained unanswered, and a new health crises of unprecedented scope arose.

As Zimbabwe grappled with these issues, how much support did the U.S. give? What, if any, concrete steps did the Clinton administration take to assist the people of Zimbabwe? Did African Americans continue to play a special role, pushing for progressive policies? While it is still too early for a definitive assessment on U.S. relations with Zimbabwe during the 1990s, we can examine some of the key events and begin to consider the above questions.

In the mid-1990s, the situation in Zimbabwe warranted a mixed review. However, on the positive side of the ledger, peace reigned. Race relations remained generally good, although Robert Mugabe was loosing ground in his effort to retain the white population. The number of whites continued to dwindle, and the black percentage of the population approached 99 percent. Of approximately twelve million people, fewer than one hundred thousand were white.

The shrinking percentage of white citizens was not bad in and of itself. However, their ongoing possession of an incredibly disproportionate stake in the economy threatened to prompt a violent uprising. In 1995, whites accounted for less than 1 percent of the population, yet they held approximately 97 percent of the wealth. Some four thousand white farmers owned about 30 percent of the best farmland, and at least 60 percent of the land overall was owned by whites. At the same time, seven million blacks struggled to survive in areas severely struck by droughts. Mugabe talked about land reform, but refrained from concrete action. However, even a redistribution of the land would not have appeased everyone. Black Zimbabweans, students in one of Africa's best educational systems, were unable to find work; unemployment among blacks hovered somewhere around 30 percent.[1]

A more serious problem, literally an issue of life and death, became evident in Zimbabwe in the 1990s—AIDS. By middecade the epidemic raged out of control, devastating young adults and resulting in about two hundred thousand deaths a year. Funeral directors, running out of cemetery plots, requested permission to bury people vertically or in layers. Experts estimated that one-third of Zimbabwean youth would be orphans within fifteen years. In 1998, a UN analytical report concluded that the impact of AIDS in southern Africa rivaled the effect of the Black Death in Europe during the Middle Ages. Zimbabwe was the worst case, with over 25 percent of the adult population infected with HIV.[2]

The task of leading Zimbabwe's fight against AIDS and other less drastic problems remained in the hands of Mugabe and his ruling Zimbabwe African National Union (ZANU) party. As the end of the millennium approached, opposition to Mugabe spread throughout Zimbabwean society. Military veterans protested the government's failure to pay their pensions. Ian Smith accused the ZANU elite of fraud and corruption, while Ndabaningi Sithole allegedly plotted to kill Mugabe. Rising food prices sparked riots in Harare, resulting in five deaths and army intervention in January 1998. In May, the major labor unions struck and thousands of disgruntled students demanded that Mugabe resign. Yet he and ZANU seemed as entrenched as ever.[3]

For the Clinton administration, as for its predecessors, dealing with Zimbabwe meant dealing with Mugabe. President Clinton, offering hospitality comparable to that of Carter, Reagan, and Bush, hosted Mugabe at the White House for an official working visit in May 1995. The two leaders discussed ways to improve Zimbabwe's economy, particularly by increasing trade and foreign investment. Clinton thanked Mugabe for his efforts to resolve conflicts in southern Africa, especially in Angola.[4]

Such state visits, while of symbolic value, made little concrete impact. Substantive relations between the United States and Zimbabwe remained significant during the Clinton years however. The official American contribution to Zimbabwe's well-being included economic aid administered by the United States Agency for International Development (USAID), whose programs focused on fighting AIDS, conserving wildlife, and helping low-income Zimbabweans buy homes.[5] American taxpayers also funded Peace Corps projects in Zimbabwe and the largest Fulbright exchange program in sub-Saharan Africa. Members of the U.S. special forces from Fort Bragg, South Carolina, began training the Zimbabwean army.[6]

The mining industry remained a central component of the Zimbabwean economy in the mid-1990s, and desire for strategic minerals continued to be an important element of relations with the United States. Chromite was still a mainstay of Zimbabwean mining, with over a half million tons produced in 1994. The United States, in turn, imported massive quantities of related alloys. In 1995, over $25 million worth of Zimbabwean ferrochromium was shipped to American factories. Only Russia, Turkey, South Africa, and Kazakstan supplied more. Furthermore, Zimbabwe was the third leading source of ferrochromium-silicone for the United States in 1995.[7]

Mining, of course, had long been one area of the southern African economy in which Americans had interests. By the mid-1990s, U.S. involvement had expanded to include many other products. By 1995, the U.S. was Zimbabwe's fourth largest trading partner. During that year Zimbabwe imported about $110 million in American goods and shipped about $160 million worth of goods to the United States.[8] Leaders on both sides of the Atlantic hoped to continue expanding such activity, and the call was particularly strong among blacks in the United States.

In July 1997, Leon Sullivan organized the fourth annual African-African American Summit, which met in Zimbabwe and was hosted by Mugabe. The theme of the gathering was economic development. Jesse Jackson led a U.S. delegation, that included Transportation Secretary Rodney Slater. Slater announced that the Clinton administration intended to provide $500 million to improve African infrastructures as a way to lure investment. Ruth Davis, the former U.S. ambassador to Benin and one of few African-American female ambassadors, hailed the summit as evidence of a "thirst for communication" between Africans and African Americans. She also noted the rising number of black American tourists visiting Africa, estimated at one hundred thousand per year in the late 1990s.[9]

Many of the Zimbabwe summit participants, including Jackson, Sullivan, and Slater, reconvened early in 1998 at a meeting on Africa for American mayors. Denver's Wellington Webb chaired the session, advocating Africa as a higher priority for U.S. investment. He explained his intention to name Harare as Denver's sister-city and thus promote business and cultural exchange. The conference featured dialogue, primarily on economic issues, among over two hundred U.S. mayors and many African ambassadors. Amos Midzi, Zimbabwe's ambassador to the United States, praised the conference's focus: "You cannot overemphasize the economic aspect, because that is what we need."[10]

While many key leaders espoused an increase in American trade and investment in Africa in the late 1990s, the Clinton administration manifested a desire to promote democracy simultaneously. With that in mind, in October 1997 Clinton appointed Jesse Jackson as his special envoy for African democratization. Jackson was well-suited to the task, having tremendous experience in boosting voter registration in the U.S. and a strong reputation in Africa. Clinton asked Jackson to facilitate democratic reform in African nations, instructing him to work closely with Secretary of State Madeleine Albright.[11]

Secretary Albright herself visited seven African nations in December 1997 on what was billed as a "pro-democracy" tour. She praised the nations she visited as states with potential for democracy and free markets. Her itinerary drew criticism, however, with critics contending that South Africa was the only stop that featured true democracy. Albright experienced particular frustration in the Democratic Republic of the Congo, when its new leader Laurent Kabila mocked democracy and human rights at a press conference. Kabila, evidently, was no role model for progressive government. It seemed that Albright's visit to the Congo was more an effort to prevent escalating violence than a reward for Kabila's democracy. Similar assessments could be made about stops in Uganda, Ethiopia, Rwanda, and Angola.[12]

Albright's visit to South Africa and meeting with Nelson Mandela was the only stop that was virtually above reproach. From there she went to her final destination on the continent, Zimbabwe, and to more controversy. After meeting with Mugabe, Albright announced that the U.S. would be providing $1 million to combat drought and a smaller grant that would facilitate a meeting between the Zimbabwe Parliament and members of the U.S. Congress to discuss democratic reform. As the press conference wound down, Albright was grilled about the corrupt and repressive nature of Mugabe's government. Albright replied that while she and Mugabe had discussed the importance of human rights, she recognized that every country had its own "local context."[13]

By referring to a "local context" for human rights in Zimbabwe, Secretary Albright may well have been alluding to the lack of rights for homosexuals. Since late 1995, Mugabe's blatant antigay stance had been an international issue. In August of that year, he prohibited a gay rights group from participating in a book fair in Harare. Mugabe later defended his action and described gays as perverts who were "lower than pigs and dogs." Barney Frank (D-Mass.), one of three openly gay members of the U.S. Congress, co-authored with Congressional Black Caucus chair Maxine Waters (D-Cal.) a letter of protest to Mugabe. The letter was signed by seventy other members of Congress. Frank also urged the State Department to indicate its displeasure with Mugabe's government, which U.S. ambassador to Zimbabwe Johnnie Carson soon communicated.[14]

Although Mugabe never repented, the 1995 reactions from members of the U.S. government may have prevented him from taking more aggressive actions against gays, at least in the short run. However, in April 1998 he again manifested his views on gays.

He exclaimed: "Animals in the jungle are better than these people." His homophobia again prompted a response in the United States. Mugabe had been invited to deliver a June commencement address at California State Polytechnic University in Pomona. The faculty senate denounced Mugabe in a May resolution, and Mugabe cancelled his speech.[15]

The ironies of Mugabe's verbal attacks on gays and the subsequent reactions were many. The theme of the August 1995 book fair that sparked his initial discriminatory actions was human rights. Perhaps more ironic is the fact that some of the most strident reaction against his views came from groups who had long been his allies. The Congressional Black Caucus (CBC) was instrumental in maintaining the sanctions that had helped bring Mugabe to power in 1980, and yet CBC chair Maxine Waters took the lead in denouncing Mugabe in 1995. Academics had consistently praised Mugabe's conciliatory policies towards whites as a great example of racial justice, yet in May 1998 they blasted him for denying justice to gays.

During a visit to Harare in the late 1980s Jesse Jackson suggested that Mugabe tour the United States, where he was a hero. Jackson called Mugabe "the center of hope for reconciliation around the world." By the late 1990s, Mugabe's views on gays made him an international pariah. In the words of an editorial in *The Nation*, the "once-venerated freedom fighter" had turned into a "cranky old bigot."[16] His sinking reputation, moreover, probably contributed to President Clinton's decision to skip Zimbabwe when he made his historic trip to Africa in 1998.

In March and April of 1998, Clinton spent twelve days touring Africa, on a six-nation junket. He paid short visits to Ghana, Uganda, Rwanda, and Senegal, and spent three days each in South Africa and Botswana.[17] His sightseeing with Nelson Mandela, including a tour of Robben Island, provided the most dramatic footage of the trip. Mandela scolded Clinton for U.S. policies towards Cuba and Libya, two nations who had greatly assisted the anti-apartheid struggle. He also criticized trade legislation pending in the U.S. Congress, arguing that it would place unwanted controls on South African trade. Nevertheless, Mandela concluded by praising Clinton's character and his decision to tour Africa.[18]

Clinton, for his part, emphasized the positive throughout his stay in South Africa. He characterized South Africans as a people "unshackled," and underlined the fact that both South Africa and the United States featured multiracial democracy. During a visit to Soweto, he spoke in tribute to the people who had died in the fight against apartheid.[19] From South Africa, Clinton and his wife Hillary went on to Botswana for a safari. Their final stop was Senegal, where they saw a notorious outpost of the slave trade. Both Botswana and Senegal generated more powerful images for the American media.

For Clinton, the 12-day trip was a success in many ways. For one thing, it took some of the media's attention away from his problems at home, most notably the allegations about an affair with Monica Lewinsky. More importantly, the trip demonstrated his interest in a continent that had generally been ignored by his predecessors. For at least twelve days, an American president had been thinking about Africa. Even Jimmy Carter, the only other sitting president to visit southern Africa, had stayed just a few days in Nigeria and Liberia. How much of a concrete impact the visit will have on the people of Africa remains to be seen. Nonetheless, Clinton succeeded in turning the spotlight on an area of the world that typically only received attention for tragedies of disease, war, and famine.

Clinton's spotlight did not illuminate Zimbabwe, however. Considering the history of U.S./Zimbabwe relations, it was shocking that Clinton bypassed it. Indeed, it would have been just as convenient for Clinton to have gone on safari in the game preserves of Zimbabwe as it was in Botswana. He could have emphasized American efforts to aid Zimbabwean wildlife conservation. Perhaps he could have stopped at Victoria Falls, or at the ruins of Great Zimbabwe. Instead, Clinton skipped Zimbabwe altogether. The choice to skip Mugabe's nation in 1998 suggests much about what had made Zimbabwe a high priority in the 1970s and 1980s.

It will be many years before the documents that record the planning of the trip become available to scholars. Even then, the reasons for skipping Zimbabwe might not be explicit. The answer, however, seems clear. The most compelling reason to be concerned with Zimbabwe, for most American policy makers, had been its potential influence on South Africa. Whether they supported Robert Mugabe or Ian Smith, or fell somewhere in between, most U.S. officials believed the greatest significance of Zimbabwe was what it meant for South Africa. Indeed, U.S. relations with Harare in the 1970s and 1980s eventually contributed to the end of apartheid in Pretoria in 1994.

Mugabe and most Zimbabweans were certainly pleased with the triumph of multiracial democracy in South Africa and with their contribution to the victory. Ironically, however, a side effect of the ascendence of Mandela was a decline in Mugabe's importance to the rest of the world. A free and democratic South Africa, with its tremendous human and natural resources, dwarfed the neighbor to the north. All of the characteristics that earned Zimbabwe a significant place in U.S. foreign relations could be found in South Africa, and in much greater amounts.

Finally, in addition to diamonds, gold, and beaches, South Africa possessed one other critical advantage over Zimbabwe. Quite simply, Mandela was possibly the world's most heroic figure. Like Mugabe he had triumphed over racism. Yet, unlike Mugabe, he was generally humble and gracious. Furthermore, he championed equal rights for everyone, including homosexuals. The new South African constitution was the first in the world to protect gays from discrimination. On no other issue was the contrast more pronounced between Mandela and Mugabe, whose anti-gay tirades had sullied his international reputation.

For the Clinton administration, which strongly supported gay rights in the United States, Mugabe's homophobia may have been the deciding factor in leaving Zimbabwe off the itinerary. Photos of Clinton with Mugabe, a "cranky old bigot," were not the kind of publicity that the administration sought.[20] Mugabe, who had benefitted from the influence of African Americans during the Carter administration, may have suffered due to the influence of gay Americans during the Clinton years. The key to why Clinton skipped Zimbabwe was probably the fact that freedom had reached South Africa, and therefore Zimbabwe was no longer considered important; however, Mugabe's verbal attacks on gays had only made the decision easier.

Zimbabwe had been a high priority in U.S. foreign relations in the 1960s, 1970s, and 1980s, mainly because of its relevance for American domestic politics and events in South Africa. In 1998, these same forces pushed Zimbabwe off the agenda. The common thread that ran through U.S. relations with Zimbabwe from 1953 to 1998, in fact, was that American officials generally judged Zimbabwe for its influence on other places. Zimbabwe's significance had always been its potential impact on U.S. relations with the Soviet Union, Great Britain, and South Africa, or its importance in domestic politics. The only U.S. leader to take significant action toward Zimbabwe chiefly out of concern for its people was Jimmy Carter. His influence on Clinton's foreign policy, however, was minimal.[21] So, at the end of the millennium Zimbabwe finds itself once again off the radar screen of U.S. foreign relations, back where it had been in the 1950s. The more things change, the more they stay the same.

NOTES

1. Donald McNeil, "Whites Face Seizure of Land in Zimbabwe," *Denver Post*, 12 February 1998; Paul Taylor, "Zimbabwe: a Pattern for S. Africa?" *Washington Post*, 9 April 1995, a23; Keith Richburg, "Despite Problems, Zimbabwe `Works,'" *Washington Post*, 3 August 1994, a1 and a20.

2. Paul Taylor, "AIDS Overwhelming Zimbabwe's Advanced Defenses," *Washington Post*, 12 April 1995, a1 and a30; United States Agency for International Development, "The USAID FY 1998 Congressional Presentation," copy from internet in author's possession.

3. Ian Smith, *The Great Betrayal: The Memoirs of Africa's Most Controversial Leader* (London: Blake Publishing, 1997), 399-406; Angus Shaw, "Minister Convicted in plot to kill Zimbabwe president," *Rocky Mountain News*, 6 December 1997; Holger Jensen, "Political Woes Threaten Zimbabwe food supply," *Rocky Mountain News*, 25 January 1998, 39a; "Strike called in Zimbabwe," *Denver Post*, 2 May 1998, 18a; "Students Demand Mugabe's resignation," *Denver Post*, 30 May 1998.

4. The White House, "Statement by the Press Secretary," 18 May 1995, copy printed from internet in author's possession.

5. USAID efforts to combat AIDS, in "The USAID FY 1998 Congressional Presentation." USAID assistance for home buyers in United States Agency for International Development, "USAID Congressional Presentation FY 1997," copy from internet in author's

possession. Film star Alicia Silverstone visited Zimbabwe in 1998 to help fight drooping trunk disease among elephants, and discussed it on Jay Leno's *Tonight* show on 10 July 1998.

6. Discussion of Peace Corps and Fulbright in confirmation hearings to consider the nomination of Johnnie Carson as ambassador to Zimbabwe, Senate Foreign Relations Committee, Africa Subcommittee, 16 February 1995, copy from internet in author's possession. Special forces mentioned in Douglas Brinkley, *The Unfinished Presidency: Jimmy Carter's Journey Beyond the White House* (New York: Viking, 1998), 196.

7. United States Department of the Interior, *Minerals Yearbook: Metals and Minerals*, Volume I (Washington: U.S. Government Printing Office, 1995), 177, 188-189.

8. Trade statistics in "The USAID FY 1998 Congressional Presentation."

9. Lupi Mushayakarara, "African-African American Summit Focuses on Economic Development," *The African* (November/December 1997), 4-6; Interview with Ruth Davis, ibid., 12-13. Tourist estimate by Randall Robinson in James Brooke, "Blacks in U.S. Heartland Put New Focus on Africa," *The New York Times*, 22 March 1998.

10. Bruce Finley, "Allying Africa, America," *Denver Post*, 29 January 1998, 1a and 22a.

11. "Jesse Jackson Appointed to Push Democracy in Africa," *Rocky Mountain News*, 9 October 1997.

12. Norman Kempster, "Albright Vows 'New Chapter' with Africa," *Denver Post*, 10 December 1997, 22a; Howard French, "Albright in Africa: The Embraceable Regimes?" *The New York Times*, 16 December 1997.

13. U.S. Department of State, "Albright and Mugabe Joint Press Conference," 15 December 1997, copy from Africa News Online (www.africanews.org) in the author's possession.

14. For details on Mugabe's initial actions and remarks see "Mugging Dissent," *The Economist*, 19 August 1995, 38; Lynne Duke, "Mugabe Makes Homosexuals Public Enemies," *Washington Post*, 9 September 1995, a19. For the U.S. reaction, see John Gallagher, "Counterattack: U.S. Protest Keeps Homophobia at Bay in Southern Africa," *The Advocate*, 14 November 1995.

15. Mugabe's April remark in *The Advocate*, 26 May 1998, 18. Incident at Cal Tech from "Queer News You Can Use," 21 May 1998, copy from internet (www.planetout.com) in author's possession. Eliakim Sibanda, a former member of Joshua Nkomo's army and a

graduate student in Denver in 1998, first informed me of this incident and of the general controversy over Mugabe's views on gays.

16. Marshall Frady, *Jesse: The Life and Pilgrimage of Jesse Jackson* (New York: Random House, 1996), 424; *The Nation*, 18 September 1995, 261.

17. For overviews of Clinton's itinerary and objectives see Howard French, "Africa in Metamorphosis Awaits Clinton's Arrival," *The New York Times*, 22 March 1998, and R.W. Apple, "Into Africa," *The New York Times*, 24 March 1998.

18. Terence Hunt, "A Trip to the Painful Past," *Denver Post*, 28 March 1998; Jodi Enda, "Mandela Lectures Clinton," *Denver Post*, 28 March 1998, 1a and 9a; "Mandela Assails U.S. Trade Bill," *Rocky Mountain News*, 30 March 1998.

19. Bob Deans, "Clinton Hails South Africa as 'a people unshackled,'" *Rocky Mountain News*, 27 March 1998; Kathy Lewis, "'Call of conscience' honored," *Denver Post*, 29 March 1998.

20. For discussion of the South African constitution and the description of Mugabe, see Mark Gevisser, "Mugabe's Mantra," *The Nation*, 18 September 1995, 261.

21. For discussion of Carter's postpresidential efforts to help the people of Zimbabwe, and his strained relations with Clinton, see Douglas Brinkley, *The Unfinished Presidency*, 194-196, 368-374, 383, 454-456, 474-475.

INDEX

Sullivan Principles 256, 296, 321, 330, 334

Tambo, Oliver 328, 341-342
Tempelsman, Maurice 156
Thatcher, Margaret 244, 274, 276, 304
Thomas, Norman 19
Timmons, William 202
Tower, John 173, 191
Tshombe, Moise 74
Tsongas, Paul 263, 325
Tunney, John 209-300
Tutu, Desmond 327, 349

Utt, James 152

Vance, Cyrus 5, 9, 12, 118, 125, 137, 182, 228, 244, 290-291, 296, 309, 314
Verwoerd, Hendrik 113
Vorster, John 205, 252

Wallace, George 30, 35, 327
Walters, Ronald 4, 10, 304, 353
Warnke, Paul 244
Warren, Earl 201
Waters, Maxine 365-366
Webb, Wellington 364
Welensky, Roy 15-16, 27, 29, 45, 50-51, 54, 58, 61, 66, 75, 82, 96, 158, 185
Whitehead, Edgar 35, 69, 73
Whitfield, Mal 31
Wilkins, Roy 70, 115, 123, 126, 140, 148, 180, 232
William, J. Fulbright 172
Williams, G. Mennen 7, 37, 49, 84, 86, 90-92, 95, 97, 123, 130, 132-134, 136, 139, 178, 180, 191

Wilson, Harold 102, 108, 134-135, 140, 181, 186
Wilson, Woodrow 213
Wisner, Frank 321, 323
Wonder, Stevie 317

Young, Andrew 2, 5, 9, 70, 154, 183, 202, 215, 228, 243, 245, 261, 270, 280, 282, 286-287, 290, 292-293, 296-297, 299, 302, 306, 314, 320, 331, 345, 350
Young, Whitney 70, 123, 126, 129, 139

Zaire 248, 265, 292, 294